D0983692

EMPIRE OF FEAR

Empire of Fear

by

VLADIMIR and EVDOKIA
PETROV

FREDERICK A. PRAEGER
New York

First published in the United States of America in 1956
by Frederick A. Praeger, Inc., 150 East 52 Street, New York 22.
Copyright © 1956 by Vladimir and Ekdokia Petrov
All Rights Reserved
Library of Congress Catalog Card Number 56:13225
Printed in the United States of America

Contents

CONTENTS

Illustrations

Foreword

This book is a book of evidence rather than opinions. We did not set out to write an anti-Soviet book, but to tell a true story, whatever picture might emerge; the order is important. We challenge anybody to disprove a single word of what we have written. We know it will have to face the most searching examination by the public in the West and by a few senior Intelligence chiefs in the U.S.S.R. We do not fear this test.

Some of this evidence, concerning our life and work in Australia, has already been given under oath in the court room and tested by cross-examination, before the three impartial judges appointed as Commissioners of the Australian Royal Commission on Espionage.

Their opinion of us as witnesses will carry more weight than anything that we could say ourselves. Here is what they have reported:

> During the many months of our Inquiry we have had the credibility of the Petrovs under constant scrutiny. In this regard they started with a heavy handicap: they were persons who had deserted their country and its service, and were prepared to divulge its secrets, and for this purpose Petrov had taken documents to which he had no right; both of them had become dependent for their protection and subsistence on the Government, a fact which might induce them to invent or embellish evidence to please that Government; the vicious attacks upon them by some Communists and like-minded persons in the court-room and in a section of the press might cause them in revenge to strain their evidence; they were ostensibly recent apostates from Communism, a creed in which—reputedly—a lie may be justified by the end to be served.

> Such considerations made it imperative that we should scrutinize their evidence and assess their credibility with the utmost care. But during the long period in which they gave evidence we had many and extraordinary opportunities of testing their credibility and their accuracy.

> Petrov was in the witness-box on thirty-seven days for approximately seventy-four hours in all, and Mrs Petrov on twenty-one days for approximately thirty hours in all. During that time we had their demeanour under constant scrutiny and, as we have pointed out,

9

their evidence was capable of being checked and was checked in a variety of ways at a multiplicity of points. We ourselves had opportunities of checking which were not available even to counsel assisting us: certain wire recordings of conversations and other material were available to us only.

We feel that in the final result we should find, and we do find, that the Petrovs are witnesses of truth.

We also found their accuracy to be of a high order, which is not surprising seeing that they had long training in a service which demanded accuracy.

The volume of facts about which they were questioned before us was enormous; and meantime, during many months, they were being questioned on behalf of the counter-espionage services of other Western countries on matters not directly relevant to our Inquiry, with results which we know to have been of the greatest value to those countries.

In all the circumstances, it is not surprising that occasionally their memories were at fault in respect of such things as dates and sequences of events, and that sometimes they differed between themselves in their recollections of such matters. Any person of judicial experience knows that such faults of memory and such divergencies are normal, even in highly intelligent witnesses—indeed the absence of them would be suspicious.[1]

But most of the story told in this book lies outside the scope of the Royal Commission's inquiries. It is the story of our lives in the Soviet Union, and especially of our lives as permanent career officers of the most secret organ of the Soviet State, at various times known as the O.G.P.U., N.K.V.D., M.G.B. and M.V.D. Two vital functions of this secret state-within-a-state are internal security and foreign espionage; and we have much to tell from personal experience in both these fields.

The story of our break with Soviet communism and our flight as refugees from the system which we had served for so long has peculiar interest for several reasons. We are both second-generation children of the Soviet Revolution.

We were both born into the primitive poverty of a Russian village; the Revolution gave both of us opportunities which we would never

[1] Report of the Royal Commission on Espionage; Sydney, 1955. pp. 63–65, paragraphs 183–185, 193–196.

have enjoyed otherwise; we each rose to positions of comfort, prosperity and privilege in the Soviet service.

In the twenty-and-more years since we both joined the O.G.P.U. we have both been members of that select minority of Soviet citizens who are the governing bureaucracy of modern Russia and who enjoy a life of comparative comfort. Thus we can tell of the terrible hardships of the mass of the Soviet people unembittered by personal deprivations of the material necessities of life. We have belonged to the favoured few.

But what we have to describe is something far more dreadful than a country of general poverty and shortages. It is a society which we see in clearer perspective since we left it—a régime of universal fear.

That is why we have called our book the Empire of Fear. The word 'fear' needs no explanation. For a definition of 'Empire' we turn to a Soviet source, The Dictionary of Russian Language:[1]

EMPIRE—A large imperialistic colonial state pursuing aggressive policies and cruelly exploiting dependent people.

Our book shows that no better description could be found of the Communist empire whose capital and heart is Moscow: its victims are the helpless dependent masses exploited by a small governing clique for whom their own power and military strength always takes precedence over real improvement in the life of the people.

The Soviet empire is not confined to the peoples and nationalities within the actual boundaries of the U.S.S.R. It reaches westward into Europe, where it has established its sway over the so-called 'Peoples' Democracies', and it drives eastward into Asia. Our book shows something of this expansion. In every country and corner of the world it sways people by the power of fear.

Of the dreadful and appalling things that are done in the Soviet Union by Soviet citizens to Soviet citizens more are done through fear than through hatred and malice.

Fear is the essential instrument of Communist domination.

Fear is the master wherever the power of the Kremlin can make itself felt. That fear ruled our lives in the Embassy at Canberra and drove us to seek refuge and freedom from fear in Australia.

Even the Soviet leaders, though they enjoy power, luxury, and freedom from any material necessity, can never know freedom from fear.

[1]3rd Edition, compiled by S. I. Ojegov, published under the Editorship of Academician S. P. Obnorsky, by the Government Publishers of Foreign and National Dictionaries, Moscow, 1953.

For the régime under which they live destroys ruthlessly and systematically the only source of such freedom—confidence and trust between one human being and another.

There is a Russian saying which has an ominous aptness in the Soviet Union today—'Don't dig another's grave, or you yourself will be the first occupant of it.'

And yet, as we show in our story, our Soviet people are not different from other people in their basic impulses, hopes and desires. They long for freedom and a better life, though they can spare little time to think about such things; they have the ordinary human instincts of kindliness and friendship and they have a deep loyalty towards their native land and a deep love for their families and their own flesh and blood. It is that love and that loyalty in particular that the Soviet Government so cruelly and inhumanly exploits.

Are we traitors to our country? That is the agonizing question which everyone in our position must ask himself. Moscow has denounced us as traitors (the sentence on us will have been already passed) and we have had the charge flung at us by a Communist barrister at the Royal Commission.

To anyone who asks that question we reply: Read our story, study the picture we give of our life in the Soviet Union, follow step by step the development that led to our break with our country. If, having done that, you can say confidently that in our position you would have returned to the Soviet Union, then you are at liberty to call us traitors. But read our story first.

We believe in our country and in the people of Russia. But we believe that in escaping we did the only thing possible. By telling the truth as we have seen and known it about life in the Soviet Union, we may help you in Western countries to understand what it is you have to deal with.

The worst enemy of all is fear; his rule is more terrible than chains, prison, or death. You in the West, who still enjoy freedom, have the only hope of finding something better and stronger, which can free the whole world, and the people of Russia, from the bondage of fear.

EMPIRE OF FEAR

I

Our Village

I WAS born in the village of Larikha in central Siberia on the 15th February 1907 and was christened Afanasy Mikhailovich Shorokhov in the village church, according to Russian Orthodox rites. I will explain later about my name, and how it was twice changed, once at my own request and once without my knowledge. For simplicity I call myself Vladimir Mikhailovich Petrov throughout this book. Our village had a church, a fact which gave it a status above the nearby hamlets which had not, and it numbered about three hundred and sixty houses. It was a good-sized village for those parts, though not to be classed with the market town of Ishim, nineteen miles away.

My father was a peasant, and his fathers before him for generations back; my mother was a typical Russian peasant woman. I grew up in the village; my early formative years were spent close to the soil and to the countryside of Siberia. Now, after all that has happened, I am still happiest in the open air, with my gun or fishing rod, and I have a liking for animals that goes back to my boyhood. When I talked in Sydney with Dr Beckett about what I could do if I stayed in Australia, I told him, 'I am only a countryman'; and that is how I began.

It is important to the story too, because in all my later work in Moscow and abroad, as a diplomat and as a colonel of the M.V.D., I have never lost my feeling for the land, or my sympathy for the peasant people of Russia.

The house where I was born was a typical village house for that part of Siberia. It was built of logs, packed on the inside with moss, and ad-joined a group of buildings—woodshed, stalls for the sheep, cattle and horses, steam bath house, grain store and poultry sheds—all built round a central yard. The house itself consisted of two large rooms; its focus was the brick oven where we slept, my father and mother, myself and my two brothers. Sometimes during the night my mother would turn away from me to give more attention to my younger brother, and I would feel jealous and kick him. We brothers often fought among our-selves; but if an outsider intervened, we would immediately close our ranks and stick together, according to the good old village custom.

Our village, as I remember it in those pre-Revolutionary days, was

by no means a community of oppressed tenants groaning under the
heel of a tyrannical landowner. Serfdom in Russia had, of course, been
abolished many years before, in 1861, under Czar Alexander II; but, in
our village, which was typical of Siberia as I knew it, we were not even
tenant-farmers. Each family owned its own land and was entitled to a
share of the common land, which was apportioned by the headman and
elders of the village on the basis of three acres for each male in the
family. After that they could buy or sell as they wished. There were no
big landowners in our part of Siberia. The most prosperous farmers in
our district had four sons, and owned about forty acres, with perhaps a
hundred cows, as well as horses and some farm machinery. Later, when
the terrible purge of the so-called 'Kulaks' was unleashed, only three
farmers could be found in Larikha who hired any labour, and they were
not wealthy men, but lived very much as the rest of us did. Our farms
were certainly poor by European standards; and of course there were
inequalities, according to the individual farmer's skill, industry and
luck. But we enjoyed a simple peasant independence, together with a
real and unforced community life.

As there were three sons in our family, we had twelve acres of tillage;
we grew wheat, rye, potatoes and oats in rotation. With these crops,
and our vegetable garden beside the house, we were able in good years
to eat well enough. The vegetable garden grew beetroot, cabbage (from
which we made the Russian form of sauerkraut), cucumbers, which we
salted, and potatoes, which we stored for the long winter. We had
brown bread, and occasionally white bread, when my father went by
horse-drawn sledge to the market fair in Ishim. That was only in
winter; he, like everyone else, was too busy in the fields in the summer
months. Mother set fish-traps in the Ishim river, and sometimes Father
would take us boys fishing for minnows or roach. We had no pigs,
unlike most of the villagers, who dried the pork in the sun for roasts and
to use in soups. But we had other Siberian delicacies, whose names can
still make my mouth water. There were *blini*, or pancakes, eaten with
melted butter, on which we feasted in the 'Butter Week', before the
forty days fast from meat which we observed during Lent. And in
winter there were *pelmeni*, or meat dumplings, which Mother used to
make. She rolled the dough very thin, and cut it out in circles with a
cup. Into each circle she put raw minced meat—beef and mutton
mixed, or mutton and pork—then turned each dumpling over and
pinched it into a ball. Then she put the raw dumplings, hundreds at a
time, out on trays to freeze. When they were frozen hard as rocks, she
hung them up in flour bags in the icy air outside, where they kept in-

definitely. Coming in tired and cold, we would take a few frozen
pelmeni and throw them into simmering water, where they cooked in a
few minutes, to become juicy and delicious. Mother also made various
soups which were favourites of mine; some days we would have a
roast, and on special occasions one of our ducks or chickens. We always
had a big earthenware jar of milk standing in the kitchen; we drank
milk and mother made junket from it. Sometimes we had eggs, when
Mother would put a towel inside the steaming samovar, and boil the
eggs in it.

How hard Mother worked, from dawn to dark! She milked three
cows, fed the poultry and calves, worked in the vegetable garden and
prepared our meals. We had fourteen sheep, which we sheared ourselves; Mother then washed the wool, dried it, spun it into thread,
wove the thread into coarse cloth, and made us our clothes from it. The
only bought clothes I remember having were my Sunday and holiday
outfit of long trousers, jacket and top boots; all the rest of my clothes
Mother made herself. In the short, hot, summer months we ran about
barefoot in shirt and trousers; in winter we wore fur jackets, overcoats
made of sheepskins, fur caps with ear-flaps, and boots of felt with
leather soles stitched to them. The Siberian winters were long and
bitterly cold. For eight months of the year our stock had to be stalled
and fed; keeping warm and keeping alive were the two constant problems for animals and human beings alike.

During the summer months we all worked in the fields, starting early
and ending only when it was too dark to work. But we strictly observed prescribed holidays—a week at Christmas, and of course New
Year's Day, Good Friday, Easter Day and Palm Sunday. Mother was
patient and devout, and it was considered a sin to work on the holy
days. We attended a church service every Saturday night, and on Sunday morning we stood or knelt throughout the celebration of the
Russian Orthodox Liturgy which started at eight in the morning and
went on till noon. We were not allowed to touch food till it was over.
Our church at Larikha was large and well-endowed; it was one of the
few brick buildings in the village. There were many ikons on the walls
and wax candles burned before the altar. The clergy, consisting of three
priests and a deacon, also looked after the seven other villages in our
parish. The priests, like everyone else in the village, had plots of land
which they cultivated, in addition to celebrating all the church services,
and officiating at the christenings, marriages, burials, and thanksgiving
services of our whole village community. They received a small pit-
tance from the voluntary collections at services, but they were certainly

not rich and lived very simply. I remember them as gentle, kindly
men, very much part of the life of the village, who were always ready
to give advice, visit and comfort sick folk, and help the poorest
villagers.

Before the Revolution, every house in the village had ikons on the
walls and a Bible. When I went to school and became the first and only
member of our family who could read, it was my duty to read passages
from the Bible to the family round the table at night. This would have
been the task of my elder brother, but his schooling—school was not
compulsory in those days—lasted one day only. When he got back with
the books they had given him, my father said, 'That's all the school for
you; I need you in the fields; you're helping me from now on,' and
that settled it. My brother did not mind. But I was quick and learned to
read in one year. I suppose my father thought one scholar was enough
for one peasant family.

School was voluntary and was only held in the winter. I attended for
two winters. Mother would send me off after breakfast with a very
simple lunch—perhaps no more than a slice of brown bread—and I
would trudge through the snow to the schoolhouse, where the school-
teacher lived with her mother. It was a one-storey house of logs lined
with moss, and one room of it was our school. Our teacher, Olga
Grigorievna, was elderly and kindly, and managed with remarkable
success her fifty pupils, divided into three classes, who sat all together
in the single schoolroom, with its stove and blackboard and wooden
benches. We studied Russian, reading and writing, simple arithmetic
and the Bible. I never remember our teacher using cane or strap or
losing her temper with us. We village children on the whole were
timid and docile; and we had all had drilled into us the privilege that
we enjoyed in attending school when we might be making ourselves
useful to our hard-pressed parents.

I enjoyed school, and was proud of my progress; I looked forward to
going on from primary to secondary school. But all such hopes were
brought to a sudden end by a family disaster of the first magnitude.

It was in the sultry August of 1914; there was much talk of the war,
which had just broken out, and already the whole village had been
stirred to its foundations by the arrival of foreigners in our midst—a
batch of Austrian prisoners-of-war taken early in the fighting, who had
been sent to work in the fields. Already, too, some of our younger men
had been called up to the Army, and my father had heard with foreboding that his age group was the next due for call-up.

My father had a local reputation in the countryside round Larikha as a good slaughterer, and on this fateful day he had been asked to slaughter a pig for a neighbour on the outskirts of our village. He took me and my younger brother with him; I was seven at the time. He and the neighbour took the pig a little way off, slaughtered it, skinned it, singed the skin over a fire, and then scraped it clean of bristle. Just as they finished the scraping, it started to rain, huge heavy drops, a real August thunderstorm; they had seen the black cloud and hurried to get their job done before the downpour began. The owner of the pig joined my brother and me in the shelter of the slaughterhouse wall. My father at first crouched against the fence; but finding he was getting wet, ran to the shelter of a windmill which stood nearby. We saw him dodge under the lee of the windmill, its great vanes spinning in the gusty wind, and huddle under its overhanging bulk. The next moment there was a blinding flash of lightning and an ear-splitting crash; and the neighbour cried, 'The mill is struck and perhaps Mikhail Danielo-vich also!' We ran to the mill and saw my father lying on his back on the ground. The lightning had stripped off his clothes, and there was a huge red weal the whole length of his body. His knee-boots were split in half, his coat and shirt lay a few feet away twisted into a ball by the force of the lightning.

My brother and I stood by our father, crying in terror, while the peasant ran to fetch the village policeman. By the time they got back a little knot of awestruck villagers had gathered round, and a girl student from Ishim who was staying in the village with relatives came forward with a mirror, which she held in front of Father's mouth; it became misted, showing that he was still breathing.

At this point the Austrian prisoners-of-war came up with shovels; it was explained that they proposed to bury my father up to his neck in the earth, as cold earth was a remedy for the effects of lightning. We of the village were impressed with their proposal; we thought that as they were foreigners, educated people from Europe, they must know much more about the proper treatment of such cases than ignorant Russian peasants like ourselves. But our village policeman forbade it; he declared that warmth would be better, and ordered the neighbours to bring Father home to our stables, and bury him there for a while in the warm dung of the stable floor.

My brother and I, barefoot, crying and soaked to the skin, ran home through the pouring rain. Mother had already heard the news. Amid her grief she was strangely fatalistic; through her tears and sobs I remember her saying, 'When I heard the lightning and thunder, something told me of this. It was only this morning that your father was so full of foreboding. He strode up and down in the yard there, and cried, "Today I shall either be called up for the war, or I shall be dead".'

Presently they carried Father in and buried him in the stable, as our policeman had instructed. But the debate of friends and neighbours went on; argument as to what should be done swayed this way and that, and the advice of the Austrian prisoners-of-war began to prevail. After an hour or two they dug Father up from the stable floor and buried him, with only his head above ground, in the earth of our vegetable garden. Though it was summer the night was cold, and when they came again in the morning they found that he was stiff and dead. Then they took Father and buried him properly in the village cemetery, among his relatives, as was the old Russian custom. Though I was only seven at the time, I remember every detail of these tragic happenings as though it were yesterday.

The cemetery was surrounded by great old birch trees and had a fence and moat around it; there were plots of flowers and painted wooden crosses with inscriptions. Each family was careful to look after the graves and gravestones of their own folk; neglected graves were a disgrace to a family.

Naturally when I revisited Larikha in 1949, I went to look for the graves of my ancestors and family, but I could find no trace of the old cemetery. The trees were gone, the ground had been ploughed over, there were no graves or gravestones to be seen. Instead, the village had a new, smaller cemetery in a different place. I should not have been surprised, for I knew well enough that it was part of Soviet policy to destroy everything old; all links with the past that might carry dangers of counter-revolutionary 'reaction' against the new socialist state. But standing there on the earth of my native village, where my father and ancestors lay buried, I felt uneasy and disturbed.

My father was much missed in the village. He was a simple man, a good neighbour who hurt nobody and in quiet ways had helped many, and the whole village mourned him.

For us, Father's tragic death, apart from the shock and grief to ourselves, brought urgent practical problems. It is a very serious business for a village family to lose its breadwinner. However, in a village community one is rarely left to face such disasters alone. Neighbours assisted in all sorts of practical ways, and my mother had a brother living also in Larikha, Efim Ivanovich Gregoriev. He had fourteen children, and after Father's death he and his family helped us at each harvest, and we in turn helped them. My schooling came to a sudden end; every pair of hands in the family was needed to look after our fields and garden and animals. The help which friends and neighbours gave us in our trouble was something taken very much for granted, an unwritten law. Before the imposition of collective farming and communal ownership it was a normal thing for villagers to share and help one another; our community life was spontaneous and customary, rather than enforced.

I remember old Marfa Ivanovna, the village midwife, who was always at hand, at any hour of day or night, when there was a birth in the village; she assisted my two brothers and me into the world and never dreamed of asking a kopek of anyone for her services. She had a small plot of land, and on Sundays (work of such kind was allowed on Sundays) the village people would come to plough, sow and reap. She would ask them into her small house and would offer them modest hospitality with vodka and a simple meal.

Likewise, when anyone in the village needed to build a house, his neighbours would leave their own work for the day, bring their own horses and wagons and go with him to the forest, to help cut, trim, and haul the logs for the house.

For four years after Father's death we kept ourselves alive by hard relentless work in which we all shared. Then in 1919 the shortages caused by war and revolution brought about a famine. Our own horses died because we had not enough fodder to feed them through the winter, and we had great difficulty in ploughing. I was then twelve, and though short, I was strongly built. Mother decided to take me to our village blacksmith, who was better off than most people because at this time he was paid for his work in food and produce instead of money, and because his whole family worked and lived together. He had a smithy and house which he had inherited from his father before him. I had often stood at the door of his forge while he blew up the fire and set the sparks flying, and had thought how fine it would be to have such a skilled and impressive trade.

'Evgeni Pavlovich,' said my mother, 'will you take Volodya here as an apprentice? He's a willing boy and will work well for you.'

'Certainly,' he answered, 'I hear he's a good lad; I'll give him a job.'

It was agreed that I should do farm work for him as well as my work in the smithy. For the first year I would get nothing but my keep; after that, if he was satisfied, he would pay me a wage.

I went to live at the blacksmith's house, which was fairly large by village standards, having two good-sized rooms and a big courtyard. He gave me my meals, which were adequate, and in the winter months I slept on the plank bed, or sleeping shelf, above the stove in the kitchen. In summer I preferred to sleep on straw in one of the wagons in the courtyard.

The blacksmith, Evgeni Pavlovich Niskovskikh, was a tradesman of wide accomplishments, and besides his ordinary work in the forge he could repair anything from farm implements to sewing machines. He did his best to teach me, when he was not too busy himself, and in the eight years I worked for him I became a qualified blacksmith; I could make axles, mend guns and repair locks. At the beginning of my second year with him, we signed a contract whereby he undertook to pay me the wage of nine roubles a year. It was not much, but to me it was a new experience to have money of my own in my pocket. For nine roubles you could buy a horse; a pair of topboots could be had for a rouble and a half. During that year I got various advances from my master, who noted every kopek carefully in a notebook. My wages increased each year, until eventually I was earning five roubles a month, out of which I was able to help Mother and have a little over for myself.

My greatest prize was a gun of my own. The blacksmith himself was a good shot; he had a double-barrelled shotgun and an English setter called 'Jack', which he used to take with him in the spring and autumn when he visited the lakes and marshes round Larikha after ducks and geese. Occasionally, when he was in a particularly good humour, he would take me with him; and these expeditions fired my boyish enthusiasm for shooting. I got my gun from poor old Dmitri Stepanovich, the wainwright, who lived opposite our house with his blind mother. He made a new butt for an old gun, and I got it from him for two roubles.

Whenever I took my master's horses to plough, I would take my gun with me, and occasionally had some luck. Once I had a narrow escape. The gun was an ancient hammer-lock. I had cocked it, and was crawling on my stomach, stalking some ducks, and trailing the gun after me with the barrel close to my head. It went off with a tremendous bang; the ducks rose and flew off, and I lay on the ground cursing with annoyance and fright.

When I was seventeen I fell very much in love. My cousin Tatiana, the daughter of my mother's brother, had a friend called Capitolina. She was the adopted daughter of the Tarasov family, whose house and garden backed on to ours. I first met Capitolina along with Tatiana; we were both children, and I took no particular notice of her. As we grew up, I used to see her often, especially on Sundays when the boys and girls of our village would gather for singing and dancing in the evenings after church, and I played the accordion. It happened quite suddenly, when she was sixteen and I a year older. We boys had a habit of hanging around the dairy at milking time, when the girls came from the cow byres with their full pails of milk. This evening there was no one else about. I met Capitolina as she came out of the dairy. Her bare arms were shapely and rounded, her skin a lovely golden-brown from the summer sun, her figure full and trim. Her black hair was drawn back neatly from her pretty face, which glowed with health and her work in the dairy; and her black eyes opened wider at our unexpected meeting. I was quite overcome at the sight of her; all at once she seemed to have become something wonderful and strange and desirable. I had nothing to say; I mumbled something unintelligible and rushed off in confusion.

It was some little time before I plucked up courage to tell her that I loved her, and found to my joy that she did not reject me. After a little while she told me that she too loved me, and we agreed between us that we would marry.

For four years we kept company; our families, of course, knew all about it and made no objection. After a while, according to the recognized custom with courting couples in the villages of Russia, we slept together at her home. Of course, we also kept the recognized and strict rule in such cases, that there should be no question of intimacy. Village custom was quite clear and practical about the matter, and no self-respecting girl would have dreamed of consenting to such a thing before marriage. In the close-knit community of our village there were few secrets and public opinion was a strong force.

At the end of four years, when there had been no cloud between us and no change in our mutual plan to marry, I received a shock from another direction. I learned from friends that professional match-makers had visited Capitolina's parents with an attractive offer, and that without any reference to me she had been betrothed to a man in another village whom she had never seen. Her parents were, alas, within their rights, according to village custom; but human feelings are not to be ignored. The betrothal was announced, girls who were her particular friends came to help her get ready her dowry of bed-linen, underclothing, personal treasures; and the customary evening visits by her friends, boys and girls alike, began. I came with them, lighthearted in my manner but with an aching heart; I left a note with her, begging her to reject her new suitor, and renewing my solemn promise to marry her. I was overjoyed next day when I got her reply: she had done what I asked, and had told her parents that she would not marry the stranger. That same evening my mother and elder brother visited her parents; and it was agreed between the two families that Capitolina and I should be allowed to marry. My mother told me that her parents had objected to me because I was now a member of the Komsomol, the Communist Youth Organization, but they had given in to Capitolina's pleadings.

Three days passed without a chance to see Capitolina alone; her parents still kept her closely under their eye. Then I heard from friends, as one does hear these things in a village, that Capitolina's parents had double-crossed me, and were still negotiating for the match with the stranger in the other village.

In a cold sweat of rage and fear I waited my chance. Just before dusk, when I knew her parents were out of the house, I took my favourite horse from the blacksmith's stable, a mettlesome black which no one else could handle, and harnessed him to a sleigh (it was winter-time). I drove quietly to Capitolina's house, walked in, and found her alone, except for her stepbrother.

'Capitolina, I have a horse and sleigh at the door. Would you care to come for a drive with me?'

'Oh Volodya, thank you. Yes, I would.'

She was startled and excited, but kept her composure as I helped her into the sleigh and we drove away over the snow. I took the road to Voroninov, a village four miles away, where some distant relatives of mine lived, the Smirnovs. They were pleased to see me and my friend and we had a drink of tea with them. I had planned that we would stay the night with them, because I knew that preparations were afoot to take Capitolina away that very night to the village where my rival lived. But after tea she began to cry and begged me to take her home. I could see that, even though she loved me, her parents' pressure was stronger still. Her tears and distress were too much for me. I took leave of the Smirnovs and with a heavy heart drove Capitolina back the cheerless miles to Larikha. Her father was waiting in the house when we went in.

'Vladimir Mikhailovich,' he shouted, 'what right had you to take Capitolina off with you like this?'

'Because we are betrothed,' I answered, 'and you agreed to our betrothal.'

He had no reply. Capitolina sobbed in a corner. I wished them good night and drove back to my quarters with the blacksmith. Wearily I unharnessed the horse and climbed up to my plank bed above the stove.

For two hours I lay in restless misery, and sleep was as far away as ever. At about ten o'clock I got up. Whatever happened, I must see Capitolina again. Pulling on my boots, I stumbled through the snow towards her parents' house. But outside the house were a group of lads I knew who told me the worst. Capitolina's parents had decided to allow no further risks to the plan they had in mind, and had lost no time in making good their decision. She had been taken away by force to the other village a little before I arrived.

Sick and miserable I went back to my lodging with the blacksmith. That was the end; there was nothing more I could do. Her parents had won. After all, I was still only the blacksmith's apprentice.

Three days later Capitolina was married to the suitor of her parents' choice; I never saw her again.

Of course all the village knew everything that had happened, and my master, the blacksmith, took pleasure in teasing me about the affair. As we worked together at the forge, he would sing romantic love-lorn ditties. One of them went—

> *Why, crazy woman, do you destroy the one*
> *who dotes on you?*
> *If you don't love me, God be with you!*

I would grit my teeth and once I hit the cutter he was holding a tremendous bang with my hammer, breaking it and jarring his arm. Jauntily he replaced it with another cutter and went on with his song.

As for Capitolina, when I revisited Larikha in 1949, a friend of hers told me that her husband had been killed in the war and that she was living with her two children in the same village of Pakhomovo, a few miles from Ishim, to which she had been taken as a bride by her determined and masterful parents on that winter's night that I remember so well.

II

The Revolution

THE REVOLUTION came to Larikha in a gradual, piecemeal fashion. It began with the soldiers returning from the front, with their talk about Communism and the remarkable benefits that the Revolution would bring; they used to hold meetings in the large District Council building, which had a hall attached to it. Agitators, who were introduced as 'Commissars', began to come regularly from Ishim; they would call all the village folk into the hall, announce that the Czar was deposed and the Soviet now in power in Moscow and (which interested their audience more) would promise that the new régime would bring abundance of things that had become almost unobtainable of late—cloth, manufactured suits, axes, scythes, ploughs, kerosene.

Despite these promises, the first effect of the Revolution which was really felt in our village was movement of goods in the opposite direction. On instructions from Moscow, the whole village was divided into sections of ten households each, with one peasant householder, now termed the 'Inspector', in charge of each group of ten. Under the direction of the village Council (or 'Soviet'), it was his duty to inspect the stores of grain, livestock and other property, and to assess how much each household should contribute to the village Soviet, for disposal by the supreme Soviet in Moscow. In Czarist days the villagers had paid only a small poll-tax in money; these large exactions of the food by which they lived were a much more serious matter.

Our 'Inspector' was Maxim Stepanov, who lived two doors away; I remember the first day he came. He called my mother, looked over all our sheds and storehouses, and announced authoritatively: 'You must leave so much for yourselves; the rest you must take to the village Soviet.' My mother was timid and made no protest; she took for granted that an order from any authority must be obeyed without question. Other households were less amenable, especially where the head of the household was a man of strong character; Stepanov and the others were abusively nicknamed 'District Police Inspectors'.

The constant confiscations of food eventually brought our village to the verge of starvation; so much grain was appropriated that there was not enough left for next year's sowing, and at the same time severe inroads were made into the livestock of every household. But we were urged to be patient, and contribute loyally; since our food was all going to help the factory workers in Moscow to produce the manufactured goods we so badly needed, and to support the gallant Red Army fighting the Whites for the survival of the Revolution.

We had spasmodic glimpses of the civil war. Larikha was off the main roads and the railway, but there were skirmishes in the nearby countryside when Admiral Kolchak's White Army was retreating. I remember hearing desultory rifle fire in the distance and once or twice small bands of Reds or Whites galloped through the village but did not stop.

The Whites had already set up a recruiting station at Ishim and among a number who were summoned and mobilized from our village for Kolchak's Army was my elder brother Ivan. He went off on service with them till his unit was surrounded and he was taken prisoner at Omsk; he then transferred to the Red Army and served for a period without suffering any penalty for his service under the Whites, so confused and haphazard was the whole situation at this time. After he had gone I took one of our horses to Ishim, hoping to raise a little money by selling it to the Army; but after inspection it was rejected.

In 1921 the peasants in our district rose in desperate protest against the continued confiscations. The rising began in the village of Gagarino, twelve miles from Larikha, under the battle-cry 'Soviet Power without the Communists': its sole motive was to arrest the tide which was sucking away the peasants' livelihood. The authorities brought up artillery; a few shells fell near our village and the rising collapsed. But in some other villages Communists were killed and in Larikha groups of angry peasants formed units and armed themselves with whatever they had—shot-guns, pitchforks, home-made lances—so that our local Communists had to take refuge in Ishim till it was all over.

My master, the blacksmith, was among the more enlightened and progressive of our villagers. He could read, and subscribed to two papers published in Moscow—*The Peasants' Gazette* and *Poverty*. Both of these were Communist publications, but their accent was on agricultural progress and improved methods of farming rather than on theoretical questions. The blacksmith studied them keenly and tried to put their ideas into practice in his household and on his farm and to set an example of improved farming to the rest of the village. At this time he was one of the eight Communists in our village and he influenced me greatly. During the winter I was allowed to read these journals, and was much interested by articles about agriculture and also about the Komsomol, the Communist Youth Organization.

One Sunday in 1923 an agitator arrived from Ishim and called a meeting of the village youth in our local hall. He was young, earnest, neatly dressed, spoke well, and impressed us as a man of education. He made no mention of Marx or Lenin or of Communist theory, but explained to us that the Komsomol organization was the focus of culture in towns and villages. Youth had a vital part to play in shaping the future, and youth should set an example and take the lead in advancing culture and progress. It was our duty to do this, to help the village Soviet, and to take an active part in civic affairs in our village. If any of us would like to join the Komsomol, he would be happy to enrol us at once.

He was given a respectful hearing, but afterwards most of the youngsters were timid and dubious, while the elders were frankly suspicious and hostile. However, a handful of us came forward to answer the speaker's appeal, I among them. We said we would like to join the Komsomol, and were each given a membership card marked 'R.K.S.M.', standing for 'Russian Communist Union of Youth'. We formed a village cell, obtained a room for a library, which was stocked with newspapers, periodicals and books from Ishim, and held meetings every week.

When I told Mother what I had done, and showed her my membership card, she shook her head.

'Volodya,' she said, 'this will be the death of you before you're finished.'

She said this because during the Ishim revolt the peasants had killed some Komsomol as well as Communist Party members. Likewise many of our younger friends warned us and jeered at us, but we argued strenuously that the Komsomol, as the organ of culture and progress, was badly needed in backward villages like ours, and had the authority of the new Moscow Government behind it.

I was sincere enough about this; the blacksmith's journals and the agitator from Ishim had convinced me. But what really fired my enthusiasm was the thought of the opportunities for study, education and advancement which, we were assured, would be specially available to Komsomol members. Of this I shall have more to say presently.

But first I want to finish the story of our village, for it is typical of the story of thousands and thousands of peasant villages across Russia whose life and economy were ruined by the relentless exactions of the

Soviet Government in Moscow and the rigid imposition of collective farming. In the policy-made famine of 1932-35 three and a half million peasants died of needless starvation, according to official Moscow figures; foreign observers put the figure much higher. But I have had no official connection with agriculture in the Soviet since my work in 1928 and I will describe only what I have seen myself, or what I have heard from persons whose word I believe, and who had no reason to exaggerate or falsify at the time they spoke. Today, not even the Soviet Government can hide the fact that agriculture represents the most disastrous and damaging failure in the whole history of the Revolution in Russia.

As I write the fallen Malenkov has just been announced as the scapegoat for his government's 'failure to increase agricultural production sufficiently'. Quite recently General Nikishev told our former M.V.D. colleague, Yuri Rastvorov, that 'Soviet agriculture must be rescued from the blind alley into which it has drifted'. And in September 1953 when Krushchev, then the Soviet's agricultural chief, launched a drive for greater agricultural production, he spoke of current 'serious shortcomings'. It was then admitted that the total agricultural production of the U.S.S.R. was actually less than it had been in 1938, and that despite the huge population increase, the total livestock in the country was less than it had been in 1913. In the ten years after 1928 more than twenty million peasants left the countryside to swell the proletariat of the towns and cities.

I cannot trace in detail the tragic and terrible story of the villages of Russia; but certain of my own personal experiences were signposts on their road to ruin.

First, the case of my master the blacksmith, with his enthusiasm for communism as a road to culture and better farming methods. How could he foresee what his own fate would be, once the doctrines of Marx and Lenin became the infallible Bible of the Soviet Government? His first setback was expulsion from the Party. After his first wife died, the blacksmith proposed marriage to a widow who lived in Ishim. She was a devout woman, the daughter of a village chanter, one of the church servants who intone the psalms during the Orthodox Liturgy of the Russian Church. She consented, on condition that they were married in a church, to which the blacksmith agreed. At a subsequent Party meeting in the village he was accused of being married in church, which was contrary to communist teaching. He acknowledged his offence (there was no question of concealing it) and was duly expelled from the Party. He accepted his fate philosophically; and in fact suffered no very great hardship at that stage. The only immediate penalties were that he lost social contact with Party members and forfeited his chances of membership of the District Committee and of appointment to the various positions of influence and profit which were now open only to persons whom the Party favoured. Apart from that he was left pretty well alone.

It was later, about 1929, that the crushing blow fell, during the purge of the so-called 'Kulaks'. The order came down from the Supreme Soviet in Moscow to all the local Soviets that all peasant proprietors who employed labour were exploiters, enemies of the people, and counter-revolutionaries, and must be ruthlessly expropriated. The most dreadful results followed this license to persons with personal grudges and to mistaken fanatics. Thousands of peasants who were relatively prosperous perhaps through their own hard work, were denounced as 'Kulaks' and were swept away to miserable exile. Later on, when I was working in Nadejdinsk (Serov), I saw many trainloads of these wretched dispossessed people passing through on their way to wild frontier settlements, often in forest regions, where they had to suffer the most desperate hardships and start life all over again. Whole new Kulak villages were established in desolate regions of Siberia and Kazakstan, as the Government made the purge an opportunity to open up un-developed areas with this reservoir of forced labour. These Kulak villages had no elected council or soviet; they came under the direct control of an o.g.p.u. 'Commandant', who was in fact an absolute autocrat over the life and death of his workers. I would watch the trucks as they passed by the factory at Nadejdinsk; they were crammed with families who had had to leave their homes at a couple of hours' notice, taking with them what few belongings they could carry. They travelled and lived like cattle; but they had the ordinary thoughts and feelings of human beings, at least when they started on their exile. Once there was an accident, and one of the closed trucks was overturned. A young girl climbed out of the wreck and cried to me, 'I was not a Kulak, I was working for the Kulak, I was being paid by him!' She had been swept up in the wholesale dispossession of families and house-holds. Stronger than the shock of the accident was her tragic burning desire for justice, and her protest at the wrong she had suffered.

In this holocaust, which occurred after I had left the village, Evgeni Pavlovich Niskovskikh was branded as a Kulak. His shop and farm, with his cattle and all his property except a few personal items, were confiscated and he and his religious wife and all his family were ban-ished to a Kulak settlement, I do not know where, at a few hours' notice and with only the things they could carry with them. I never heard of them again.

Apart from its toll of human suffering, the effects of the purge of the Kulaks on agriculture were severe. When any peasant who had three horses, or was a little more prosperous than his neighbours, might be condemned as a Kulak, many of the best peasants left the villages to work in factories in the cities. Collectivization drove off many more; villages were depopulated, and agricultural production slumped disastrously. Later on, after some years of experience with collective farms, improved methods and greater mechanization did result in a recovery in production. But the collective farmer did not benefit; rents on machinery and levies paid to the Government were immediately raised, so that the collective farmer in Russia today remains, even by Russian standards, a creature who lives on the margin of existence.

Originally, no doubt, the Government's intention was that collectivization should go forward by persuasion rather than by force; but they reckoned without stubborn human nature, especially peasant human nature. The method was that in a village of, say, a hundred houses, one house with a large courtyard would be selected and all the poultry of the village collected there. In the courtyard of another house would be all the pigs or cows; and so on. When this process had been completed, the village Soviet could claim to have established its 'Kolhoz', or collective farm. Competition was encouraged between communities in the speed with which it could be reported to Moscow that a 'Kolhoz' had been set up.

There were some amusing incidents. At the village of Kakva, which I knew, the village Soviet called a meeting of the peasants to discuss any mistakes which might have been made in establishing the Kolhoz. A heated and turbulent gathering resulted, at which the peasants attacked not just the mistakes of execution, but the whole idea of the collective. In the end each peasant 'collected' his own cows, horses and fowls and went home to his own property.

Later, of course, the collective was rigorously enforced upon them.

In the first flush of the Revolutionary epoch, a series of enthusiastic campaigns were launched—schemes for loans to the Government, for self-imposed taxation, and so forth. Being an active Komsomol and Party worker I was appointed a Government official and in that capacity I went round many local villages and towns sponsoring and enforcing these campaigns.

It was in 1928, when a policy of wholesale collectivization was decreed by the Soviet Government, that I was given direct responsibility for enforcing the Government levies on villages in our district. That year the country was passing through a great industrial crisis, and the campaigns for greater production and returns from the land were called the 'horror' campaigns, because they stripped the peasants to the bone. Plans were drawn up, whereby each area had to provide a certain quantity of grain by a certain date, to be handed over to the local Soviet at prices fixed by the Government. It was a grim business for us too, who as Government officials had to justify and enforce these orders from Moscow upon our own folk whose life and hardships we knew so well.

I was sent to the village of Sajimo as adviser to the village council there. There were no Party members there, only one candidate; I was alone as a representative of the Communist Party and the Soviet Government. I discussed with the head man of the village council, with whom I stayed, the position of each family in the village—how many acres each had under cultivation, how much livestock, how many members in the family. After we had fixed the amount of the levy on each household and the list had been submitted to the village council for amendment, I called a meeting of the poorer peasants first. Their quotas were negligible. Then I summoned a meeting of the whole village at which I explained the urgent reasons for the Government's drive for greater production. As I expected, there was uproar and fierce protest, the dominant cry of the more prosperous peasants being, 'How can I supply such a quantity as this? I have no grain, you can inspect my store yourself. Have I got to buy grain to fulfil the quota?' Then some of the poorer peasants, who had been let off lightly, chipped in with the reproach, 'We are contributing our quota; why can't you do the same?'

Quarrels and fights broke out among the peasants, who were violently rebellious at the threatened demands. I sat quiet. Finally I interviewed each peasant individually, asked him whether he could fulfil his quota, and tried to persuade him that he could. Some reluctantly agreed; others fiercely refused. These I asked to wait outside the schoolhouse where I saw them; and after a night of sleeping in the open, some more of them agreed to fulfil their quota. In the morning many came to me with the plea, 'Comrade Chairman, I have to do my ploughing this morning; may I be excused?'

I allowed some to go, without releasing them from their obligation; but the more prosperous, whom I believed to be well able to supply the quota, I kept waiting indefinitely. They knew that if they finally refused, their stock and property would be inventoried and most of it confiscated. I was acting on the orders of the Soviet Government, enforced by the District Police; and they had no redress.

In that same village I had a narrow escape. There was one old peasant with a large house who had five sons, all living at home and all working; his substantial holding included some fine lime trees and he kept bees. With the head man of the village council I summoned this old man and told him that we had assessed his liability at forty-five 'pouds' of wheat (a 'poud' being about 35 lbs.).

'Comrade Chairman,' he said sorrowfully, 'I can't possibly fulfil such a huge quota; but I suppose I will have to buy it on the open market for the Government.'

I suggested that he could supply the quantity out of his own stock; whereupon he protested that it was impossible, and invited us to inspect his grain store. An inspection committee duly visited his house, and we found that his store did indeed contain only enough grain to provide his family with flour for a few days; the rest of the bins were empty.

But we had received a tip-off from a poor neighbour. We went to the steam bath house which stands in the courtyard of every village house, and lifted the floorboards. Below the bath house, was a great pit full to the brim with grain. Looking round, we saw no sign of the old man. Inquiring at the house, we were told by an old woman that he was sick, nor were his five sons anywhere to be seen. We worked out how much would be required by the family to take them up to the next harvest; the rest was appropriated. It amounted to more than eight wagon-loads of grain.

Our orders were that in cases of evasion, we should confiscate without repayment; nevertheless I told the head man to pay for what we had taken at the fixed rate, which he did. Though I had my duty to do, I could understand the old man's feelings in the matter.

That same night I was sitting with the head man in his house when there was a crash of splintering glass and a bullet, fired through the window, shattered the kerosene lamp on the table two feet away from me. The head man ran to the door and peered out cautiously; but it was a pitch black night, there was no means of getting in touch with the police and nothing could be done. That same evening he lost a horse, killed by an unknown hand. Mine was a hazardous duty, and several of my colleagues were killed, especially on forest roads at night.

In spite of my innate sympathy for the feelings of the peasants, I did not at the time question the need for these exactions; I regarded my function as an unpleasant but necessary duty. If the factory workers were short of food, they must have it to produce the machines and the

goods which would enable our backward and stubborn people to progress in spite of themselves. I was young, and as a Party member, my
first loyalty was to the Soviet Government, which could alone rescue
and develop our country along wholly new and revolutionary lines.

What I found most frustrating and heartbreaking was the regularity
with which, as soon as one campaign had been successfully completed,
another would be launched. It would be necessary to go through the
whole process all over again and try once more to convince the angry
and embittered peasants that having with great efforts fulfilled one
quota, they must immediately set to, and fulfil yet another. That was
quite the worst part of it. Even then I wondered at the blindness of a
policy which seemed so utterly callous and impersonal in the ruthless
reduplication of demands. Officially all mistakes were traced not to the
Soviet Government itself, but to the stupidity of intermediate officials.

Who was ultimately to blame? Victims were regularly found. There
was young Gerasimov, who studied with me at the Party school at
Nijny-Tagil. He was an enthusiastic Party worker who did his utmost
to enforce collectivization to the letter of his instructions. Later, as a
reward for his tireless zeal, he was accused of treating the peasants with
excessive severity; he was expelled from the Party, arrested, charged
and condemned. Scapegoats were always being found, to convince the
peasants that it was not the Government but bungling and officious
administrators who were responsible for their hardships. But somehow, as one of the administrators, I was never quite convinced.

Nor could I see with complete revolutionary disregard the fearful
sufferings of the village folk of Russia. Were these just a necessary stage
on the way to a happier life for all, as we were everlastingly assured,
and as I had, in duty bound, to assure the villagers whom I visited? Or
was this mountain of injustice and suffering avoidable, or too great for
any recompense it might bring? I kept on conscientiously with my
duties, but these questions worked away like a mole beneath the surface,
as they must with all Russians who care about the sufferings of their
own people.

In the famine of 1921 in Larikha I remember collecting the bark of
trees and the dried tops of potato-plants, and sunflowers which had
been stripped of their seeds, and breaking the ice on ponds to grub the
roots of reeds; out of these things Mother made soups and stews to keep
us alive. That year so many people died in Larikha that the ordinary
funeral services lapsed; the dead were buried all together in shallow
graves, since people had not the strength to dig deeper.

But from what I heard later of famines in other parts of Russia, I

realize that we were among the lucky ones. In 1934 my friend Korob-
kin, who was a Deputy Chief of an N.K.V.D. Section, visited his native
village near Petropavlovsk in Kazakstan, formerly considered a prosperous area. He found cannibalism there—men who robbed graves and
ate the bodies, women who were known to have eaten their own
children.

In Cánberra Mrs Lipniakov told us of a woman friend of hers working in Leningrad who decided in 1933 to revisit her native village in the
rich grain-growing Ukraine. She arrived by train at the nearest station
and as there was no transport she decided to walk the six miles to her
village. When she got within sight of it she saw that there was no smoke
from any of the chimneys, which struck her as strange, seeing that it
was winter. In the street there was no one to be seen; the village appeared uninhabited. Even her own home, the house where she was
born, was dark and deserted as she pushed her way in and called, 'Is
there anyone at home?' Then she heard a husky voice from the top of
the stove and saw lying on it the emaciated figure of a man with long
hair and a straggling beard. After a little talk with him she discovered
that he was her own brother. He told her that he was the sole survivor
of the famine. She gave him a little bread which she had brought and
stayed with him till the next day, when he died. She left him there
where he was—the horror of the dead village was too much for her;
she could not bear to stay even to bury him—and returned to Leningrad. She was bitter beyond words that the Soviet Government could
allow this to happen; but there was not a thing she could do. To complain would mean dismissal and probably arrest for disloyalty as well.
So she was silent, and told only a few of her closest friends.

This happened sixteen years after the Revolution which was to bring
prosperity to all, and do away with injustice and inequality in the model
socialist state.

Stamped indelibly on my mind is the picture of my native village of
Larikha as I saw it for the last time in the autumn of 1949. A letter had
come to me in Moscow to say that my mother was seriously ill, and I
had been able to get three weeks' compassionate leave from my Department to visit her.

As I sat in the grain-truck jolting along the familiar road from our
nearest railway station at Ishim, I wondered what I should find. The
reality was worse than anything I had imagined. Countryside and
village as we approached reminded me of a desert. Barely a third of the
three hundred and sixty houses of my boyhood remained standing in
anything like reasonable repair; many were gone completely. Roofs

and walls had fallen in, gardens were neglected, everywhere was desolation. One brick building remained in the village, the 'Kolhoz' council house. The church had been pulled down. (I discovered later that it had been intended to use the bricks to build a tractor-station, but the mortar was too strong, and so many bricks were broken in the course of demolition that they were used for road-making instead.)

I drove right past our house without recognizing it and I had to get the driver to go back. The roof was gone, grass and earth covered the ceiling; the stables, outbuildings and the vegetable garden were nowhere to be seen. During my stay I found that most of the remaining houses were in a similar state.

I found my mother lying in bed; she was dying of cancer. She was like a child in her delight at seeing me, which she had never expected to do again. I was her only remaining son. My brother Ivan, who was a postman, had been murdered many years before; and Alexander had been killed during the war, fighting on the Leningrad front. I had sent money regularly to help out her meagre pension, and had many times asked her to come and live with us in Moscow, but she had always replied:

'No, I was born here in the village and here I'll die.'

I found that she was being visited by a doctor from the Kolhoz clinic, which was one of the benefits which collectivization had brought; but there was not much that could be done. She was being cared for by her nephew's wife, Evlampia, and by an old lady who had been deported from Estonia as a Kulak and sent to Larikha as her place of exile. Though her son had been killed fighting in the Red Army, this old lady got no pension because she had been deported and Mother divided food, money, everything she had, with her; they were very good friends.

One episode brought me back to the crude realities of village life again. On the first night I slept in the house on a bench in a fine sleeping-bag which I had brought back from Sweden. It zipped up to the neck and so protected most of my person but, during the night, I was terribly bitten on the face by bed bugs. When I mentioned it to Mother, she only laughed.

'Son, we are used to it. You have forgotten.'

But after that I slept outside.

Whenever I spoke of her health she answered directly and with resignation:

'I can do little around the house now; I am very weak and have much pain; I am near my end.'

She told me that she had never changed her mind about religion; and I asked her how she managed to pray to God. 'Oh, I pray every day myself,' she answered, 'and when I am well enough I ask the truck drivers to take me to Ishim. There is still a church in Ishim; out of the five or six you remember, one is still standing.'

She died soon after I returned to Moscow. I had left money to provide fully for a funeral service in Ishim, for a funeral and a wake-feast for her friends and neighbours in Larikha, and for her burial in the new cemetery, since the old cemetery where Father lay had been destroyed.

The chief of the Kolhoz wrote to me about her few belongings but I did not ask for anything and told him to give them to her friends in the village. With Mother's death my last close family tie in the Soviet Union was gone, and my last direct link with the soil and earth of Russia.

III

A Foot on the Ladder

'KOMSOMOL youth must study! They must educate themselves to be the vanguard of culture and progress in the new Russia!'

The words of the Ishim agitator rang in my ears. The objective and the opportunity which he held out to us in that first meeting in our village beckoned me on, and stirred my ambition to its roots.

The benefits of education bulked large in the early programme of the Revolution; and to many of us village youngsters it seemed an intoxicating possibility. My forebears had been illiterate since the beginning of time; neither my father nor my mother nor my elder brother ever learnt to read. For generations we had been peasants, tied to the earth, bound to our native village, with no possible chance of fitting ourselves for any other life than ignorant tillers of the soil from birth to death. The accent on education was one of the real benefits brought by the Revolution. For the first time an opportunity for self-improvement and self-advancement was offered to the ambitious and diligent among workers and peasants, by way of the Communist Party. Here was a chance to rise above the backwardness and stagnation of our origins, into a new era of enlightenment, education and privilege.

With that prospect before me, I threw myself energetically into Komsomol work; and I was typical of hundreds of thousands of our Soviet youth at that time. There were some—children of privileged and even aristocratic families—who espoused the revolutionary cause from purely idealistic motives. But for the vast majority, including myself, the motive of self-advancement was the first and chief incentive to membership of the Communist Party.

Soon I was elected to the executive bureau of our Komsomol cell in Larikha, first in charge of political education then as secretary. Politics, culture and agriculture were mixed together; I would find myself taking a study group on the significance of May Day one week, and attending a course on butter-production or tractor-driving the next.

Most of the older people, like Capitolina's parents, regarded us with deep suspicion. But we could put up with that, since we had the future, and the victorious Party on our side.

My reward came in August 1926, after three years of hard work, when I was selected out of our local Komsomol to attend a course of study at the new Workers' High School in the town of Perm (now Molotov). It was with high hopes that I said good-bye to my mother, my village comrades and my master the blacksmith, and boarded the train for Perm. Komsomol funds had provided fifteen roubles, of which thirteen had gone on the single ticket; and I had got an advance of three roubles from my employer; so that I had about the equivalent of £5 in my pocket.

The town of Perm impressed me immensely: it made Ishim seem provincial. There was a large agricultural-implement factory, which actually made guns of up to 12-inch calibre, as I believe it does today. Perm, on the river Kama, was a busy river port, and I gazed in wonder at the big river steamers with their huge paddles, and at the jetties, docks and wharves. For the first time I saw buildings four storeys high, and marvelled at the smart women in silk dresses, and the neatness of the men in their tailored suits, with coats and trousers.

I gazed open-eyed at the shop windows with their array of goods for sale; for this was at the height of Lenin's New Economic Policy—that short-lived period of concession to private enterprise which gave the Soviet people an interlude of abundance which they have never enjoyed since.

Among the wonders which I saw for the first time at Perm were bicycles and telephones.

On the second day we candidates faced an entrance test in Dictation, Reading, Arithmetic and Political Education; it was necessary to pass in all four subjects. I passed in Reading and Political Education but I failed in Arithmetic and Dictation. In the latter I made thirty-six spelling errors out of seventy words.

When the results were posted, I saw my name among the three failures out of the seven candidates for the course. It was a bitter disappointment. I pleaded for leniency and for admission to the course; but the authorities were adamant and rigid. Competition was keen, they could not be concerned with the difficulties of every self-taught blacksmith's assistant. The best they could do was to provide me with a set of books called *Workers' High School At Home* for study by correspondence.

In fact, the setback was severe. It was to be eleven years before I qualified for higher education; and then only after four years of gruelling evening study carried on in conjunction with my exacting duties in the Special Department of the N.K.V.D.

The three of us who had failed were drawn together by our common

disappointment, and after discussion we decided that there was nothing
for it but to go back to our villages. But how? None of us had any
money, the question of return tickets not having been considered in the
excitement and optimism of our departure. We decided to 'jump the
rattler'.

Having discovered when a train heading in the direction of our home
district would pass through Perm in the hours of darkness, we
scrambled up the back of the tender and stretched ourselves out on the
coal, where we could see the fireman as he stoked the engine, but he
could not see us. We were undetected, but apart from the violent jolting of the tender, we were choked by the coal dust and were soon as
black as negroes from head to foot from the smoke of the engine. It was
unbearable. At the first stop we jumped down, made our way along the
train and eventually found more tolerable accommodation in an empty
goods-wagon, where we even dozed off to sleep.

I awoke with the strangely peaceful sensation that the wagon was not
moving. Cautiously we peeped out. It was now dawn, and the reason
for our restful state was apparent. During the night our wagon had
been uncoupled from the train and had been shunted into a siding in
what was evidently a big railway junction. In the distance were the
station buildings and trains being shunted over points.

After a hurried conference, we climbed down from our wagon,
crawled underneath, and began to pick our way cautiously across the
lines towards the station.

'Halt! All of you! Put up your hands or I shoot!'

Our knees knocked together and we held aloft shaking hands as the
armed sentry advanced on us with his rifle at the ready. We thought
he was really preparing to shoot us; especially when we saw that he
was guarding a train of sealed wagons that stood nearby.

'Don't try any funny business; this rifle is loaded! Come with me!'

The sentry escorted us to the station platform, flung open a door
marked 'Private' and motioned us to enter. It was the office of the
O.G.P.U. Transport Controller. We saw this awesome uniformed figure
fully dressed except for his boots, sleeping on an elevated bunk like my
platform bed at the blacksmith's house.

The sentry shook him vigorously till he roused himself. 'Here are
three unidentified persons who were prowling on the lines. I've arrested
them and brought them here for identification.'

The O.G.P.U. man jumped down from his bed in a moment and
searched our pockets and our persons for arms. Finding no implements
for sabotage or robbery, he made us produce our documents—those

documents without which one cannot move an inch in the Soviet Union. Mine included my Birth Certificate, and an identity certificate from the Larikha village Soviet giving personal particulars about me and my employment, with a photo and a notation that I was a Komsomol and a candidate for membership of the Communist Party.

The regularity of our documents slightly tempered the fierceness of our examiner; we plucked up courage enough to explain our difficulty and to ask whether he could help us to get back to our villages.

'No, no,' he grumbled, returning to his bunk, 'you must get home as best you can. You are released from arrest but I can't help you any further, it's no business of mine.'

Outside, frightened but relieved, we held another conference and decided to carry on 'jumping'; there was nothing else to do.

About midday an eastward-bound passenger express arrived at the junction. We split up, in search of carriages without conductors.

I perched myself on the ladder of the mail-van, holding on to the two iron handrails; and in this way I hung on while we passed several major stations. But it was autumn, the air was keen and I was nearly frozen. At the first stop we compared notes, and I thawed out a little. But the mail-van guard must have spotted me for he came and stood at the top of the steps just before the train started.

Frantically I hunted along the train, looking for a dog box or a rubbish box such as were carried under some Russian railway carriages. I found neither, and in desperation I decided to crawl in underneath a carriage and stretch myself along one of the axles. My precious study books were my undoing. I had tucked them tightly under my belt for safe keeping but as I stretched out horizontal, they all fell out on the line. Luck was against me. A little boy who was standing near on the platform saw the whole thing, and as I tried to recover the books he called in a shrill excited voice:

'Hares! Hares! Look, father, look; there's a hare!' ('Hare' is the Russian nickname for anyone who is 'jumping' a train.)

His father bent down to see also and this brought the conductor along.

'Get out of there,' he shouted at me, 'you'll get your head cut off when we start!'

Guilty and frightened I climbed out from under the carriage, picked up the books and moved off. But I kept close to the train, for it was my only hope. Somehow or other I must manage to board it.

My luck changed. As the train began to move I saw an empty conductor's cabin, jumped and got into it. I travelled on in this good fortune till late that evening, when the train stopped at a fairly big station. With my two partners, who had had similar luck, I went in search of food. We were all famished but we had to be content with some bread which we begged from peasant cottages near the station, and a drink of cold water from the chained drinking mug on the station platform.

We slept that night in the waiting-room of the station and next morning boarded another passenger-train. This time we were more accomplished in our technique. We sat boldly in a compartment with the other passengers, and secreted ourselves in lavatories whenever we heard the warning approach of 'Tickets please!'

About 1 p.m. that day we reached Sverdlovsk—almost home terri-tory. Worn out, we decided to go to the District Committee of the Communist Party, tell our story and ask for help. At last we got it. They gave us a letter to the Department of Education where we were given ten roubles each.

What a meal we had!—*shchee*, or cabbage soup, tasty cutlets and a fruit dish to conclude. And then we had money enough for our tickets.

That evening we boarded the train for Tyumen as authentic ticket-holding passengers, no longer as hunted 'hares'.

At Ishim I left the train, said good-bye to my two comrades, and trudged along the nineteen miles to Larikha with the news of my failure.

My reception there was characteristic. My Komsomol comrades were sympathetic and disappointed.

My master the blacksmith welcomed me cordially back into his employ.

'But you should have prepared for the exam more thoroughly before you left,' said he.

I answered, looking at my calloused hands, 'Yes, with more spare time and more help with my letters, I would have prepared better.'

My mother shook her head when I told her what had happened.

'Son, it is as I said. You should realize that you have not sufficient education for such high ideas. You should stay here in the village and work.'

I bit my lip and said nothing. But secretly I determined that, by hook or by crook, I was going to get the education that would open so many doors. Every day, after my work in the smithy, I took newspapers and magazine articles and copied them out with painstaking care to give me practice in expression and to improve my handwriting. Those thirty-six errors in dictation were not going to clip my wings for ever!

My Party career was not ruined by my failure, but I now had to work my passage and come up the hard way. The Party District Committee at Ishim were impressed by my determination; after a year they sent me to a Teachers' Training Course in a former monastery near Sverdlovsk. In the venerable building with its high whitewashed wall, the students occupied the cells of the dispossessed monks and ate in the great hall that had been their refectory. At the end of this course I passed all the tests and received a certificate qualifying me as a Pioneer teacher and physical training instructor. It was a step.

Back in Larikha, a further, and vitally important, promotion awaited me. On the 15th July 1927 I was admitted to membership of the Communist Party of the Soviet Union. I had joined the *élite* band who were the real holders of power, privilege and responsibility in the new Russia. I had to apply in writing, filling in a detailed questionnaire and citing three guarantors, two of whom had to be Party members. The accuracy of my biographical details had to be confirmed by the District Komsomol.

Even so, I qualified after only a year's probation. Joining the Party was a much simpler matter then than it is now. In those days the Party was optimistic about the early achievement of the ideal socialist society and the workers' paradise. It was generally assumed that anyone of peasant or working-class stock would support the cause of the Party which was the chosen instrument of the Revolution. Today both the educational requirements and political tests are much more searching. Competition for privileged posts is intense and the Soviet people are disillusioned about the Utopia that has failed to arrive.

My first assignment as a Party Member was to the large village of Vikulovo, in charge of the Cultural Centre. I lived in lodgings, and was on duty from nine in the morning till midnight. I managed the library and reading room, helped illiterate villagers to write letters—mostly to their sons in the Army, or in connection with lawsuits—and gave readings of the Russian classics. My audiences were almost entirely women who brought their foot-looms and wove cloth while they listened, preferring a companionable gossip with their neighbours to sitting at home alone. Some of the young men came to a class in shooting and arms-drill which I organized with the help of a Red Army veteran and they would wait to take some of the girls home after the cultural evenings. The main patrons of the library were village teachers and a number of political exiles, well-educated, intelligent people, mostly Jews, from Moscow, Leningrad and Sverdlovsk, who had been banished from their homes on suspicion of Trotskyist sympathies. It was not always an advantage to have been educated *before* the Revolution.

Next came my gruelling ordeal as a Government collector in the
villages which I have already described. Then, after a course in trade-
union work at a Party school at Nijni-Tagil, I had my first experience
of the new industrial Russia. I was appointed Youth Organizer to the
great new steelworks at Nadejdinsk in northern Siberia at the northern
end of the Ural Mountains.

The Nadejdinsk works produced high quality steel at the price of
severe human hardship. Smoke and acrid fumes from the furnaces
sometimes enveloped the whole town. The summer was short, the
winter long and harsh. The fifteen thousand workers got only one meal
during their eight-hour shift and that was miserably meagre. I was
supposed to receive my rations at the works, but I had to supplement
them substantially out of my pay in order to exist.

Accommodation was very short, and twelve of us had to sleep in two
bug-ridden rooms. I preferred to sleep on the table in my small office
at the works.

Soviet trade unions were not so disciplined and subservient at that
time as they are now and while I was there the workers' factory committee actually staged a protest. When no wages had been paid for two
months they organized a march on the factory manager, aired their
grievances and presented him with a flag made of straw matting as an
insulting emblem. The wages were promptly paid. However, the
secretary of the factory committee, who had led the march, lost his job
soon afterwards, as the manager was himself a Party member. The
episode was part of my education in the school of hard realities. The
monolithic Soviet state has no place for trade unions as separate independent organizations such as exist in Western countries.

Among the older workers I gained few recruits to the Party. 'Why
should I join the Party?' they would say, 'I'm better off as I am without
going to meetings and paying dues and having more to worry about.'
But I had some success with the younger workers when I gave them a
rosy picture of the chances for education and improvement in their
station in life which the Komsomol and Party organizations offered.

My own political education, in terms not of programmes but of
personalities, was also taken a step forward by an episode at Nadejdinsk
which had a grim and significant sequel. We received a visit from
Rykov. Rykov was one of the old Bolsheviks who had served the
cause from the earliest days with great energy and distinction. He had
held a succession of offices, had succeeded Lenin as head of the Soviet
Government and, when we saw him, was Chairman of the All-Union
Council of Peoples' Commissars. He was in the district representing the

Party's Central Committee at a Party conference of the Urals region. It was a privilege and an experience to have this important official and renowned veteran of the Revolution in our midst.

Rykov addressed a selected audience of about a thousand in a big circus tent from a specially-erected platform. He was of middle height, bearded and looked ill. He had a plain-clothes bodyguard, but his un-assuming dress and simple language were in accord with his humble peasant origin. He spoke quietly but with a deep earnestness, stressing the vital importance of greater production to build the true socialist state, and urging everyone on to greater efforts. His modesty and sincerity made a great impression on all of us.

When he finished his address one of the workers sprang to his feet and exclaimed with enthusiasm:

'Alexei Ivanovich, you should come to our factory more often, you are too rare a visitor, we would like to see Government people here more often.'

'Well, comrade,' answered Rykov cordially, 'we shall do our best to visit you here as often as we can.'

It was more than official formality. Rykov represented the old school of Revolutionary leaders, who really believed that it was a revolution for the masses, and not for the privileged minority, and who, whatever their official responsibilities, kept in close personal touch with the ordinary people. His visit brought stimulus and incentive to all of us at Nadejdinsk.

When I saw Rykov again he was a broken man, charged with treason to the State. It was during the third great trial of 1938. Yezhov, the new chief of the N.K.V.D., under Stalin's direction was sweeping away thousands of old Bolsheviks and former government officials in a blood-bath and holocaust of maniac proportions.

Rykov was arrested and tried along with a number of these old Bol-sheviks, including Bukharin, the distinguished theoretician, and Yag-oda, the displaced chief of the N.K.V.D. The trial was held in the Trade Union Hall of Columns, practically opposite the Hotel Moscow. How-ever, there was no question of admitting the general public as in Western countries. The trial took place in a small chamber upstairs, holding only about two hundred people, and admission was by special pass only. Blocks of these passes were allotted to selected Government agencies and I received a ticket for the last two sessions on 11th and 12th March.

Vyshinsky, the Government Prosecutor, was aggressive, violent and overbearing. He shouted, screamed, thundered, gesticulated. The accused had lawyers who were nominally defending them but these offered only the feeblest of defences and in all important matters supported the charges against the accused. All the accused pleaded guilty to the charges heaped upon them. As they sat in the dock they were pale, worn, half-alive.

Their 'confessions' have been published in the Soviet official record of the trial.

This 'verbatim report' which I have read in its English version, has obviously been carefully edited. Yagoda's last plea, for example, after a confession of guilt, contains the words: 'It is hard to live after such crimes, it is hard to sit in prison for tens of years. But it is terrible to die with such a stigma. Even from behind the bars I would like to see the further flourishing of the country which I betrayed.'

But I can see now Yagoda's emaciated face and hear his low fear-ridden tones as he pleaded to the court to spare him from death and to sentence him to prison where at least he would be able to read in *Pravda* how the Soviet people were building their new life.

He was sentenced to death and executed with the rest.

Rykov was accused of collaborating with the Germans. It was said that on a visit to Germany he had drunk too much, had met a representative of German Intelligence, and had later been recruited as an agent for Germany.

Rykov himself, in his last plea, declared himself guilty of Rightist counter-revolutionary terrorism and wrecking activities in agriculture. But his peasant origin perhaps gave him a tougher fibre than the abject Yagoda. Beaten and helpless, he did not lose control of himself.

As I listened, I felt stunned and mesmerized. I wondered how he would stand up to execution by a bullet in the back of the head, and what would happen to his family, friends and relations.

Vyshinsky's speech for the prosecution was a monument of unrestrained invective. He lashed himself into a fury, appealed to the judges for the death penalty and concluded with the words: 'Our whole country, from young to old, is awaiting and demanding one thing only —the traitors and spies who were selling our country to the enemy must be shot like dirty dogs! Our people are demanding one thing— crush the accursed reptile! Time will pass. The graves of the hateful traitors will grow over with weeds and thistles. They will be covered with the eternal contempt of honest Soviet citizens, of the entire Soviet people.'

The President of the court, Ulrich, had an enormous head that hung almost on a level with his shoulders, a full round face, and looked like a prosperous country landowner of Czarist times. He asked the accused in turn if they had anything further to say before the court retired to consider its verdict. Some of them made a final appeal, but when it came to Rykov's turn, he answered in a scarcely audible voice, 'I have nothing further to say.' The former Chairman of the All-Union Council of Peoples' Commissars had nothing further to say.

All the accused, except three minor figures, were sentenced to death and shot.

In recalling the scene of the trial, I cannot entirely dissociate myself from what I know now, nor fully recapture my own feelings and impressions at the time. Fear and bewilderment were probably uppermost in my mind. It was a time of universal fear. I was present at only two days of the trial, and all my other knowledge of the cases was derived from the official *Pravda* version. Apart from *Pravda's* account, one did not discuss these matters with anyone. On the whole I accepted Vyshinsky's charges. I heard with amazement and alarm that treachery could apparently reach so high into Government circles, and could corrupt old revolutionaries like Rykov and Bukharin.

Now I see the whole trial in perspective, as a monstrous hoax. Was it likely that an old devoted Bolshevik like Rykov would lend himself so readily to the service of Nazi Germany, Socialism's most menacing enemy? This trumped-up charge was a regular device by which Stalin represented every form of political opposition as treason to the Soviet Union, and thus paved the way for the liquidation of anyone who opposed his will, or knew too much, or was required as a scapegoat for the public.

The 'Rightist' charge against Rykov was no doubt his real offence in Stalin's eyes. Rykov had dared to question Stalin's policy and to champion agriculture at a time when Stalin was pushing industrial production at any cost. Perhaps if Rykov's views had prevailed, agriculture in the Soviet Union would not be in its present disastrous state, which the Soviet Government can no longer conceal from the Soviet people and which undermines the whole economy and strength of the u.s.s.r. How impossible to foresee such an end to Rykov's life as I listened to the veteran revolutionary's inspiring words at Nadejdinsk!

But I am running ahead of my story.

IV

Red Sailor to Blue Cap

'PETROV. Vladimir Mikhailovich, to report to Naval Headquarters, Leningrad, for service with the Red Navy.'

It was in the autumn of 1930 that I began my three and a half years of naval service, an interlude which I look back upon with pleasure and gratitude, though at the end of it I was as ready as most sailors for a spell ashore.

There was no naval officer on our district Selection Board, which was responsible for allotting recruits to the various services, and it was a Red Army colonel who spoke.

I was delighted at the news. Most recruits wanted to serve in the Army, thinking that it would give them better opportunities to master a skilled trade which would be useful to them after their release. But I had admired the sailors I had seen on leave in our district, and had envied them their breezy confidence, their neat uniform, their smart ribbons and cap-tallies. The Navy appealed to me from the start.

But there was another branch represented on the Board beside the Army and the Air Force, in the person of a colonel of the O.G.P.U. troops, whose special tasks include frontier defence and internal security. He was instantly distinguishable by the light blue top to his uniform cap, and red cap-band.

'Would you like to serve with the O.G.P.U., comrade?' he asked.

'Comrade Colonel, I would prefer to join the Navy—that has always been my wish.'

I had no desire to join the O.G.P.U. troops. Despite their privileged position, they were generally hated and feared by the mass of the population, both in towns and in the country.

The O.G.P.U. colonel made no demur; and a few days later I was rolling across the breadth of Russia in one of the trucks of a recruit transport train, bound for Leningrad. It was a slow four days' journey, but most of us were in high spirits, and there was plenty of talk, singing and accordion playing on the way. Youths rejected for military service, whether on medical or political grounds, were generally disappointed, and felt that they had lost both an adventure and an opening for further education.

At Leningrad we naval recruits were met and quickly marched off to barracks in the Baltic Fleet depot. Next morning we faced a barrage of tests relating to colour blindness, physical fitness, intelligence and quick thinking.

Then we had to report to the captain of the Manning Depot, impressive in his uniform and black beard, to hear our results and appointments. I had passed all the tests, but I had some anxious moments as to what lay ahead when I heard that I was going to the Electric Mine School at Kronstadt. When the Captain mentioned my duties, I misheard the Russian word 'Shifrovat' (cypher) and thought he said 'Shlifovat' (polish).

'D-do you mean I'm to polish the mines, sir?' I stammered, with a ghastly sinking in the stomach. If he took the point he did not move a muscle. 'Comrade Petrov, you'll find out when you get there.' It was some little time before I discovered, with inexpressible relief, that I was to be a cypher-rating, not a mine-polisher.

To me, whose whole life had hitherto been spent in the vast interior of continental Russia, the Kronstadt Naval Base was a fascinating and impressive sight, with its swarming sailors, some at work, others in their smart 'going-ashore' rig, and its variety of naval vessels, including destroyers, the rescue-tug *Paris Commune*, and the two battleships *Marat* and *October Revolution*.

Immediately my ambition was fired to make my mark in this new world. I was mortified to find that my new uniform was too tight for comfort, and that we recruits were not allowed to wear cap-tallies, bearing our ship's name, for a month, and I squirmed to hear the old salts referring to us contemptuously as '*Salaga*' (new chums). The nine of us who had been selected for cypher work went through the ordinary training course, which included chemistry, physics, mathematics, Russian, English and stenography. But we also had a special position. We were not allowed to discuss our work with any of the other ratings, and we filled in an additional form with many more biographical and family details. We knew that every point would be checked and cross-checked by the o.g.p.u. in Moscow, with whom rested the final decision on all appointments to such privileged and important work as handling secret cyphers. If the slightest trace of any 'compromising material' were found about us or our relatives or friends, we would be disqualified, probably for life, from obtaining any responsible or confidential work.

However, no such calamity occurred. I finished the course with marks above the average and was posted for six months' sea service in the training cruiser *Aurora*, a vessel famous in the history of the Revolution. When the Revolution in the Fleet began, in Leningrad, *Aurora* was the first ship to open fire on the Czar's winter palace. To serve aboard her was a historic privilege for a keen young Party member.

The technical course which qualified me as a cypher specialist took two years to complete, after which I was posted to the destroyer *Volodarsky*, based on Kronstadt and attached to the Soviet Baltic Fleet. I was the senior cypher rating, and had a small cabin under the bridge where I lived and worked. I handled the ship's confidential books and was responsible for coding and decoding any secret signals originated or received by our ship. Morale was good in the Red Navy in those days. Most of us recruits put on weight on the ample naval rations, at a time when food was short and life full of hardships for the masses on shore. Discipline was strict but reasonable.

Almost all our officers had risen from the lower deck. Any penalties they imposed were usually fair and just. Our c.o. was respected and liked. He gave his orders in a quiet restrained tone, and the crew realized that he was an experienced seaman who handled his ship with skill and competence. Particularly during Fleet manœuvres we were always keen to acquit ourselves well, and to reflect credit on our ship and our Commanding Officer.

The Political Commissar, who was responsible for the political education of the ship's company, was the only severe and unpopular officer. But in my time he was not in a position to interfere with the running of the ship, apart from his special responsibility to supervise the political education of the ship's company.

Whenever we got shore leave we were popular and welcome visitors in the sailors' city of Leningrad. Our ship was adopted by the girl workers in a chemical factory there who arranged concerts, excursions, and visits to theatres for members of our company on leave. A number of marriages resulted from these acquaintanceships. We in turn would invite parties of the girls on board, and would give them a good dinner, such as was all too rare for the hungry civilian population in those years. Permission was even given for the leader of this cultural group to come for a six-day cruise during our autumn manœuvres. Alas, our kind intentions were misplaced! It was heavy weather and the poor girl spent the entire cruise being sick in the cabin of the Political Commissar—who was also seasick. The experiment was not tried again.

The thing that I appreciated most of all in my years of naval service, and which I look back upon with the greatest pleasure, was the comradeship of life afloat and the friendships I made among my shipmates. I kept in touch with many of them long after we had all left the Navy. We sailors felt pride in our service and would always come to the rescue of any other sailors who were in trouble with folk ashore or got into fights with soldiers.

Life afloat seems to make for what Russians call a 'good collective', or community spirit. This is an experience common to seafarers of all nations. But it seemed to me to come nearest to the reality of the Communist ideal expressed in the term *Tovarish* or comrade, which Lenin and the great pioneers of the Revolution had striven to achieve in the Party.

While in the Navy I wrote articles for the Navy paper *Red Baltic Fleet*, describing with genuine proletarian enthusiasm my experience in Komsomol and youth work for the Party in the country and in industry. And it was in December 1929, in the flush of that enthusiasm, that I changed my name from Shorokhov to Proletarsky, 'man of the people'. The change, according to the regulations, was advertised in *Izvestia*; and anybody who likes to study old *Izvestias* of that period will find it recorded. At that time there was a wave of fashion to demonstrate one's proletarian and revolutionary zeal by adopting such a name. Besides 'Proletarsky' other popular names adopted at that time were 'Oktyabrsky' (referring to the October Revolution) and 'Maisky' (referring to the 1st of May).

The change had to receive official sanction, and it necessitated getting a whole new set of documents. I had to get a new internal passport (which everyone over sixteen must carry in the Soviet Union) and a new identity card stamped by the local militia in each town, village or district where I had ever resided. Later I regretted my impulsive action. I had to be equipped with another name and a fresh set of documents for foreign service, as the name Proletarsky was considered too militant to be diplomatic. In fact, a case was recorded of a Proletarsky who was included in a delegation to visit Warsaw, but who was refused a visa by the right-wing Polish Government of the day because of his name.

When I set off for Sweden, and later for Australia, as 'Petrov', I left all my 'Proletarsky' documents with the Ministry of Foreign Affairs in Moscow, where they were to be reissued when I handed in my 'Petrov' documents on my return to Russia. No doubt they are still there. I have no plans for collecting them.

Apart from this complication, I came to regret the change for more personal reasons. When someone asked me, 'Why did you change your name?' I would feel an access of irrational embarrassment; I regretted my abandonment of the good old Russian name of Shorokhov. When there was a telephone call in the office for 'Proletarsky', I had a feeling that my colleagues were laughing at me behind my back.

My wife Doosia never liked the name Proletarsky, and refused to adopt it (as she was entitled to do) when we were married.

Towards the end of my naval career I had an experience which marked the climax of my youthful enthusiasm for the Party and my belief in its mission to lead, inspire and uplift the ignorant, toiling masses of the Russian people. I was chosen as one of the five naval delegates to a conference of Komsomol leaders in Leningrad, and there I heard Kirov speak.

Kirov's life and death mark a phase in the history of the Soviet Revolution. He was an old Bolshevik, a man of the stamp of Rykov, who believed with every fibre of his being that the ordinary people of the Soviet Union ought to share fully in the making of the new Russia, and who acted on that belief.

Kirov, when I saw him, belonged to a species that was soon to become extinct; he was one of the few remaining Revolutionary leaders who were not afraid of the people they led. As a member of the Politburo, he was obliged to have a bodyguard, but he always strove to give his escort the slip. He would visit factories, and talk on man-to-man terms with the ordinary workers, an unheard-of procedure on the part of Stalin, Molotov and the new hierarchy. While I was in the Navy, Kirov came to sea, aboard one of the cruisers during Baltic Fleet manœuvres, and the sailors reported that he showed a personal interest in their well-being and their life in the service. I heard a story of a worker who had a grievance about the conscription of his son to the Navy. He received an unexpected visit from Kirov, who explained the importance of what his son was doing in the Navy and convinced the old man that it was necessary and right. On another occasion, at a meeting of factory managers, Kirov brandished samples of inferior household equipment, called out the culprits who were responsible, and demanded that the public be given better quality articles in future. No other Soviet leader dared or troubled to do such things. No wonder that Kirov enjoyed an immense popularity in the whole Leningrad region.

Kirov had another gift which marked him out among the Soviet leaders—he was a magnificent speaker. Short, stocky, and broad-faced, a typical peasant, he had the capacity to identify himself with his audience and to capture their interest and sympathy with his first words. He used simple graphic language, accompanied by forceful gestures where necessary, but never to excess; and he had a particular faculty for appealing to young people.

Our conference was held in the Smolny, which had been the Czar's palace; it was set in a beautiful garden, and the big hall where we met comfortably accommodated the five hundred delegates of the Leningrad District Komsomols.

Kirov's speech on the role of Komsomols in building the new Russia made a tremendous impression. In forceful, compelling words he touched on the inadequacy of results so far achieved, and passionately urged all Komsomols to win more recruits, and to work with fresh zeal and self-sacrifice for the future of the Soviet youth. It was inspiring because of Kirov's own character and example.

Four and a half years later, in December 1934, I looked out of the window of the old O.G.P.U. building, and saw the gun carriage bearing Kirov's coffin pass through the snow-covered streets of Moscow. In front marched the leaders of the Politburo, including Molotov, Kalinin and Kaganovich; while a huge crowd of mourners, most of them deeply and sincerely stricken as though by a personal loss, followed behind. Stalin met the cortège at the Trade Union Hall, where the coffin was taken for the lying-in-state.

What lay behind the violent death of this old Bolshevik, Politburo member and popular hero? The bare facts were recorded in the Moscow Press. Kirov was shot by the assassin Nikolayev on 1st December 1934, in his office in that same Smolny where our conference had been held, and which became the Leningrad District Party Headquarters. The whole affair, which has since been unravelled in detail by Alexander Orlov,[1] was shrouded in mystery and contradictions at the time. The absence of the guards at the moment of the assassination was never explained. Stalin personally conducted the investigation and there were strange contradictory announcements. First the murder was ascribed to a large number of White Guardists who had infiltrated into the Soviet Union from abroad; then, without explanation, the blame was shifted to the Opposition leaders and the old Bolsheviks Zinoviev and Kamenev, who were later convicted at the first of the great Moscow trials and executed.

The Soviet people, trained in the docile acceptance of the line laid down by the official Soviet press as a condition of safety and, indeed, survival, were told that Zinoviev and Kamenev had murdered Kirov

---

[1] *The Secret History of Stalin's Crimes*, by Alexander Orlov, Jarrolds, London, 1954.

through the medium of Nikolayev; there were many popular execrations of them as 'wicked Trotskyites', etc.

Like everyone else, I accepted that story myself at the time; at least I did not indulge in too much profitless and dangerous speculation. Today I am convinced that Kirov's real crime was his independence and popularity; and that his murder took place under the control and direction of Stalin, as the first step in his programme of systematic elimination of all possible rivals. According to the Soviet newspapers, when Stalin saw Kirov's body on the bier he rushed forward and kissed it, overcome by grief and affection for his old comrade. Such hypocrisy would be quite in character.

Kirov's death was a milestone in the steady separation of the Soviet leaders from the Soviet people which has been going on ever since. Apart from the interlude of the War, when the Nazi threat of annihilation created a temporary unity of interest between Government and people, there has probably never been more widespread discontent, or deeper distrust between the Soviet people and their rulers, than there is in the Soviet Union today.

If it were not so, what would be the need for the immense machine of internal surveillance, employing millions of workers and covering every aspect of Soviet life, by which the Soviet Government detects and suppresses the slightest suspicion of political opposition among its people?

I have been a part of that machine; I am not writing from hearsay, but from personal experience and inside knowledge.

I joined the O.G.P.U. in May 1933. My reasons were simple. I was married, I wanted a job, and I wanted enough to eat. I had refused the invitation to join the O.G.P.U. Internal Security troops, remembering how ordinary folk avoided the sight of the dreaded uniform. I remembered the hatred aroused when O.G.P.U. men came to our village to arrest rebellious war-veterans who grumbled about the shortages; I remembered how peasant mothers frightened their naughty children with the threat, 'If you don't behave yourself, the O.G.P.U. men will get you!'

But when I finished my years of naval service and came to Moscow, I was glad to be issued free with that warm uniform jacket with its mauve shoulder-tabs, and to put on those breeches, leggings and peaked cap with its blue top and red cap-band, and to acquire the rank of 'Assistant Operational Functionary' of the O.G.P.U. And I was very glad to possess a pass to the excellent O.G.P.U. restaurant. We had fared well in the Navy, but the ordinary people of Russia, without these special privileges, were cruelly rationed and desperately short of food and clothing in those hard and hungry years.

During one of my last shore leaves I had married; and for that reason I refused an invitation to stay on in the Navy as a Political Commissar. I felt I was due for a spell ashore. It was a sailor's marriage, and it did not last. Lydia was young and flighty; I was of a quiet, perhaps phlegmatic, disposition. Besides finding my feet in my new job, I had a heavy programme of evening classes which the Party insisted that I should attend; and then I was posted abroad for a period of foreign service in China. We separated in 1938, and Lydia afterwards married a Red Army officer. At that time marriage and divorce were much easier and more casual than they have since been made in the Soviet Union.

Former shipmates who had done the naval cypher course with me recommended me for entry to the o.g.p.u., and my Komsomol and Party record was unblemished. After completing innumerable forms, and being subjected to a severe lecture on the importance and secret nature of the work, I was admitted to the Special Cypher Section which, at Lenin's suggestion, had been attached to the Foreign Department of the o.g.p.u.

Shortly afterwards I assisted another shipmate to join the same section. He filled in the five special forms, and wrote out his biography; but the Section Chief returned them to him with disapproval; they were crammed with grammatical errors. I helped him correct these till the forms were faultless (I had worked very hard at my Russian in the Navy) and he was accepted. But his renderings of decyphered telegrams remained very faulty, which puzzled the Section Chief, after his good showing on the entrance papers.

o.g.p.u. workers were from the start an important and privileged *élite* in the Soviet Union; they were the chosen corps whose task it was to protect the Revolution against foreign foes abroad and insidious counter-Revolutionaries at home; and to discharge this responsible and confidential task they must be provided with the best in such matters as food, clothing and accommodation—so the logical argument ran. In fact, I found myself working harder than ever before in my life for these privileges. Besides the exacting work of a cypher clerk, I embarked, at the instigation of the Party, on a heavy course of part-time education in a 'Workers' Faculty'. Three nights a week I attended evening classes from seven o'clock till eleven-thirty, and had preparation to do on other nights. Even on Sundays, when most of my colleagues took time off to go to a park or cinema, I stayed at home with my books. Of the thirty who began the course with me, nearly half dropped out. But in 1937, after four strenuous years, I passed in all subjects and received the reward of a large certificate. At last I had made amends for my failure to gain entrance to the Workers' High School so many years before. Henceforward I was qualified to enter any institution of higher study, equivalent to University level.

But my qualification had come too late in the day for that. Twice I tried to leave the O.G.P.U., once to rejoin the Navy and once to go to the Stalin Tank Academy and become a regular army officer.

'Volodya, why do you sit crouched at a desk all day?' asked my breezy friend Babushkin, who was an engineer in a tank regiment. 'Join the Army! See a bit of life!'

I tried hard to follow his advice. By that time, after four years of the gruelling yet impersonal work of a cypher clerk, I was tired of sitting in a chair all day and half the night dealing with an endless stream of incoming and outgoing signals. I wanted something more active and more in touch with people. But on each occasion my Chief refused to release me, on the grounds that he was too short of trained cypher staff. So an O.G.P.U. cypher clerk I remained.

It was a hard grind for the seven of us who worked in the big room on the fourth floor of No. 6 Lubianka Street—the old O.G.P.U. building that had been an insurance office in Czarist times. (It has since been demolished to make way for the imposing new building.) The chief clerk was a hard-driving taskmaster, and a stickler for absolute accuracy. Out of working hours we tried to persuade him to be more lenient and understanding towards our errors, but without success. Often we toiled till nearly midnight to complete the day's quota of cables. The flow of inward and outward cable traffic was relentless; for our section handled all the foreign communications between O.G.P.U. representatives abroad and headquarters in Moscow. There were only twelve of us altogether when I joined. The section's strength had been increased to forty-five when I was last in the Soviet Union in 1951, and it had been elevated to a Department. But in my experience the increase in staff never kept pace with the increasing traffic, as our foreign espionage networks spread wider and wider, and as secret intelligence about the countries of the non-Soviet world became more and more urgently necessary.

The cables which passed through my hands were all from Soviet 'legal' representatives, that is, O.G.P.U. representatives who were appointed to Soviet diplomatic establishments abroad under cover of some legal office, such as I myself later held in Sweden and in Australia. Any 'illegal residents'—that is, agents who operated independently of

Soviet official missions—had their own methods of communication to another department of the O.G.P.U.

During the day I saw only the cables that were handed to me personally; but when it was my turn to do night duty I saw the whole of that day's intake. From these secret communications I got some fascinating insights into the relations of our Socialist homeland with the capitalist powers that encircled it, and into the operations of our agents in all parts of the world.

In the West it was the era of the rising threat from Fascist Italy and Nazi Germany, and I recall a flood of cables from our agents in Rome and Berlin.

Then came the Spanish Civil War. The Soviet's active intervention made it easy to infiltrate our agents there, and to maintain excellent intelligence coverage; and I sweated till late into the night decoding lengthy cables reporting on the situation in Spain. I remember a whole series concerned with the shipping of arms to the Spanish Republican Army through Finland, where the arms were bought to conceal the extent of Soviet intervention.

The man in charge of this operation in Finland was Shpigelglas, Deputy Head of the O.G.P.U.'s Foreign Department. One night when I was on duty I received a telephone call from Shpigelglas who asked if there was anything of particular interest to him; I knew that Spain was his special concern. Soon afterwards he walked into the office—a rare thing for any chief of his rank to do. He was correct, polite, business-like, and agile in movements and mind. Physically he was short of stature, sandy-haired and looked like a Russian though he was actually a Jew. He looked quickly through all the cables from Spain; they came from Madrid and Barcelona, where we had Residents working under legal cover. Among other things, Shpigelglas directed sabotage work in Spain; where special groups had been formed, under Russian instructors, which achieved considerable successes. Shpigelglas was an able and ruthless man. I have since learned that it was he who had organized the murder in Switzerland of Ignace Reiss, an O.G.P.U. undercover operative in Western Europe who had refused to return to Moscow and be purged.

There was one dramatic cable from Madrid in July 1938, which I can still visualize as it lay decoded on the table before me. In laconic official language it reported that our O.G.P.U. resident 'X' had deserted the Soviet service and had fled to Paris with his wife and daughter. (Later I discovered that 'X' was Alexander Orlov, Chief O.G.P.U. Representative with the Republican forces in Spain.) In Paris, the cable continued,

'X' had instructed a lawyer, if he should be assassinated or should meet with any mishap, to publish his memoirs which contained the names of all his agents and contacts in Spain, and a description of his important and highly secret work there on behalf of the Soviet Government.

Orlov subsequently took refuge in the United States where he is now a naturalized American citizen. It was not until 1954, when Orlov published his book, that the dramatic story behind that cable was released to the world and that Orlov disclosed how he became aware that his own life was threatened, how he evaded his recall to Russia and made his escape, and how he threatened Stalin, who knew him personally, with a public revelation of Stalin's monstrous crimes if he or his family became the victims of yet another assassination.

At the time, during Yezhov's reign of terror, it would have been madness for me to make any comment or to pursue any unnecessary inquiries about the case. But I recall the cable now, and the impression it made upon me, with a particular personal interest. In those purge years, when fear was universal and danger everywhere, every escape story had an acute and poignant fascination. I wondered secretly what would be the fate and fortune of such an important State Security official, who had dared to defy Stalin and had fled to the forbidden world of the West. I little guessed then that I myself was fated to take the same road fifteen years later.

V

Red Sickle over China

THE victory of the Chinese Communist armies in 1948 and the rise of Communist China as one of the great and growing world powers seems to have come as a bolt from the blue to many people in Western countries. But Russia has been an Asian power, deeply concerned with her eastern frontiers and neighbours, since the time of the Czars. In the east, as in so many other fields, Soviet imperialism has taken over where Czarist imperialism left off, with the added instrument of Communist ideology.

In the late 1930's, while one eye of Soviet policy looked westward with alarm at the menace of Nazi Germany and Fascist Italy, the other looked eastward with apprehension at the Japanese, who became our neighbours by their occupation of Manchuria. I decoded many cables from our N.K.V.D. Residents in Manchuria, Harbin and Mongolia, which was in fact completely under Soviet control, though nominally independent. I handled the cable traffic between Moscow and a special N.K.V.D. operational group which was dispatched to Mongolia.

But it was in Sinkiang Province, in the far south-west of China, that I acquired vivid first-hand experience of Soviet intervention in foreign territory. Sinkiang has recently been in the news following Krushchev's visit to Peking at the end of 1954 when the Soviet is reported to have conceded important industrial holdings in Sinkiang to Communist China. When I was last in Moscow a party of geologists was leaving to investigate the huge mineral wealth of Sinkiang. And the proximity of Sinkiang Province to India gives it a strategic importance which is greater than ever in these days of air transport.

Before I went there, I had handled enough cables to and from Sinkiang to know that it was the scene of a powerful effort on our part to oust British and American influence, represented by missionaries and traders, and to bring the province wholly into the Soviet orbit. The cables reported that the missionaries were foreign agents, propagandists and smugglers. And when the pro-Soviet puppet government at Urumchi, the capital of Sinkiang, was threatened by a revolt of army officers and tribesmen, a detachment of N.K.V.D. border troops with tanks and aircraft was sent to help put down the rising, carry out a thorough purge, and eliminate anti-Soviet elements. To prevent ill-disposed persons such as foreign press representatives asking what Soviet Border Guards and N.K.V.D. Internal Security troops were doing on Chinese soil, instructions were given that our troops should wear Chinese uniforms and that every effort should be made to conceal their part in suppressing the revolt and in carrying out the purge.

One day my section head, Ilyin, sent for me. 'The Chief of Communications with our troops in Sinkiang has asked for a capable man to take charge of cypher duties at the Headquarters there. I've decided that you're the man for the job. Hand over your present duties and be prepared to move at once.'

It was September 1937, and early autumn tints were showing on the trees as I set out on the five-day train journey through the heart of Soviet central Asia. I felt pleased and excited. After four years of slogging desk work, this assignment promised to be a stimulating change. Moreover, it was an important step up in my career; for with eight subordinates, I would now have my own independent cypher unit at the staff headquarters. I settled down in the comfortable train, and decided to enjoy the journey. As we left behind the settled farm and forest districts near Moscow, travelling south and east, the weather grew warmer and the country wilder. Near Kazakhstan we ran out on to steppes—great flat, sandy wastes with patches of coarse grass here and there, and rocky streams full of tortoises. The wayside stations were piled high with watermelons and fish from the rivers and from the Aral Sea and we saw the wild Kazak tribesmen, famous as horse-breeders, in their fur hats and coats of wool felt; they wore these thick clothes, it was explained, to ward off the hot sun. Further on, the line ran along the north shore of the Aral Sea itself, and I saw fishing boats drawn up on the beach.

I left the train at Frunze, capital of Khirgiz Province, so renamed after the famous military leader who succeeded Trotsky as Commander-in-Chief of the Red Army. There I reported to the N.K.V.D. representative who informed my new Communications Chief, Voitenkov, of my arrival, and issued me with a fur jacket for the next stage of the journey, which would be over the mountains. The town of Frunze was developing rapidly. Overtopping the mud houses of the indigenous population were imposing public buildings including two new N.K.V.D. buildings and the headquarters of the Khirgiz Soviet Republic. Much of the labour was supplied by exiled Kulak families; and I heard that there were further transfers of population to Frunze from the Baltic countries after the Soviet occupied them in 1940, following the Nazi-Soviet pact. The toil of these miserable exiles has been the basis of the development of all the frontier regions of the u.s.s.r.

The next stage of the journey was dramatic. With an Army convoy of forty trucks, we wound our way through the precipitous passes of the famous Tien Shan mountains (The 'Heavenly' Mountains) towering 23,000 feet above us, to the military outpost of Turugart. The road was still under construction, and we passed gangs of prisoners, pale, haggard, and scarcely human-looking, watched over by armed n.k.v.d. guards. The road was so dangerous that the Moscow drivers were afraid of it, and had been replaced by locals; it was a succession of sharp curves, loose stones and sheer falls; and accidents were frequent.

Presently I began to doze, but felt a violent poke in the side. 'Do you want to see us both dead?' exclaimed the driver.

'What do you mean?' I asked.

'The sight of you dozing alongside gives me the same idea. Talk! Keep me awake if you want to live!'

I did as he asked.

We stopped for the night at a settlement of the Khirgiz tribesmen whose *yurts*, or goatskin tents, dotted the floors of the valleys. I was told that among these primitive Khirgiz the collective farm principle was regarded favourably. The explanation was simple. The less poverty-stricken among their number had been purged as 'Kulaks' and their possessions distributed among those who remained. In this way the remainder were enabled to see the value of collectivization.

The next stage of the journey was by air. From the breathless eyrie of Turugart, the border post, we flew through the passes of the Tien Shan to Yarkand, where the army unit was stationed and where our headquarters was now set up.

Yarkand, third city of Sinkiang, is nearly 4,000 feet above sea level, but is on flat ground, and is surrounded by a moat and a great mud wall with Chinese towers. The gates are shut at nightfall and when we arrived after dark we had to batter on the gate to wake up the sleeping Chinese sentry, who thought his duties were over. We were conducted to the fort which was our headquarters, and were led into a dining-room with long tables and hurricane lamps hung from the rafters; where a meal of cooked mutton awaited us. Then we were shown to our sleeping quarters. We slept in Chinese huts on wooden frame beds with straw palliasses. Carpets covered both floors and walls; indeed, so many carpets (which are a local product) were received by our troops as presents from the Chinese Command that we did not know what to do with them when the time came to return home.

Yarkand was to me at once fascinating and repellent.

The Russian who looks westward, is, by a tradition which all the efforts of the Soviet Government have not been able to overcome, subject to a sense of inferiority, however it may show itself. But in the primitive Chinese city of Yarkand, set on the ancient caravan routes of central Asia, we Soviet troops were present as representatives of a more advanced westernized civilization.

Russian towns seemed progressive compared with Yarkand's jumble of mud huts with paper windows, the mingled stench of drainage, sewage and cooking in the narrow streets, the primitive shops with wooden shutters, which nevertheless carried an impressive stock of Soviet manufactured articles. When kneading dough, it was the custom for a woman to roll up her skirt, and work the dough on her leg with filthy hands. I never touched their pancakes once I had seen this process.

On the first day we inspected the kitchen of our mess and found the walls black with flies. After our Medical Officer had mixed up some disinfectant and sprayed the kitchen, we carried out dead flies by the bucketful.

Everywhere we saw people sick and deformed by diseases which ran unchecked, even among the upper-class Chinese. When wives of the Chinese High Command consulted our Medical Officer on their child-lessness, he found that they and their husbands were all suffering from venereal diseases, some of which he was able to cure. Qualified doctors were unknown even among upper-class people. Prostitutes had a red mark painted between their eyes. They would stand in the street out-side their establishment with their 'barker', who would shout and beat a drum to attract customers. The city folk of Yarkand were the most degraded I had ever seen.

On the other hand I was impressed by some of the mixed nomadic tribes that roam the great spaces of Sinkiang—the hard-riding wild Khirgiz, the Tadjiks and the handsome Uigurs, famous as caravan-drivers. And I was interested in the country round Yarkand, light sandy soil which grew excellent vegetables and fruit, especially grapes. It never rains in Yarkand but I saw a network of irrigation channels, fed by the abundant rivers which rise in the south, in the glaciers of the high Pamir.

The majority of the tribesmen were Moslems, and many had refused to recognize the pro-Soviet Urumchi government. But the revolt was collapsing by the time I arrived, and the mopping up process was going on. One of my first tasks was to handle the cypher traffic for an opera-tion by which the rebel Chinese General in Hotan was captured. The business was carried out through an N.K.V.D. agent in the area, a Chinese who was on good terms with the rebel General. This agent was in direct radio touch with Moscow and with us in Yarkand. Acting on our instructions, he told the General that a plane from Chinese Nationalist Headquarters was coming to the area, and would take him on an aerial tour of inspection of the battle positions. A Soviet plane arrived at the arranged time, with the crew in Chinese Nationalist uniform. When embarking in the plane, the General, at our agent's suggestion, took his confidential seals with him for safe keeping. Once on board the plane he and his escorts were overpowered, disarmed, and flown straight to Yarkand. When the General was marched into the presence of our c.o., General Kraft, and was told that he must send false instructions to his troops, signed and sealed by himself, he was so terrified that he committed a physical indiscretion. The faked orders threw the rebels into confusion and the revolt quickly collapsed. The Chinese General was sent to Moscow, but I heard nothing further about his ultimate fate. It would depend on his further usefulness whether he was kept or disposed of.

In Sinkiang, since the majority of the people were devout Moslems, the soil was not favourable for an indigenous Communist Party, and the Soviet Government operated through the privileged Chinese ruling class. Our assignment, after putting down the revolt, was to carry out a 'drastic purge' of British, American and anti-Soviet elements and on these terms a breath of suspicion, a single unfavourable report, would be sufficient to condemn the victim. In fact, the most common charges were that the accused was either a friend of the British or had been to Mecca.

Soviet agents were in every party of pilgrims to Mecca; for the Communist anti-God campaign was much more overt then than it is now. I remember one fine-looking Uigur tribesman, tall and grey-bearded, who had been several times to Mecca, and who was in touch with our Soviet Consul from Kashgar. He was accused of being a double-agent, working for the other side, probably on the strength of some report from another agent. He denied the charge, but was executed all the same. 'Safer dead' was the burden of the direction which we received from Moscow on the conduct of affairs in Sinkiang.

I did not personally see any of the British, Americans or Europeans who were executed during the purge in Sinkiang. Most of them had been arrested by the Chinese Urumchi Government before our arrival. But I saw batches of indigenous prisoners at exercise with hands bound behind their backs and bandages on their eyes, and I was present when some of them were interrogated through an interpreter by Colonel Missurov, the N.K.V.D. interrogator. The business was very brief. The charge would be read out—'This man is accused of being a British or foreign spy.' Whether the man admitted it or denied it, as most did, made no difference. A few personal details would be recorded for filing purposes and the Chief of Staff would sign the order for his execution.

My colleague Nikolai Karpov, head of the Administrative Section, had to attend all the executions as representative of the C.O., and he described the process to me. The condemned prisoners were taken out by night in truckloads, fifty to seventy at a time, to the outskirts of the city, where Khirgiz troops had already dug the allotted number of graves. Alighting from the trucks, each prisoner had to kneel beside his grave with hands tied behind his back. A Khirgiz soldier would then shoot him in the back of the head and push him into the grave. When all the executions had been carried out the graves were filled in.

It was a minimum procedure. Once, however, insufficient care was taken. A strong wind blew away the light sandy soil from the graves, revealing the bodies to the local population. The episode led to some troublesome rioting, and to more careful measures of concealment from then on.

Once Karpov brought back to our headquarters a hooded hunting hawk and a couple of old muzzle-loading shotguns. I went over to stroke the bird and asked him how he came by it. He told me that two of the local population had been out hunting and were returning late when they stumbled by accident on the scene of an execution. It was a standing order that any strangers who might discover the secret of what was going on should be executed along with the prisoners. That explained the guns and the hawk.

To me it seemed a dreadful business. Karpov, however, treated it as a matter of routine. Orders were orders; that was how he looked at it.

With the completion of our task, and the coming of the New Year, the thoughts of most of us kept turning to the subject of our return to the Soviet Union; and I, as cypher chief, was constantly being asked privately if I could tell when we would be going home.

Then the order for our recall arrived, and with hearty relief we packed our kit and equipment, calculating just how much we could take with us as presents and souvenirs on the return journey.

It was on the very eve of our departure that I received a signal from Moscow marked 'Top Secret and Priority'. I decoded it personally and took it at once to the Chief of Staff, Voitenkov. The C.O., General Kraft, had left for the Soviet Union that afternoon. Voitenkov spread it out on his desk and his eyebrows twitched a little. He nodded, but said nothing.

The signal read: 'Render harmless Agent 063, found to be a British spy.'

Now Agent 063 was no ordinary agent. Before I left Moscow I had decoded many reports supplied by him which were of the highest value to the Soviet Union. Agent 063, I discovered when I arrived in Sin-kiang, was actually the Chinese Governor of Yarkand, a huge man who could hardly squeeze his fat legs into an ordinary chair. He was a well-known figure to most of us, and came frequently to our headquarters with his adjutant to visit General Kraft. On these occasions he wore Chinese-style trousers, top-boots which had to be specially made for him, and a light leather civilian top-coat. Owing to his eminence, he met all important visitors to the district, and was able to supply us with a mass of inside information about missionaries, traders and others who were said to be carrying on pro-British propaganda. There is no doubt that Agent 063 had given immense help to the Soviet expedition. It is also certain that he had acquired an intimate and accurate knowledge of our activities.

As for the rest of the signal, 'Render harmless' is a recognized formula used in secret communications with places outside the Soviet Union; it simply means 'execute'.

Voitenkov quickly drew up a plan to implement Moscow's instructions. A Chinese interpreter whom we knew as 'Peter' and who was on good terms with the Governor, was at once sent to invite him to visit our headquarters that evening, as General Kraft wished to say good-bye before his return to the Soviet Union. It was not likely that the Governor would refuse such an invitation from the Soviet Commander, and he duly appeared.

As soon as he entered he was seized and bound, and was taken to the interrogator's room. The interrogation lasted about fifteen minutes. Though I was not present I later saw the brief interrogation report, which indicated that Agent 063 had been accused of being a British spy but had denied it. Apparently he had been completely dumbfounded by the charge and by the speed of events.

Meanwhile, three of my wireless operators had been given the task of digging a large grave in the earth floor of the corridor outside our office.

Agent 063 was carried out, his mouth gagged and his hands bound behind his back and was laid face downwards in the corridor alongside the grave. While the engine of a motor-truck in the nearby courtyard was accelerated with tremendous din, one of the interrogator's assis-

tants fired three revolver shots into the back of his head. Above the
noise of the truck engine I heard the sound that came from him as the
bullets were fired into him. It was something between a long gasp and
groan; I will not easily forget the sound. His great bulk was then rolled
into the grave and petrol was poured over him and set alight to make
his body unrecognizable. Then the earth was filled in and stamped
down again, and the bamboo mats were replaced in the corridors.

It was my concluding task to report to Moscow that their instructions concerning Agent 063 had been carried out to the letter.

So much for the facts. What did I feel; what did I think about this
episode at the time? If you had been there, and had asked me my views
on the matter, I would have given you a smart, regimental and conclusive reply; Moscow had given us our orders; Moscow had all the
information and Moscow had told us that Agent 063 was a British spy.
There was no more to be said. But if you had tried to discover my
private opinion about Agent 063, you would not have got it at the time
for all the roubles in Russia. My private opinion is that Agent 063
knew too much to be allowed to survive.

We left by air next morning, taking with us three volumes of reports,
amounting to several thousand in number, on people executed in the
course of our 'drastic purge' in Sinkiang. It was considered best that
Moscow should hold the records of this aspect of the Soviet's civilizing
mission in Central Asia.

VI

The Nightmare Years

WITH the N.K.V.D. troops in Sinkiang I had seen the operation of a Moscow-directed purge against 'anti-Soviet elements' on foreign territory. As an N.K.V.D. officer in Moscow in the years 1936, 1937 and 1938, I had an inside view of the great internal purges; I lived through the most fantastic reign of terror ever imposed by a modern government on its people, and a bloodbath almost too fearful to be believed. To a few people at the top, or perhaps only to Stalin himself, the course of events reflected a ruthless and calculated policy. But for anyone else those years can only be described as a nightmare, in the blind inexplicable, capricious terror which they unleashed.

My position gave me a special insight into the scope of the great purges and their effects among the population of the Soviet Union. Soon after my return from Sinkiang I was transferred to the section of the N.K.V.D. which handled internal communications within the U.S.S.R.; later I was for a time head of that section. The signals which passed between N.K.V.D. Headquarters in Moscow and the N.K.V.D. heads in the Provinces and at distant penal establishments have left an indelible impression on my mind.

In itself, terror was not new. Terror was a weapon recognized by the founders of the Revolution. Lenin stood for a ruthless policy towards foreign interventionists, reactionaries and counter-Revolutionaries and he believed in the rule of a single 'monolithic' Party. It was Lenin who created the 'Cheka', which became the O.G.P.U., and gave it extraordinary powers unrestrained by law.

But under Stalin, in my time as a Party official, there were two huge changes. By the exiling of the 'Kulaks', the O.G.P.U. acquired a vast pool of prison labour, and expanded its functions and powers enormously. And Stalin used terror on an undreamed-of scale. Kirov's murder in 1934 was the beginning of Stalin's systematic elimination of all the old Bolsheviks, who had made the Revolution, and of every real or potential sympathizer with the Opposition leader Trotsky, who had been exiled in 1929. That was the first wave of purges. Then came the second wave, when Stalin tried desperately to eliminate the N.K.V.D. officers who had been his instruments and who knew his secrets.

The pattern of events is clearer to me now than ever it was amid the panic and uncertainty that gripped all official Moscow in those days. Thousands of the rank and file simply disappeared, shot or exiled without trial. But for the important public figures Stalin required another method, and the pretence of a confession, and so staged the notorious Moscow 'trials'.

The first trial was held in August 1936, behind closed doors, before a small hand-picked audience. I, and the rest of Moscow, read about it in the newspapers, and learnt that the accused, including the old Bolsheviks Zinoviev and Kamenev had 'confessed' to being spies and traitors, to plotting the murder of members of the Politburo and to responsibility for the murder of Kirov (which Stalin had in fact contrived through his N.K.V.D. Chief Yagoda). The accused were all summarily shot, despite the promise of mercy by which Stalin had extorted their confessions and obtained collaboration in the frame-up.

The second trial in January 1937, continued the liquidation of old Bolsheviks and former adherents of Trotsky's Left Opposition. Among the notable defendants were the industrial genius Pyatakov, the former Ambassador to Britain Sokolnikov, and the writer Karl Radek. All except Radek were sentenced to death and executed.

I have described the last two days of the third great trial in March 1938, when I saw Yagoda in the dock and heard the faint reply of the broken Rykov.

At the time I was incredulous, mystified and shaken. If such a fate could suddenly overtake the greatest and most powerful men, who was safe?

The fate of Yagoda, who in his fifteen years as N.K.V.D. Chief had planned and conducted the earlier purges and trials, was the most dramatic revelation of Stalin's methods, by which almost all his closest associates and most faithful tools fell victims to his dread of disclosure.

Yet even in Stalin's Russia, secrets got out. Even the orgy of bloodletting directed by his favourite Yezhov, who succeeded Yagoda as N.K.V.D. Chief, could not obliterate all the traces of his murderous perfidy. In all sorts of ways, clues and whispers got through the curtain of concealment; facts and stories filtered through and fragments of the truth came to light.

Take the case of Karl Radek. Perhaps I am the only man outside Russia today who can tell exactly what happened to Radek. His story is significant.

The effusive, garrulous Radek, editor and chief of *Izvestia*, was known to many visiting foreign journalists in the 'thirties. Radek, one of the Bolshevik Old Guard, had outstanding literary abilities and a wide knowledge of foreign affairs; but Lenin, while respecting his gifts, was wary of a certain irresponsible strain in him. After Lenin's death, Radek joined Trotsky's Left Opposition, and in consequence, was sent into exile. A year and a half in Siberia was enough; Radek changed sides, began to slander his old leader Trotsky and became a high favourite of Stalin's, with ready access to the Kremlin. In 1933 with his brilliantly-written book *The Architect of a Socialist Society*, Radek tickled Stalin's immense vanity; for he took an imaginative leap into the future, and showed a prominent historian at the end of the twentieth century giving a lecture in which Stalin appeared, overshadowing the great men of the past, as the genius who had reformed human society. In consequence, Radek was made editor of *Izvestia*, and an adviser on foreign policy.

When Radek was arrested, he was intensely indignant at Stalin's gross ingratitude for his services. He refused to sign the 'confession' that was presented to him. But after an interview with Stalin, Radek reversed his attitude and threw all his literary talents into improving the dramatic quality of the faked confessions which were required from himself and his fellow-prisoners. He introduced negotiations between Trotsky and the German Government, wrote the version of Trotsky's directives to the conspirators which was used at the trial, and himself confessed to conspiring with Hitler against the Soviet Union. There is no doubt that Stalin had promised him special consideration in return for his help in touching-up the picture which Stalin wished to present.

The trial ended on the 20th January, 1937. All the accused were sentenced to death except Radek. It is said that when, after a succession of death sentences, he heard his own penalty 'ten years', his face lit up and he shrugged his shoulders as if puzzled by his own undeserved luck. That accords with his flair for the colourful and dramatic.

After the trial Radek disappeared and his friends inside and outside Russia have wondered ever since what became of him. Here is the answer.

Some time in 1938, I decoded a telegram from one of the northern prisons—it was either Irkutsk or Novo-Sibirsk. It referred to Radek, and reported that a fellow-convict who occupied the same cell as Radek had quarrelled violently with him, and in the ensuing fight had lifted Radek into the air and dashed him down on the cement floor, causing a head injury from which death had resulted. Of course it could have been just an unfortunate accident. But Radek certainly knew many of Stalin's most compromising secrets.

One day soon after I had joined the O.G.P.U. before the great purges began, I witnessed an unusual incident. In the door of our office, there was a small hatch, through which we spoke to anyone who knocked and wanted admittance; the door itself was bolted on the inside. There was no knock, but I saw an arm come through the hatch and pull back the bolt, after which the door was pushed open and a man strode into the office, and without ceremony began to examine the office furniture. The Section Chief, Mrs Titov, bristled.

'Stop, you're not allowed in here! What do you mean by walking in without knocking?'

The man looked up. He was of middle height, with a round face and a squint; his eyes seemed to be looking in different directions.

'You needn't worry about your —— secrets,' he answered coarsely and offensively. 'Do you think I want to pinch 'em? I've got to check over this junk.'

There was silence in the office. Mrs Titov was an important person. I was amazed to hear her addressed in such rude and abusive language. But she hesitated; and some of the more senior members, who had witnessed the incident, intervened. They smoothed the matter over and suggested to the man that he could take his inventory of the furniture after office hours. He agreed and slouched off.

'Who was that?' I asked one of my colleagues privately, when it was all over.

'Oh! that was Savushka; he works in the Administration Section.' I thought the reply seemed a little evasive. Later still I discovered what most of the older members of the staff already knew, that Savushka's administrative job was only a cover.

Savushka was one of the N.K.V.D. executioners. He belonged to a group controlled by Lieut.-General Blokhin.

As such he enjoyed a special independence and privilege. He never altered his rough manner, or showed any deference to his superiors. Savushka had a flat of his own in No. 5 Komsomolsky Lane; he was married but had no children. I heard that he drank heavily.

His job was not one that everyone would covet.

Important political prisoners are executed in a cellar of one of the N.K.V.D. buildings No. 11 Dzerjinsky Street. The gates of this building are always kept closed, no interrogations are held there, and entry to it is strictly controlled. Such secrecy was maintained that the only people who knew of the cellar and its function were officials of the First Special Department of the N.K.V.D., which handled records and dossiers, and high N.K.V.D. officials such as Heads of Departments. I only discovered the details about it by accident, in 1950, just before I left for Australia. It happened in this way.

At a sanatorium near Moscow, where I took my annual leave, there was also staying a certain L——who had been a colleague of mine a few years before. We spent a good deal of time reminiscing and talking together. L——also introduced me to a friend of his, T—— who joined our party. But T——'s holiday was interrupted by a summons to Moscow; and thereafter he had to go up to Moscow regularly, leaving in the morning and returning to the sanatorium in the evening. We would meet him at the station. He invariably arrived back drunk. Then L—— told me the story. He explained that T—— had taken over duties which he himself had performed in the First Special Department, and that T——had been ordered to Moscow to attend executions, as he was the case officer and handled the files of the condemned persons.

L—— then confided in me the following facts. The N.K.V.D. cellar is the centre for all important political executions, including those of political prisoners from Rumania, Czechoslovakia, Poland, East Germany, etc. The cellar, which is really the basement of the building, is subdivided into a number of rooms, for the use of the executioners, for changing the prisoners' clothes and so on. Before execution the prisoner changes into white underclothes only; he knows that he has been sentenced and is about to be executed. He is led to the death cell, where he is shot in the back of the head by the executioner, either as he stands facing the wall, or just as he walks into the cell. The weapon used is a 'T.T.' 8-shot automatic pistol, so called after its inventor Tokarev. If the first shot does not dispatch the prisoner, the executioner follows it up with others. A doctor certifies death; his certificate is the last paper placed on the victim's file. A tarpaulin is spread on the floor of the cell, and a woman is employed to clean up afterwards. The bodies are taken away and buried immediately in a common grave. In the case of important figures like Beria or Zinoviev and Kamenev, the execution is publicized next day in the newspapers. But with the rank and file there is no such publicity. When the relatives of the executed man inquire, they are usually told that he has been sentenced to ten years' imprisonment, without right to correspondence; and that is the last they hear.

The executioners are highly paid, by secret Ministerial decree. They are usually selected from ignorant and illiterate men, not burdened with too much imagination. Even so, they are men, and therefore not exempt from the feelings common to human beings. They drink heavily, and Savushka, the surly Savushka, committed suicide. He shot himself in a lavatory.

But the judicial murder of individual opponents and suspects is one thing. Indiscriminate mass terror against thousands and thousands of innocent persons is another and far more horrible thing.

I can testify to this as an eye-witness, who myself coded and decoded the signals that passed between N.K.V.D. Headquarters in Moscow and the towns and provinces of the Soviet Union.

I estimate that two million Soviet citizens must have been shot without any proper trial and without any examination of the stereotyped charges brought against them, in the nightmare years of 1936, 1937 and 1938. This hideous carnage was sheer madness by any standard of right and justice; but its director, which means Stalin himself, was not a madman. The purges were a calculated policy which seemed to make sense on the basis that expediency is the only law. Reversing Western principles of justice, Stalin argued that the death of innocent thousands did not matter provided all possible threats to his own power were swept away in the holocaust.

That is clearly how Stalin thought. Of course his announcements to the Soviet people were quite different. When he became aware of the horror and hatred which the purges had aroused among the people, he executed his favourite and instrument, Yezhov, who had succeeded Yagoda, and blamed Yezhov for all the excesses of the reign of terror known as the 'Yezhovschina'. Beria then came in as head of the N.K.V.D., figuring as an apostle of moderation and the better deal which Stalin demanded on behalf of the Soviet people.

When Yagoda fell and Yezhov first took over as Chief of the N.K.V.D., he began a purge which eliminated about 3,000 higher-ranking N.K.V.D. officers, including almost all those who had ever served abroad. The Chief of my own Department, Boki, an old comrade of Lenin, was arrested, followed by his three deputies, on fantastic charges of being agents of foreign espionage. They were first exiled, then shot.

I personally handled correspondence about all these. The signals from the Camp Commandants followed a stereotyped pattern:

'Prisoner X confessed to spying on behalf of the British [or the Germans or the Japanese] and was therefore executed by shooting.'

It was invariably reported that the executed persons had confessed their crime. This matter of confession is a subject in itself, and has aroused widespread controversy outside the Soviet Union, following the astounding 'confessions' of prominent figures such as the defendants at the great Moscow trials, and since the war, of men like Cardinal Mindzenty in the Peoples' Democracies. These confessions follow a pattern; the accused not only confesses to incredible and unlikely crimes, but goes beyond his prosecutor in reviling himself, and in praising his oppressor.

There is one significant point in the debate, however. The only real question is the method by which these confessions are obtained. No honest critic really believes that the accused is freely and voluntarily uttering his own thoughts. It has been suggested that the Soviet interrogators possess some particularly subtle psychological approach, which breaks down the resistance of their victim's will-power; and it is often said that physical violence and torture are not used to get confessions.

That is probably true in the case of notable public figures; and it may be that Stalin's interrogators, and Stalin himself, were able to mix an appeal to the old Bolsheviks' Party loyalty with the hope that they would save their lives or their loved ones. But it is quite untrue that N.K.V.D. interrogators never resort to violence. Colleagues of mine who worked in the Taganskaya and Butirskaya prisons in Moscow told me of screams and howls which they heard coming from the interrogation cells, of prisoners made to stand against a wall for days on end without sleep, and beating and tortures which made the prisoners look forward to death, and ready to sign anything to escape their pain. I myself have seen discharged prisoners who were lifelong invalids as the result of what they had been through.

Once when I came in to our cypher section after a day's absence, I heard that one of our clerks had been arrested. As he worked in Berlin, he was accused of conspiracy with the Germans. He was in prison for eight months, during which he was interrogated under torture. When he was discharged all his front teeth had been knocked out. I did not actually see him being subjected to violence, but it takes a very strong argument to knock out teeth.

Most terrible of all were the indiscriminate mass purges. During this time I handled hundreds of signals to all parts of the Soviet Union which were couched in the following form:

'To N.K.V.D., Frunze. You are charged with the task of exterminating 10,000 enemies of the people. Report results by signal.—Yezhov.'

And in due course the reply would come back:

'In reply to yours of such-and-such date, the following enemies of the Soviet people have been shot.'

At first, personal particulars of all the victims were reported; but soon that became impossible, and only lists of names were sent. Even then our section worked day and night trying to keep up with the mass liquidations.

The alleged determination of the Government was to destroy the Fifth Column of foreign sympathizers who were said to be lurking everywhere. Actually, Stalin's aim was ruthless elimination of all (and particularly all the old generation of the Party) who might constitute a political opposition.

The quotas of victims for each district and town were fixed at N.K.V.D. Headquarters in Moscow. I remember one order to the town of Sverdlovsk for 15,000 'enemies of the people' to be exterminated.

What happened when these signals from Moscow were received? The District N.K.V.D. officials would draw up a plan based on the number necessary to meet Moscow's demands. Then the local officials would ransack their lists and records to collect together every sort of incriminating trace; for example, 'associated with the White Army, bourgeois background, Trotskyist, Menshevik, Esdek, Nationalist.' Often they were hard put to it to fill out their quota; but they dared not fail to carry out Moscow's orders speedily and to the letter.

Usually the summary executions were carried out by N.K.V.D. troops; but a cypher clerk whom I knew told me after a visit to Georgia that there the victims were simply thrown into old mine-shafts, as the quickest method, and left to die.

Any district officials who were dilatory in carrying out their instructions would be terrified by a visitation from Moscow. A colleague who was in hospital at the same time as myself in 1949 told the following story: He was head of the N.K.V.D. District Office in the town of Rostov in 1938, at the height of Yezhov's purge. Out of the blue they received a visit from Yezhov's toady and lieutenant, B——. Armed with all the arrogance of his Moscow authority, B—— marched into my friend's office, accused him of inefficiency and slackness and shouted, 'Get cracking, you son-of-a-bitch, and do something or I'll have *you* arrested!'

B—— then called a meeting of all the terrified officials of the Rostov District, N.K.V.D. and assailed them violently.

'You Rostov officials have failed in the task allotted to you! Moscow will not tolerate such laxness on the part of so-called Chekists! You are incapable of your jobs of hunting down enemies of the people! Why, there are some of those enemies in this room—there, there and there!' As he spoke, B—— pointed to several of the N.K.V.D. officials whom he had evidently selected beforehand. The trembling head of the Department immediately had them arrested, charges were trumped up and they were shot.

B—— was in charge of N.K.V.D. border troops in the Far East when his master Yezhov fell. He saw the writing on the wall and fled to Japan.

The cases of these executed N.K.V.D. officers in Rostov were then re-examined, the victims' names were cleared, and the Soviet Government undertook to pay a life-pension to their dependents.

By that time Stalin had decided to attach to Yezhov's name all the hatred and resentment which such outrages had generated even among the submissive Soviet people. And perhaps by that time also he considered that the object of the purges had been sufficiently accomplished.

How did it happen that local officials, many of whom were quite ordinary decent human beings, with a normal hatred of injustice and cruelty, were prepared to carry out the merciless indiscriminate purges prescribed for them?

There is a simple word which explains most things in Russia that puzzle and baffle the outside world. It is 'fear'. It is almost impossible for people in Western countries to understand how constant, universal, and ever-present is the element of fear among the people of the Soviet Union.

A friend in my Department whom I will call M—— told me of his own experience as an N.K.V.D. official in a country town in the Novo-Sibirsk region. The number of victims demanded by Moscow from this town was five hundred. M—— went through all the local dossiers, and found nothing but trivial offences recorded. But Moscow's requirements were implacable; he was driven to desperate measures. He listed priests and their relatives; he put down anyone who was reported to have spoken critically about conditions in the Soviet Union; he included all former members of Admiral Kolchak's White Army. Even though the Soviet Government had decreed that it was not an offence to have served in Kolchak's Army, since its personnel had been forcibly conscripted, it was more than M——'s life was worth not to fulfil his quota. He made up his list of five hundred enemies of the people, had them quickly charged and executed and reported to Moscow: 'Task accomplished in accordance with your instructions.'

M——, himself a Siberian, detested what he had to do. He was by

nature a decent, honest, kindly man. He told me the story with savage
resentment. Years afterwards its horror and injustice lay heavy on his
conscience.

But M——— did what he was ordered. Apart from a man's ordinary
desire to remain alive, M——— had a mother, a father, a wife and two
children.

★ ★ ★

Fear ruled us all, and drove underground any murmurs of protest and
revolt. When old Revolutionary heroes like Zinoviev, Kamenev,
Bukharin and Rykov were executed, when my chief Boki and all his
deputies were likewise shot as spies, I found it unbelievable that all these
distinguished men, who had given their lives to serve the Revolution,
were really traitors to their country. But I did not breathe a word of my
suspicions, except perhaps very tentatively in the close company of one
or two old shipmates. And even that was a risk.

All the same, in the depth of my being, as in the hearts of thousands
and millions of my countrymen, there began to smoulder a hatred of
the treachery, falsehood and injustice of the régime under which we
lived, and which already seemed so remote from the hopes and ideals
which the Revolution had set before the Russian people.

Why did I myself come unscathed through the capricious fury of the
purge years? Probably for a number of reasons. I was not an old Bolshevik; I had no pre-Stalin Party history which could link me with any
trace of political opposition. As an N.K.V.D. cypher clerk I was a useful
technical worker, and at the same time I was not so elevated as to
arouse the envy of malicious slanderers who wanted my job, or to have
connections with senior officials whose downfall would involve me
also. Nor had I served in a Soviet establishment abroad at this time.
Anyone who had done so came under immediate suspicion of having
foreign sympathies.

Even so I had one or two close calls. When my friend and former
shipmate Novikov was arrested—an active, honest Party worker if
ever there was one—a photograph was found in his possession, dating
from our Navy days, in which I featured. I heard from his wife that the
investigators were asking a lot of questions about me; and for a time I
went in fear of arrest and interrogation. I never heard what happened
to Novikov; to make inquiries would have been the height of folly.

The other escape was from a greater and more certain destruction,
involving issues of state. After my return from Sinkiang, I used to act at
times as Personal Secretary to Voitenkov, who had been chief of com-

munications for the N.K.V.D. troops there. I preferred the job to cypher work, and applied for a permanent transfer. However, once again my section chief refused to let me go, and I remained in the section on ordinary cypher duties.

His unhelpfulness probably saved my life. In April 1938 Voitenkov was arrested at Kazansk Railway Station in Moscow. Soon afterwards Frinovsky, who as Deputy-Minister in Moscow had directed the whole Sinkiang operation, was also arrested. Both disappeared; I have no doubt that they were shot. I got the impression that the authorities were now anxious to hush up the whole Sinkiang business and intended to silence all the senior officers who knew the inside story.

If I had been officially appointed as Voitenkov's secretary, I would without doubt have been swept to destruction in the wake of his downfall.

One day our Section Chief summoned us all to his office and questioned each member closely. My own case was under investigation. Apparently the Ishim N.K.V.D. had forwarded to N.K.V.D. Headquarters a document which showed that a person who was thought to be my brother had taken part in the old 'Ishim Revolt', in bygone days. I answered that my brother had taken no part in it and had been serving in the Red Army at the time. The document evidently referred to someone else of the same surname (which was common in our district). Though this was the truth I went about in fear and alarm. I heard afterwards from my brother at Larikha that there had been inquiries in the village about me and about my change of name. Fortunately confirmation of my story was found.

The announcements which suddenly appeared in the Moscow papers during this reign of terror were bewildering and seemed incredible even at the time. When practically the whole of the Red Army High Command were liquidated, including great names like Tukhachevsky, Ubarevich, Kork, Edemann, what could we believe? Old Marshal Tukhachevsky was a Revolutionary hero who had joined the Red Army in its earliest days—it was unbelievable that he could have been a spy for the Germans. And Yezhov, whose downfall marked the end of the worst excesses, Yezhov was in his turn denounced as a German spy, who had all the time been carrying out an assignment for the German counter-intelligence to destroy the stout old Bolsheviks and the re-nowned Heads of the Armed Forces. Here was a man who had held the post of Secretary of the Communist Party of the Soviet Union and had been personally installed as Peoples' Commissar at the head of the N.K.V.D. by Stalin himself. It was a fantastic and unlikely tale.

Nevertheless, in the hush which terror imposes, it was impossible to draw a line between truth and falsehood, or to get anything like a coherent picture of what was going on behind the scenes. Much was incredible; but surely there must be elements of truth in what we were told? Vigilance against insidious foes, at home and abroad, is a constant feature of the climate of life in the u.s.s.r.

Thus, when Beria took over as n.k.v.d. Chief, and condemned the excesses of the purged traitor Yezhov, he was also careful to add that Yezhov had destroyed, along with thousands of innocent persons, a number of real enemies of the people.

If the purges were bewildering to a person in my privileged position in Moscow, they must have been absolutely incomprehensible to the toiling officials and loyal Party workers in remote provinces, who suddenly found themselves denounced as secret enemies of the cause they served.

In 1939 I spoke with a friend who had been an official in China and far Mongolia at the time of the 'Yezhovschina'. He told me that, in his area, some of the accused, just before they were shot, shouted, with wild abandon, 'Greetings to Stalin! Long live our great leader!' I was puzzled and questioned him about it. He explained that they were not sarcastic cries, but sincere. Unable to understand what was happening to them, or why they had been forced to sign confessions to crimes they had never committed, these innocent victims nevertheless felt an urge to proclaim with their last breath their unswerving loyalty to the Party and their Leader, little realizing that it was Stalin's deliberately calculated policy that had sent them to their death.

★   ★   ★

The purge in the n.k.v.d. began with the Chiefs, Heads of Departments and their deputies, and worked down through the rank and file. In general the penalties varied in accordance with the importance of the victim, ranging from death to exile, imprisonment or dismissal. In any department and section investigations were conducted into the whole staff and everyone went about in fear that each day would bring to light some fresh charge, some new basis for suspicion against him.

In those times of panic and insecurity, it was dangerous even to defend one's friends. A clerk in my section called Yermakov who had done the cypher course at Kronstadt with me and had served in our sister-destroyer *Uritsky*, was accused at our Party meeting of being a Trotskyite. He was found guilty, dismissed from his job, and expelled from the Party. The case against him was that at the age of sixteen he had distributed some Trotskyite pamphlets. At the meeting Yermakov wept and protested his innocence of all Trotskyite sympathies, saying that the pamphlets had been handed to him without his realizing what they were all about.

Convinced of his innocence, I went as far as I dared in his defence. I gave my personal testimony to his excellent naval record, and his keenness as Komsomol secretary of his ship when I knew him, adding that his wife was also a loyal Komsomol worker. To go further than that would have laid me open to the charge of condoning Trotskyite views.

But even that was going too far for Yermakov's closest friend, Belov. Belov rose to his feet and denounced Yermakov as a Trotskyite, as one guilty of a grave offence who should have known better, and who deserved to be punished. Then he rounded on me.

'Petrov, I have heard what you say! I warn you, you and I are taking different roads! You go your way, and I'll go mine!'

In days past the three of us had been friends and companions, in the office and out of it. Belov was not a bad fellow at heart, he had no wish to harm anybody. But fear drove him. Belov feared desperately for his own fate. Just because he was known as Yermakov's closest friend, he outdid everyone else in denunciation and severity, to prove that he himself was blameless.

Such incidents repelled and disgusted me, though I said little at the time. I am not a man of great ambitions, but I value honest friendship and comradeship—things which become dangerous and impossible when terror is everywhere.

VII

Big Boss Beria

WHEN Beria became chief of the N.K.V.D. in place of Yezhov in the autumn of 1938, he put into effect a rapid reversal of the actions of his purged predecessor which had aroused such hatred and revulsion among the Soviet people. Cases were re-examined, prisoners liberated, exiles recalled home, expelled officials and Party members reinstated in their positions. At the same time a small group of Yezhov's most intimate colleagues were liquidated.

In this way Beria, and of course Stalin, who stood behind him, earned some popularity and a reputation as a setter-right of wrongs and injustices. Beria also gave official voice to a fact that was well-known to the Soviet people—namely that many of the failures in government departments and industry which had been too readily blamed on the sabotage of 'hostile elements' were really due simply to inefficiency and bad management.

With Beria's accession to power, the reign of terror was curbed and controlled; and ordinary innocent citizens were able to breathe more freely.

But it was a change in degree only. The principle of purging political opponents and liquidating 'enemies of the people' remains an intrinsic element of the Soviet system. Excesses and misuse of this principle are denounced whenever it is necessary to find a scapegoat to satisfy the people. But the purge-principle is unquestioned.

It was at the end of 1938 or early in 1939, when I was Deputy-Chief of the 6th (Cypher) Section of the 5th Directorate of the N.K.V.D., that my chief Degtjarov came to me and said that the Commissar, Beria, wanted a man for an important task. It was necessary to liquidate the Soviet Ambassador in a Middle-Eastern capital (I believe it was either Teheran or Kabul) who, it had been reported, was planning to defect from the Soviet service. One man had to be selected for this task out of our section; did I agree that Bokov was the right choice? I thought for a moment. Bokov, one of our cypher clerks, was tall, fair-haired, and unusually strong. He had served in the Red Navy, was taciturn by nature, and was a single man. Yes, Bokov was probably the best man we had for the job which the Commissar had in mind.

The rest of the story I heard later from Bokov himself. Two men had been chosen, Bokov and a man from the highly secret Administration of Special Tasks. This group, which was then headed by Colonel Serebriansky, worked directly under the Commissar on special assignments of this kind.

Bokov and his colleagues were summoned to Beria's presence. The Peoples' Commissar for Internal Affairs and State Security was grave and impressive; he warned them that a particularly secret and important task had been assigned to them. Then, turning to Bokov, he said:

'Comrade, I hear that you are a man of unusual strength. Are you strong enough to kill a man with a single blow of an iron bar?'

'Yes, Comrade Commissar,' answered Bokov.

Beria explained to them that there was a Soviet Ambassador who was guilty of treachery to the Soviet Union and who must therefore be disposed of. It had been reported that he was planning to defect from the Soviet service. The detailed plan for the operation against him would be explained to them in due course.

After this interview we supplied Bokov with a special code for direct communication with Moscow, and the two men left for their destination. They had been issued with passports by the Ministry of Foreign Affairs, by whom they were allegedly being sent on a special mission to the Ambassador. However, the N.K.V.D. Resident knew what this 'special mission' was about, and that its purpose was to 'render harmless' the Ambassador. No doubt it was through the Resident that Moscow had been informed of the Ambassador's intending defection. When the two men reached their destination, the N.K.V.D. Resident met them. He provided Bokov with a short iron bar which could be concealed under his clothes, and took them both in to the Ambassador. While the Ambassador was engaged in conversation with the other conspirator, Bokov struck him on the head with the iron bar, from behind, splitting his skull and killing him with one blow, as he had promised. They then rolled the Ambassador's body in a carpet to conceal the bloodstains and took it to the outskirts of the city, where they buried it.

I decoded the cable addressed to the Commissar, which reported: 'Task carried out according to plan.'

The Ambassador's wife was told that her husband had been summoned to Moscow on such urgent business that he had not had time to say good-bye; she and their two children were to follow by train. I heard no more about their fate, but it is unlikely that they reached

Moscow. They were probably taken off the train somewhere along the line and sent to a labour camp, as was usual with the families of 'enemies of the people'.

Bokov continued to work at the Embassy as a cypher clerk for another twelve months, to cover his traces. When he returned to Moscow he was awarded the Red Star for his services; and after I got back from Sweden I saw him working in the Directorate which kept a security watch on the Armed Forces.

He showed no remorse about his deed, though what he felt in secret I cannot say. No doubt he told himself that he had acted in the line of duty against a public enemy. He was certainly flattered to receive a personal commission from Beria himself, and to be able to prove that the physical prowess which he claimed was no empty boast.

In Australia, years afterwards, when I was myself considering the stark choice which faced me between returning to Moscow and forsaking the Soviet service, I naturally remembered the story of my colleague Bokov and the Ambassador. I was in real fear for my life. I would like that fact to be appreciated by people who have never lived under a régime of fear, and who have suggested that while waiting to make my break I amused myself by forging and fabricating documents concerned with minute details of Australian internal politics.

From that time until his dramatic arrest in June 1953, not long before my own decision to seek political asylum in Australia, Beria was my big boss at a time when he probably wielded more real power in the Soviet Union than any man except Stalin. He remained Supreme Chief of the wide-reaching empire of the N.K.V.D. for fifteen years—longer than the office had ever been held by any man previously in the history of the Soviet Union. But he worked behind the scenes and was evidently more interested in the substance of power than in its trappings and display. Beria remained almost as little-known to the rank and file of the Soviet people as he did to the world outside, apart from his formal public appearances at the Bolshoi Theatre, or at Stalin's side during reviews and parades in the Red Square. A foreign journalist has recorded an impression of Beria on these occasions, 'gazing enigmatically and unmoved at the crowds through his pince-nez from under a large Homburg hat which always seemed a little too big for him'.[1]

But the outlines of Beria's life and career were generally known. Like Stalin, Beria was a Georgian; he was born in 1899 in a village near the

[1]*Stalin's Heirs*, by Gordon Young, Verschoyle, London, 1953.

Georgian capital Tiflis, where Stalin studied until the age of twenty in a theological seminary. Like anyone else in the Soviet Union who is able to do so, he claimed poor origins; but his family were evidently able to give him an excellent education at the Baku High School. Stalin retained a strong Georgian accent—I could hardly understand him when I first heard his voice on the radio—but Beria spoke Russian clearly and with little Georgian accent. As a Bolshevik before the Revolution, Beria did undercover work with Mikoyan; and in 1921 he joined Lenin's 'Cheka', which later became the O.G.P.U. He became head of the Caucasus branch of the O.G.P.U. and was prominent in pushing forward the first Five-Year-Plan for the region; later, as Secretary of the Caucasus Central Committee, Beria purged and galvanized the local Party with ruthless efficiency.

In 1935, when Stalin was in the middle of his struggle to oust and destroy every shade of political opposition, Beria published a book which set him on the direct road to Stalin's highest favours; for it described Stalin's heroic feats in the early days of the Revolution and depicted the comradeship and mutual regard between Stalin and Lenin, who was said to have described Stalin as 'the fiery Colchian'. Beria's book was just what Stalin wanted at that time. It was a compulsory study and a standard text-book for all Komsomol and Party members up to the time of Beria's arrest, when all his writings and photographs were withdrawn.

During my time in the U.S.S.R. I was never in a position to question, much less verify, the truth of such accounts. I had heard rumours but no precise details about Lenin's 'Testament', in which he praised all his former close comrades except Stalin, and urged that Stalin should be removed from his position as Secretary of the Party's Central Committee. Only after I left the Soviet service did I discover that, according to Trotsky and others, Beria's book created 'a romantic early revolutionary career for Stalin' which he never had. If so, it would be all the more valuable to Stalin. From that point it seems that Beria's career was assured, culminating in his stepping into Yezhov's shoes as Commissar at the head of the N.K.V.D. But it was the war that carried Beria to the summit of his power. As chief of the N.K.V.D.—'Peoples' Commissar for Internal Affairs'—he was responsible for the mass transfers of population which were carried out, first from the occupied parts of Poland and the Baltic States, then from the areas of Russia threatened by the Germans. He was responsible for morale and internal security, including security supervision over the Armed Forces; for all the Foreign Intelligence Services of the Soviet Union except that of the

Red Army; and for Armaments and Munitions. As a member of the Defence Committee, it was Beria who organized the huge transfer of industry beyond the Ural Mountains, and the conversion of peace-time industry to war-production.

I knew to my cost the volume of work that these vast responsibilities involved. In our cypher section we filed stacks of signals inches thick drafted and signed by Beria concerning the transfer and conversion of Soviet industry for war. No one has ever questioned that he was a hard driver of others and a prodigious worker himself.

It was the war that led to my two personal meetings with Beria. When Hitler attacked the Soviet Union, and the German armies advanced across Russian territory with such formidable speed, something very like panic set in. On 16th October 1941, a general evacuation from Moscow of all Government establishments, including the N.K.V.D. was ordered; my wife Doosia was evacuated to Kuibyshev. But I stayed on with a special cypher group attached to Beria's headquarters. Our orders were, if the Germans captured Moscow, to burn all our files and escape as best we could to join one of the Partisan units operating behind the enemy's lines. On the day of the evacuation, when all the main records were being packed for removal to Kuibyshev, I have a vivid memory of the scene in our office—files and papers strewn all over the floor in confusion, until they were hastily collected and bundled into bags for the transfer. It must have been a huge job sorting them out again.

We retained only skeleton working files in Moscow, and we quite expected at any moment a signal with the special prefix indicating a general emergency, and the transfer of all lines of communication to Kuibyshev, because Moscow was in German hands.

About four days later, when the evacuation was practically complete, and there were only six of us cypher clerks left in the section, I received a telephone call from Beria's personal secretary Mamulov to say that the Commissar wished to see me. Mamulov was a Georgian, like Beria. He was calm and capable and had already done me a service. When I became head of a section I often went to his office with signals for the Commissar and once I asked Mamulov whether he could get me a car for our section, which now numbered forty people. The car was provided, and though my Department chief Shevelev was annoyed at my going over his head, it proved very useful. During the evacuation I helped many of our staff by transporting their baggage to the station in the section car. When I was last in Moscow, Mamulov was Deputy to Kruglov, who stepped into one pair of Beria's shoes. But I am certain that Mamulov is not alive today; he was much too close to Beria to survive his chief's downfall.

As I knocked and entered Mamulov's office, the door on the other side of the room opened and Beria came in. Mamulov introduced me.

'Comrade Commissar, this is Comrade Petrov, head of the 6th Cypher Section, whom you wished to see.'

He then handed me a signal which lay on his desk; I saw that it was addressed to Beria personally.

'Comrade Petrov, can you decypher that for me?' asked Beria.

'I will do my best, Comrade Commissar.'

'Do, and if you succeed report the contents to Mamulov.'

I took the signal back to my office, and sat down at my desk. It was all numerals, no letters, and I began to apply to it the principles which I had learned at the cypher school. On examination I found a number of repeated numerals, and soon came to the conclusion that it was a simple form of cypher, in which figures were substituted for letters. I wrote down the Russian alphabet in sequence, and put a 2-digit numeral opposite each letter—01, 02, 03, etc. According to the law of averages, the commonest letter in Russian is 'P'; and I knew the order of frequency of the rest of the alphabet. Separating the numerals in the cable into groups of five, I looked for the letter 'P'; then, by a process of elimination I was gradually able to substitute letters for all the numerals, and got the text of the cable.

It was marked Top Secret and Personal to the Commissar and was from the N.K.V.D. representative in a factory in a town near the front line through which our Soviet troops were retreating. It read:

'Group in charge of dismantling and removing equipment is abandoning valuable machinery to the Germans. Consider them traitors in consequence.'

I did not handle the Commissar's reply. I have no doubt that he ordered summary action against the suspects.

My second interview with Beria was in December 1941. This time it was on my initiative. My section was desperately overworked at the time, and I had discovered that the clerks evacuated to Kuibyshev were having a fairly easy time of it. I went to Mamulov and asked to see the Commissar. In the stress of war access of this sort to the top was much easier. Mamulov rang through to get his chief's O.K.; then nodded to me, saying:

'All right; he'll see you. Go ahead.'

Because of the German bombing, Beria at this time had his office in the strong air-raid shelter in the basement of 'Number Two' Dzerjinsky Street. Another part of the shelter had been taken over to house our more important files, but there was no room for us to sleep there. When the raids were on we went to our own less effective shelter. After all, we were replaceable, but the files were not.

I knocked on the door and asked, 'Comrade Peoples' Commissar, may I enter?'

'Yes, come in.'

Beria was sitting at his large green-topped desk, on which was a thick pile of papers and three telephones, one to Stalin direct, one to other Government offices and Ministries, and one for long-distance calls to any part of the Soviet Union—from Murmansk to Vladivostok. There were no windows, of course, and air entered the room through a forced-draught vent. The room was furnished with a sofa, armchair, wardrobe, a large safe and a portrait of Stalin.

Beria, wearing his uniform of Peoples' Commissar, asked: 'What is it you want?'

I recited my case of our overworked and under-staffed section, reminded him that a large part of the traffic we handled served his Commissariat, and mentioned the extra clerks in Kuibyshev.

Before I finished speaking he cut me short. 'Of course. What was Shevelev thinking of when he sent so many away? See Mamulov and ask for the number you want.'

Five additional clerks arrived that day by plane from Kuibyshev. Some foreign visitors who met Beria described his manner as precise and schoolmasterish. During my interviews he gave me the impression of a serious, responsible official, intent on getting things done quickly and efficiently. Without doubt he was a first-rate administrator.

In N.K.V.D. circles Beria had the reputation of a good boss, who went to a great deal of trouble to look after the welfare of his staff. N.K.V.D. personnel who were transferred to Moscow and could not get accommodation could often put their case to Beria himself, who always saw that something was found for them. As a result of his forcefulness and drive we N.K.V.D. personnel had the best of what there was. Houses were found for us when the staffs of other Ministries could not get them, and throughout the war the N.K.V.D. restaurants were amply stocked with food when not only the civilian population but other officials, such as employees of the Ministry of Foreign Affairs, were on very meagre rations. When epaulettes (an old Czarist symbol) were reintroduced for the Red Army during the war, Beria insisted that we should get an extra payment for rank, as Army officers did. It was the same with holiday sanatoriums, hospitals, office buildings, medical treatment; Beria insisted that N.K.V.D. staff should have the best. In this he differed from Molotov and other Ministers, who lived in great luxury themselves, but took less trouble about the living and working conditions of their staffs. Naturally his drive and success in these matters did not increase his popularity with his fellow-Ministers and jealous rivals.

After the war, in March 1946, Beria seemed to divide and delegate his empire. The all-embracing N.K.V.D. was separated into two Ministries, the Ministry of State Security (M.G.B.) and the Ministry of Internal Affairs (M.V.D.); the M.G.B. was headed by Merkulov, the M.V.D. by Kruglov.

What happened to Beria? He was certainly not under a cloud, for at the same time he was made Vice-President of the Council of Ministers, and a full member of the Politburo; and in 1949 he was awarded the prized Order of Lenin.

The explanation is, that Stalin had given him a new and vitally important task. The vast labour resources of the N.K.V.D., with which he had built huge projects like the Moscow-Volga Canal and the White Sea Canal, were now to be used for the development of the Soviet's atomic power, and Beria was put in charge. I have no exact knowledge on this subject. I believe that some of the great establishments are in southern Russia, perhaps in the Crimea; and after the war, when I was in charge of the 6th Section of the K.I., we sent a man to a uranium mine somewhere in Poland. But I have no doubt that Beria was in supreme control both of this vital industry, and of the Soviet atomic espionage which advanced our atomic knowledge by at least two years and gave the Soviet Intelligence Services their first large-scale publicity in the western world. But this was while Stalin lived.

Stalin died on 5th March 1953. The next day the two Ministries, the M.G.B. and the M.V.D., were merged in one, under the title M.V.D., and Beria once more took direct control of both.

Then, a month later, the former M.G.B. was publicly disgraced by an 'exposure', unknown before in Soviet history, of the fact that 'impermissible methods' had been used in the extraction of confessions from accused persons. This referred to the 'confessions' of a number of doctors who had been arrested before Stalin's death on charges of plotting the death of members of the Politburo. Now the doctors were freed, their oppressors were rebuked and there was a reference to the 'rights of Soviet citizens'.

I left the Soviet Union in January 1951 and my opportunities to discuss these events with later arrivals at our Embassy in Canberra were limited. But my opinion is that, with Stalin dead, Beria felt it necessary to recover direct control of State Security and Internal Affairs to ensure his own future; and that the business of exposing M.G.B. methods was a bid for popularity with the masses, similar to the display of moderation which Beria had put on when he rebuked the excesses of Yezhov, years before.

Three months later, in June 1953, Beria himself was arrested by Malenkov and his allies; and on 23rd December Beria and his associates were executed. What Beria's thoughts were as he stood in the death cell to which he had sent so many 'enemies of the people', and which had seen the end of his two predecessors, Yezhov and Yagoda, would be a significant piece of history, if the secret could ever be known.

Beria was charged with trying to put the State Security Service above Party and State in order to liquidate the present socialist régime and restore capitalism; he was accused of being an agent of British and American Intelligence, together with a long list of other crimes and misdemeanours, including picking up women who caught his fancy from the streets of Moscow.

We had a Party meeting in the Canberra Embassy at which all these charges were solemnly read out. No one commented. What lies behind them? Of Beria's private life I know little. A friend of my wife's once lived underneath a flat in Moscow which Beria occupied and she described sounds of revelry which she had heard overhead. I can only say that Beria did not have the look of a dissolute man when I interviewed him. The picking up of women from the Moscow streets was a preposterous charge to bring against a man of Beria's public position and secret power, for whom such conduct would have been both dangerous and unnecessary.

Our M.V.D. colleague Yuri Rastvorov, who escaped to the Americans in Japan a little before my own break, has suggested a reconstruction of the events in Moscow at the time of Beria's arrest, based on what he was told by prominent Soviet visitors to Japan. His version suggested that Beria was on the point of seizing total power himself, when his plans were unveiled and anticipated by Malenkov and his allies. I cannot shed any light on this particular matter.

What is certain is that Beria was the loser in a naked struggle for supreme power, which is not yet ended. Beria, by seniority, record, abilities, achievements, was the most natural successor to Stalin among the leaders who remained. The charges of espionage for a foreign power and plotting to restore capitalism are now formalities without which the epitaph on any fallen Soviet giant is incomplete. I do not believe that they have any substance in Beria's case. Beria's real crime was a simple and fundamental one in the eyes of his rivals. Beria was too powerful.

Beria's fall had a direct and decisive influence on my own fate and my decision to escape from the Soviet service, and to take refuge in Australia, as I shall presently relate.

VIII

War and Marriage

'HALT! Let me see your pass!'

I stopped in my tracks. Though I was wearing my N.K.V.D. uniform with the insignia of a Lieutenant of State Security I had no intention of arguing with a Kremlin guard on such a point. Moreover, this was 1938, one of the purge years.

I handed him the special pass authorizing me to enter the Kremlin on this date. He examined it and handed it back in silence.

'Hold up your hands!'

I did so, and he went carefully through all my pockets in search of a concealed weapon. Finally he came to my hip-pocket and pulled out the bulky object which had attracted his sharp eyes. It was a newspaper which I had thrust into my pocket absent-mindedly as I dressed for the occasion. I should have been more careful. We had all been strictly warned against bringing any sort of weapon into the Kremlin precincts. The bulge gave possible grounds for suspicion. The guard handed the paper back with a grunt and signed me on. For all he knew I might have been concealing a revolver and have been planning the assassination of the President of the U.S.S.R.

In fact, I was entering the Kremlin on a less dangerous mission. Some weeks before, not long after my return from Sinkiang, I had been reading through *Pravda* when I suddenly saw my own name. To my pleasure and surprise I found that I had been awarded a Red Star in recognition of my services. At that time it was an unusual distinction; out of those who took part in the Sinkiang expedition, only about fifty were decorated with Red Stars.

Telephone calls poured in all day; I had no idea I had so many friends. Then on the appointed day I went to the Kremlin to receive my award. The presentations were made in a large hall especially devoted to such ceremonies, which is on the right as you enter the main public gate of the Kremlin. While the Secretary of the Supreme Council read out the citation, President Kalinin handed us our medals and shook hands (we had been warned not to do this too vigorously!) after which we retired to our seats and each pinned his own medal on his chest. The Red Star is a silver five-pointed star with an embossed Red Army soldier in the centre. I left mine in my office in Moscow when I went abroad to Sweden and then to Australia. It is a rule that on foreign stations only the Ambassador and his wife are allowed to wear their decorations, as such decorations might assist foreign intelligence services to determine the background and real function of our Soviet representatives.

Besides the gratification and reassurance which this distinction gave me, there were practical and material perquisites. The holder of a Red Star was entitled to an extra fourteen roubles a month, one free rail ticket per year to any part of the Soviet Union, a free tram pass, and a free pass to any bathhouse. In addition, I was entitled to use the special privileged ticket window at the big Moscow railway stations; and at smaller stations, which had no such special window, I was entitled to go to the head of the queue. In the Soviet Union, land of patient and perpetual queues for all except the privileged few, this was no small advantage.

Then in 1940 I married again. Since my return from Sinkiang and my divorce, I had occupied a room in Karmanitsky Lane, between Smolensky Square and Arbat Square; but I spent little time there apart from sleeping. I practically lived at the office. Although I had completed my studies by this time, the pressure of cypher work was continuous. I had all my meals, breakfast included, at the N.K.V.D. restaurant, and frequently in the evenings I went back to the office and worked, to keep up to date with the day's traffic, till one or two in the morning.

On other evenings I was busy with Party work. I conducted a study group on the history of the Communist Party and as Party organizer for my section I was also a member of the Party Bureau of our whole Department.

One of my more ticklish duties was the allocation of clothing coupons among our staff. All clothing, and especially shoes, were very scarce, and coupons were jealously coveted. Several of my predecessors had abused their privilege and had been detected unfairly favouring their wives and friends. But I had no wife, and in any case I disliked such abuses and did my best to be fair to everyone. I prepared a list, considered each case personally, and then made my distribution. Needless to say, whenever I appeared I was mobbed by my colleagues of both sexes; indeed, I found myself a very popular man.

However, there was a testimony that I valued more. After my first term of office I was overwhelmingly re-elected by secret ballot of the whole Department.

Now that my studies were completed, I made a habit of taking Sundays off, and usually spent the whole day out of the city. Sometimes I went to the shooting range; for it was a matter of keen competition between different Departments to have the greatest number of qualified 'Voroshilov's Marksmen' among their staff. At other times I went for picnics in the country with office colleagues; and in the winter we organized skiing parties to the outskirts of Moscow.

It was on these expeditions that I began to see a lot of Doosia.

Doosia worked in a different section, which was housed in what had formerly been the Hotel Select, whereas my section was in No. 2 Lubianka (also fronting on Dzerjinsky Street). In our building were the offices of the Chiefs of the N.K.V.D., including Beria and his Deputy Merkulov. (I occasionally saw Beria with his bodyguards on his swift passage from car to office; he entered by a special side door, never by the front entrance which the rest of us used.) Doosia did not normally visit our building but I often went to her office block to attend Party meetings and saw her at work and in the N.K.V.D. restaurant. Just when her fair hair, blue eyes and animated personality made their first distinctive impression on me I cannot say, but presently I found that it was unusual for me to visit the office where she worked without stopping to speak to her. And increasingly in the train on the way back from our skiing trips I would find myself in the same compartment as Doosia. I think it all began when one of my colleagues—I can't remember who —said to me half in joke, half seriously, 'Volodya, it's time you were married. Look at Doosia! She has charm and intelligence, she's an excellent mother to her little girl and you are now a single man again. What about it?'

I told him to be quiet and not be a gossiping busybody, but his words kept recurring to me with curious insistence in the days that followed.

I was lonely; I admired Doosia's charm, vivacity and intelligence; before long I found myself determined to marry her.

For a long time she was friendly but elusive. But I was persistent. After a while I became a constant visitor at her flat and I became very fond of her little daughter Irina who would run to me and always greeted me as 'Uncle Volodya'.

I knew about Doosia's previous marriage and the stigma and threat that hung over her from her first husband's arrest. In those years especially, the safest policy would have been for me to keep away, lest I too should become involved in any future penalties that might suddenly descend on her. I had seen too many such cases at first hand.

But by this time I was prepared to disregard the risk. That fact, and other things, turned the scale with Doosia. She will tell her side of the

story in her own words. In June 1940 we went through the simple
formalities of registration by which in Soviet law we became man and
wife.

We had not quite finished redecorating our flat when the Germans
invaded Russia.

It was the culmination of years of mounting tension. For as the
purges and internal terror began to abate, the external threat grew
greater and greater. Although I was fully occupied on internal communications we were inevitably in close touch with other branches and
departments of the N.K.V.D. which dealt with Foreign Intelligence and
from them I gathered many rumbles of the approaching storm. Apart
from that, it was obvious, even from the Soviet newspapers, that
Mussolini's Italy and Hitler's Germany were advancing from strength
to strength. Soviet policy remained wary, watchful to defend the
socialist homeland and to take advantage of the fratricidal strife of the
capitalist powers.

There was the failure of our support for the Republican Government
in Spain.

Then came the war against Finland.

For many Soviet sympathizers in Western countries, the Soviet attack on Finland came as a severe shock. It seemed to them that the
Soviet Union, to which they looked as the champion of social justice
and peace, had blackened its record and had followed the sordid example of Mussolini's and Hitler's aggressions. A former British communist who fought in Spain and visited Moscow as a Comintern delegate, Fred Copeman, has described the Finnish war as an important step
in his disillusionment with Communism.

With us it was different. The war with Finland caused dismay, as
stories of the Finns' stubborn and skilful resistance came back from the
front, as Soviet casualties mounted, and the slow progress of our troops
became obvious. But we were not surprised or shocked. We accepted
the official explanation that the proximity of the Finnish border consti-
tuted an acute threat to Leningrad, and that the war was necessary, in
view of the international situation, as a measure of protection and
defence of the socialist homeland.

The argument of defence can be stretched indefinitely, especially if
you regard the whole outside world as your inevitable foe. And that is
how Soviet leadership regards the whole non-communist world, whatever tactical agreements and compromises it may make for the time
being.

A perfect example of such a tactical agreement was the Nazi-Soviet

Pact of 1939. This political move was another staggering blow to idealistic Communists in the West, who had cherished the belief that the Soviet Union was the main bulwark against Fascist aggression. I have read that in the case of Whittaker Chambers in the United States, the Nazi-Soviet Pact was the last straw in his disillusionment and decision to break with the Party.

It may be interesting to compare the reaction within the Soviet Union. Such an outstanding reversal of policy did certainly provide the Soviet Government with a problem of explanation. For years our propaganda had been whipping up violent anti-Fascist feelings, and focusing on Hitler's Germany and Mussolini's Italy as the chief menaces to peace and socialism. Suddenly, overnight, the Soviet people found themselves allies of their most feared and hated enemy. Radical adjustment was necessary to the new line.

But the Soviet people had over long years become so accustomed to policies of total expediency, and to startling shifts and contradictions in what they were told to think and feel, that they experienced no shock comparable to that felt in Western countries. I remember my own surprise—less sudden because I had learnt from signals that preparations were afoot for Molotov and his delegation to meet Ribbentrop.

But the Pact was explained, and accepted by most of us, as a stroke of policy designed to lessen the danger of war for the Soviet Union. With the ever-present threat of a Japanese attack in the Far East, this agreement with Germany might secure our western frontier. There was hope, too, of trade benefits; under the Pact Germany placed a large order for wheat from the Soviet Union. When the Pact was signed, Molotov explained that it was a necessary move which would make possible peaceful co-existence between our two countries.

For simplicity's sake Molotov made no reference in his speech to the partition of Poland between Germany and the Soviet Union, nor was it mentioned in the papers. However, I learnt in advance that something of the sort was planned from a top-secret cable which I handled, signed by Beria and addressed to Minsk and other border cities warning them that Soviet occupation of Polish territory was imminent, and instructing them to make ready N.K.V.D. operational units to follow in the wake of the occupying forces.

However, Hitler was not prepared to yield pride of place to Stalin as a master of cynicism and perfidy. I was in hospital when his troops invaded on 21st June 1941; but for weeks previously there had been an accumulation of evidence—dispatches from Soviet agents in Poland and elsewhere—of intensive German preparations across the border.

Also (though I knew nothing of this at the time) the Soviet Government had received precise information as to the date of the German attack, as well as an authoritative assurance that Japan had no intention of attacking Soviet territory in the Far East. This information came from Dr Richard Sorge, the German newspaper correspondent who ran an outstandingly successful Soviet spy network in Japan.

Morale inside the Soviet Union in the early stages of the war was shaky. Hasty action had to be taken to disabuse the people of what they had been told at the time of the Nazi-Soviet Pact and to explain to them that the war, which had been interpreted on Marxist lines as an inevitable struggle for markets between capitalist powers, was now a crusade for the survival of Russia and socialism. Factory meetings and speeches by Soviet leaders accompanied the call to total mobilization, and overnight the watchword became patriotism and defence of the homeland. Stalin, in his broadcast speech soon after the outbreak of hostilities, invoked the Czarist military heroes Suvarov and Kutuzov, who defeated Napoleon. Citizens not conscripted were required to build fortifications behind the lines. In the office we were all issued with new weapons and gas-masks.

But the news that came in from the front was ominous and alarming. It was clear that the German attack had caught us off our guard, despite all warnings. Big detachments of our border troops were taken prisoner, with quantities of equipment; at Minsk many Soviet planes were captured on the ground. Soon remnants of the defeated units began to stream through Moscow for regrouping and the people of Moscow saw trucks, soldiers, wounded men and refugees, jamming the overcrowded roads and railways in their retreat before the Germans.

More disturbing still for those of us 'in the know' were the signals that came in from the border districts. Whole sections of the population were welcoming the Germans as liberators. Then the Soviet General Vlassov's army was surrounded and surrendered. Convinced that the Germans were going to win, Vlassov and a part of his army went over to the German side and this anti-Soviet Russian force was augmented by many more Russian p.o.w's. This army of Vlassov's, I learned, could have been much bigger had not the Germans feared that they would ultimately be unable to control it.

When Smolensk fell, civilian morale was further depressed.

German air-raids were now a constant occurrence and Doosia and I used to go down to the air-raid shelter each evening in time for the regular seven o'clock raid which the methodical Germans put on. Once, caught in the street on our way to the shelter, we crouched in a doorway while a low-flying raider passed right overhead. At other times we saw rescue parties cleaning away débris and picking up casualties. The N.K.V.D. garage was hit, and a bomb fell in the road between my office and the next building. However, not even at the worst period of the raids on Moscow was the damage anything like as severe as that which we saw later in London. The German Air Force had to fight a war on two fronts. And after a while the Moscow anti-aircraft barrage became too formidable for the raiders. I arranged for Doosia, after a brief evacuation to Kuibyshev, to return to Moscow and to transfer to my section. She was glad to return. She was convinced that we would be all right and that our flat would not be hit, and her conviction proved to be justified.

As the German advance continued, partial evacuation of Moscow was ordered. Then on 16th October, as I have described, the order for general evacuation was received. Amid the confusion and chaos, as all the Ministries and the Diplomatic Corps removed to Kuibyshev, and whole factories and their workers were in process of transfer eastward beyond the Urals, there was disorder and much bewilderment among the frightened population of Moscow who remained behind.

The sight of the N.K.V.D. troops getting into trucks for departure increased the panic. People remarked that, 'Things must be pretty bad when the N.K.V.D. are shifting out instead of staying to defend Moscow!' I stayed on, with my cypher group, but Doosia was evacuated with her section to Kuibyshev.

When she was due to leave and a truck came to pick up her bags, a woman neighbour exclaimed, 'What are you running away for? Aren't you going to stay and defend Moscow? I suppose all the N.K.V.D. are getting out?'

She would not believe it when I told her that only my wife was going and that I was staying behind in Moscow. A few days later my chief, Degtjarov and I were walking along Kuznetsky Street, in our N.K.V.D. uniform when another woman stared at us and called:

'Fancy that, the N.K.V.D. men are still here! They all went away, but look, these two are still here!'

To the people of Moscow, the N.K.V.D. represented a privileged governing class, but it was clear from these incidents that in such a crisis the mass of the people did not trust us as their friends and protectors even in face of the foreign invader.

For the majority, war-time conditions meant a desperate struggle for existence. Food was bad and very scarce and there was much black marketing. A loaf of bread on the black market cost 100 to 120 roubles.

A woman friend of Doosia's refused to be evacuated. 'No, I'm staying here,' she said bitterly. 'Why should I move? Perhaps I will be better off under the Germans.'

If the Germans had been shrewd they might have turned this situation to immense advantage. Had there been evidence of decent treatment for those who submitted, in addition to the enemy's formidable military gains, it might even have altered the course of the war.

But, instead, stories poured in of German ruthlessness, brutalities and atrocities in the conquered areas. There were too many of them, and their evidence was too strong, for them to be disbelieved.

The arrogance and cruelties of the German armies in the early stages of their invasion, together with the appeal to Russian national pride and patriotism in an all-out struggle for survival, stiffened the morale of the soldiers and the civilian population alike. They showed their spirit in the successful defences of Moscow and Leningrad, the victory at Stalingrad, and the daring effective exploits of our Partisan units operating behind the German lines.

A story widely publicized throughout the Soviet Union was that of the girl-partisan, Zoe Kosmodemyanskaya. She joined a Partisan unit while still a schoolgirl of sixteen. Captured by the Germans, she was stripped of her clothes, exposed in the snow, tortured and eventually hanged. To the end she refused to divulge information about the military dispositions of her comrades and as she went to the scaffold she cried:

'You can't hang every Soviet citizen! Long live our leader Stalin!'

The overriding need for national unity in those desperate and critical days induced Stalin to bid for the positive support of even the religious leaders. With curious and characteristic cynicism he arranged a conference in the Kremlin, to which he invited the robed and bearded patriarchs and all the important dignitaries of the Russian Orthodox Church. At the conference there was also a certain Karpov. Now Karpov was a permanent career officer of the N.K.V.D. who, over a long period, had made an assiduous and exhaustive study of Russian Orthodox ceremonies, ordinances, and theological teaching, and was able to converse earnestly and learnedly with the church dignitaries on their own ground. At this conference Stalin suggested that the character and erudition of Karpov made him an ideal man to represent the Church on the Soviet Council of Ministers. His suggestion was applauded, and Karpov was appointed.

I have seen Karpov. In 1951 he was Minister for Cults and Religious Affairs and may still hold that office. His N.K.V.D. training would be a valuable preparation for the post. After all, Stalin studied in a theological seminary.

But there was no question of relying on appeals to individual loyalty in the maintenance of war-time morale, whether among the civil population or in the armed forces. Fear and severity, normal instruments of Soviet rule in peace-time, were not likely to be discarded in the heat of war.

There was a ruthless purge of all prisoners. Those whose cases were still being investigated were sent away, if there was time, to camps in remote regions. But prisoners in towns close to the German advance were executed without further inquiry, lest they should be captured and go over to the service of the enemy. Punishment battalions were formed, in which political prisoners and criminals were told that they could expiate their crimes by death or glory; these battalions were sent wherever the fighting was hottest.

A story with a happy ending was that of my shipmate and fellow cypher-rating, Lebedev, who served at Murmansk. In 1942, when Mr Eden came to Russia in a British destroyer, a flotilla of our destroyers was ordered to meet and escort him into harbour. Owing to a coding error, the officer commanding the Soviet flotilla was given the wrong latitude and longitude for the rendezvous and Mr Eden was not met. The mistake was traced to my friend Lebedev. It was a serious matter; Soviet prestige had suffered. Lebedev was sentenced to death. However, his sentence was commuted to service in an infantry Punishment Battalion. But after a grim ordeal in which he was several times wounded, Lebedev was decorated with the Red Star, and was reinstated in his post.

Retribution and precautions were swift and sweeping. My wife's friend Jenya Chistova had a brother, a senior M.V.D. officer and a member of the Supreme Soviet, who was in charge of the Leningrad fortifications, and who was captured by the Germans while carrying documents concerning these defence works. Immediately Jenya and two other sisters who worked in the N.K.V.D. were all dismissed and deprived of their flat. Jenya was evacuated to Ufa, where she died of tuberculosis.

During the war the N.K.V.D. kept a strict watch over all the armed forces through the organization known as 'Smersh'. Its name is made up of two Russian words, *Smert Shpionam*, meaning 'Death to Spies'. But its real task was not the apprehension and punishment of foreign spies; it was the detection of the slightest sign of disaffection, or even the expression of discontent, among the Soviet soldiers, sailors and airmen.

My colleague M——, who was for three years a cypher clerk in Mongolia, worked in Smersh; after the war it became the 3rd Chief Directorate of the M.G.B.

Every battalion, regiment and company of the Red Army had a Smersh representative attached to it, as did all parallel units in the Navy and Air Force. His position was quite open but he had to recruit and organize a number of secret agents to spy and report on the rest of the unit: the average number was ten agents to every hundred men. The Smersh representative had conspiratorial meetings with his agents as though he were running a spy network on foreign soil. My friend Y——, who was a Smersh representative attached to the Moscow fortifications, once peevishly told me that the Germans were interfering with his work, as his agents kept running for cover during bombardments. Smersh agents furnished detailed reports on their comrades, noting any defeatist talk, complaints about conditions, or criticism of the authorities. These reports went through Smersh channels, circumventing the Commanding Officer and staff of the unit. No wonder that the professional soldiers detested Smersh—though they had to pay lip service to the need for this relentless vigilance. This hatred is said to have played a part in Beria's downfall, and may well have done, particularly if it is true that the redoubtable Zhukov suffered a setback through the activities of this Department. But it had the backing of Government and Party, to whom it offered a means of keeping in check the menace of a successful and ambitious military leader.

It was effective. In the war Smersh was a potent, ever-present reality. It meant that in the last resort waverers had to fear more certain retribution from the bullets of their countrymen than from the guns of the enemy. Smersh was just another province of the empire of fear.

An example of the severity meted out to all offenders was the case of my wife's brother. Early in the war, when he was fourteen, he was evacuated with his father to Ufa and went to work in an arms factory there. Factories were largely self-supporting units and while in Ufa he was sent with a party of men to another area to fish for the factory. One morning he found that the ration cards of the whole party, which had been entrusted to him, had been stolen. He had a shrewd idea who had done it, but as the culprit was a powerful and influential person, he dared not take action against him.

Terrified of what might happen to him, he ran away to the front and tried to join the Red Army. He was apprehended, charged as a deserter from the labour front, and sentenced to five years in a 'Corrective' Labour Camp.

At the end of the war an amnesty was declared and Doosia's brother was released. He was ill, bed-ridden and nothing but skin and bone when her mother went to meet him, and but for the food which we had by this time sent from Sweden, he might never have recovered from what he had been through in the camp.

Severity and fear were employed as instruments to produce obedience. On the other hand, if Doosia's brother had not been so afraid of the penalties for his loss of the ration cards, he would never have run away from his factory.

This may be the point for me to say a word about the Labour Camps which are such an important element of the Soviet system, in peace no less than in war. Knowledge of the existence of these camps provides a background of dread to the thoughts of the most obscure and inoffensive citizen of the U.S.S.R. and they constitute an ever-present threat that no Soviet official can afford to forget. If I had gone back to the Soviet Union from Australia, I would probably now be serving at least a ten-year sentence in a Labour Camp as a result of the intrigues against me and the hostile reports to Moscow sent by the two Ambassadors.

'Slave Labour' is the term commonly used by Western writers to describe the miserable inmates, estimated to number twelve or fifteen millions, of these Soviet Labour Camps. Technically they are not slaves but convicted prisoners serving their allotted sentence of hard labour. But when one considers the severity of sentences imposed in the Soviet Union, especially for any political offence, and the conditions of life of these prisoners, the distinction does not seem very real. Slavery could easily be preferable. There are, however, two distinct types of prisoners —political offenders and ordinary criminals. These latter receive much more lenient treatment. Their camps are often situated near centres of population, where they work on building construction, roads, and other public works. I frequently saw gangs of these criminal offenders working on projects in and around Moscow. They are allowed the right of correspondence with their families and recently capital punishment has been abolished in their case, even for murder.

But the death sentence has not been abolished for political offenders. In prison or camp, these 'enemies of the people' are debarred from correspondence with their families and friends, and are sent to penal colonies in remote regions far from towns and cities, generally to the far north of Siberia.

All these camps, for criminal and political prisoners alike, are under the control of the vast organization known as Gulag, which works under M.V.D. direction. Its head office in Moscow alone employs a staff of about 2,000. For a short time during the war I was chief of the cypher section of Gulag, with twelve cypher clerks under me. Our task was to handle the secret telegrams between Moscow and the hundreds of camps scattered throughout the length and breadth of the Soviet Union. I remember many telegrams from the main political camps in the far north—Solovky, Vorkuta, a huge camp, Norilsk, Nagayevo, near Kamchatka in the Far East, and many smaller ones in the Yakutsk area. Most of the telegrams were reports on particular prisoners, but others were administrative. Gulag includes an Operational Section, a Political Section, an Administrative Section, a Guard Section, and a Construction Section, which supplies the armies of prison labour for great construction projects like the building of canals, roads and railways.

I was lucky enough to escape personal experience of Soviet Labour Camps, either as a prisoner or as a Camp official, but I knew a number of N.K.V.D. colleagues who had been stationed at camps, including my friend Byelov, who was a cypher clerk at Vorkuta. The picture they gave of human degradation in these penal colonies was terrible, but it was too consistent to be doubted.

The guards, who have direct control of the prisoners, are specially selected for their brutality and severity. The prisoners live a marginal existence. They wear prison-issue grey cotton jacket and trousers and are marched to work from their huts each day in a straggling column, each holding the man ahead of him under the arms in order to keep together. Their diet is miserably inadequate. In the morning, weak tea and bread; at mid-day, thin soup; at night, a mug of water and a little more bread. Scurvy is prevalent, decaying teeth and gums are general. But even this minimum ration is only for those who can fulfil their daily allotted quota of work. Once a man becomes too weak to fulfil his quota, his ration is reduced also. Not many prisoners from political camps return to tell their tale at the end of their term. At Norilsk camp one winter when there was a shortage of food, the prisoners were dying so fast that neither time nor means were available to dig graves for them, and their bodies were stacked out in the open like firewood, until warmer weather should make it possible to dig the ground and bury them.

Non-political offenders had a chance of serving their sentence and returning to normal existence. Such was the case with Chesnokov, an N.K.V.D. cypher clerk who, after four years at the Soviet Embassy in Washington, was accused of misappropriating N.K.V.D. funds and was sentenced to ten years' penal servitude. He denied the charge. It may have been true or it may have been trumped up as the result of intrigues against him. His sentence was later reduced to five years, which suggests the latter reason. I saw him soon after his release. He found that during his imprisonment his wife had sold up all his belongings and had gone off with another man. As we had known each other in the Red Navy (he was a cypher rating, junior to me, and had served in a submarine in the Black Sea) I did my best to help him. His career was ruined, but through a friend of mine he eventually got a job in the railways.

Chesnokov described the dreadful food, the disorder, thieving and violence among the prisoners. Because of his intelligence and education, he was put in charge of a working party which consisted of ordinary thugs and criminals. His fairness and moderation earned their respect. As a reward his gang offered to kidnap for him the best girl they could find (newly-arrived) from the women's barracks, and to steal extra bread for him, but Chesnokov refused their well-intentioned offers.

Nothing could be more ironical than the official description of these establishments as 'Corrective Labour Camps'. The grim and ghastly conditions, the hooliganism, stealing and violence among the prisoners, have the effect of corrupting instead of reforming anyone who is sent there.

This was dramatically demonstrated in Moscow in recent years. Immediately after Stalin's death the new Government, with the object of gaining popularity, declared an amnesty for all prisoners serving sentences under five years. The results were alarming and unforeseen. I heard about them from later arrivals at our Embassy in Canberra. Such hordes of prisoners were released that all the railway stations were crowded and Moscow was flooded with them. A reign of lawlessness and banditry followed. Gangs of thugs held up people in trains, trams and buses; the ordinary militia were quite unable to cope with such widespread crime; even Government officials were afraid to travel home at night. Eventually the released prisoners were rounded up and sent back to camps again. Those who had not been hardened criminals when they were first sentenced had become so as a result of their camp life.

Scapegoats for the blunder were sought and even Molotov was questioned about it at a Party meeting in the Ministry of Foreign Affairs.

As Beria was by that time under arrest, Molotov gave the standard classic reply: 'The amnesty to prisoners was decreed on the initiative and insistence of Beria.'

★　★　★

My wartime interlude as chief of cypher communications for Gulag certainly did not make me any more anxious to see the inside of a Labour Camp, even though it were labelled 'corrective'. But it was an instructive experience.

It was in June 1942, in the grimmest stage of the struggle against Germany, that I received the appointment which carried Doosia and myself from grey, war-clouded Moscow to the peace and abundance of neutral Sweden.

But before I describe that phase of our lives, it is necessary that she should tell her story up to the time of our marriage, and our setting out on that adventure together.

Childhood

LIKE my husband, I was born in one of the primitive villages of Russia a few years before the Revolution, but unlike him, I moved with my family to Moscow when I was ten. That fact made an enormous difference to our upbringing and outlook. He, apart from his service in the Red Navy, lived and worked in villages and provincial towns until his middle twenties, when he joined the O.G.P.U. in Moscow; his youth and early manhood were spent largely among country folk. But I grew up in Moscow, close to the hub and heartbeat of the Soviet régime, and was able to take full advantage of the special privileges and opportunities open to children of the Moscow proletariat.

Our village of Lipky, in Ryazan province, not very far from Moscow, was smaller and poorer than Volodya's Siberian village of Larikha. There were only about a hundred houses, many of them without chimneys, so that the smoke of the fires had to find its way out of the doors or the windows; and the countryside was bare and treeless. My earliest memories, like those of most citizens of the Soviet Union, are set against a background of hardship and fear.

The people of Ryazan province have a reputation for courage—which their soldiers proved true in the last war—and for quick wits. My mother had both, and she certainly needed them. She was seventeen when I, her first child, was born. Father left soon afterwards to seek work in Leningrad, leaving Mother and me with his parents.

Grandfather was an imposing and terrifying figure; he had a beard and looked rather like the great Leo Tolstoy. He favoured his elder son Yasha, who was in the house with his wife and family, but he regarded my father as the black sheep of the family. In his eyes Mother and I were unwanted interlopers.

'Just one more mouth to feed!' was all he said to Mother when I was born.

He encouraged Anna, Yasha's eight-year-old daughter, to cheat me of my proper food when Mother was out at work in the fields. Anna would chew up some bread, put it in a piece of cloth and give it to me as a dummy when I cried with hunger. I remember the day—I must have been about four at the time—when Mother tried to give me a cup of milk and Grandfather snatched it and threw it out of the door rather than let me have it. A child's mind does not forget such things.

Breaking-point came in the great famine year of 1919, when I was five. I had wandered into the vegetable garden near the house and picked up a cucumber, when Grandfather saw me. With a roar of rage he rushed out, seized my arm and dragged me to the stable. He tied my ankles together, fastened the rope to one of the rafters, hauled me up and was belabouring me with a switch as I hung head downwards, screaming with pain and fright, when Mother reached the scene. Her fury made him desist, but that was the end as far as she was concerned. At last Father came from Leningrad, and with three or four other families from famine-stricken Lipky we decided to migrate to Siberia, where it was said that there was more food to be had. We travelled in wagons to the town of Ryazan, the capital of our province, where we were to catch the train. It was night when we got there, and I fell asleep on the floor of the wagon, which had been drawn up in the station yard. Suddenly I was wakened by the sound of an ear-splitting whistle, and through the darkness of the night—it was ten or eleven o'clock—I saw a thunderous glow and rows and rows of moving lights. I had never seen a train, and I cried with fright, and felt as though I was on the brink of a precipice, or had suddenly been transported to another world, till Mother comforted me and reassured me that it was only the engine and carriages of the train that would take us to our new home.

Vividly I recall the long train journey, our arrival at the city of Semipalatinsk, foraging through the countryside, sleeping under wagons in the open fields, Mother begging food from house to house, the prosperous-looking homestead where they set their dogs on us, the kind villager and his family who took us in while Father helped him in the fields. When Mother caught typhoid, we took her to the *Feldsher*, the village medical wiseacre who advised us to reduce her temperature by keeping her wrapped in wet bed-sheets. She was then twenty-two and must have had a strong constitution, for after six weeks she began to recover in spite of this treatment, though she was so weak at first that we had to teach her how to walk.

We had moved into a derelict mud house on the outskirts of the village of Alexeevka, when Father in turn fell sick with typhoid, became delirious and tried to murder us all with an axe. I remember how our animals died either from frostbite or through inadequate feeding and how every morning that winter we had to dig our way out of our snowbound house.

Then things took a turn for the better. Father recovered, Mother sold her precious dowry and with the money we bought a better house and a plot of land where we grew watermelons, rockmelons and sunflowers.

One summer's day Father took me with him in the wagon to visit our plot. It had been a beautiful spring. I remember the scent of the pinewoods when we went for firewood and the riot of blossoming flowers, poppies, carnations, sunflowers, daisies and violets. We reached our plot in the evening and went for water to a large nearby well with wooden sides. The well was dry, but at the bottom of it was a big buck hare. 'Doosia, there's our dinner,' said Father. As the well was deep, he went back to the wagon, removed the sides, which were detachable, and lashed them end-to-end to make a ladder. I watched him climb down into the well, and dispatch the unfortunate hare; but when he began to climb out again, the lashing broke and the ladder came apart. I began to cry, fearing that I would be left alone in the gathering darkness.

'Now, now, Doosia,' he called. 'Don't cry, be a brave girl. I'll soon get this ladder mended. Just wait there, I'll soon be with you.'

It was nearly an hour before he got the ladder mended and climbed out to join me. How relieved I was, and how I clung to him!

We went across to our field and got ready for the night. We were to sleep in a small wooden hut with a shelf at one end which he had built for these occasions. It was dark when we got there.

'Wolves are our next danger,' said my Father as he gathered some wood and lit a fire. There were many wolves in that part of Siberia, and sure enough before long we heard distant howling. I shivered and began to cry, but Father cheered me up.

'Don't be afraid, Doosia, they are frightened of the fire; they won't dare to come near us.'

He skinned the hare and began to cook it over the fire, and promised to make me a fine hat from its fur. Thus comforted I ate my supper and went to sleep safe inside the hut.

We stayed in Alexeevka till late in 1924, when my parents decided to return to Lipky again. Famine by this time had struck Siberia, and we had heard that things had improved in Ryazan. However, we did not settle in impoverished Lipky.

Father went to Moscow, where he got work as a tram-driver and wrote to say that he had found accommodation for us as well. Late that year, when I was ten years old, we came, Mother, myself and my younger brother Ivan to join him. From that day, until I sought asylum in Australia in 1951, Moscow was my home.

The accommodation which Father had secured for us is worth describing. It represented quite common conditions of life for ordinary humble folk in Moscow at that time, and even in 1951, when I was last in Moscow, despite the many imposing public works and public buildings which have arisen under Soviet rule, the mass of the people still lived under conditions little if at all better than those of 1924. I am not speaking now of the show places, the special blocks of flats and the selected shops and factories which are shown to visiting Western delegations on their conducted tours, but of living conditions in Moscow as they exist for the ordinary citizen without special privilege or influence.

We lived three families in one room on the third floor of a big six-storey tenement building, which had formerly been a hotel, in the centre of Moscow, near Lubianka Street, ten minutes' walk from Sretensky Boulevarde. The room was of medium size, with a big window on one side, but as this looked on to a well, of which one side was formed by the wall of a factory, it was a dark room. In all there were ten people in this one room, which also served as the only passageway for the occupants of other rooms. Our room had four beds, one against each wall. In one slept Mother and Father, in another a childless couple, in another my aunt (who was also my godmother) and her husband. My brother Ivan and I took turns sleeping in the fourth bed or on the floor, where my aunt's two children also slept. None of us had very many clothes; what we had we kept in boxes under the beds.

A communal kitchen served twenty people who occupied five rooms on our floor; each family had its own primus stove to cook on and a small table with drawers. There was a tap with running water in the kitchen, and a cool cupboard for food.

In the room I have described we lived for two years, and did not consider ourselves outrageously overcrowded by Moscow standards. Only when Mother brought my brother back from a sanatorium where he had been lying ill were we able to appeal and get relief.

Do not imagine that Russian people are any different from Westerners in their longing for living space and privacy. They have exactly the same instincts. They have an equal desire to lead their own lives and to have somewhere that they can call their own for themselves and their families. But they have no choice and no standards of comparison, and they are constantly assured that conditions in the decadent capitalist countries are far worse. Thus, for example, most Russian girls in their wildest dreams do not hope for more when they marry than a room of their own. Separate flats and houses are the prerogatives of the elect minority, the governing bureaucracy whose envied privileges carry their own perils but are comparatively lavish while they last.

For us, some relief came with the tragic death of my brother Ivan. When we went first from Lipky to Siberia, Ivan and I were the only children. While we were in Siberia, Mother had another boy, Valentin. He died of typhus when he was three. Then she had twin boys, Nikolai and Sergei, who died of dysentery when they were a few months old. Then she had another daughter, Serafima, who died, also of dysentery, after our return to Lipky. Mother's experience was not unusual. This terrible wastage of human life is a burden familiar and commonplace among the ordinary women of Russia. But it seemed that these bereavements were not enough. In Siberia Ivan had a serious fall. He was a lively boy, and was playing by himself, sitting astride a wooden fence and pretending that he was a daredevil Cossack horseman, when he fell backwards on to a heavy wooden post and broke his back. From then on he was a chronic invalid. There were no trained doctors in the village, only an ignorant villager who had a reputation for medical knowledge and who prescribed hot baths. They did him no good. Poor Ivan recovered, but he was hunchbacked and always ailing; yet he was clever at school and showed artistic gifts which he had perhaps inherited from Father, who was always painting pictures and writing poems. After we came to Moscow Ivan got worse; Mother suffered deeply for him and devoted herself passionately to his welfare. Though she had had little education in the village, she battled tirelessly with officialdom and with innumerable forms and eventually succeeded in getting him into a sanatorium. There it was found that he had a tubercular bone infection, and later, meningitis. For a long time he was in and out of the sanatorium, and during this time, to make conditions a little better for him when he was at home, Mother launched many appeals to the Health Department. At last an inspector came and we were moved to another room with a small annexe in another part of the building. As a family, we were now lucky enough to have a room of our own. When I last heard from them in 1954, a few weeks before my flight, my parents were still living there.

Eventually it became clear that Ivan was sinking and that nothing could be done for him, so Mother brought him home to be with her and nursed him till he died.

To complete the story of our family, it was in 1926 that Ivan died, and the following year my younger brother Valentin was born. Years afterwards came the last of our family, my sister Tamara, born in 1937 within a few days of the birth of my own daughter Irina. I, the eldest, was thus twenty-three years older than Tamara, the youngest. Even as a child, after we first moved to Moscow, I became increasingly Mother's companion and confidant. Father gave her money for the housekeeping; he was always good-natured, casual, easy-going and somehow remote. Mother's was the thought, care, energy and self-sacrifice that held our family together. This quality of care for others must have been part of her character very early in life, judging from an amusing incident she told me of her early childhood in the village.

Her father used to come home drunk; he could not carry his liquor and would be flushed after one glass of beer. Her mother bitterly resented this failing of his and used to rate him soundly, which caused Mother much distress, as she hated her parents quarrelling and thought that her mother was too severe on her father. One night he came home tipsy, but with guilty prudence had bought two salted herrings which he presented to his wife as a peace-offering. But she was so furious that she wouldn't even look at them and threw them under the bed. Grandfather was shocked and wounded at this treatment of his present. A state of war existed between them. Mother, who was then about nine, could not bear the enmity between her parents and deplored the waste of the fish. She retrieved the herrings from under the bed, cooked them, put them on the table, and invited her father and mother to dinner.

Though she said nothing to me at the time, Mother went through awful conflicts on the question of having my brother Valentin christened. By this time I was a member of the Pioneers, the officially-sponsored movement for children not yet old enough to be Komsomols, or Young Communists. This meant that, young as I was, I had taken the first step towards a career under a government which had made plain its practical hostility to religion. In Moscow Mother did not go to church even at Christmas. But when Valentin was three or four months old, and had not been christened, she began to have dreams and nightmares and could not sleep at night. At last she decided to have him christened. The church opposite our home had been demolished, but there was another church a few streets away and she set out with my aunt, carrying Valentin and a kettle of hot water, as it was winter, for the total immersion which the Russian Orthodox service requires. But when they reached the church there was no priest in attendance and they came home disappointed. They went again, and again there was no priest. Then one day when they were going to market, my Mother carrying Valentin, they passed another church and went in. There was a priest there but they had no warm water. Mother decided to wait no longer and to have Valentin christened in cold water, though it hurt her to do it. But they still had no godfather for the child. However, they were not to be put off by this difficulty. They went out into the street and asked the old *dvornik*, or yardman, to be godfather. He agreed; Valentin was christened, and after that Mother slept soundly.

Many years passed before she told me this story. She had watched my career in the Pioneers, Komsomol and O.G.P.U. and she feared to put a strain on my loyalties. Mother loved me very much and she had a shrewd understanding of the realities of life in the new Russia. Though she had had little education, Mother was intelligent, capable and wise.

At an early age I showed an interest in clothes and Mother sympathized with and encouraged me in this. She herself had had an unusually large range of dresses when she was married, but they had gone when she sold her dowry during the famine years in Siberia. She would have liked to dress well, but she had very little money and what she had she spent on me.

Sometimes she was quick-tempered and our ideas did not always coincide. Once she was trying a new frock on me which she had made herself. I didn't think it suited me and at last Mother lost patience, pulled it off me and threw it away, exclaiming, 'I'll never make you another.' After that we had a seamstress who came and made my clothes for me. She would work all day for no other wage than her meals at our table, but it was Mother who provided even that small wage.

What I owe to my mother's generous, unstinting care for me, I can never say. That is the terrible heart-ache of my story.

Living in Moscow meant exciting opportunities for education, both at school and in the Communist Youth Organizations, which I would never have had in the village.

My first day at school was a double ordeal. Wearing my best dress and feeling very scared and very much a country cousin in the great metropolis, I set out and had successfully crossed several side streets when disaster overtook me. A car came up behind me and suddenly sounded its horn. Such things were unknown in the villages where I had lived, though quite common by that time in the capital. Panic took hold of me. I darted out on to the road and began to run backwards and forwards like a frightened rabbit, while the car stopped, its driver mystified by my behaviour. Eventually I ran to a lamp-post and clung trembling to it, crying and waiting for my last moment to come. After a few minutes I looked around. To my immense relief the car was nowhere to be seen. Some passers-by then politely asked me where I was going and kindly directed me to the school, which I reached in due course, breathless but unharmed.

The school occupied the fourth floor of a large building. I climbed the stairs with a beating heart and paused outside the door, afraid to go in. What would these Moscow children be like, I wondered; would they think I was a silly peasant girl and jeer at me for my village accent?

With a desperate effort at boldness I opened the door and went in. A crowd of children were inside, racing about and playing with one another; but when they saw me they all stopped and came crowding round. I shrank back, wondering if they would smother me.

One of the biggest girls, who seemed to be a leader, looked me up and down and said:

'You're a new girl. You must have come from a village.'

'Oh no,' I faltered, 'I live in Moscow.'

'Well, you're a newcomer here, anyway, we never saw you before. What class are you in?'

At this point the teacher came up and introduced me to my schoolmates (Mother had previously interviewed her) explaining that I had recently arrived from the country and asked them to be nice to me and not to tease me.

I soon made friends and came to love school. My favourite subjects were arithmetic, Russian, geography and physical culture. Music would have been my first favourite, but unfortunately our music master was too odd and eccentric to be a successful teacher. Carried away by emotion, he would shut his eyes when playing the violin; the children would titter and the poor man's artistry would be entirely lost in the laughter and disturbance.

At this time Soviet ideas on education were of a 'progressive' and experimental kind. All corporal punishment was abolished after the Revolution and the teachers did not always find it easy to maintain discipline, as they had to do, by persuasion. Sometimes they had to approach parents and ask them to speak firmly to their children, with the ultimate threat of expulsion in the background. On the whole they managed our class of about thirty boys and girls, seated in two long rows of desks, remarkably well, except during music lessons and physical training, when we moved about, often with confusion and noise. Then, too, there were the inevitable naughty boys, who would put chalk on their hands then pat the teacher's arm, leaving a pattern of finger marks, or who would surreptitiously put snow under the teacher's seat. After a while the snow would melt and form a pool, to her great embarrassment. Because I was both timid and interested in lessons I gave the teachers very little trouble and accordingly got good marks for 'discipline'.

But school was less than half the story.

One day, a few weeks after we came to Moscow, I was walking along Lubianka Street, quite close to where we lived, when I saw a crowd of boys and girls coming out of a large building. They were chattering gaily to each other, and all wore red scarves. They looked the happiest, liveliest crowd of children I had ever seen, and I immediately felt I wanted to find out who they were and what they were doing. Shy but fascinated, I went in at the door by which they had come out. Inside there was an entrance hall full of more children all wearing the same red scarves; with them a woman who was obviously their leader. Greatly daring, I went up and asked her what the place was and who the children were.

She answered me quite kindly.

'This is the o.g.p.u. building, little girl, and these children are all Pioneers.'

'Can I join them? Can I be a Pioneer too?'

'Well, that depends. This is the o.g.p.u. group of Pioneers. Does your father work in the o.g.p.u.?'

'Oh, yes. Can I join?'

It was true. Father had recently got a job as wagon-driver in the Transport Section of the o.g.p.u., and so I was entitled to join this section of the Pioneers. The woman gave me the necessary sheaf of forms, without which nothing can be done in the Soviet Union, even where children are concerned. I had to fill in all sorts of details about myself and my parents. But in due course I was notified that I had been accepted as a candidate for membership in the Pioneers and that I should attend on a given night at the 'Summer Garden' Club of the o.g.p.u., to take the oath. When I told my parents what I had done, they made no demur. It had been my own decision. I had not asked their permission. They listened carefully to my enthusiastic story, but made no comment. A new Russia was being created under the direction of the Soviet Government and the youth movements were the road to advancement in its service.

The investiture was an exciting occasion. The candidates were lined up on the stage in the crowded hall, while all the Pioneers of the o.g.p.u. section made up the audience. The Chief of Pioneers—a woman—came forward holding a number of red scarves and badges and spoke the Pioneer oath, which we all repeated after her:

'I, a young Pioneer of the Soviet Union, in the presence of my Comrades, solemnly promise to the Soviet Union that I will firmly and unfailingly fulfil Lenin's covenant and direction. I solemnly promise to set an example at school and at home.'

She added, 'Pioneers, be prepared to serve the cause of Illich [Lenin]!' We all saluted, and replied, 'Always ready!'

Then she put the scarves with the badges pinned on to them, around the necks of each of us in turn and tied them in the regulation way, with one end longer than the other. She reminded us that scarves and badges must be worn at all times and that whenever two Pioneers met out of doors they must salute each other.

Finally a Communist Party official, representing the Party Presidium, addressed us. I cannot even remember now who he was, but he spoke to us very much as follows:

'Children, from today you are Pioneers. You have promised solemnly to carry out Illich's directions. Make sure that you keep that promise faithfully.'

Our Chief then called us to attention and we marched out to a stirring roll of drums.

It was all tremendously thrilling for an eleven-year-old girl fresh from the primitive simplicity of a Russian village. I used to gaze with enormous pride at my Pioneer badge with its design of a golden flame on a background of red, and the motto 'Be Prepared'. I enjoyed saluting so much that whenever I saw another Pioneer I would cross the street, if necessary, in order to exchange salutes.

The great event to which we looked forward all the year was the annual two months' Pioneer Camp, held sometimes on the outskirts of Moscow, but sometimes in distant and exciting regions of Russia. One year the Camp was at Anapa in the Crimea. The journey was an adventure in itself—a thousand boys and girls in six special trains travelling across Russia for three days to Sevastopol. It was all carefully organized with a Chief of each train and an adult Leader to every twenty-five Pioneers. We travelled in four-berth compartments with wooden bunks; we each took our own sheets, blankets, pillows and food for the journey and spent our time in singing, sleeping, talking and playing chess or dominoes.

From Sevastopol, a fleet of buses took us to the beautiful seaside camp at Anapa, where the cooks had a hot meal waiting for us, after which we were directed to our tents and our waiting camp stretchers. Everything had been thought of!

Our days were organized with military precision and ran to a strict routine. Morning and evening we paraded by companies to salute the hoisting and lowering of the Red flag, while the drums beat and a bugle played the Pioneers' Song.

The day was filled with camp duties, study and excursions, and there were fixed times for recreation. How we revelled in sunbathing or swimming in the crisp waters of the Black Sea! How satisfactory it was to gather round the camp fire at night and listen to eerie, blood-curdling stories told by a camp Leader in the flickering firelight!

Back in Moscow, our room always seemed so small and restricted after the scope and variety of life in camp. With Mother and Father both out at work (as is normal with all Russian families) I missed the regular meals and fixed framework of camp routine. However, as a Pioneer and later as a Komsomol, I had a busy enough programme in Moscow. My comrades and I did regular spare-time services (*Subbot-niki*) such as collecting scrap-iron. We had meetings and social events; we were urged to set an example to other children at school, to help our mothers and to give up our seats in trams to older people.

All that I have described so far may seem the normal and necessary framework of any movement in any country which aims to appeal to young people. Certainly Soviet children and Soviet youth respond to the same things as their brothers and sisters in other countries. But the Pioneer and Komsomol organizations are instruments of the Soviet Government and express the special character of the Soviet system.

Looking back, I can see things in our training which I took as a matter of course at the time, but which would strike an observer from a Western democratic country as strange and significant. There was the constant emphasis on political education. Its theme was more or less as follows: 'Now you are Pioneers; at fifteen you will become Kom-somols, after that, members of the Communist Party. The Communist Party is the Party which led the fight against capitalism and which provides the leaders who are leading our country into new prosperity, especially Stalin, our father whom we must love very much.' We had these ideas impressed upon us constantly in talks, discussions, and in articles in the *Pioneers' Pravda*. Most children accepted what they were told without much thought or question; Russian children are certainly no more naturally 'political' than any other children; and there were always a good number of glazed eyes, yawns, and wandering thoughts during political education classes.

More effective were the lessons impressed on us in the stories told by our leaders. Fear and hatred of the class enemy were instilled into us as

Communist virtues. For example, there was the story of Pavlik Moro-
zov, the young Pioneer in a village who, during the collectivization
campaign, gave such help to the Party workers in persuading the
peasants to collectivize their property that vengeful villagers seized and
killed him. We were told that Kulaks were the ones who had done this
and that Pavlik's own father sided with them. Pavlik was publicized
across the length and breadth of the Soviet Union as a young martyr
who had given his life in the fight against Kulaks, reactionaries, exploiters and enemies of the Revolution. He was quoted as an example
to all Communist youth.

I heard this story, accepted it and repeated it without questioning its
implications. I had never seen at first hand what collectivization meant
to the village people who underwent this costly revolution imposed
upon them by the far-away Government in Moscow. My knowledge
of collectivization was a paper knowledge, based on books, articles and
the published statements of our leaders. Later on, when I was studying
hard as a candidate for membership of the Communist Party, I read an
article by Stalin, 'We are giddy with the success of collectivization.'
He criticized severely the mistakes made by over-conscientious Communists in enforcing collectivization, and not adhering to their instructions that it should be carried out voluntarily. The local administrators, he said, had frequently been over-zealous, and competitive in
their eagerness to gain credit for impressive results; in their reports they
had exaggerated the percentage of their villages which had been collectivized. It had been necessary to question the peasants again, and to
revise the quoted figures. All this, the article implied, was the result of
deviation from the wise restraint of the policy laid down by the Soviet
Government.

I accepted all this at its face value, never realizing that the unfortunate
officials who had to implement Stalin's policy of ruthless enforcement
were being made the scapegoats for the hatred and resistance which it
aroused among the stripped and starving peasants.

In those days I did not see that the real blame lay with the Government's inhuman policy. But I had no illusions about the contrast
between life in the city and life in the country. In our second or third
year in Moscow Mother decided to revisit her relatives in our old village of Lipky, and took me with her. I will never forget the shock
which the abject poverty of everything made upon me. It was strange
how much I had forgotten in the short time since I had lived in a village.
Our crowded quarters in Moscow seemed a paradise in comparison
with the dingy cottages, the thatched roofs with gaping holes in them,

the crumbling walls patched and propped up against total collapse. And the village people, in their threadbare clothes, their feet bound only with the *lapty* or bast-shoes made of strips of lime-tree bark—how poor, dull and wretched they seemed after the vitality of life in Moscow. Even the village children ran after us, laughing at our clothes and our speech, and jeered at us as 'Muscovites'. Mother took me to our old cottage, so small and dilapidated, and asked me if I would like to come back to live there.

I shrank back and said, 'I want to go back to Moscow.' Mother laughed and said, 'It's all right. We're going back.' I felt as though I was turning from death to life. The little girl with the village accent had become a passionate Muscovite.

Hatred and fear, which most Western countries try to minimize in the education of their young people, are preached as virtues to Communist youth. At Pioneer Camps we were told the ghastly story of *The Man Who Laughed*, about a boy who was captured by a circus troupe and was subjected to an operation to give him a permanent smile. He grew to be a man but still could not cease smiling, even at the most solemn moment. In the end his grotesque deformity alienated and lost him the woman he loved. The moral of this children's story was the wickedness of the mercenary masters who had exploited the boy.

Even our Pioneer scarf symbolized a warning and a threat. We were told that the short end represented the Pioneers, the long end the Komsomols, while the point at the back stood for the Communist Party of the Soviet Union. The knot represented the unbreakable unity of these three. 'But if the knot is wrongly tied and slips then enemies will do this!' As she spoke, the Leader drew the scarf tight in a throttling movement round my neck. She was deadly serious; there was menace, not humour, in her voice and eye.

An eleven-year-old Pioneer was not too young to be imbued with that fear of insidious enemies lurking everywhere which is the hallmark and characteristic obsession of life in the Soviet Union.

X

Four Friends

In the Pioneer and Komsomol organizations many friendships were formed, some short-lived but some lasting into later life. It was in these organizations, rather than at school, that I found my own closest friends and companions.

Several boys whom I met at Pioneer Camps became pressing in their attentions, but at that stage I shrank from any special boy friend relationship and always took one of my girl friends along with me, to the boys' annoyance.

In my Pioneer days, and for a long time afterwards, I was really quite heart-free as far as boys were concerned. My closest companions were my three girl friends, Maroosia, Nina and Sara. We were all members of the O.G.P.U. branch of the Pioneers, all became section leaders and went on to the Komsomol together. We were inseparable both at the summer camps, and at home in Moscow. Together we carried out our *subbotniki*, our allotted spare-time tasks; we went skating together after school, and used to meet regularly at one or other of our homes for schoolgirl chat and society.

Our favourite resort was Maroosia's home, because she had the rare privilege of a room of her own. The four of us would crowd in, shut the door on all strangers and intruders and in the cosy warmth of our own society, arrange our lives and futures very much to our own satisfaction. We even had a pact to read out any letters from boys which any of us had received, and to compose the answers jointly. It was a pity that the boys could not hear our candid comments, as we discussed what we really thought about them. I remember how we compared Yuri, with his handsome face and undersized physique, with another boy who was very well-built but had an ugly face; and we would exclaim, 'Why not Yuri's face on Ivan's body? Why is Nature so cruel?'

Maroosia's room gave us an exquisite sense of privacy which we relished to the full. There we could talk undisturbed about ourselves, what sort of husbands we would have, how many children we wanted, what we would do, what the future held for us. Often the others said to me, 'Doosia, you are the luckiest of us. You will have the happiest life.'

As I compare our subsequent lives, I remember their curious prophecy. Strangely different though our stories have been, they are also strangely alike. For each reflects in a different way some characteristic feature of the Soviet system and its drastic impact on the lives of the men and women who live under it.

In Maroosia's case, tragedy sprang from the fact that her father was a foreigner. There is irony in the situation when one considers the international claims of Communism. Maroosia was born in Russia and claimed to be a Russian, but her parents were Estonians by birth. Though she herself was a dark-eyed pretty brunette, her father was a typical Balt, fair, blue-eyed, tall, good-natured. He was a veteran Communist who had worked in the Finance and Administration section of the O.G.P.U. from the time of its institution (as the Cheka) under Lenin, and had given years of faithful service to his adopted country, the Soviet Union.

Maroosia took after her mother, an affectionate, warm-hearted woman who treated me like her own daughter. There were two sisters and a brother, and the family lived in a three-roomed flat which was a second home to me. Whenever I went there I felt at ease; a sense of peace and hospitality seemed to possess it. I particularly noticed how Maroosia's father seemed to adore his children and they him, and I felt very envious. My relationship with my own father was so different. He never punished or scolded me, but neither did he show me any particular affection. On the rare occasions when he kissed me good-bye, perhaps when I was going off to one of the Pioneer camps, I used to feel embarrassed because it was such an unusual thing for him to do. Whenever I went to Maroosia's house and saw how the children hung round their father and kissed him I felt an ache of loneliness and a longing for the same sort of family affection in our own home.

Maroosia was an intelligent girl. After qualifying at High School and the Foreign Language Technicum, she got a responsible job as telephonist and secretary at the Butirskaya Prison. There she met and married one of the prison officers, as she thought, for love. At first they lived happily together with her parents and had a son whom they called Yuri. But her husband turned out to be a wastrel and unfaithful, and they separated. However, one day in 1939, not long before the outbreak of war, he turned up again, confessed to Maroosia that their troubles were all his fault, and asked her to take him back. Largely for the sake of young Yuri, Maroosia eventually agreed. All her husband brought back with him was a black trench coat and his prison officer's uniform, which he was wearing; the rest he had lost or sold. So

Maroosia bought him a new outfit of clothes out of her own money, hoping that he would reform and that they might really make a new start together.

But with the outbreak of war a major disaster struck the family. When the Soviet armies, as a result of the Nazi-Soviet Pact, occupied the Baltic countries, there was a drastic precautionary purge of Balts in the Soviet Union. Maroosia's father was dismissed from his O.G.P.U. post simply because he was of Estonian origin. The veteran Communist was heartbroken at this blow; eager to prove his loyalty, he joined the Red Army and in 1941 was posted to the front line. Maroosia's husband, panic-stricken at his father-in-law's dismissal, left her again in the hope of safeguarding his own job. Nevertheless he too was dismissed. After a while, her father, whose nerves had gone to pieces under the shock, was released from the Army as a mental case and came home. I had a meal at their house soon after his return and was horrified to see the change in him and the bitterness of Maroosia's mother. Then I was posted abroad, and it was not until 1948, after my return from Sweden, that I saw Maroosia again. She looked an old woman. I could hardly believe it. Was this the Maroosia I had known as a charming, popular girl who loved skating and swimming, in whose room we friends had enjoyed so much gay and animated chatter? She and her mother were living in destitution, having sold all their belongings in the war years to buy food. Her father had died, her brother had been killed at the front, her husband had disappeared. Because of her father, Maroosia found herself debarred from any responsible job and had become a manual worker in a 'Kolchuk' rubber factory, trimming the edges of moulds. Her fingers were swollen from the hard, unhealthy work and from the constant struggle to fulfil the ever-increasing quotas which were demanded.

I gave her a dress, a woollen pullover and some shoes which I had brought from Sweden. It seemed little enough but she was pathetically grateful.

When I asked her if she was now a Party member, she said no, she had resigned even from the Komsomol. 'When a family gets into trouble with our rulers, Doosia, there's no hope for them. All I want is to die in peace.'

Maroosia had at least known what it was to have a happy home. Not so Nina, who lived near us and was a year younger than I. Her father was a dark-haired, handsome man but a harsh domestic tyrant. We children always had to talk in whispers when he was at home. I never heard loud conversation or laughter in their house. No wonder Nina

spent as little time as she could in her own home and always preferred
to be at Sara's or Maroosia's. Nina was tall like Maroosia, with brown
hair and eyes, an upturned nose and very thin lips. When I first got to
know her in the Pioneers she was very thin, and whenever the rest of
us went swimming she always excused herself and said she had something else to do. Later I found out that this was because poor Nina
suffered from eczema, brought on by nervous strain, which she was
anxious to hide from us.

At eighteen Nina developed into a pretty girl. She joined the O.G.P.U.
just after I did and was put on to surveillance duties as a member of a
group including both men and girls who shadowed persons whom the
O.G.P.U. was keeping under observation. She visited restaurants, began
to dress smartly and started smoking. Her team of shadowers had a
special secret house which they used as a base for operations and for
writing up their reports. They worked under code names, Nina's being
'Carmen'. It was difficult and arduous work. One winter Nina was
following an elusive quarry who made a habit of changing from one
moving tram to another. While trying to follow Nina slipped on the
icy street and knocked out three front teeth.

Nina's undoing was a craving that is general though disguised within
the jealously-guarded frontiers of the Soviet Union: the dream of her
life was to go abroad and see the world.

While working in the O.G.P.U. she met a young man called Nikolai
who fell in love with her. She liked him and enjoyed his company, but
at first would not consider marriage. His father was then living in
Rumania as a Soviet trade representative, with his wife, Nikolai's stepmother, and Nikolai sported foreign-made clothes which caused quite
a stir in the Moscow streets and made him very conspicuous. When all
his efforts to capture Nina's heart had failed, he devised a stratagem. He
told her that he had written to his parents in Rumania with the news
that he had met a wonderful girl whom he loved and adored who was
dying to travel abroad, and who would greatly appreciate an invitation
from them to do so.

After she heard this Nina softened noticeably towards Nikolai and
began to spend a good deal more time in his company.

Presently he produced a letter apparently from his parents, congratu-
lating him on his good luck and hoping for a visit from Nikolai and
Nina in the near future. Meanwhile they asked Nikolai to go to the
trunk in which his stepmother stored the things she had brought back
from Rumania on the last furlough and select some suitable gift for his
beloved. Nikolai read the letter out to Nina, then took her to the flat,

opened his stepmother's trunk and invited her to choose for herself what she would like best. She chose a grey woollen tailor-made suit, and a woollen pullover in electric blue.

After that their romance progressed with remarkable speed. Before long they were married and in due course had a daughter, whom they called Ella. The dream was shattered when Nikolai's father died in Rumania and his stepmother returned to Moscow to occupy a room in their flat. Almost at once she noticed that Nina was wearing a suit and pullover remarkably like the ones she had bought in Rumania. She looked in her trunk; there was no mistake about it, they were hers. She was furious. 'Nina Ivanovna, what are you doing in my suit and pullover? How dare you wear them without my permission! I demand them back immediately!'

'*Your* suit and pullover? Nonsense, these are my own now. Nikolai gave them to me as a present!'

It took some time to sort the matter out, but when poor Nina eventually discovered the truth and realized how Nikolai had tricked her, her resentment and bitterness knew no bounds. Relations between them got worse and worse and finally they separated. Two years later Nikolai married again. For a long time he had no children by his second marriage and he asked Nina to return to him, saying that he would divorce his second wife, as was permissible under Soviet law if both parties were agreeable. But at this time Nina would have nothing further to do with him.

After this Nina had various men friends but did not find any permanent partner, and she went steadily downhill. When I got back from Sweden in 1947 I found her working in the 'K.I.', the Committee of Information, where I also worked, though in a different department. Soon afterwards her ex-husband Nikolai returned from an appointment abroad and also came to work in the K.I. From then on Nina pursued him desperately by all the means in her power, begging him to return to her again. But by this time he had settled down. He already had a child by his second wife and all Nina's pathetic efforts were unavailing. I felt very sorry for her. Such a series of disasters seemed to have sprung from her understandable passion to travel abroad.

Sara's story reveals most clearly of all the cynical injustice of the Soviet system.

Sara was the youngest and gayest of us. Two years my junior, she was a Jewess, five feet tall, with a nice figure, curly auburn hair, large wide eyes and a typically Jewish face, with a slightly curved nose that might be compared to Susan Hayward's. She was a happy, vivacious person, who loved singing, music, ballet and the theatre. As both her parents had jobs in the N.K.V.D. they were comfortably off and constantly entertained on a generous and hospitable scale.

We all envied Sara when she sat down at her own piano and played pieces or accompanied herself as she sang. Sara married, but her husband was killed at the front during the war, leaving her with a little daughter. Being a qualified engineer, she got a confidential job in the Wireless Communications Section of the M.G.B.

Suddenly she was dismissed.

The blow fell soon after she had attended a party at a friend's house, at which most of the guests were Jewish. There were songs, musical items, dancing and games with plenty of drinking, laughter and funny stories.

Two days later Sara was summoned to the M.G.B. Personnel Section. The official who interviewed her was quiet, polite and serious. He asked her to describe the party which she had attended on the night in question. She did so as well as she could.

He studied her carefully and asked, 'Comrade, can you not recall anything particular that occurred?'

Sara racked her brains. What was he getting at?

'Not to my knowledge,' she answered. 'Nobody was drunk.'

'Were not some anecdotes told?'

'Oh yes, several, but none that seemed to me of any significance. I didn't hear them all. Some were told when I was in another room, out of earshot.'

'You admit then that anecdotes were told? Why didn't you report about them here the next day?'

'Because any stories I heard were purely humorous and of no importance. Some were told by Jews against themselves.'

'The anecdote I am concerned with was anti-Soviet in tone. As an M.G.B. worker it was your duty to be the first to report it here, not to wait until it was reported by someone else.'

'Certainly that would have been my duty had I heard it, but how could I report an anecdote without knowing what it was?'

'Comrade, it is known to us that at the social gathering which you attended a certain young man related an anecdote which ridiculed a Soviet official. I much regret that this occurrence was not reported by you. That is all, you may leave.'

Two or three weeks passed. Then Sara was again summoned to the Personnel Section. She was told that she had been dismissed from the M.G.B. as it had been found that the background of her late husband's father revealed certain undesirable features which made it impossible to retain her in such a confidential post. Sara flared up.

'Even if my husband's father did not have an unblemished record, that does not alter the fact that my husband gave his life at the front, fighting the enemies of the Soviet Union! Surely that wipes out any black mark! Why should I be held responsible for my husband's father?'

'I cannot comment any further on your case, Comrade. I am acting on instructions. The subject is closed.'

On the way back to her office Sara's anger ebbed away into a sense of hopelessness and despair. Thinking carefully back over the whole sequence of events she came to the conclusion that the business of her husband's background was no more than a pretext and that the real reason for her dismissal was her failure to report the offending anecdote. It had evidently been heard and reported by someone at the party, possibly an outsider, possibly by an agent belonging to some other Intelligence organ. A matter of departmental pride had evidently been involved. There was no appeal and no redress. There was nothing whatever she could do about it.

After her dismissal from the M.G.B. Sara was for a long time out of work. She applied for many jobs but met a blank wall everywhere. At last she succeeded in getting an inferior post as an engineer in a small factory which did no confidential work. All avenues of advancement had been closed for ever to her because she had been dismissed from the M.G.B. for a reported omission of which she was entirely guiltless.

Sara's story was by no means exceptional. Similar catastrophes were only too common. Accordingly, whenever friends came to a party at my flat, however gay they became, I never allowed the telling of anecdotes. I knew too much about the deadly consequences which could follow. Witty anecdotes can be too costly a luxury in the Soviet Union.

So much for three of the four friends of Pioneer and Komsomol days who were so inseparable and planned their futures together with such schoolgirl enthusiasm.

Against that background their prophecy that I would be the luckiest was perhaps not so wrong after all.

XI

Joining the O.G.P.U.

EARLY in 1933, when I was nineteen, I joined the O.G.P.U. I took this step, which proved so decisive for my whole future life, because at the time it seemed the most normal and obvious thing in the world to do. The name of the O.G.P.U. (later called N.K.V.D., M.G.B., M.V.D. and now K.G.B.) became notorious as the instrument of political terror, especially at the time of the purges. 'O.G.P.U. men' suggests a uniform type of ruthless thugs with all the power of the Soviet State behind them. That picture is true enough, as our story shows, but it is not the whole truth. The O.G.P.U. organization is much more than just a 'Secret Police' force. It is the body set up by Lenin and the old leaders of the Bolshevik Revolution to protect the Revolution from its political enemies. Its enormously wide functions include a relentless watch within the Soviet Union for the first signs of anti-Soviet views, and a continuous programme of political espionage abroad against the capitalist enemies of the socialist homeland. No one can begin to understand how people think and behave in the Soviet Union until he grasps this perpetual obsession with lurking enemies, internal and external alike.

Against this background of insidious danger, the O.G.P.U. is presented to the Soviet people as the stern defender of the Soviet state, the shrewd relentless enemy of the enemies of the Revolution. That is the official version.

And that was how I grew up to regard the O.G.P.U. when I did not simply take it for granted. The imposing O.G.P.U. building was not far from where we lived. One of my earliest impressions in Moscow had been the happy children of the O.G.P.U. branch of the Pioneers, where I made friends and found all sorts of interests. Both my parents were connected with the lower levels of the O.G.P.U. edifice, for Father had a job for a time as a driver in its transport section and Mother worked intermittently in O.G.P.U. canteens when Ivan was not at home needing her attention. The parents of my friends Sara and Maroosia were O.G.P.U. workers, and though they never talked about their work, they impressed me as educated, intelligent people, whom I admired and looked up to. There was every official encouragement of this attitude.

In 1926, when I was twelve, and our Pioneer group was in camp at
Aprelevka, on the outskirts of Moscow, I enjoyed a tremendous privi-
lege. Felix Dzerjinsky, the Polish aristocrat and old Bolshevik whom
Lenin had appointed as first head of the Cheka, before it became the
O.G.P.U., had just died. His body was lying in state in the Hall of
Columns in the House of the Soviet Union in Moscow, and our group
was ordered to send its best Pioneers to take part in the Guard of
Honour. I was the youngest and smallest Pioneer chosen for this great
honour. I wore my green uniform, with its jacket and pleated skirt
and special Pioneer buttons and pocket. We marched in and stood at
attention facing the coffin where the body of this hero of the Socialist
Revolution lay on the bier. We were only there five minutes, but I was
so stirred and moved by the ceremony that when we got back to camp
I was in tears and was so overwrought that I had to be taken home.

Kulaks, reactionaries, spies, saboteurs, enemies of the people—we
were constantly reminded of these dangers to our homeland and the
great socialist experiment. Our class at school made regular visits to an
aircraft factory, when we were shown the whole process and were
allowed to take notes. I remember asking, 'Why are we allowed to
visit a place which is obviously secret?' I wonder how many school-
girls in Western countries would have bothered to ask such a question?

Then I used to hear Sara's and Maroosia's parents warning them to
be very careful about their friends and especially about their boy
friends. I remember that Sara once got friendly with an American boy.
She was studying languages and wanted to practise English. But her
parents warned her severely of the dangers. At the time of the 1937
purge the American boy was arrested and I think deported. Apparently
Sara's friendship with him was never discovered. She was lucky.

As for myself, I never knew or spoke to any foreigners in my own
country. The perils of any such association were well known. My first
contact with foreigners was when Volodya and I were posted to the
Soviet Embassy in Sweden. The O.G.P.U. enjoyed the prestige of the
bulwark of the state and the scourge of these lurking enemies. Besides,
there were practical and material considerations.

In 1930 when I was a Komsomol in charge of very small children, or
'Octobrists', I often took groups of them to the splendid Dynamo
Stadium which belonged to the O.G.P.U. and belongs to the State
Security Service today. There was a magnificent arena, outdoor and in-
door tennis courts under a great glass roof, and skating rinks, all of
which were only accessible by special pass supplied to O.G.P.U. workers.
Sometimes, too, my friends and I were invited to film evenings in the

theatre of the palatial o.g.p.u. Club. Everything to do with the o.g.p.u. made clear that its workers were a favoured *élite*, whose importance to the Soviet state was recognized by substantial rewards and material privileges.

Accordingly when David Kunin suggested that I might like to join the o.g.p.u. where he worked himself, I was very attracted to the idea. I had known David as a Pioneer leader and he was an admirer of mine at the time.

I hesitated as I was busy studying English at the Foreign Language Technicum, but when David assured me that I could carry on with my language studies while working in the o.g.p.u., and that in fact it would be an advantage, my mind was made up. My parents accepted this step as they had accepted my joining the Pioneers. I was now a Komsomol; I belonged to the new era. They would not stand in the way of my success in the new Russia.

David got me the necessary sheaf of forms. I had to supply complete personal particulars about myself, my parents and all the members of my family. These details included my educational record, Komsomol or Party record, activities before the Revolution (the first three years of my life) whether I was a member of the Party before the Revolution, whether I was ever in any of the Opposition parties, whether I had ever served in the Red Army or the White Army, had ever appeared in court, or been punished or reprimanded by the Komsomol or the Party, and whether I had any relations living abroad. I had to answer all the same questions in regard to all members of my family. Everything had to be done in triplicate with photos. Finally, I had to get guarantors who must be Party members and o.g.p.u. members who had known me personally for at least a year.

I remember one of my guarantors, an o.g.p.u. worker who lived in the same flat as our family. He was a fine man, a Jew, who had served on assignments abroad, and possessed such wonders as foreign furniture and foreign clothes. Probably because of his foreign service, he was arrested in one of the purges in 1937 or 1938.

After a few weeks David told me that I had been accepted and could start work next day. We arranged a rendezvous and he escorted me to a building which had formerly belonged to the Ministry of Foreign Affairs, on the corner of Lubianka Street and Kuznetsky Bridge Street. We climbed up to the top floor, which was entirely occupied by the section where I was to work. On the lower floors were flats. I showed the pass which David had given me, and was admitted. I found myself in a room surrounded by elderly people, mostly men, and felt very conscious of my youthfulness. Later I discovered that these elderly gentlemen were mostly former Russian aristocrats, including numbers of Counts and Barons, who were employed because of their knowledge of foreign languages. At that time the Soviet was short of trained linguists and had not yet been able to dispense with the services of all politically questionable persons who had high professional qualifications.

I was shepherded through these veterans and shown into a private office. A senior officer in military uniform, Colonel Kharkevich, greeted me and invited me to sit down.

'Comrade, you are a newcomer to our work and you may find it rather strange at first. I would like to explain it to you briefly.'

I sat mute and attentive. He was an impressive man. 'You have been appointed to the Special Cypher Department of the o.g.p.u. However, for the time being you will work in the Military Intelligence Section here, of which I am the Head. The people whom you see here and with whom you will work are engaged in decyphering the codes used in communications between foreign countries and their embassies here in Moscow. You will realize how important this work is. Our socialist homeland is isolated and is surrounded by capitalist countries who, by their very nature, must be continually plotting to destroy the achievements of the Socialist Revolution which spells their doom. It is vital for us to know their intentions.'

I made no comment, nor was any required.

'Now, a word of warning. I am aware that your home is not far away, therefore you doubtless know that in this building, in addition to our office, there are ordinary tenants, and a Ministry of Foreign Affairs Club. These outside persons provide good cover for our workers, who can mingle with them as they enter and leave the building and pass unnoticed. You must sign a strict undertaking not to disclose to your parents, friends, or anyone at all where you work. If we find that you have revealed the whereabouts of this office, I must warn you that the consequences to yourself will be very serious indeed. Restaurants also are out of bounds to our workers. They are dangerous places. That is all. You have been allotted to the Japanese Section. The Head of the Section will explain your work to you.'

I left, tingling with nervous importance. Colonel Kharkevich's solemn admonitions had impressed me greatly. He seemed a solid, immovable rock of official gravity and responsibility. Yet he, too, was swept away in the holocaust of the 1938 purge.

In the Japanese Section I was introduced to a number of people

whom I got to know as friends and colleagues in the following months
and years. They were an odd and interesting lot.

Vera Plotnikova was seven or eight years older than myself, plain,
broad in the beam, good-hearted, kind and friendly to me from the
start. I was always 'Doosia' to her and indeed to all of them. She was
married to a colonel in the Red Army and had three children. I often
visited them at their spacious flat, which the Army provided, and I
found that she had spent a lot of time in Japan with her father, a well-
known Professor of Japanese who had compiled a Japanese-Russian
dictionary. However, in 1937 her husband was arrested. (She heard
later that he had been shot for 'anti-Soviet activities'.) Vera was immediately dismissed from her job. She and her children had to move
into one room. She was quite unable to get a job commensurate with
her qualifications. To feed her children she managed to get work as a
typist. Vera died of tuberculosis during the war.

Galina Podpalova was tall, thin and stooping. Her nose, dark eyes
and languid manner were very much in the style of Greta Garbo. She
had been married young but had separated from her husband and had
no children. She lived alone most of her life. During the war she
married one of the workers in our Section, but he died within a year
or two. It seemed that fate intended Galina Podpalova to be a
solitary.

She was the daughter of well-to-do parents in old Russia and had
lived a long time in Japan to complete her study of the language.
Galina liked things Japanese so much that she even affected a Japanese
style of greeting people and, instead of a handbag, she carried her things
wrapped in a square, Japanese fashion. At home she always wore
kimonos and her two-roomed flat was furnished entirely in the Japanese
style with vases, fans, silk scrolls with Japanese inscriptions, Japanese
screens, low tables, much lacquer work and ivory dragons and orna-
ments. At home or in the office she was always spick and span and
usually wore clothes which she had bought in Japan. I often visited her
at her flat, and found her style of life original and fascinating.

Among my new colleagues was Ivan Kalinin, who was sent to Spain
to help the Spanish Republican Army and came back a nervous wreck,
and Kim, a handsome and brilliant young officer in one of the operational departments of the o.g.p.u. He was of Korean origin and visited
our Japanese Section as a consultant from time to time. Finally, there
was old, distinguished, vigorous Professor Shungsky, our supreme
authority on the Japanese language. He had seen military service under
the Czars and he was an expert on Japanese military terminology.

I was very much the learner and student for my first four years but at last I could read, write and translate to Shungsky's satisfaction. At our final test, after I had translated a sentence to his liking, he kissed me and gave me full marks.

About the middle of 1934 I was transferred from the Military Intelligence Section to the O.G.P.U. Section in the Special Department under a certain Gusev. (In the 1937 purge he was arrested and shot.) At the same time I became a permanent O.G.P.U. worker with the rank of Sergeant of State Security. It was about this time, too, that the whole O.G.P.U. was reorganized and became the N.K.V.D.

I enjoyed my work very much and liked my immediate colleagues and companions. My initial salary of 133 roubles a month was not princely, but I could live on it quite reasonably, and that in itself was a privilege to be cherished and clung to. I lived at home and was even able to get home for lunch; my contribution to the family budget was a help to them all. I did not tell even Mother where I was working or what I was doing. It was official and confidential; that was enough for her.

When, in 1935, our Department moved into new quarters in an N.K.V.D. building in Dzerjinsky Square, it was still very convenient to my home. Altogether I counted myself extremely lucky to have such a job.

This is not the place to follow the history of the great purges and the Moscow trials, but the atmosphere of menace and apprehension intensified as the reign of terror gripped official Moscow. There was an eerie contrast between our ordinary friendly human relations as we worked together in the office or visited one another's homes and the things that were always happening to people one knew or knew about.

The Chief of the whole Special Department, Gleb Boki, an old Bolshevik and friend of Lenin, was one of those arrested and shot in the 1937 purge. He was always a sinister and mysterious figure to his subordinates. The door of his office was always shut and he had a peephole in it with one-way glass, so that he could examine every visitor personally before admitting them. After his arrest it was found that he had a bath and bedroom attached to his office and a hoard of gold and silver coins was discovered.

I never spoke to Boki except for the times on night duty which I will describe. He was fairly tall and had a stoop. He never wore a hat but at all seasons of the year he always wore a raincoat. He had cold, piercing, blue eyes, which gave people the feeling that he hated the sight of them.

While I worked in the Special Department I heard various whispers about how Boki behaved on his vacations near Batumi, in the Mahindjaury district. Quite by accident I stumbled on some independent evidence which confirmed the truth of these stories. I went with another girl who worked in our Special Department to spend my annual holiday at a place called 'Green Cape' in that same district. We had managed to get tickets entitling us to free accommodation at a sanatorium there, even though it was not one of those under N.K.V.D. control. It was the month of May when we arrived. The magnolia trees were in full bloom, there were flowers everywhere and there was glorious sunshine to bask in. The crisp golden weather was still too cold for swimming, but we went for walks along the pebbly beach and on one of these walks we got into conversation with a youth who mentioned that a certain Boki from Moscow used to take their house for holidays each year. Without disclosing that we had any knowledge of Boki, we drew the youth out as to what went on. In peasant fashion he was extraordinarily frank. He told us that Boki used to come every year with a mixed party of carefully selected men and women friends. Certain trusted local officers, including some members of the local N.K.V.D., used also to be invited to the orgies that took place nightly. The best wines were brought from Batum and flowed freely. In due course the participants would strip off their clothes and indulge in drunken naked dances. At intervals they would go to the steam bath which was kept in readiness, or go swimming, after which they would return to their orgies and debauches. My friend and I were frightened and surprised by this confirmation of what we had heard said, but of course we gave no sign to the boy that we had any more than a passing interest in what he told us.

Back in Moscow I confided this story to a man in the Department whom I believed I could trust. His reaction was alarming.

'Doosia, Boki is already aware that you know about his behaviour. If you so much as open your mouth about this to anyone, he will make life unbearable for you. You are playing with fire. I must warn you that he may invite you to join his vacation party in order to implicate you in his debauches and blackmail you into keeping your mouth shut. So be on your guard.'

After this I lived in terror and did not breathe a word about the matter to my closest friends.

The times that I feared most were the nights when I was alone in the office on duty for the whole Department. Boki used to emerge from his sanctum, walk round and come up to me asking if there were any urgent matters requiring his attention. His piercing eyes seemed to look right through me and I would sit at my desk trembling and imagining that he was trying to make up his mind whether to invite me to his vacation house. For my nights on duty I always chose my plainest and dullest clothes for fear of attracting his unwelcome attentions.

Whether because of this, or for some entirely different reason, he never did invite me, for which I was devoutly thankful. Under a system where dismissals and penalties fall silently, unpredictably and without warning, it is a serious matter to make an enemy of anyone in a position to do you harm.

In 1934, the year after I joined the o.g.p.u., the great Kirov was murdered. Then the arrests and trials of the old Bolsheviks began, starting with the legendary figures of Zinoviev and Kamenev. Suddenly the Soviet public learned, through the pages of *Pravda* and *Izvestia*, that yesterday's heroes of the Socialist Revolution stood unveiled as traitors, enemies of the Revolution and agents of foreign powers bent on restoring capitalism in the Soviet Union. What did ordinary citizens think? It is impossible to know with any certainty. What did we say? What the newspapers told us. Or better still, nothing at all. How could we arrive at any worthwhile opinions? For the younger generation like myself, there was no alternative voice, no background of experience, against which we could test the truth of what we read every day. These matters of high politics were far above my head. I think I accepted most of what I read in the papers. I swallowed the story that these men, who had given their lives for the Socialist Revolution, had betrayed their life's work overnight. I accepted the proposition that agents of foreign powers lurked in every house and by-way, awaiting the opportunity to carry out espionage, sabotage and assassination. That was the reason, we were told, for the all-pervading vigilance of our o.g.p.u. system among the Russian people themselves. It was our vital function to be the protectors and guardians of our unique socialist experiment in its Soviet homeland.

Between my confidential job in the Special Department, the friends I made there, and my home, I led a restricted and circumscribed life. I had surprisingly few contacts with the Soviet people outside my immediate circle.

Once, however, I was called upon to do a job for the n.k.v.d. 'in the field'. It was an experience I have never forgotten and strangely unlike anything I had expected.

The occasion was the great parade which takes place each year on the first of May in the Red Square. The year was 1936. In all my life in

Moscow I never saw one of these parades except on the newsreels. All the spectators at them had special passes, the best positions being reserved for diplomats and foreign visitors and for important Soviet officials. Each parade took place under the most elaborate precautions and only after it was over and all the great ones had left the scene, were the crowds allowed to demonstrate in the Red Square, where Stalin, from a safe and remote eminence, would acknowledge their plaudits.

Security precautions on these occasions were the responsibility of the N.K.V.D. Every window looking on to the Red Square, in houses and office buildings alike, was manned and guarded. None of the occupants was allowed to go to a window or even look out; no precaution must be neglected which might lessen the possibility of an attempt to throw a bomb or commit some other terrorist act. Soviet leaders do not find it wise to rely solely upon the love and devotion of their people. For some reason I and others from my Section were chosen on the day in question to keep guard over a tenement house occupied by a number of families just behind St Basil's Cathedral, that striking mosque-like building familiar to Western eyes in photographs of the Red Square, which is now preserved as an historical relic. The tenement house was appalling—wet, dilapidated, smelly. When I got inside I thought at first that it must be a stable. However, it was doubtless the kind of place that a ruthless terrorist might well select as a base for operations. With a mixture of apprehension and vague resolution I climbed the stairs accompanied by our Section leader who knocked on the door of the room to which I had been posted. The whole building stank of dirt and decay.

A small, dark woman opened the door.

He told the woman our business and left the rest to me.

'Oh do come in,' she said. 'This is my husband.'

I went in and was surprised to find that their small room was remarkably clean and cared for and was tastefully furnished. Everything about them indicated that they were a decent, self-respecting couple.

'So you are here to watch us,' she went on. 'Well, I'm delighted that they've sent a nice girl this time, instead of one of those coarse, stupid men to lounge about the place. Every parade it's the same. Whatever they think poor folk like us are going to do, I don't know.'

She gave me a chair, and, following my orders, I placed it where I could make sure that they did not look out of the window during the parade.

I sat there from nine in the morning until late in the afternoon, when

I was notified that the parade and demonstration were over and I could go home.

The woman poured out her woes to me. They were Greeks by birth and were longing to return to their homeland. They had applied for permission to do so, but had always been refused. She hated the house, which was neglected, unhealthy and overcrowded. Six families lived in a few rooms on that floor. There was no bathroom, only one basin and a tap between them all. The other tenants made no attempt to keep the place clean, and as there was no kitchen, each family had to have its kitchen table and primus stove for cooking out in the passage. My sympathy went out to them. They were obviously so much more conscientious and deserving than their neighbours.

'Why do you think your application to leave was refused?' I asked. 'How do I know?' she answered. 'A brother of mine was once arrested here in the Soviet, I don't know what for. Perhaps for that reason we will never be allowed to go home.'

They were very friendly and made no attempt even to look out of the window. I felt strangely disturbed and found myself wondering what harm could this poor woman possibly do?

This was my first experience of defending the socialist state from its enemies among the Soviet people. It was a small enough incident in itself, but it made a lasting impression on my mind.

Before very long I was to have drastic personal experience of what it feels like to fight for one's life against the imputation of potential anti-Soviet sympathies.

XII

First Love

ROMAN KRIVOSH sidled into my life quietly and unobtrusively. He worked in the Anglo-American Section of the Special Department, and I met him, along with a crowd of other new acquaintances, soon after I joined the o.g.p.u. I can't even remember the exact time and place. It may have been round the office, or in the Department's canteen where we all had meals. He was of Serbian origin and was tall and broad-shouldered, with a wide brow and dark, pleasantly curling hair. His brown eyes were small, but twinkled with humour and intelligence; he had a good nose, but somewhat flattened at the end, like a duck's bill. He affected an engaging quizzical kind of conceit and later, when I knew him better, he would often gaze at himself in a mirror, wag his head wisely and say, 'Romulka, my boy, why ever is it that all the women run after you?'

He was always reserved and reticent about his family background but I had plenty of opportunity to learn about it later on during the investigations. His father, Vladimir, I then discovered, had been an important official in the Okhrana, the Czarist political police organization, and had also worked in the Special Department of the o.g.p.u. after the Revolution, since his knowledge of languages made him so useful to the Soviet government that his service under the Czar was for the time being ignored. During succeeding purges Roman's father was alternately arrested and released, and was in and out of custody at the Butirskaya Prison in Moscow, where he continued with his work, or at Solovky, the penal colony near the Arctic Circle. An elder brother of Roman's had fled to China either during or after the Revolution. This family background had a direct and drastic influence on my own life.

Roman Krivosh moved in literary and theatrical circles. He had written novels and poetry, some of which was published in periodicals in the early post-Revolutionary era and he was married when I first knew him to a variety artist named Tamara. I heard these details in casual gossip round the office and I certainly took no special interest in him in the early stages of our acquaintanceship.

However, in 1935, after our Department moved to its new quarters in the Dzerjinsky Square, Krivosh began to court me in earnest. He was divorced from Tamara by this time and he soon made it plain that I was the chosen object of his attentions. He was easy-going, humorous, likeable and had quite a way with him, but he was eleven years older than I and at the time I did not feel in any hurry to make up my mind on the subject of getting married. Of course, I had had numbers of boy friends from Pioneer days onwards, including David Kunin who had suggested my joining the O.G.P.U. I would go skating with them or on expeditions to the country on Sundays, or to film shows, but I enjoyed life very well on those terms and always steered our relationship into safer waters if any of my boy friends seemed to be getting too serious.

With Roman Krivosh I pursued the same tactics, but he persevered. He never missed an opportunity of coming and talking to me if he saw me in the street or passed me in the office or met me anywhere. Standing in the queue for lunch I would feel someone tickling the back of my neck and would hear him say, 'What pretty hair you have, Doosia.' Once in the canteen, I remember, I bought some chocolates of the popular 'Mishka' brand, so called after the famous picture by Shishkin of a bear and her two cubs in the forest. They were my favourite sweets. Roman noticed this; he was a most attentive observer. Whenever he saw me in the canteen he would place one or two of these chocolates on my plate and retire in silence. Likewise when I left my office desk I frequently found a similar offering sitting on top of my papers when I got back. My woman's heart found it hard to be impervious to these small, silent tokens of esteem but I felt embarrassed at the openness of his attentions and wondered what my colleagues would think. There was certainly no secret in the office about the way Krivosh was courting me.

Comments varied. Some of my colleagues wagged their fingers in warning and said, 'Doosenka, just you be careful; Krivosh is a dangerous man.' But others protested against these reproving wiseacres. 'Why should she be careful? What's the danger? After all, he's divorced and Doosia's young and single. Don't be so stupid and interfering!' I tried to cover up my shyness and embarrassment at this public discussion of my affairs but I could see that many people admired Roman's pertinacity and skill in courting me.

One holiday our whole Department went for a picnic in the country outside Moscow. At the railway station I bought a copy of a children's paper called *Murzilka* for the children of some friends of mine. While I was looking at it Roman came up and asked me what I was reading.

'It's *Murzilka*,' I answered.

'May I see it, please?'

'Certainly.'

He took it, tucked it under his arm and walked off.

I ran after him along the platform calling in protest, 'Wait! I didn't say you could have my *Murzilka* to keep, give it back, it belongs to me!'

'From now on,' he answered, '*Murzilka* belongs to me.'

From that moment he always called me his '*Murzilka*'.

But in spite of his persistent attentions, his presents, and his playful devotion I was not going to be hustled. I doubted whether he was really serious.

I had been once or twice to his flat while he was still married to Tamara and he invited me there frequently after his divorce. He was an excellent cook and made some delicious meals. But I would not go alone and always took someone with me, usually Nina and her husband Nikolai, before they separated.

Then suddenly, I can't say just how or why, all my careful defences collapsed. I fell deeply and overwhelmingly in love with him. From 1936 we lived as man and wife. We did not register the marriage. Later, the Soviet law on the matter was altered and it became necessary to register marriages before one could apply for alimony if there was a separation. But at that time in the Soviet Union the registration of marriages was quite optional and the authorities had not yet embarked on their policy of stricter marriage laws. In any case, calculations and considerations about alimony were then far from my mind.

Looking back upon the months that followed my going to live with Roman, I have a sense of something fragile and dreamlike and I wonder whether the shadow of later events has touched my memory of them with a poignancy that I did not feel at the time. I know that my heart was full with joy and gratitude at my blessings. I was young and healthy. I had an interesting and privileged job; I had my family and my friends. I had a home with the husband I adored. It was no wonder that when my girl friends came to visit me and spend an evening with us they would say enviously:

'Doosia, you *are* fortunate to have such a lovely home and such a charming husband.'

I would smile and kiss them good-bye and think myself the luckiest girl in the world.

My life with Roman opened up for me a new and exciting world in which I found continual delight. Though lively and sociable, he was also a bookish man, widely read, and able to speak a number of languages. He often spoke French with other tenants in nearby apartments who were also N.K.V.D. workers, and he talked with easy familiarity of the fascinating countries beyond the guarded borders of our own Russia. Our apartment consisted of one very large, pleasant room, full of things which had intrigued me even before I came to live among them. Every detail stands out clearly in my mind. On the floor was a valuable hand-made Persian carpet with a delicate floral pattern in blue-green and gold on a crimson background. This carpet had a history. It was a family heirloom. Long years before, the Krivosh family had had a dog which had died of bubonic plague lying on the carpet. Fearing infection, they had cut off the strip where the dog had died but the remainder was large enough to cover most of the floor in our spacious apartment. Facing the door, and screening off the rest of the room, was a huge high bookcase, and there were more bookshelves along the near wall. Our divan bed occupied one corner, and Roman's writing desk, piled with papers and his typewriter, stood in another corner. There was a large window with curtains and a dining-table and chairs in the Rococo style and a big leather armchair. In the corner, diagonally opposite the door, stood a large bronze Apollo Belvedere which I particularly liked.

Roman worked a lot at his writing and sometimes discussed the plots of stories he was working on with me. Often my friends or his would come to spend the evening with us and at other times people from neighbouring flats would drop in. One woman neighbour, Valentina Sergeevna, was a particular busybody. Young and bounding with energy herself, she was married to an elderly and ailing husband who always went to bed at eight o'clock. Roman told me that in earlier days when they used to have rowdy parties with some of Tamara's theatrical friends, this Valentina used to be consumed with curiosity and desire to be in things. She would knock on the wall as if to say, 'You are making too much noise,' whereupon Roman would rush out and say, 'Do come in and join the fun, I know that's what you really want.' Whenever we had visitors Roman would say, 'Valentina will be here in a minute.' Sure enough, in a matter of minutes she would come bursting in saying, 'Here's your kettle, it was boiling.'

'That's strange,' we would say, 'we didn't put a kettle on.'

'No,' she would say, not a whit put out, 'I put it on for you, I thought you would be wanting one.'

She was perfectly happy, having achieved her object of getting inside the door. Once or twice, when we had had too many of her uninvited visits, Roman played a trick on her. He waited behind the door until he heard her step, then he rushed out in a tremendous hurry, colliding with her and slamming the door violently in her face. He would then apologize profusely. She was thick-skinned and required firm treatment. But she proved a friend indeed to me later, when I desperately needed a friend. Her help then far outweighed her occasional intrusions on our privacy.

On many evenings at home after the day's work, Roman and I would be just ourselves.

★   ★   ★

On the 4th June 1937 our daughter was born. We called her Irina, after my mother's mother.

The hospital was so overcrowded that at first I was put in a corridor; then they put a fifth bed in a four-bed ward and marked it 'Additional'. When Irina was brought to me I noticed that the label on her wrist was 'Additional', and from then on, whenever the nurses brought the babies in on their arms they always asked, 'Who is the mother of "Additional"?' At her first feed she took the breast straight away and took so much that she choked. I looked down at her wrinkled-up face coughing and choking and thought she had stopped breathing. 'Quick,' I screamed, 'my baby is dying! She's choking!' Doctors and nurses came rushing in and quickly unwrapped her—babies are always firmly wrapped in Russia—then my fears subsided as I saw that she was alive and was already getting over her choking fit.

There was a strange moment when Mother came to visit me and spoke to me through a nearby window which looked out on to the hospital yard. She herself was expecting a baby any day and when the other women in the ward asked me who my visitor had been I felt too shy and embarrassed to tell them that my mother was pregnant, so I said that it was my sister. Nine days later Mother went to hospital and my young sister Tamara was born.

When we were both out of hospital, during the forty-five days' statutory leave granted to mothers in the Soviet Union after the birth of a child, Mother and I used to meet and take our babies for walks together in the nearest park.

How wonderful it was to come home with my baby! Irina was healthy, fat and cuddly. She was the joy of my heart. Roman, too, was delighted, and was tremendously proud of his daughter.

When Irina was a month old the thing happened. Arrests are common enough at any time in the Soviet Union, and those were years of mounting suspicion and terror. Already I have mentioned many of my chiefs and acquaintances who were purged at one time or another during these years, and families who were ruined by the arrest of one of their members. People were continually disappearing; sometimes there would be a paragraph in *Pravda* announcing their arrest and the charge against them; usually there would be nothing at all. The effect of this nightmare uncertainty on ordinary people was to silence all comment, especially all discussion on the fate of others, and to make everyone cling desperately to the irrational human hope—'Whoever else may be affected, perhaps nothing will happen to *me*.'

But now it was to me that it happened.

It was at two o'clock on a morning in July. We were in bed, but were not asleep. Irina had been fretful and I had been up attending to her. There was a knock on the door. Roman got up mumbling drowsily, 'Confound it, it's probably our neighbour Irishka—no doubt she's had another quarrel with her husband and wants us to put her up for the night!'

At the door, he called, 'Who is it?'

The voice of our yardman answered, 'It's the *dvornik* here.'

'What's the trouble? It's late and we're in bed.'

'Yes, I know, but I want a word with you. Please let me in.'

Roman switched on the light and opened the door.

The *dvornik* walked in, followed by two uniformed N.K.V.D. men who had been standing behind him.

I sat erect in bed, rigid.

The leader spoke.

'You are Roman Krivosh? We have here a warrant for your arrest.'

'A warrant for my arrest? What for? I've committed no offence. I'm entirely innocent, it must be a mistake.'

'These are our orders. We have to search your room.'

Irina began to cry. I scrambled out of bed, huddled a dressing-gown round me and sat on the edge of the bed, holding Irina to me, stiff and tense, trying to comfort her.

They went to work. They were neither abusive nor brutal, those N.K.V.D. men; their faces were like blocks of wood. We might as well not have been in the room. They went through every box and trunk we possessed, tipping the contents out on the floor and rummaging through our clothes in search of anything concealed. Then they turned their attention to Roman's library. They examined the titles and the contents of every one of his seven hundred-odd books and looked through each book for any traces of anti-Soviet or Oppositionist literature. They did not confiscate any of the books, but they took his typewriter and all the papers in his desk, including the typescript of the book he was writing. They did not pause or hurry. By the time they had finished their search the day was beginning to dawn.

I sat on the bed through it all, stunned, dazed, incredulous, feeling— 'No, this can't really be happening to *me*.'

Then I broke down and sobbed with unutterable misery and despair.

Roman meanwhile had got dressed as they ordered. He kept patting my shoulder, comforting me and saying, 'Don't be afraid, I'm sure it's a mistake.' He was very calm and matter-of-fact to the end. When it was time to go he hugged me again and said in a firm voice, 'Don't worry, my little Doosia—Pusilka; I've done nothing wrong; I'm sure it's all a mistake. I'll soon be back with you again.'

Then he went with the men down to their car and drove away. That was how Roman Krivosh, the father of my little daughter, the man who had so patiently won my heart and had strolled so gaily and nonchalantly into my life, went out of it for ever.

I sat on the bed holding Irina to me and staring at the piles of books and clothes that littered the room where I had been happier than ever before in my life. It was broad daylight now. There was not a breath of wind, not a cloud in the sky, and the sun streamed in at the window with the abundant promise of a lovely summer's day.

★ ★ ★

I said 'for ever'; but I did see him once again, years later. In the interval I had heard scraps of news about him from the head of his section in the Special Department who took work for him to do in the Butirskaya Prison where he was held. It seems that he wrote to me from prison, but the letters were never delivered. After four years, in 1941, in the stress of war, he was released from prison and returned to the Special Department, but according to my colleagues he began to drink heavily and was eventually dismissed.

I saw him in 1947, after my return from Sweden at the home of a mutual friend, the widow of a man who had died on a military mission to Japan. When I entered the room he greeted me with a gentle courtesy. He had changed a great deal in appearance. He seemed shorter, he was thin and shabbily dressed and had several front teeth missing. He knew of my marriage to Petrov. We talked as friends; the past seemed so very long ago. I asked him the real reason for his arrest.

'It is quite simple, Doosia; they treated me as they treated my father before me. We are always under suspicion, not for anything we have done but for our bourgeois background and what they think we *might* do. At times when the Government gets alarmed and apprehensive they arrest people like us as a precaution, a preventive measure, to isolate us from the community. That's all there is to it.'

'But when were you released from prison?' I asked.

'In 1941. after war broke out. They needed me then. That proves that they knew I was innocent. They would never have taken a chance on my loyalty in wartime. I was allowed to go back to the Department —I was even decorated for my services.'

We talked a little more. Roman spoke of Irina and told me that he still had the photo of her which I once gave to his mother. His own father had not been arrested again, since he was considered too old and feeble to do any possible harm to the State. Roman congratulated me on my marriage to Petrov and said he was glad that things had turned out so well for me.

Then for a moment the Roman I had known seemed to return.

'Doosia, I am delighted to see that you look as charming as ever. As for me, I ask you to forgive me for all the trouble and distress that I brought you by persuading you to marry me.'

That was good-bye, and his last word to me. I never saw him or spoke to him again.

XIII

At Bay

MY BROODING on the morning of Roman's arrest was cut short by practical necessities. I heard movements in adjoining rooms and realized that the neighbours would be looking in before long. Hastily I got to work replacing the books in the shelves and picking up our clothes—they were not so very numerous when gathered together—and putting them back in the trunks. Sure enough, when I opened the door there were three or four of our neighbours in the passage. I could see that they were torn between curiosity and apprehension. 'What's happened?' they asked in awed whispers. 'We heard the noise of people walking about, saw your light on and then heard a car drive away. What was it?'

'My husband has been arrested. We have no idea why; he said it must be some mistake. I expect him back any time.'

They went about their business with that awed fascination that people feel when a major disaster strikes someone near them.

Later in the morning I rang up the Special Department and reported my husband's arrest, as I was bound to do. I spoke to Gusev, head of my Section. I could hear the tremor of panic in his voice.

'Dear Comrade, this is serious news indeed. I'm afraid we shall have to part company—in view of the fact that your husband has been arrested. But yes, do come in and see me in a day or two when your leave is up. We shall see about it then.'

That was the first rumble of thunder, the first indication of what I must expect on all sides now that my partner and protector had gone and the cloud of official suspicion hung over me also.

I thought of my friend Anna, who worked in the Chinese Section of the Special Department. She, too, had been arrested some time ago. After twelve months in prison she was released, but when we passed in the street I did not recognize her till she came up and spoke to me. She had been a gay, healthy, rosy-cheeked girl when I knew her last; now she was clad in a shabby ill-fitting coat which could not conceal the fact that she was nothing but skin and bone.

'Anna,' I cried, 'I didn't recognize you. Tell me what happened. Why were you arrested?'

She shook her head as the tears rolled down her cheeks; all she would say was, 'You see I am free now. Would they have released me if I had really been guilty?' She was too frightened to give any more details of her experiences.

I thought of Charlotta Stashevskaya, whom I had known from Pioneer days. Charlotta's mother, from whom she took her name, was French; her father was a Soviet representative in Paris. Up to 1928 Charlotta lived with her parents in France. Later, in 1937, she acted as a guide in one of the Soviet pavilions at the Paris Exhibition. In Moscow she studied at the Institute of Communications with my friend Sara. In the middle of her course, her father was arrested, and a few months later her mother also. All their property was confiscated and Charlotta was expelled, first from her Komsomol branch and then from the Institute. It was too much for flesh and blood to stand. She went into the bathroom of their flat, turned on the gas and put an end to a life that had lost all hope and purpose. I was with a group of relatives and friends at her funeral, and the expression on her face as she lay in the coffin was striking in its peace and serenity, as though she wanted to tell us, 'Now I am very happy.'

I thought of Maria Byeliaeva whom I had met at Charlotta's funeral. They had been friends in the Pioneers. Maria had married an engineer who was posted to Vladivostok. They were devoted to each other and to their children and were very happy. But one night, just as had happened to me, the N.K.V.D. men came to the house and arrested her husband. Their three children woke to see strange men turning the house upside down and their mother and father in tears. After he had been taken away, she came with her children to Moscow. I do not know the whole story but in the end Maria became a prostitute on the streets. I saw her several times with men going into restaurants. She was smartly dressed and had the look that cannot be mistaken.

My thoughts were interrupted by the ringing of the telephone. It was Ludmilla, a girl who had been to see us once or twice and who I thought had been in love with Roman at some time.

'Hullo, Doosia, it's Ludmilla speaking. How are you?'

'Oh, I'm quite well, thank you.'

'I've been away on holidays, and I wondered how you all were. I often think of you and how happy you must be with Roman and your lovely little baby.'

'Oh yes, I suppose you do,' I said bitterly, but she did not catch the irony in my voice and asked, 'Is Roman there? May I have a word with him?'

'He's out at the moment, but he may be back soon.'

'Oh, I see. Well, may I come round?'

'Of course, do come. I'll be here.'

Before long there was a knock on the door and Ludmilla came in. She was attractive, in a plump blonde style, well dressed and looked a picture of health after her holiday. She gave me a broad smile and a warm greeting; then she saw Irina in her cot and went over to talk to her. Presently she asked casually if Roman had come back yet.

'No, he's not back.'

She looked at me hard. 'What is it, Doosia? Why, you've been crying! What's the matter?'

'Oh, my happiness, I suppose.'

This time she could not mistake my tone.

'Doosia, what is it really?'

'Roman was arrested this morning.'

'Oh, Doosia!' She burst into tears and I guessed that she had in fact been fond of him. She stayed with me for a time, while we talked and I told her all that I knew. Helpless though we both were, our common grief brought us closer together.

Then, as ordered, I reported at the office to my chief Gusev and heard ominous news.

'Comrade K, now that your husband has been arrested as an enemy of the Soviet people, the question of your continued membership of the Komsomol becomes acute. That is not for me to decide, of course, but I must insist that until that vital question is decided, you are suspended from all official duties here. You will be summoned in due course to state your case.'

The hunt was on. I had seen it before, the sickening scramble to escape the taint of anyone who seemed to have fallen from official grace, the panic rush by everyone round about to prove by increased sternness that they at least harboured no hint of anti-Soviet sympathies. The only difference was that now, instead of hearing about the victimization of others, I myself was the victim.

Well, I determined to fight my case tooth and nail. My husband had gone, but I had Irina, that small, precious bundle that was utterly dependent on me for food and protection and life itself. If I was expelled from the Komsomol I could lose my job; if I lost my job, where would I get another? I would be marked for life. I had seen it happen to too many other wretched people. I understood what was at stake.

Gnawing fear made me feel sick in the stomach. Yet the need to fight for life, for my life and Irina's, kept me taut. I could not afford much self-piteous brooding on my misfortune. To that extent the struggle was a spur, a blessing even.

A few days after my interview with Gusev, I was summoned to attend a General Meeting of our Departmental Branch of the Komsomols.

Not unnaturally, the atmosphere was tense and highly charged. Each member was terrified lest he should be accused of supporting someone connected with an arrested person. When I entered the room even my close colleagues avoided greeting or speaking to me. I understood.

Our Komsomol branch consisted of about thirty people. The usual procedure was followed; a Presidium of three was proposed and elected, after which the Secretary presented the agenda; 'Personal Case of Comrade K.' The issue to be discussed by the meeting was then defined, namely, whether, when the case had been heard, Comrade K. should be (a) expelled from the Komsomol, or (b) allowed to retain her membership under stern admonition and reprimand.

The Secretary spoke first. He outlined the history of my marriage and my husband's arrest and concluded, 'As Secretary of this Komsomol organization, I consider that, as Krivosh has been arrested as an enemy of the people and as Comrade K. was then living with him as his wife, she has shown herself unfit to be a member of the Komsomol and must be expelled.' I was in tears, but I defended myself passionately.

'Comrades, I assure you that I am absolutely innocent of any wrongdoing. If my husband has been arrested, what does that prove against me? I lived with him for ten months only; in that time I never had the slightest suspicion of any anti-Soviet activities on his part. When I married him, I assumed that as an N.K.V.D. worker, his character, honesty and loyalty must be beyond question—I know how carefully every one of us has to be examined and screened for employment here.'

There was an uneasy stir at this; I saw my chance and seized on the point.

'Let's face facts, Comrades. Any one of us here today could be arrested tomorrow—it could even happen to our Secretary.'

Everyone in the room thought anxiously of the skeletons in their own cupboards. (By an irony of fate, the Secretary actually was dismissed a little later. It was found that in his biographical record he had concealed the fact that his father had possessed quite a large farm, had employed labour and had been branded as a Kulak during the collectivization drive.) I asked the meeting to consider my peasant background and my good record as Pioneer, Komsomol and N.K.V.D. worker. Finally I quoted an old Russian proverb: 'Had I known the spot where I would slip, I would have put some straw there to break my fall'—indicating that if I had known the trouble that Krivosh would bring on me, I would never have married him.

My pleading had no effect. Fear ruled everyone. There was no real discussion. No one dared to support me, and the view of the senior member, the Secretary, was all that mattered.

They voted unanimously to expel me from the Komsomol. However, the resolution of the branch Komsomol was not binding. According to the constitution it had to come up for consideration before the Committee of the Komsomol for the whole N.K.V.D.

I spent the week's interval between the two meetings in an agony of suspense. The decision meant everything. In a Western democratic country it would be different; there would be some alternative. I might have been disgraced and dismissed without being ruined for life. But in the Soviet Union there is one political party only, one channel of official approval or displeasure, and a black mark on a person's record remains there for life. If I were expelled from the Komsomol I would be dismissed from the N.K.V.D. I would never be allowed to hold a confidential job again. All avenues of advancement would be blocked. I was fighting not just for myself but for my family and for the food, clothing, health and future of my baby daughter.

On the morning of the vital Committee meeting I took Irina to Mother's to leave her there. I felt sick with fear and foreboding.

To my surprise I found Mother cheerful, buoyant, and happy. She kissed me gaily as she took Irina from me.

'Doosenka dear, don't worry about the meeting. I know everything will be all right; you won't be expelled.'

'I'd like to know how you're so sure of that, Mother; I'm half out already.'

'No, this time you'll be all right; you won't be expelled from the Komsomol. That was the dream I had last night and I'm certain it will turn out true.'

It was unusual for Mother to talk like that. Normally she did not attach much importance to dreams. But I could not share her confidence. I had been too badly shaken already. I was almost hysterical. The Committee meeting began with a review of the case. The Branch Secretary spoke as before and I repeated my defence. This time there was a little more discussion and one or two people plucked up enough courage to say a few tentative words in extenuation of my offence.

The last to speak was the Secretary of the Communist Party in the Special Department. He was the senior man present.

'Comrades,' he began, 'we all know Comrade K. We know that she comes of a poor peasant family, that she was a Pioneer for many years, then a Komsomol with a fine record for keenness and discipline and that until the birth of her own child she did excellent work as an Octobrist leader. The whole of her adult life has been spent in the N.K.V.D. service, where she is reckoned as one of the most efficient workers in her own special field. As for her marriage, even though it only lasted for ten months and was not registered, we must grant that she made a most serious mistake. She lacked the experience and wisdom to read her husband's character aright. As we now see, she has realized her mistake and admitted it. To expel offenders is easy; to educate them is more difficult, but it is the function of the Komsomol organization. I therefore propose, for my part, that, rather than expulsion, the punishment recorded against her should be "Severe Reprimand and Serious Warning".'

The big man had spoken. The issue of the vote was not in doubt. At the last moment I had been snatched back from the brink of total disaster, even though the reprimand would stand on my record for the rest of my life.

Sobbing with gratitude and relief I rushed to tell Mother the good news. She was happy, but took it calmly: 'I told you so. I knew it would be all right.'

In after years we often spoke about her dream and how, though normally a matter-of-fact person, she did sometimes have a gift of intuition, especially in times of stress.

It had been a life-and-death struggle, in which I had gained the best that could be hoped by a mixture of luck, desperate energy and tactics. I had secured a reprieve for myself and Irina; Roman was beyond any possible help that I could give him.

One thing was taken for granted by all of us—the Secretary, myself, everyone in the room. It was the madness of even seeming to question the justice of Krivosh's arrest. His guilt had to be assumed as a starting-point for all argument. He himself would have expected nothing different of me in the situation which he understood so well.

I had escaped the worst and was allowed to return to my job, but immediately I had to face a second serious threat. There are too many hungry eyes in the Soviet Union, and the vultures who gather quickly when anyone falls were already busy.

It was Valentina, our good-hearted busybody neighbour, who rang through to me at the office. She was excited and breathless.

'Doosia, it's urgent. I must tell you. The caretaker of our building is

trying to get you out of your room. He wants to put someone else in.'
'How dare he try that! What has happened? What have you done?'
'I saw him nosing about and realized what he was up to. He was
planning to get in and put your furniture out on the landing! He was
trying to force the lock of your door! He says you're not registered
here. I phoned you at once; you'd better act quickly!'
'I will. Thank you for ringing, Valentina Sergeevna, thank you
indeed!'
As I put down the telephone I was shaking with rage and alarm. I saw
clearly what was afoot. The caretaker knew that I was not registered as
a tenant in his building (I was still registered with my parents), and he
thought that now Krivosh had been arrested he could get me out and
make room for one of his friends. But he had reckoned without the fact
that I was an N.K.V.D. worker and the room was an N.K.V.D. apartment.
I went straight to the administrative head of our Section, a charming
and intelligent woman, who listened sympathetically. She phoned
straight through to the caretaker and spoke to him briskly.
'You know that this room is N.K.V.D. property. You are under our
orders in allotting the accommodation.'
'But Krivosh has been arrested; his wife is not registered as a tenant
here.'
'She will be tomorrow. Do nothing till you get further instructions.'
Next day she arranged for me to be excused duty in order to be
registered as tenant of the room. The militiaman who came to register
me was puzzled and surprised at his assignment.
'This is a queer job,' he said. 'Your husband's been arrested, yet you
still work in the N.K.V.D. and the N.K.V.D. is telling me to register you
in this room!'
'I advise you to carry out your orders,' I answered sharply.
'All right, all right.' He put the necessary stamp on my passport.
'From now on you are registered as the tenant of this room.'
He went away still pondering the mystery.
I had warded off attack number two.
But on the third point I had to give way. A certain Evdokimov, who
worked in the Special Department and toadied without shame to the
administrative head, appealed for the room as soon as he heard that
Krivosh had been arrested. His case was upheld and, with regrets, I had
to move out and transfer to the room which he had occupied.
It was long and narrow, not more than a third the size of Krivosh's
room, but I had no choice. I moved all our furniture and belongings
and arranged them to my taste in the new room which was on the third

floor of a building in Ermolaevsky Lane, near Mayakovsky Square (so named after the young poet whom Stalin praised after his death as the greatest poet of his epoch). However, this room, where I lived with Irina for three years, had one great advantage. It was not N.K.V.D. accommodation. Therefore, if the blow which I still dreaded should suddenly fall on me, and I were summarily dismissed from my job, I would not be automatically evicted from house and home. That was something. Soon our narrow room became a home which Irina and I grew to love and cherish dearly.

For a long time I lived with the spectre of dismissal and arrest never far from my mind. It was quite common for wives to be arrested months or even years after their husbands.

I was especially fearful whenever a periodic wave of inquisition and purging passed through the N.K.V.D. Three or four Chiefs of our Department were arrested in quick succession. The panic was universal. No one knew who would be the next victim.

After Boki's arrest, Shapiro became Chief. Soon after his promotion he summoned the whole Department to his office. We sat on several rows of chairs facing him and his secretary, who sat behind a table. Each person had to describe his life and background. This time my friend, Madame Moritz, was the victim. She was married to a German, a brilliant linguist who worked in the Special Department. She, too, was an intelligent, gifted person, who spoke English, German, French and some Japanese. She and I were responsible for checking over the typed copies of the day's messages against the written translations.

When it came to her turn to describe her family background, she mentioned that her father had been an admiral in Czarist times (to omit such a fact would have been suicidal). She insisted that he sprang from a very poor family. But the interrogators sniffed the breeze.

'In that case, how did he rise to such a position in the old Russia?'

'He made his way up, by hard work and long service.'

'That is incredible, Comrade.'

'What I tell you is true. He was a very good officer to his sailors; he always did his best for them; he hid Bolshevik sailors in his house on the eve of the Revolution.'

It was no use; she was dismissed the next day. Shapiro could not risk the charge of leniency to the daughter of a Czarist admiral.

A month later Shapiro himself was arrested.

What could I expect myself?

XIV

Uncle Volodya

ALTHOUGH I had been lucky enough to escape disaster by a hair's breadth, the dread of dismissal and even arrest hovered for a long time in the background of my thoughts. People who had no such black mark recorded against them—no father or brother who had been a Kulak or had served in the White Army, no relative who had been arrested—went demurely about their business, determined that no action of theirs should connect them with any such tainted person. Anyone like myself whose record bore such a spot had to be doubly careful. 'Walls have ears' is not a figure of speech in the Soviet Union, but a grim reality of everyday life. A caution and reticence unthinkable in a Western country become second nature. We in the N.K.V.D. were, of course, particularly careful. We knew even more specifically than other people about the intensive surveillance system, which in the Soviet is not just directed against certain persons whom the Government has special reason to suspect, but is a network designed to cover the whole population, official, military and civilian alike. Every large house has its regular agents, often women, whose function is to pick up gossip and report it to the authorities. Any criticisms of Government policy, any complaints about living conditions or shortages, were highly dangerous and we in the N.K.V.D. were even more vulnerable than ordinary citizens because of our privileged position and special knowledge.

However, as time passed and nothing happened, my fears gradually subsided. I went on with my job in the Special Department and continued my Komsomol membership and duties as before. In due course I was able to apply to have the reprimand rescinded and eventually, in 1940, this was done. Do not imagine that the record of my offence was torn up. The difference was that my dossier would henceforward bear the notation that I had been reprimanded in 1937 and that the reprimand had been officially rescinded in 1940. I was bound to report the whole story in all future applications, statements, and references for the rest of my life. In the Soviet Union personal dossiers may be amended or altered; they are rarely destroyed.

Meanwhile Irina and I lived quietly and undisturbed in the new room, where I arranged the furniture left by Roman to fit the more restricted space—my divan bed along the wall on the left as you entered; Irina's cot and the old mahogany Venetian bookcase against the adjacent wall; then the two comfortable chairs under the windows at the end; and finally, my desk, the Apollo Belvedere, and the tall bookcase along the fourth wall. The old carpet covered the floor. I had the same dining table and chairs and on top of the bookcase I put a very old porcelain vase which gave me great pleasure. It was a fine and delicate piece of work with a graceful bird in pink and gold on a light blue background.

But my great joy and delight was Irina, who was growing fast. She had short golden-brown curly hair, brown eyes with long lashes, very dark eyebrows, a small turned-up nose and an olive skin. She had my mouth and chin, but the rest of her face was so different that no one would believe she was mine. She got prettier as she grew. Out walking everyone stopped to look at her. I took great trouble with her clothes and searched the Moscow shops for nice frocks and dresses which were rare indeed, but could sometimes be found.

When Irina was tiny I used to take her to Mother's every day on my way to work and leave her there with Tamara until the evening. This arrangement served a double purpose. Although Mother was only seventeen years older than I, my troubles had upset her so much that she was not able to feed Tamara, so I fed both babies myself.

For nine months, while feeding my baby, I was allowed to finish work two hours earlier than usual, but even so it was a long tiring journey in the crowded trams. I always managed to get a seat, as mothers with children are entitled to special seats which are reached by the conductor's door. Prams are not allowed on the Moscow trams; they are a rare luxury anyway and I never had one.

As Irina grew it became too laborious to carry her to and fro each day, and I searched about for a suitable maid to look after her in my absence.

The first one, Maroosia, was pleasant and efficient. She cooked, cleaned and looked after Irina while I was at work. But she fell in love, her mind was always on her boy friend instead of her job and she became careless. I was sent away to the Crimea for a short break to recuperate and I left her in charge. When I got back I was horrified at Irina's appearance, and found that Maroosia's boy friend had been living in the apartment in my absence. So Maroosia had to go without delay.

The next candidate was a girl I picked up in a nearby park and decided to try, as she seemed clean and suitable. But when I got back from work on the first evening I found that she had left, having tried to force open my cupboard doors, damaging the locks in the process. However, I had her passport, which everyone must carry at all times in the Soviet Union; without it she could do nothing, and was liable to be arrested. Sure enough she came back, begging me not to take her to the police. I let her go with a warning.

After one more unsuccessful venture, I at last got Frosia, who turned out to be a conscientious and trustworthy girl who was particularly good with Irina.

When Irina and Tamara reached the crawling stage, Mother used to bring Tamara over and they would play together on the floor. The difference between them was amusing. Tamara was active and solidly built, and would soon take possession of all the toys. Irina was fatter and softer and was quite content to sit by and watch what Tamara was doing.

Mother used to say, 'Tamara is the daughter of ordinary working folk, but Irina is clever like her parents.'

Irina loved music and always looked forward to Sundays. Then we would have records on the gramophone, including some children's records of her own, both stories and songs. She would dance and sing herself and was very quick at picking up the melodies. I was determined to bring her up properly and she was wonderfully responsive. She began to feed herself very early and quickly learnt the right spoon to use for each dish. When I began to give her tea to drink she would stir it herself and put the spoon down on the saucer before drinking and she soon learned to say 'Thank you' when she was given anything. She had a place for her own storybooks in the bookshelf and always put them back there after she had finished looking at them.

Once when I was busy she was very quiet. I looked round and saw that she had been to my bag. Her mouth and chin were all smeared with lipstick with blobs of powder smudged over the top. She had put on my hat and scarf and came up to me asking engagingly:

'Mummy, do you like me like this?'

I made her promise not to touch my things again and she kept her word.

Gradually, as time went on and my worst fears began to seem unnecessary, I returned to a more peaceful frame of mind. Roman was gone. I had heard nothing from him and never expected to see him again. On the other hand, the fury of the purge had eased in Moscow, and the arrest which I had feared day and night for many months after his disappearance had not occurred. I was still a Komsomol member, I had my job, I had my room and my daughter was growing apace. I found it possible to look ahead a little and even to think of marriage. Two old friends from Pioneer days, Anatoly and Yuri, were both attentive, and often dropped round to see me in the evening, but they were both married and while not wishing to lose their friendship I did not consider them seriously. For some time I had also been aware that Volodya Proletarsky, who worked in the 6th Section of the Special Department, was also being very attentive. I liked him and we often exchanged friendly words round the office when we happened to meet, but I did not at first think very seriously of him either. However, I heard people discussing him in general conversation and learned that he had been married before but was now divorced. I made a mental note of that and tucked it away somewhere in a corner of my mind without giving it any special thought.

In the summer of 1939 I spent my annual leave at Odessa. When I got back I noticed that Volodya was even more attentive and pressing than he had been before; I began to believe that he was really serious. He always spoke to me whenever we met in the office and it seemed to happen that we met very frequently. One Sunday a party from the Special Department, including Volodya and myself, went on a skiing expedition to the outskirts of Moscow. Coming back in the train we girls began to discuss where we would like to go for dinner and various ideas were suggested. But I was quite clear about my plans.

'Home for me,' I said. 'I've got something nice in the pot and I'm going to have a quiet dinner at home.'

'How I wish someone would ask me to dinner,' said Volodya in a general but pointed way.

But I only teased him and he had to find his own dinner that evening.

It was early in 1940, when he started calling at my apartment, that I saw Volodya in a new light. He took to Irina at once and she to him. Uncle Volodya, *Dyadya Volodya*, soon became her favourite visitor.

'*Dyadya Volodya*,' she would cry with delight and run to greet him; he would lift her up in the air and she would sit on his shoulders with her hands over his eyes. At other times, to make her jealous, he would sit next to me on the couch; then Irina would run to him and belabour his knees, crying 'Don't touch my Mummy, my Mummy not yours.' We would laugh and give way to her jealous mood. She always insisted that she must sit in the middle, between the two of us.

However, I still had many reservations about Volodya. He offended me at times by taking altogether too proprietary a line, such as checking up on all my movements, and even ringing up when I was late getting home to find out where I had been. A cooler, more reserved attitude was my reply to these tactics of his.

That was how matters stood between us when fate decided to take from me the most precious thing in my life.

Two earlier incidents came back to me afterwards, though I thought little of them at the time. Once when Irina was very small I took her for a walk, and sat down to rest at the window of Mother's home. A poor, tottering old woman came up and looked at Irina asleep in my arms. 'Oh my dear, I'm sorry to say that she will not live.' I was startled and upset; it was so unexpected. 'What do you mean? Why do you say that?' 'My dear, you will remember my words one day.' 'Go away,' I cried, 'go away, you old witch!' The strange, unpleasant incident soon faded from my conscious mind. But I did remember it later.

Another time I became engrossed in a story by Maupassant about a wife whose husband left her. All her love became focused on her son. Then the son fell ill with pneumonia and she lived in constant fear of losing him, as in the end she did.

I read this story in the evenings after work, sometimes reading on till eleven or twelve at night. While reading I felt wholly absorbed and identified with the fear and grief of this unhappy woman. But when I put the book down and looked at Irina sleeping peacefully in her cot, my heart filled with gratitude for the life and glowing health of my little daughter.

On the last Saturday in April I got a telephone call at the office from Frosia to say that Irina was not well. When I got home Irina complained that her leg felt sore and I made a compress for it, thinking that perhaps she had knocked it or had had a fall. But I wasn't happy about her and rang for a doctor. A woman doctor from the N.K.V.D. hospital called in and looked at Irina but she said that it was only a feverish cold. I had also rung Volodya to let him know that 'Irishka' was not well, and when he arrived, Irina, for all her sickness, gave her usual joyful greeting to *Dyadya Volodya* from her cot and was sad when he had to leave. Later in the day I took her temperature and found that it was very high; and she was sick several times. I passed an anxious night.

In the morning Irina felt better though she still complained about her sore knee. She had her usual breakfast and lunch, which encouraged me, but towards evening she began to get worse and worse. I rang through to the doctor and told her the situation but she answered, 'Don't worry, it's only a cold. I have some other patients to see first, but I'll call round later in the evening. Mothers are always over-anxious about their children. You are young and it's all new to you.'

Irina got worse and worse; she was delirious most of the time. Whenever she was conscious she called for me or for *Dyadya Volodya*. I tried repeatedly to get him on the phone but I couldn't get through to him. The best I could do was to leave a message for him to ring as soon as he came in.

That night, at eleven o'clock, Irina died.

Five minutes later the doctor walked in. She blanched white and nearly fainted when she saw that she was too late. I was hysterical. I flew at her and sent her away; whenever we passed in the street afterwards she always avoided meeting me. At the post mortem it was found that Irina had died of meningitis.

Volodya arrived soon after the doctor's departure. He had received my message in the office and had hurried straight across. All that night he and I sat with Irina's body; his comfort and sympathy were all that saved me in the bottomless pit of my misery and desolation and were something I will remember as long as I live.

Later that evening Mother came also. She cried terribly because she entered so deeply into my grief. She said, 'Better if it had been Tamara instead of Irina; I am old and have had children, but you, Doosia, are young.' But I stopped her.

'No, Mother, you mustn't talk like that. It is my fate. From now on Tamara is my daughter.' And that was how I felt about Tamara from that time onwards.

Irina died on 30th April 1940 and in June Volodya and I were married. We registered our marriage at the Marriage Registry and in the evening my parents came round to wish us well. Irina's death was so recent, we were in no mood for celebration. As is permissible under Soviet law, I retained my own name, instead of taking Volodya's, for a number of reasons. First, I shrank from the fuss and publicity that one must go through in the Soviet Union in changing one's name; there are so many documents to be amended and so many authorities to be interviewed. Secondly, I didn't like the name Proletarsky; it had an adopted, artificial kind of sound about it. And perhaps, too, I wanted to remain myself, Doosia K., to retain something of my independence.

What finally made me decide to marry Volodya? Many things had built up towards that decision in the time that I had known him. The opinion of my colleagues influenced me in his favour. Both the men and the women in our office spoke of him as a man of kind heart who was generally considered the best chief in the Department and the most popular with his subordinates because he treated them humanely and kept on friendly terms with them all.

I found too that his professional reputation stood high. Not only had he won the N.K.V.D. Distinguished Service Badge, but he was the first man in our Special Department to get the Red Star, which had been awarded to him for his work in China.

Not only by name, but also by origin and background, he was a man of the people. He was of peasant stock; he was on the Committee of the Communist Party unit in our Department, and led a study circle on the history of the Communist Party. Here, if anywhere, was surely a man with his foot set firmly on the stairway of solid progress and safe orthodoxy within the framework of the Soviet Service. After the experience of my earlier marriage, there was a particular appeal for me in that.

Moreover, Volodya had convinced me of his love and devotion in the face of real opposition. I could not ignore the fact that, although he was fully aware of the slur against me on account of my former marriage and of the real risk he ran in linking himself with me, he still wanted to marry me. I felt that he must be sincere and that I would have in him a staunch supporter and defender.

After we were married I glowed with pleasure whenever I heard someone say to Volodya, 'How happy you have made her,' or when one of his friends remarked, 'You're a lucky fellow, Volodya, to have such a clever and charming wife.'

But perhaps the thing that swayed me most of all was my knowledge of the bond which there had been between Volodya and Irina, and the memory of her childish spontaneous joy as she ran to welcome him:

'Dyadya Volodya! Dyadya Volodya!'

XV

Perilous Passage

IT WAS in July 1942 that Volodya and I set out from Moscow to join the staff of the Soviet Embassy in Stockholm. We reached our destination in March 1943 after seven months of dangers and vicissitudes that took us as far south as the Cape of Good Hope. We were very lucky to arrive at all.

What emotions does a Soviet official feel when he is offered the opportunity of a posting to a foreign country? Whatever his feelings may be, if he is wise he keeps them severely in check and displays a certain calculated indifference to the proposition. On the one hand it is proper for him to show a readiness to serve in any capacity and in any situation where he may be of use to the Soviet Government. On the other hand he will be most unwise if he shows any undue enthusiasm at the prospect. Such enthusiasm, if reported, could be interpreted in the most dangerous light. Indeed, I knew of one official who lost his foreign appointment and his job because he showed himself too eager to go abroad.

One day early in 1942, while the Soviet armies were locked in a life and death struggle with the Germans, Volodya said to me after work, 'My chief, Degtjarov, called me in today. He told me that there's a position vacant in Sweden—someone's been recalled—and he's recommended me for it. He asked me if I liked the idea.'

'What did you say?'

'I told him that I was interested, but that I would like to consult you. I also told him that I had some misgivings because in my job I'd seen too many cases of our people coming back from posts abroad with a black mark on their record.'

'What did he say to that?'

'Oh, he brushed it aside. He said, "Don't worry about that, Volodya. I know your background; you're a sound man; you'll be quite all right on that score. Besides, you're just married. You want to set up a nice home. You need to buy all sorts of things that you can't get here. Doosia is still very young and I notice that she has a taste for nice clothes. Take the chance; go abroad; you'll find it a stimulating experience".'

I laughed at this.

'That's just the way Fedor Filipovich would talk. I've heard him speak of his own service abroad; he's often patted my arm and said in his breezy way, "Go abroad, Doosia, go abroad; see how other people live".'

It was Volodya's turn to chuckle.

'Yes; but he didn't forget his own interests either. As I was leaving he added, "By the way, Volodya, when you come back, mind you bring me a nice leather coat like that one of yours." I promised I would.'

A leather coat is still a great prize in the Soviet Union and Degtjarov had admired the one that Volodya had brought back with him from his expedition to Sinkiang. (When we got to Sweden, incidentally, we noticed that, apart from our Soviet Embassy people, such leather coats were worn only by chauffeurs.)

Now another thought struck me. 'Sweden? That means going by Archangel to London. It will be a dangerous journey.'

Volodya shrugged his shoulders.

'We are officers of State Security, under orders. We must go where we are sent.'

Of course, Degtjarov's inquiries and Volodya's hesitation were both formal gestures. The appointment had already been referred to and approved by those on high. In the Soviet service, whether in war or in peace, there is no question of applying for a particular post—which would be a highly dangerous thing to do—or of refusing such an appointment when it is offered, apart from such valid reasons as serious ill-health. The Soviet official goes where he is sent, submissively and demurely. There is a general understanding that that is much the best course.

The pose of indifference is not easy. An appointment abroad is normally regarded as a coveted prize, a golden opportunity, which may occur only once in a Soviet citizen's lifetime, of seeing beyond the guarded confines of his own country and of acquiring possessions totally unobtainable in quantity or quality inside the Soviet Union.

All the propaganda resources of the Soviet Government have not been able to conceal from the Soviet people the huge discrepancy in general living standards between themselves and their Western neighbours. And not only their Western neighbours. A colleague of Volodya's who had served in Japan used to puzzle over the paradox that a small crowded country like Japan seemed able to provide a better standard of life than a huge country like the Soviet Union with all its far-flung resources.

Though I had never had poor Nina's consuming passion to go abroad, this appointment to Sweden was an exciting prospect. Hitherto I had never spoken to a foreigner in my life but I had seen numbers of them in the streets of Moscow—instantly recognizable by their clothes, which stood out in sharp contrast to the ungainly sameness of our Russian garments.

We have a Russian proverb which aptly describes a foreigner in the streets of Moscow—'a parrot among the crows.'

Whenever foreigners passed, people stared inquisitively at their shoes, hats, bags, suits; everything about them was strange and interesting.

Once, after my return from Sweden, I was walking in a Moscow street wearing a topcoat that I had brought back with me, when a woman overtook me and put her hand on my arm. 'Do you mind,' she said, 'I have been following you a long way admiring your coat from the back; may I see the front view also?'

Before I ever left Russia I had seen plenty of pictures of life in foreign countries. My friend Sara's father worked in the Customs Department, which zealously confiscated quantities of foreign literature, including film magazines, at the frontiers of the U.S.S.R. Some of them found their way to his home, where Sara would produce them for the awe and edification of the rest of us. Each of us adopted the name of a foreign film star or actress. I was Mary Pickford, Sara was Sarah Bernhardt, Maroosia was Lya di Putti and Nina was Pola Negri. Moreover, my colleagues in the Japanese Section of the Special Department lent me books and illustrated magazines, many of them British and American, which they had to read in the course of their duty. I took them home and studied the types of houses, the trains, buses, cars, the cities and streets, the shops, window displays and fashion designs.

My girl friends stared fascinated at these windows on to another world, and would exclaim, 'Fancy that! They've got everything! That's what I call life!'

On the eve of our departure from Moscow, Volodya showed me our new foreign passports, which had just been handed to him at the Ministry for Foreign Affairs. There, for the first time, I saw myself described as 'Mrs Petrov'. The authorities, as Volodya has mentioned, had judged 'Proletarsky' too militant a name for foreign service and had chosen 'Petrov' instead. Thus we received the name by which we were to be officially known in Sweden and later in Australia. Inside Russia, among our N.K.V.D. colleagues, we would still be Doosia K. and

Volodya Proletarsky. But anywhere outside the Soviet Union we were henceforth to be Mr and Mrs Petrov, destined to be the eventual authors of this book.

Volodya's official posting, as notified to the Swedish authorities, was 'Clerk' to the Soviet Embassy. His secret functions, which no one but the Ambassador and the N.K.V.D. Resident must know about, were twofold; he was cypher clerk to the N.K.V.D. chief in the Embassy (whose function was also secret from the other Embassy members) and was responsible to the N.K.V.D. for keeping watch on the security and loyalty of all Soviet representatives in Stockholm, including, as it turned out, the Soviet Ambassador, Madame Kollontai.

As for me, although I remained a cadre (that is, permanent) officer of the N.K.V.D., I had no official posting to the Embassy; I went simply as Volodya's wife.

As the train rolled over the north Russian plain on its way to Archangel, one thought gave me particular satisfaction. A foreign posting is a sign of official confidence in the Soviet Union; no one who is regarded as in any way a 'doubtful' case is ever allowed outside the borders of the U.S.S.R. After all I had been through as a result of my first husband's arrest, this posting abroad was significant and encouraging. Whatever lay ahead, I determined to prove myself in every way a worthy daughter of my Soviet homeland.

At Archangel our first problem was the refusal of the Intourist Hotel, where bookings had been made for us, to admit us until we produced a certificate to show that we had had a bath. This, we discovered, was a wartime regulation to guard against epidemics, though it may have been designed also to impress the various foreigners, including officers of foreign ships, who patronized the Intourist Hotel. On inquiry we were directed to the public bath house, which normally provided steam baths in the Russian style. Here a fresh difficulty met us. Because of wartime shortages, there was no fuel to heat the bath or the bath house. Even though it was July, the weather was sharp enough and we were afraid of catching colds. Russian adaptability provided a solution. We quickly undressed and dressed again, washed our hands and faces and gave the attendant a few roubles each. He in turn provided certificates and stamped them with the date. A great deal of unnecessary bother was saved and the hotel authorities were happy to admit us as guests.

The Intourist Hotel represented the lap of luxury to us after wartime Moscow. We had a room of our own and ample meals. The reason for this good fare was evident. With convoys arriving from Britain and the United States, it was important that the ships' officers who stayed there should get a favourable impression of their ally, and so the best was supplied. However, to conceal from these foreigners the high prices prevailing in Russia, two menus were provided. On the menu offered to visitors the same items were half or a third less than we Russians had to pay.

The local residents of Archangel were not allowed to visit the hotel, with the exception of two women whom we very soon spotted as N.K.V.D. workers. They were in their early thirties, attractive, and had better clothes than we possessed, though we had our kit for foreign service. They were not difficult to identify as N.K.V.D. workers, though of course we gave them no sign that we knew their business, or that we ourselves were N.K.V.D. I knew something of this 'field work', which Nina had been engaged in for a time. In all Intourist hotels which cater for foreigners there are girls who act as guides and interpreters, and who are almost without exception either cadre or co-opted N.K.V.D. workers. In direct contrast with all other Soviet citizens, they are encouraged to spend time with foreigners in order to pick up information and intelligence.

We were amused and interested to watch these two women at work. They were always in the hotel when ships' officers were dining there, drinking and flirting till the early hours of the morning. I heard that one of them later married a British officer.

We waited ten weeks at Archangel for a passage to London, but nothing materialized. The convoys were suffering heavy losses at that time, and perhaps the ships' captains did not like the responsibility of taking several Russian families, including a number of women, who are said to bring bad luck to a ship.

At last we were recalled to Moscow, where we waited another six weeks for Teheran visas and nearly starved to death. It was one of the penalties of our secret role and it gave me a first-hand insight into the hardships which the ordinary citizen had to endure. As we were now officially on the books of the Ministry of Foreign Affairs, we were strictly forbidden to betray any N.K.V.D. connections and therefore could not go to the N.K.V.D. dining-room, which even during the war was relatively well-provided. Instead, we had to eat at a very inferior canteen of the Ministry of Foreign Affairs. Moreover, as Mother and Tamara were on the terribly meagre civilian ration, I used to take them along to share my meal with me. It was a desperately hard time, even by Russian standards.

At last we were off, by passenger plane to Kuibyshev, then to Teheran.

My first impressions of an Eastern city remain a vivid memory—the magnificent palace and fine official buildings in dazzling white, the miserable hovels of the poor quarters, the crowds of beggars and children in loin cloths. But after Moscow the abundant food made our eyes open—tomatoes, cucumbers, all sorts of fruits and vegetables. At one meal I ate six or seven eggs, with vegetables, grapes and other fruit.

Then on we went again, to Cairo, where we saw the East in a different aspect. I was stunned by the noise, confusion, and especially the cries of newspaper boys; I had never heard such a din before. There were the noisy crowds of Arabs in red fezes, the big opulent shops and houses in the centre of the city, the spacious hotel, an oasis of quiet, where Arab servants appeared as if by magic when we clapped our hands.

A very young, very polite Englishman at the British Consulate (which was acting for our own Government) supplied us with money and saw to our onward travel arrangements. Tours were arranged; we visited the pyramids and a great mosque and rode on camels. Volodya took a picture of me sitting on a camel with a fez on my head; but the camera and pictures were lost at sea with the rest of our belongings.

At lunch at our hotel all our Soviet party sat together. The ample meal ended with fruit, after which the servants silently placed a finger-bowl in front of each of us. I watched to see what our people would do. The children in the party took the matter into their own hands; they picked up the bowls and began to drink from them. Their elders saw the servants laughing and joined in their laughter.

Behaviour is so free and easy in the Soviet Union that it is an ordeal for most Soviet visitors to be faced with the strict etiquette and formal manners of the West. As part of their preparation for foreign service the Ministry of Foreign Affairs gives all Soviet representatives an official paper to read on the subject of etiquette. There is no indication of the author, but I have heard it attributed to Maisky, the Soviet Ambassador who, with his wife, spent so many years in London. I remember instructions on the correct way to eat nuts and fruit. For example, it was explained that rock melons should be eaten with a spoon, instead of with a knife and fork, Russian style, and that a knife and fork should be put together when the course is finished instead of being left anyhow, as happens in Russia. I think, too, that there' was a warning to remove the spoon from a teacup before drinking. This is practical; too often I have seen our people leave the spoon in the cup, with the result that it comes into violent collision with the nose. But the principal advice given is to watch the habits of the foreigners carefully and do as they do.

For my part, I was determined that we Soviet people should give a good account of ourselves and show that we were equal to all occasions.

With the Mediterranean closed to ordinary shipping, we embarked at Suez in a British passenger ship, the *Llandaff Castle*, for the long voyage down the coast of Africa and round the Cape of Good Hope. Volodya and I had a two-berth cabin and all our party were very comfortable in first-class accommodation. The atmosphere on board was most cordial towards us; all the stewards were polite and attentive and our fellow-passengers praised the Russian Army for its heroic fight against the Germans. Volodya made friends with some British army officers, who taught him English and the song *Tipperary*. Among the crew, the radio operator was particularly friendly to us Russians. He invited us to the crew's quarters when he was off duty, to have tea and to hear him play his guitar. We felt very much at home and settled down to enjoy the long voyage.

A few days after we left Aden some alarming news went round; a ship had been torpedoed in waters which we had just passed through; but our ship's crew spoke quite confidently when we asked their opinion. 'Don't worry, we've been on this run for two years and we've never yet been attacked by sea or air.'

We were glad of their reassurance, but our apprehensions remained. That night was hot and oppressive beyond anything we had yet encountered. Our cabins were unbearably stuffy, despite the ventilation, and we all brought our bedding up and spread it out on deck. It was a restless, uneasy night with a gusty wind and a heavy swell, which made the ship roll uncomfortably, even though no spray was coming over the deck. Few of us got much sleep and some of the women were crying from a mixture of discomfort and foreboding.

But nothing happened; the day dawned calm and sunny and our fears of the night disappeared. A spirit of relief and cheerfulness pervaded us all and though it was still very hot we were able to relax and enjoy ourselves, sitting about in tropical clothing, while the children played on the deck or on the swings in the children's playroom. I was quite comfortable in a light summer frock and sandals. It was November 30th, 1942.

Just before dinner we went as usual to the bar with our husbands as we saw that the English women did. I also noticed that they wore evening dress. The only woman in our party who possessed an evening dress was Mrs Vinogradov, wife of the First Secretary, who had served abroad in Bulgaria. She had a long evening dress of black velvet.

I urged her to wear her evening dress in spite of the heat to show the

English women that we Russians could do as well as they could and after some demur she eventually agreed. She was grateful later, though reluctant at the time.

Darkness fell suddenly and at half-past seven we went down to dinner. We had just finished soup when the whole ship shook, there was a loud crash and the ship listed over violently. Everyone in the dining saloon sprang up and there was a simultaneous cry, neither a scream nor a shout, but a prolonged gasp—'Ohhh . . .!'

There was shattered glass everywhere. Looking across at Volodya I saw that he was bleeding from cuts on the face and arm where glass from a broken porthole had fallen on him.

Everyone began to surge up the stairway to the upper deck. It was not easy because the ship was listing so heavily towards the starboard side, where the torpedo had struck. Our cabin was on the port side. The equivalent cabins on the other side had all been destroyed by the explosion. Volodya's first thought was to get his jacket, which contained all our documents. Even at that moment of crisis our long years of Soviet training in security and the vital importance of documents, did not desert us. But I was in a panic and pulled Volodya away.

'No, Volodya, no! Your jacket is too heavy! It will weigh you down in the water! You'll sink!'

He seized our passports from his inside pocket, thrust them into his trouser pocket and we hurried up to the boat deck. I was frantic and my memory of those hectic minutes is confused. There was much shouting and crying, as everyone clustered on the higher side of the deck away from the side where the torpedo had struck. Some of the crew were already sitting in a boat; but there was a roar from the Captain and they scrambled out to make way for the passengers. As we were standing waiting our turn to get in, one of the ship's officers seized me by the arm and tried to drag me along the deck. I have no idea to this day what he had in his mind—whether to take me to another boat, or to a raft but Volodya rushed after us, took me by the other arm and pulled me back. I remember that twice I tried to scramble out of the boat and twice Volodya had to push me back into it. The sailors were struggling to get the boat swung out. At last it began to bump down the side of the ship towards the water. Just then another torpedo struck on the other side. There was a roar and a column of spray, and the ship leaned over yet more sharply. When our boat was in the water and had pulled a little way from the ship I looked up and saw our Soviet colleague Kalugin standing in another boat which was still at deck level, while the sailors worked feverishly to lower it. He was holding a rope.

Suddenly the boat fell to the water and the rope ran through his hands so fast that it tore them to the bone. Later, in the boat, he suffered terribly before we were picked up.

There was a worse sight than that. One Englishwoman was trying to get down the side of the ship on a rope ladder, clutching her eight-year-old daughter in her arms. The double effort was too much for her strength. Her daughter slipped from her arm into the sea. At the time it seemed that she must have been drowned, but in 1955 we discovered, through an Australian newspaper report which mentioned the sinking, that happily the little girl had been saved.

At last all the undamaged boats were lowered into the water and began to move about, picking up people who were swimming or clinging to rafts and floats; some of them were black from head to foot from thick oil which spread across the water from the damaged ship. Our boat picked up the Captain who had waited till all the boats were lowered and had then jumped through a window into the water. We found him clinging to a float. He sat hunched up, shivering and trembling from cold and shock.

The abandoned ship was now ablaze. A lurid light showed up the loaded boats, the rafts and the wreckage. Then a third torpedo struck the ship; she broke in half and in a few seconds slid beneath the waves.

Among those lost was the radio operator who had been such a friend to us Russians. He stayed behind sending out the s.o.s. signals which saved our lives.

I had never before seen a ship sink, and sick and terrified as I was, I was awestruck at the quiet completeness and finality of it. One moment there was a ship, even though shattered and burning. The next moment there was no ship at all, only the moving sea, with the boats and the rafts bobbing and stirring like insignificant corks on its restless surface. Not one of us could be immune to the eerie solemnity of the moment. I have never experienced anything like it before or since.

Twenty minutes after the ship sank, as the boats lay bumping and nosing together in the gentle swell, the submarine came up, fifteen yards from us, like a fat pig, snorting and blowing, with the water running off it. We were all frightened and one of the ship's crew lost his head completely. Thinking that the submarine meant to turn its machine-guns on us, he dived over the side into the water. Soon afterwards, realizing his mistake, he began to cry and call to us to pick him up, but we could not reach him or see him in the darkness and he was drowned.

We Russians were also very frightened. We feared that the English would tell the submarine commander about us. We took it to be a German submarine and we had no doubt that they would single us out for any special severities which they had in mind. Communist teaching and wartime experience alike confirmed our belief that the hatred of the Germans towards the Soviet Union was more bitter than their hatred of their enemies in the West. We whispered among ourselves and made ready to tear up our Russian passports. But it turned out to be unnecessary.

The submarine turned a searchlight on the boats and the commander called in very bad English, 'What ship, what nationality, what cargo?' The Captain answered briefly, giving the name of our ship, *Llandaff Castle*, the British company and the cargo, which included some gold.

Our worst fears were not fulfilled. The commander did not turn his guns on us or take any prisoners. He simply shouted, 'Save yourselves as best you can!' and with a churning of his propellers, disappeared into the night.

We were alone on the sea.

Volodya and I were in one boat with Mrs Vinogradov and another family; the rest of our Russian party were in another boat. I had kicked off my shoes as I got into the boat and had nothing but the light frock I was wearing at dinner, and even that was badly torn. During the night it got very cold, with a keen salty wind, and Volodya grumbled at having been persuaded to leave his jacket behind. Mrs Vinogradov, on the other hand, was extremely grateful for her black velvet evening dress which kept her comparatively warm throughout the night.

Fortunately there were some blankets in our boat. Like most of the women, I lay in the bottom of the boat feeling sick and wretched with a blanket over me, while Volodya and the men sat huddled on the seats.

The next morning dawned calm and sunny, for which we were profoundly thankful. Before long the warmth began to cheer us all up. The Captain had recovered and saw to the rationing of the water and biscuits which were stored in the boat. We did not know how long they might have to last. Luckily all our Soviet people had got off safely, as well as most of the passengers and crew, but the boats were very crowded. The English people were all very thoughtful and considerate. It wasn't the kind of situation where differences of nationality seem the most important thing.

But there were other problems besides food and warmth. With men and women adrift for days in a boat, there is the inevitable problem of providing privacy for the needs of nature. However, it was tackled in a practical way. At certain times a canvas screen was raised across the middle of the boat to make a ladies' retiring room, which the sailors, despite some playful pretences at dropping the screen, treated with due respect.

Another cold night followed the warm day and our spirits sank with the thermometer. We were all tired, and listless. We did not row, for our best hope lay in keeping as near to the position of the sinking as possible, in the hope that the s.o.s. had been heard and help was on the way. We simply floated with the boats roped together.

Next morning brought us excitement and fresh hope. An aeroplane appeared, flew over us as we waved and shouted wildly, and circled round us several times before it flew off. Obviously our s.o.s. had been heard, and steps were being taken to rescue us.

However, our delight was premature. Nothing happened all that day and by the evening it was windy and choppy. We were soon drenched, sick, miserable and in considerable danger. During the night the lines that kept the boats together broke. Three of the boats kept together, but the third drifted away and disappeared. We never saw it again. In it was the mother whose daughter we had seen fall into the sea, while her husband and their three-year-old son were in our boat. His grief was terrible.

Daylight brought no improvement; the boat pitched and rolled and had to be baled out continually. Then at last, to our unspeakable joy and relief, we saw a ship approaching us. We were found! How we waved and cheered. It was a British destroyer and presently our boat was bumping alongside and they threw us down a ladder. I was the first person of all the survivors to step on to the haven of the destroyer's deck.

For what remained of the day the destroyer searched the area for a sign of the other boat, but at last they had to give up and set a course for Durban.

We had been picked up in the nick of time. A gale was now blowing, lashing the sea and making the destroyer roll and pound and groan. Our boats would have been swamped and sunk.

How kind and courteous they were to us in that destroyer! We women had the officers' wardroom put at our disposal and were able to rest wrapped in dry blankets. It was a rare luxury in itself to be warm and dry again. As most of our frocks were dirty and torn, the ship's officers lent us all that they had to offer on board—khaki shorts and shirts. Some of the officers were amused at our women, who were broader in the beam than the English women, but we took it all as a joke and laughed with them. I preferred to wear my old torn frock and to pin it together where necessary until I could get something else suitable.

Durban overwhelmed us with kindness. Ladies from the Red Cross met us on board with complete outfits of clothes. However, most of them were too big for us; perhaps they thought that all Russians were giants. Some of our women did not mind and put on the outsize garments which had been so kindly provided. But Mrs Vinogradov stuck to her black velvet evening dress which she wore hitched up with a belt lent her by one of the sailors and a pair of white sailor's shoes. She looked like one of the shabby nuns who were still seen in post-Revolutionary Russia after the closing of the convents.

When we were ready, the Red Cross ladies took us to hotels, where accommodation had been arranged and then in parties to the shops, where they fitted us out completely, from shoes and stockings to hats. It was indeed a generous welcome which we all appreciated very much.

Best of all was the news that the lost boat had reached the African coast somewhere north of the point where we had been torpedoed, and that the occupants were safe.

Durban, with its lush green foliage, its beautiful white buildings and its palatial shops stocked with an abundance of goods, remains a vivid picture in my mind. Although we avoided publicity, we were modest celebrities. The whole town knew our story. One emigré Russian, said to be a prince, visited our hotel when we were out and left £10 'for the Russians'. However, we were on the alert. We refused the gift, indicating that our Government would look after us.

After two or three days the British authorities provided us with money for our fares to Pretoria, where our own Consul-General resided. Though well aware of our situation, he had neither come to Durban himself nor sent anyone to see to our welfare.

At Pretoria he gave us an equally unsympathetic reception. All the women in our party formed a deputation begging him to arrange for them to go by air for the rest of the journey or to send them back to Moscow. They were terrified of risking themselves on the sea again, after what they had been through.

But he dismissed their pleadings with callous impatience. 'Torpedoed? Oh, that's not so bad. You weren't burned in oil. Now when *my* wife came to Pretoria by air, she was almost involved in a plane crash. That really *was* serious.'

His offhand attitude caused deep resentment. It was obvious that he was not concerned about anyone or anything beyond his immediate personal interests and did not want to be bothered with looking after us. As one of the women grumbled under her breath (quoting a Russian saying), 'Only your own shirt touches you closely.'

Seeing their dismay and alarm I remembered stories I had read of how a bold line by some individual had succeeded in rallying others and in stemming the tide of panic. Besides, I had a strong intuition that all would be well.

'Listen,' I told them, 'I am certain that we are going to be all right for the rest of the voyage. I have a feeling about it. I'm as sure as I stand here that we will arrive safely.'

My confidence, which was not just assumed but sprang from a real conviction, helped to calm and reassure them.

From the pleasant city of Pretoria we travelled to Cape Town with its spectacular beauty. Our party was tremendously impressed by a visit to Table Mountain. We met the same friendliness everywhere during our wait for a ship. One English family kept assuring us that the Germans would certainly be *kaput* before long by Britain, America and their brave allies the Russians.

At last we got berths in a great 20,000-ton liner with deck towering above deck. But as we went up the gangway the children in our party began to whimper, 'Don't go on the ship; not again—we don't want to go on the ship!'

Once again I voiced my certainty that we would come to no harm and would arrive safely. Sure enough, this time we had a calm, comfortable and uneventful voyage. We had practice alarms, were equipped with lifebelts and went to our boat stations every day, but there were no attacks or mishaps. This time we travelled in convoy. We saw the naval vessels zig-zagging all round us, and felt a sense o security.

When we reached London, the other women kissed me and told their husbands, 'She brought us good luck.'

'How were you so certain?' they asked me, as we said good-bye. I could only repeat that I had felt this strong conviction throughout our stay in South Africa. But I remembered, too, the words of Mrs Kalugin, a devoutly religious woman who was not a Communist, after we were picked up from the boats.

'Do you know why we have been rescued?' she asked us. 'Because of my prayers. All the time in the boat I prayed and prayed to God to help us and now we have been saved.'

The rest of us ridiculed her and told her that it was just fate, but she did not seem resentful or at all disturbed in her own certainty.

London in that early March of 1943 was foggy, drizzling and grey. The people seemed to us well dressed, quiet and very polite. An Embassy colleague took Volodya to visit Karl Marx's grave in Highgate Cemetery but I did not go with them. However, I saw Buckingham Palace and Westminster Abbey which awed me by its size and solemnity. In Moscow I had never been inside a church except St Basil's Cathedral in the Red Square.

In Westminster Abbey, the tomb of the Unknown Warrior made a deep impression on me. I asked myself, 'Have we such a memorial in Moscow?' The profound and sincere reverence for the dead shown by people in Western countries always struck me forcibly, in contrast to the careless, perfunctory attitude in the U.S.S.R. Our cemeteries are neglected; funerals are without dignity or reverence; wreaths left on a grave would be stolen. I have often pondered over this difference in attitudes.

Our hotel in London was near Hyde Park and we loved to walk there and watch people feeding the swans on the Serpentine. The tameness of the birds in coming up to be fed by hand amazed us.

We had never seen such a thing before. In the Soviet Union it is unknown. There the birds (like the people) are much too frightened.

Heavy air raids took place during our fortnight in London and we went regularly to our hotel shelter. We saw numerous bombed buildings, many more than in Moscow. An air raid was in progress when our darkened train left London for the north and when we reached Aberdeen we heard that our London hotel had been hit that very night.

After two days in the clean, windy city of Aberdeen, we flew by night across the North Sea and landed in Sweden in the early morning. It was an uncomfortable flight; we flew very high, sometimes needing to use oxygen masks in order to breathe.

The precautions were not needless. Not long afterwards our Military Attaché's wife, and the wife of his secretary, with four children, were crossing by the same route. The plane was shot down by the Germans inside Swedish territory, and everyone was killed. The Soviet Embassy organized an official funeral, and all the Diplomatic Corps came to pay their respects and offer condolences.

Our journey from Moscow to Stockholm had certainly been hazardous. But we had arrived.

XVI

Housewife and Spy-mistress

VOLODYA and I remember our four years in Sweden as a happy and halcyon interlude. We enjoyed a degree of comfort, freedom and security that we had never known before and at the end of our time we were able to return home to Moscow with the knowledge that we had served the Soviet well and the hope that we were favourably regarded by the powers that ruled our fate. Our later experiences at the Embassy in Canberra were in sharp and painful contrast.

After the rigours of wartime Moscow we were immediately struck by the widespread comfort and prosperity of capitalist neutral Sweden. Even as we drove into Stockholm from the airport, I was astonished at the shoals of men and women on bicycles. I thought it must be an athletic contest. But our Embassy comrades who had come to meet us explained that it was not so, but that all these people owned their own bicycles and rode to and from their work on them every day. I was amazed at this general affluence. But I was even more astonished to see hundreds of bicycles standing in bicycle parks, propped against the kerb, or leaning against walls. Such a thing would be unthinkable in Moscow. In the first place, if one does not belong to the privileged *élite* who are whisked to and from their offices in official cars, one travels by public transport, tram, trolley-bus or the Metro. No one rides bicycles; it would be a dangerous operation in the Moscow traffic. In the second place, any bicycles left in a Moscow street, even though locked, would be stolen immediately. A bicycle is such a valuable luxury that some owners take them to pieces when not in use. I took a bicycle back from Sweden for my sister Tamara; she kept it in her room and never dared to ride it beyond the street where she lived.

Then to see the Stockholm shops, full of so many wonderful things, was like walking through fairyland. I knew more about what to expect in Western countries than many of our Soviet people did, but it was a revelation to me. I was particularly impressed by the high standard of dressing among the Swedish women and by the fact that in the Stockholm streets the average person, not just the fortunate few, was carefully, neatly and tidily dressed. In Moscow the attitude is that any old clothes are good enough for the job. Most people present that grey, drab aspect that has been noted by so many foreign observers. It is understandable. I know that many Soviet women would like to dress better, but nice clothes are simply unobtainable. In any case their life is one long struggle for basic necessities for themselves and their families and when you come to the necessities of life, food comes before smart clothing.

In Sweden, Volodya and I were, by Soviet standards, very prosperous. For the first few months I had no official appointment but, after a time, I, too, began work in the N.K.V.D. office. Our combined salaries, which at that time were paid in full abroad, gave us a relative affluence which we appreciated to the full. We had money and there were things to buy.

Our sunny flat at Rindogatan 8, in the suburb of Gärdet, was on the second floor of a large block, with its own balconies and windows on two sides and its own kitchen, bathroom, bedroom and sitting-room. I got immense pleasure out of arranging and furnishing it, which we could now afford to do. Whenever my Swedish friend Maria came to see me, she always exclaimed, 'What a charming flat you have, Doosia! I do like it.' My purchases included the furniture for two rooms and— my long-cherished dream!—an English upright piano. I longed to study music seriously and I did manage to have a few lessons in Sweden, but before long my work became too demanding and my time too full.

Volodya, for his part, recalling the days when he used to play for the village dancing, bought a fine Italian accordion and a book on 'How to teach yourself the accordion'. He practised on Sundays and mastered some simple tunes.

We loved the beautiful city of Stockholm. Its streets always seemed miraculously clean, without any evident attention. I was puzzled by this, thinking of the women sweepers who trudge the Moscow streets with brooms made of twigs until I found that, in Stockholm, the streets were swept at night by machines. We loved the tree-lined streets and many parks and the surrounding country with its numerous lakes, rivers, fjords and woods. A walk which we often chose was in the King's Forest, only five minutes from our suburb of Gärdet, and our favourite spot was marked by a huge ancient mossy oak tree. Because of its enormous girth we christened this oak tree 'Petishkin', after a very fat man of that name on the staff of our Soviet Trade Representative. This was a standing joke among our friends, who would ring and say, 'Let's call on Petishkin'; or, 'I'll meet you at three o'clock at Petishkin.'

For longer expeditions Volodya bought a motor-cycle, and I rode pillion behind him, nervous and far from comfortable as we bumped along. But it did enable us to see the countryside. Sometimes we went with Embassy friends like Volodya's colleagues Chernov or Petukhov, sometimes by ourselves. We would take a tent, a primus stove and fishing tackle and would spend the whole Sunday in the open air. Sometimes we came back with enough salmon or bream to supply the whole Embassy staff.

Best of all, there was at that time in our Stockholm Embassy a very good 'collective', or spirit of comradeship. The Ambassador when we first arrived was the famous Madame Kollontai, of whom we have more to tell. Soon afterwards she was recalled to Moscow and was replaced by Chernyshev, who was less experienced and who had a difference with our N.K.V.D. chief, Razin. But, in general, the good spirit established by Madame Kollontai continued on under the new Ambassador.

The friendliness of the Embassy women was in marked contrast to my later experiences in Canberra. Besides parties at our homes we had many gay and cheerful evenings, with film-shows, dancing and celebrations at our Soviet Club in the old part of the city. While in Sweden I had three major operations. During my illness my fellow-Komsomol members in the Embassy staff organized an additional night-and-day nursing service and showed the greatest care and concern for my safe recovery.

The Swedish people, in spite of their neutrality, were always polite and friendly to us as Russians, but there were some aspects of Swedish life which I found it hard to get used to. On Sundays I missed the crowds of holiday-makers and sightseers which throng the Moscow streets and parks. On Sunday Stockholm seemed a dead and deserted city. All the people had withdrawn to their homes.

The reserve and sober deportment of the Swedish people was also in striking contrast to Russian behaviour. Our people are by nature spontaneous and forthcoming in expressing their feelings, whether of joy or grief; they are quick to show either. On a train journey in Russia the occupants of a compartment immediately introduce themselves to one another and are soon talking, laughing or playing games. People invariably ask each other's destination, purpose in going and all sorts of other personal details. Of course, the dangerous subjects—one's work or politics—as well as all contacts with foreigners, are strictly taboo. But, apart from that, Russians give full rein to their sociable and gregarious inclinations.

In Sweden, on the other hand, I noticed that it was considered bad manners to initiate conversation with a stranger. In trains each travel-

ler's seat was his private possession where he was entitled to remain
aloof from the rest of the company. Twice I was sent to the famous and
luxurious sanatorium at Saltsjö-Baden, staying a month on each occasion. Most of the other guests were either very old or very rich and,
apart from the manageress, not one person ever spoke to me, even
among my table companions at meals. We never got beyond 'Good
morning' or 'Good evening'. I respected their ways and did not start a
conversation with anyone. Each week-end Volodya and some of the
Embassy people would drive out to see me; but for the rest of the time
I was quite on my own. Strangely enough, I was entirely happy, and
never once felt lonely. I was quite content to go for walks by myself,
to swim in the beautiful fjord, to read, to watch tennis, or to stroll to
the railway station and observe the people arriving and departing. Such
independence is a rare and novel experience in the life of a Soviet
citizen.

In those years of 1943 to 1947 we Soviet officials were greatly assisted
by the reservoir of goodwill which existed among the Swedish people
towards us. The U.S.S.R. had played a great part in defeating Hitler and
in ensuring victory for the Allies, which the Swedes, for all their neutrality, knew well enough was in their own best interests. The Swedish
Government and people had not yet been shocked by the subsequent
revelations of Soviet espionage into an understanding of what the
Soviet attitude and Soviet plans really were towards them. During our
time there a group of Soviet artists, including the novelist Sobolev and
the singer Vera Davidova, toured Sweden and received an enthusiastic
welcome. I attended a concert in Stockholm at which Davidova was
the soloist. The audience included one of my actress heroines, Greta
Garbo, whom I had seen years before in *Anna Karenina*. I craned my
neck in the theatre to see her and later ran with a crowd in the street to
get a better look. The Stockholm press reported enthusiastically on
Davidova's singing and on Garbo's presence. It seemed to me a happy
symbol of Soviet-Swedish accord.

Nevertheless, not for a moment did we of the Embassy staff forget
that, however friendly our relations with our hosts might be on the
surface, we were in fact a Soviet colony in enemy territory. Our real
social life and relaxation must be confined to our own people. Apart
from the normal necessary contacts of business and daily life, close
social relations with foreigners were strictly forbidden, apart from
those approved by Moscow as capable of exploitation to the advantage
of the Soviet Union. Any attempts by foreigners to promote closer
social relations with our people must be assumed to be instigated by an

enemy Intelligence agency until Moscow was satisfied to the contrary. This was the attitude in which all Intelligence workers and all diplomats on our staff had been firmly grounded and the humblest Embassy employee understood equally well, though less explicitly, that any close contacts with foreigners were dangerous and forbidden.

The only Soviet citizens who might not appreciate this danger to the full were those who had been too long abroad, exposed to the corrosion of decadent liberal ideas, and who were therefore out of direct touch with the ideological climate of the Soviet Union. Our Ambassador, Madame Kollontai, and her personal staff provided a case in point, but, as Volodya was personally involved in this case, and handled the correspondence with Moscow on the matter, I will leave him to describe it.

To me, as a Lieutenant of State Security, the experience in Sweden was exciting and stimulating.

After my appointment as N.K.V.D. secretary I worked regular hours in our office in the Embassy, where my duties included typing correspondence between our office and Moscow, typing stencils for the duplicator, photographing the more important documents which our agents had procured and translating material from English into Russian. From the reports which I handled I got an impression of the wide ramifications of our N.K.V.D. network in Sweden. For the first time in my career, I came into close touch with the operations of Soviet espionage abroad. I copied the reports of agents, typed out directives from Moscow and read the reports of our Soviet contact men. All the same, this was office work, paper work. I did not at first experience the danger or have the responsibility of going out into the field and meeting our agents face to face on foreign soil in defiance of the Swedish police and Counter-Intelligence. This was the situation under our first N.K.V.D. chief, Yartsev, and then under his energetic wife who carried on when he was recalled ahead to Moscow.

But when Razin arrived and took over from Mrs Yartsev as N.K.V.D. chief in Sweden I was given a new and important assignment. Razin was a highly competent Intelligence officer with a great deal of foreign experience. We got to know a lot about him from stories which he recounted, from office correspondence and from his personal dossier, which Volodya studied in connection with his S.K. duties. By accident, I also discovered a secret of Razin's personal life—with some amusing consequences.

Before the war Razin had been N.K.V.D. chief in Harbin, and later in Berlin, where, he told us, he had unmasked a Soviet agent who was double-crossing us and was actually working for the German Intelligence. In the nightmare years of the purges, 1937 and 1938, Razin fell under suspicion, along with almost every N.K.V.D. officer who had ever served abroad, and was dismissed. But he escaped the holocaust which swept so many N.K.V.D. officers to destruction and was allowed to work in the undistinguished post of a censor in an official publishing house. Eventually he was reinstated, perhaps owing to pressing wartime needs, and came out to Sweden as N.K.V.D. chief early in 1944.

On our return to Moscow we heard something of his subsequent history. After his term in Sweden, Razin was posted as N.K.V.D. chief to Finland and later to Germany. However, on his recall to Moscow he was once again under a cloud and received only a minor appointment in charge of a library.

This may have been due to the irregularities of his domestic life. Razin divorced his first wife, and lived in *de facto* wedlock with another woman, by whom he had a daughter. When he arrived in Sweden he was hoping to arrange for his *de facto* wife and their daughter to join him; correspondence between him and Moscow on this point passed through my hands. When a cable arrived to say that they would be arriving on a certain date, Razin was overjoyed. A second cable plunged him into the depths of despair. Moscow had discovered that a relative of his *de facto* wife had been arrested at some point and indicated that there was no longer any possibility of her being allowed to leave the Soviet Union because of this 'compromising material'. Razin was deeply depressed and was also very alarmed about his own future.

The gossip in the Embassy was that after a while he proposed to the eighteen-year-old daughter of our N.K.V.D. chauffeur, but that her parents put their foot down as they considered her too young for him.

Later, when I was visiting our agent 'Klara', I discovered through her that Razin was having an affair with an attractive and well-known Swedish woman. He was an intelligent and impressive man, liked and respected by his Embassy colleagues. In the office he was punctual, polite and efficient. He took care of his clothes and appearance. He was tall and broad with dark eyes, straight black hair, a round handsome face and a deeply-clefted chin. He spoke fluent English and German and, helped by his wide foreign experience, was a lively and versatile conversationalist. Finally (a quality not universal among Soviet men) he was respectful, even courtly, to ladies. His popularity with the Embassy women was not surprising.

From correspondence which I typed I learnt of a certain 'Maria', a girl whom Razin had met in a theatre and was studying with a view to

At Mascot airfield Mrs Petrov is hustled to her plane by
Russian officials

Evdokia Petrov

Vladimir Petrov

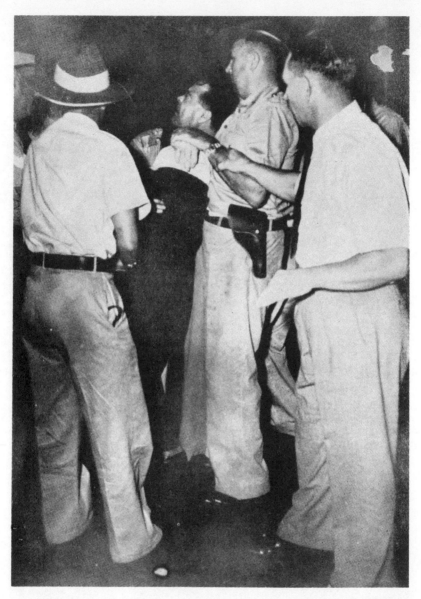

Australian police disarm Mrs Petrov's escort at Darwin airfield

her ultimate recruitment as a Soviet agent. When I came into the picture, he had requested and obtained Moscow's approval to hand over the study of 'Maria' to Lena Kondakova.

Lena was the Ambassador's secretary and it was generally believed among our staff that the Ambassador's wife kept a close and jealous eye on her. Certainly she and Lena were inseparable. Lena was about twenty-five, short and slight, with blue eyes and brown hair that fell very attractively over her shapely forehead, and she had a beautiful mouth. But alas! her nose ruined the effect. It was so crooked that every time I stood in front of her I had an almost irresistible desire to put it straight and had to restrain myself. Lena had spent some time in the United States; and after her return to Moscow from Sweden she was dismissed from the Ministry of Foreign Affairs because of some unguarded remarks she had made about the gaiety and freedom of the social life she had enjoyed in America.

Moscow agreed to Razin's proposal because Lena had been secretly co-opted as an N.K.V.D. assistant. She took over the study of 'Maria' and had several meetings with her. But soon her dual functions began to involve her in difficulty and embarrassment. The Ambassador did not know of her N.K.V.D. role and he became suspicious of Lena's close association with a foreigner, which was discovered when one of the Embassy staff called unexpectedly at Lena's flat and found 'Maria' there. Before long Lena complained to Razin and asked him to relieve her of her embarrassing task, which he agreed to do.

I will never forget the morning when Razin walked into my room in the N.K.V.D. office with a Moscow cable in his hand.

'Doosia, I have some important news for you. I proposed to Moscow that you should take over the running of Maria and Moscow have approved. Are you happy to accept the assignment?'

I said, 'Yes, of course. I am happy to serve in any way I can.'

In fact, my heart was beating with a tumult of nervousness and elation, but chiefly elation. This was by far the most important and delicate task I had yet been entrusted with in my whole State Security career. The nervousness was natural. The elation was twofold. In the first place I felt flattered, as any girl in my position would have done, at this evidence of official confidence in my professional skill and capabilities. In the second place, and with a particular personal intensity, I felt a surge of relief and gratification at this important indication that I now enjoyed the trust of Moscow and that the black mark on my record was not to be a life sentence. I determined to put everything I had into making a success of my new assignment.

My 'cover' for my meetings with 'Maria' was to be that which Lena
had also used, the exchange of language lessons. I was studying
Swedish, Maria wanted to learn Russian, of which she had some knowledge. For ordinary conversation we used English.

On the date arranged, I went to Lena's flat. Present 'Maria' arrived
and we were introduced, she, of course, by her right name, I as 'Mrs
Petrov'. Maria was Jewish; she was young, dark, attractive and intelligent and was cordial towards me from the start.

My meetings with her were quite open and took place each week,
either at her flat or mine. Any efforts at secrecy on my part would have
been pointless. At this stage my whole protection was our mutual
exchange of language lessons. Maria's parents were often at home when
I called on her and Volodya was sometimes present when she came to
see me.

All the same, it was with a beating heart that I made my way to our
first lesson and climbed the stairs to Maria's flat. She opened the door
in answer to my knock and led me to her room. Maria lived with her
parents in an unpretentious, old-fashioned, four-roomed flat which
would have been spacious in Moscow and which in Sweden represented a moderate middle-class standard of comfort. Her father was
in business of some kind. At my first visit Maria introduced me to
her parents, who were always very friendly towards me; they showed
no special curiosity about my friendship with Maria and used to ask me
about the Soviet Union without displaying any noticeable anti-Soviet
or pro-Soviet feelings.

Maria had her own small room modestly furnished with wardrobe,
dressing table, curtains and all the essentials of a girl's bedroom. Round
the walls she had hung bas-reliefs of famous composers. I found that
Maria, like so many of her race, was musical and sometimes after our
lessons she would sit down at the piano and play things for me, including some Chopin pieces which I particularly liked.

Soon Maria and I became real friends. Nevertheless on my side, as I
well understood from the beginning, there could be no such thing as a
merely personal relationship. My friendship with Maria was a planned
operation, approved, controlled and directed by Moscow. It was
tactical from the start. And yet, strangely, or perhaps naturally, that did
not alter the fact that I really did like Maria, and was sorry when our
friendship came to an end.

Through my chief, Razin, I was in constant touch with Moscow
about the development of my association with Maria, with the specific
aim of recruiting her as a spy for the Soviet. The three stages, as I knew

well enough already, were Study, Indoctrination and Recruitment. Conscious of the importance of my mission, both for my career and for the Soviet Union, I put my best into the project. I planned each step in discussion with Razin and in the light of the latest Moscow instructions and after each meeting I wrote a careful report which Razin forwarded, with his comments, to N.K.V.D. Headquarters in Moscow.

The first stage of 'studying' Maria was relatively straightforward. I had to supply Moscow with any scrap of detail about her which I could discover—her full name, parents' names, date of birth, friends and associates, her hobbies, tastes, weaknesses and needs. At the same time I had to gain her friendship and confidence. Before long I noticed that the wrist-watch which Maria wore was old and battered and I proposed to Moscow that for her birthday I should give her a new watch. Moscow approved and with N.K.V.D. funds I bought Maria a nice stainless-steel wrist-watch. She was thrilled and delighted and always said that she liked it even better than my own gold Omega. At other times I sent her flowers, for which she always thanked me most warmly.

During our lessons I gradually discovered a great deal about Maria's personal life and about her work. Maria was a secretary in the Swedish Ministry of Foreign Affairs. I got to know names and particulars of other girls who worked with her, the times when she did night duty and the sort of material that passed through her hands. Maria was already a valuable source of information to us but she was still an 'in the dark' (that is—unconscious) source. The delicate task of winning her consent to be a conscious source of information to the Soviet Union still remained to be accomplished.

The preparatory, or softening-up, process is known in Soviet Intelligence language as 'Indoctrination' and is considered essential before any approach is made. The subject must be 'ideologically prepared'; that is, imbued with a reasoned conviction of the rightness of the Soviet cause and the necessity of assisting it in every way possible.

Urged on by Moscow, who suggested that I was not sufficiently aggressive in this matter of indoctrination, I set about the ideological preparation of Maria for recruitment to our service. I worked to a standard plan, adapted to her particular situation.

As she was Jewish, I lost no opportunity of mentioning the privileged position enjoyed by Jews in our country and I told her about the privileges and status of the more than seventy other different nationalities within the Soviet Union. This was all new ground to Maria. She listened with interest to all I had to say. Then, according to pattern, I depicted the sharp contrast between conditions in Sweden and the Soviet Union. I described the great new buildings in Moscow, the vast development projects in the Soviet Union, the Soviet Constitution and the rights it guaranteed, the absence of unemployment, the free medical treatment, holidays on full pay, maternity benefits and women's rights. I represented the Soviet Union in such glowing colours that Maria was impressed and amazed and often exclaimed, 'We could never do that here.'

Finally I held up the Soviet Union as the one great champion of peace among the nations of the world. I reminded her that it was Hitler who had attacked us, not we who had attacked Hitler and told her that Hitler's Germany and other capitalist countries all aimed to destroy the Soviet Union and to capture the world's markets. 'We in the Soviet Union have no wish to impose our form of government on other countries,' I told her. 'The slogan of our Government is peace. We are dedicated to the struggle for peace. All people everywhere who are against war should rally to assist the Soviet Union in the most practical, energetic and courageous way they can. All those who do so will be considered as real friends by our great Soviet Union and will be given every assistance.'

Maria would listen with interest and seemed sympathetic to all I had to say. She had not thought a great deal about such matters herself, but it was clear that she liked me and seemed convinced by my arguments.

As for myself, I knew well enough that many of my arguments were propaganda, but I was acting under instructions; they were part of my job.

We had many lessons and conversations over the course of a year or so, and became closer and closer friends. My cultivation of Maria might have continued in this way for years, for it is characteristic of Soviet Intelligence to be prepared to wait, but circumstances outside our control brought the case to a head.

One day Maria arrived at my flat with a sparkle in her eye and burst out at once:

'Doosia, I have some exciting news. I am soon to be posted abroad, somewhere in Eastern Europe!'

'Oh, congratulations! Are you glad?'

'Oh yes, I'm very excited about it. Apart from the extra foreign service allowance, I've always wanted to go abroad and see the world. I'm thrilled at the prospect.'

I discussed the new development with Razin and we agreed that the time had come. We sent off a cable to Moscow proposing that before

Maria went abroad an attempt should be made to recruit her as a conscious agent of the Soviet Union. Moscow agreed and suggested that Volodya should recruit her. However, when we pointed out that, whereas he hardly knew her, Maria and I were intimate friends, they agreed that I should attempt the recruitment. Moscow also agreed that the attempt should be made at her flat, not mine, for fear of observation or microphoning of my flat by the Swedish Counter-Intelligence.

It was a beautiful, mild August evening when I climbed the stairs for my last fateful lesson with Maria. She greeted me warmly and we went to her room where the open window let in the soft air of the summer night. Inwardly I was tense with excitement but outwardly I was my usual self. At least, Maria did not appear to notice anything unusual; she was as friendly as ever and was elated at the prospect of her trip.

As had been our recent practice, we spent an hour on Swedish, then an hour on Russian; after which our talk drifted to general topics—her preparations for going abroad, how busy she was, what was happening in her office, what night-duty she still had to complete.

I thought, 'Here goes, it's now or never.'

I said to her, 'Maria, when you are working on night duty, are you ever visited by anyone, or are you alone?'

'Oh, it's usually very quiet,' she answered, 'but you never know. My boss sometimes works till the early hours of the morning. He may call for something I'm typing, or want me to take dictation. Why?'

'I'll tell you in a minute. I want to talk to you about something very important.'

My tone must have conveyed a lot. Maria sat still and looked at me in surprise.

'Maria, you've known a number of us from the Soviet Embassy—Razin, Lena, myself—and you and I have had some very frank talks about things, haven't we? I mean especially about the warlike plans of the capitalist countries against the peace-loving Soviet Union. Now that the war is over, there ought to be peace, but it isn't enough just to wish for peace. Everyone who really wants peace must be active in fighting for it.'

Maria nodded, slightly puzzled. We had talked like this before, but there was a new urgency in my voice. I went on, 'War is a terrible thing. Even here in neutral Sweden you have felt the effects of war, though the effects here are negligible compared with the sufferings of the Russian people. Why have you escaped? Because your Government deceived the people. They allowed German troops to pass through

Sweden. They collaborated with Hitler. Otherwise the Nazis would have overrun Sweden. Maria, you are Jewish. Think what dreadful cruelties you would have suffered under the Nazis!'

That touched her. She turned pale. I followed up my chance. 'There is only one way to fight for peace—by helping the Soviet Union, which stands for peace, against its warlike enemies. There are many ways to help the Soviet Union. It may be by campaigning for peace or it may be with information. The more information the Soviet Union has about the plans of its enemies, the more hope there is that its fight for peace will succeed.'

'Doosia, what do you mean? What sort of information?' She was staring at me open-eyed. I pressed on resolutely.

'I mean this, Maria. The Soviet Union needs to know what secret treaties there are between capitalist countries which threaten it. It also needs to know in advance the secret discussions on treaties which are being negotiated between itself and foreign countries. At this moment, as you know, your Department is negotiating a treaty between the Soviet Union and Sweden. Maria, can you get me copies of these drafts and discussions and of other material which will help the Soviet Union? From what you have told me, you are alone most of the time when you are on night duty. It should be quite easy. This would help the Soviet very much. Of course, it would be an absolutely secret matter between you, me and my boss. No one else would know.'

At these last words her face clouded; she realized beyond all doubt what I was asking her to do.

'Doosia, I'm afraid you don't understand. It would be quite impossible for me to copy documents. And in any case I don't think there would be anything of interest to the Soviet.'

I braced myself.

'Why is it impossible, Maria? Perhaps you don't realize what is of interest to the Soviet Union and what is not. I'm not asking you to decide that question; I'm simply asking you to supply the copies.'

Maria shrank and tried another tack.

'No, I don't think I could help you, really. As you know, I'm going abroad very soon. Time is short.'

'You might be able to help us in your new post. But, in any case, couldn't you let me have the drafts of this treaty before you go?'

Maria shook her head.

'Why not, Maria? Are you afraid? I can assure you that no one else need ever know. And if the worst did happen, you could count on help from us.'

'No, no! I couldn't get anything you would want; and I'd be too frightened anyway. I can't do it.'

'Well, don't decide in haste. Think it over, Maria, and let me know later.'

But Maria recovered herself and said firmly and officially, 'This is my final decision.'

I realized that my attempt had failed and that it was no use pressing her further.

My disappointment turned to alarm, as I reflected that there was nothing to prevent Maria reporting on me to her parents or to the Swedish police. I took a grip on myself. It was my turn to be firm.

'Very well, Maria, as you choose. We are still friends, I hope. Of course, you won't say a word to anyone, even to your parents, about this conversation of ours. If it came to the ears of the police, or of your Department, they would immediately suspect you, even though you denied it. You might be sacked from your job, or even arrested; certainly they wouldn't let you go abroad. For me it would be embarrassing but not serious. At the worst your Government might declare me *persona non grata* and I would be recalled to the Soviet Union.'

This was a piece of bluff on my part. Actually I was liable to arrest by the Swedish police. I was a humble Embassy worker, not a diplomat, and I had not the immunity that goes with diplomatic status. It could have been very serious for me indeed. I meant to frighten Maria for this reason, and also to prevent her being indiscreet and doing harm to herself, for I liked her as a person and did not want her to suffer.

That was how Maria and I parted. Two days later she went abroad. Before she left I sent her some roses and a card wishing her good luck for her trip. In the past she had always written to thank me, but this time there was no reply.

I reported the failure of my attempted recruitment to Moscow, who made no special comment. Such attempts and failures were all in the day's work, and were minor incidents in the vast, unceasing, worldwide espionage campaign which the Soviet Union wages against the non-Soviet world.

I have not seen or heard of her from that day to this. I was genuinely sorry to end my friendship with Maria, whose conversation and company I enjoyed. But, after all, I was in Sweden not as a private tourist but as the wife of a Soviet Intelligence officer, and as a Lieutenant of State Security on active operational service. To the best of my ability I had carried out the duty assigned to me.

My other agent, Klara, was quite a different kettle of fish. She was not an inexperienced, ingenuous girl like Maria, who had to be carefully cultivated and educated to prepare her for the Soviet service. Klara was a mature woman, a convinced, indoctrinated Communist, and a Soviet agent of long standing and experience. There were no psychological problems in my dealings with Klara; we understood one another perfectly. On the other hand, since she was an active productive agent, supplying me with documentary material for transmission to Moscow, the problems of espionage technique and operational secrecy became all-important.

Our chief, Razin, had been contact-man for Klara before I took over, but when he heard that he was to be posted to Finland he sent off a cable to Moscow proposing that I should succeed him. In support of his proposal he mentioned that I knew English (which was important, as most of Klara's material was in English); that I was now familiar with Swedish conditions and that in appearance and speech I could easily be taken for a Swedish woman. This was a fact. Perhaps because I was a blonde and studied local fashions in clothes, women several times came up to ask me the way in Stockholm, assuming that I was a native. And with the Swedish language I had picked up the local accent and intonation so well that shop assistants often assumed that I was a Swedish housewife.

'Moscow approves,' Razin told me a few days later, 'so you will take over the running of Klara. I'll introduce you.'

Again I was pleased and flattered. I had seen enough of the case to know that Klara was highly regarded, in fact was considered one of our best Soviet agents in Sweden at that time.

Razin drove me through the streets of Stockholm in his car which he parked in a narrow side lane near the heart of the city. We got out and walked carefully but casually to our appointment. Having taken precautions to see that we were not being followed, and choosing a moment when there was no one else visible in the street, we went into the building. To avoid meeting anyone in the lift we climbed the stairs to Klara's flat. She was expecting us and opened the door immediately.

Our first meeting was brief and to the point. Razin introduced me simply as 'Doosia', her new contact. Arrangements were made for our next meeting, and we left.

Even at our first brief acquaintance I took to Klara and at our subsequent meetings I got to like her more and more. I sensed a complete understanding between us. Klara belonged to the number of seasoned

cosmopolitan Communist agents who in the past have served the Soviet
Union so well. From her friendly attitude to me as a Soviet official, and
from our conversations generally, I formed the impression that she was
sincerely pro-Soviet. She had visited Moscow and spoke with enthusiasm of her experiences there. I had no doubt that she had been well
received in N.K.V.D. circles and had been made to feel the importance of
her services to the Soviet Union. Klara's wide contacts were her principal value to us. She supplied a steady stream of political information,
including gossip and character sketches of potential recruits, which
Moscow regarded as highly important. She received regular payments
out of N.K.V.D. funds for these services, but I always felt that her main
motive was ideological, not mercenary.

One amusing episode occurred during our association. In the course
of her researches, Klara discovered and reported that an attractive
Swedish woman with whom she was friendly was having a love affair
with my chief Razin.

I returned with this titbit of information and discussed it with
Volodya, before taking the report in to the Embassy. It posed quite a
thorny problem, in view of Volodya's 's.K.' functions as a watchdog on
the loyalty and behaviour of Soviet officials.

The next day I handed over the latest information from Klara, including this report, to Razin, as was my custom.

Soon afterwards he came over to my desk. It was comical to see the
mixture of casualness and embarrassment in his manner as he approached me.

'Doosia, I am studying these latest reports from Klara. Have you
read them yet yourself?'

'No, I have not had time, but I will do so as soon as you have finished
with them.'

'Yes, yes . . . Well, I will hand them on to you in due course; there's
no hurry . . .' His relief at my answer was highly amusing. I never saw
the report about the woman again. I have no doubt that Razin destroyed it.

Volodya pondered what to do about the matter. Strictly speaking
he was bound to report all such s.K. matters, and such a liaison with a
foreigner, unless conducted for Intelligence purposes and with the
approval of Moscow, amounted to a very serious lapse. However, as all
his s.K. reports had to be submitted to his chief Razin, he decided to do
othing—especially as he knew from his wife that the matter in question *had* been reported to Razin.

We were forced to the conclusion that even a supervisory system as close and pervasive as that of the Soviet Union was unable to cope with every contingency.

I had two methods of meeting Klara, one at her flat, when we had matters which required discussion, the other at various rendezvous in the city, when we did not speak to each other but merely effected the transfer of material between us.

Whenever I had an appointment at Klara's flat, I would leave the office an hour or two earlier than usual, on the pretext of doing some shopping and would go home first.

We had a simple telephone code as a safeguard for our meetings. If the meeting we had previously arranged was to take place as arranged, Klara would ring me at home at a fixed time. I would lift the receiver and answer 'Hullo' two or three times; if there was no answer, it meant that Klara was signalling to me, 'All clear'. If the arrangement had to be altered, Klara would not ring at the fixed time; that meant that I would not ring back, but would call on her at a time which had been previously arranged in case of such an emergency.

From home I would go to the centre of the city, which was fifteen minutes' walk, or five minutes by tram. Before approaching Klara's street I always took elaborate precautions against surveillance. I would visit several shops, sometimes buying something, sometimes just looking at things; I would look out into the street and watch the door to see if anyone suspicious followed me into the shop.

Owing to her influential contacts, Klara would be an object of immediate interest to the Swedish Counter-Intelligence if it were found that she was in regular contact with an official of the Soviet Embassy and, though she herself always seemed confident, I never shook off my nervous fear of detection.

When the only business which Klara had to transact with me was to hand over material, we would arrange to meet in the book section of a big department store. Our usual procedure was as follows: I would go first to the store, make my way to the book department, go up to a counter where I saw there was no salesman in attendance and put my handbag on the counter. Klara, who had sighted me outside the store, would follow me in, come up to the same counter and stand near me. She would put her report, folded very small, on the counter. I would immediately palm it and put it in my handbag as soon as I was satisfied that I was not under observation. If a salesman came up I would ask about some book, examine a few and sometimes buy one. I usually left the shop some little time after Klara.

These meetings were usually in the middle of the day when there were numbers of shoppers about. Once the report was in my possession I would go straight to the Embassy and put it in our safe for translation into Russian at the earliest opportunity. Then I submitted it to my N.K.V.D. chief, who would dispatch it, with his comments, to Moscow.

On an average I must have had two meetings a month with Klara, most of them at her flat, over a period of two years. Throughout that time I took the strictest precautions, even though I never detected any evidence of observation or interest in us on the part of the Swedish authorities.

About the end of 1946 I transmitted instructions from Moscow to Klara transferring her to Yugoslavia, where she would be contacted by our Soviet representative. But after she had left we discovered to our dismay that she had arranged for her flat to be occupied by a friend who was also a Soviet agent. This sort of private arrangement between agents without any reference to their controllers was severely frowned on by Moscow. Klara had been paid a large sum of money for her mission, but after three or four months she reappeared in Stockholm and rang me up quite out of the blue. Again she had apparently acted without any reference to, or direction from, Moscow. It further appeared that Moscow had become suspicious about Klara's sojourn in Yugoslavia, where she had not renewed operational contact with the N.K.V.D. Resident.

I resumed my meetings with Klara and found her as friendly and cooperative as ever. But Moscow's suspicions about her remained and when I handed her over to the new N.K.V.D. chief, Kirsanov, just before we left Sweden, we were under instructions to handle her with care.

On that fragmentary and inconclusive note my association with Klara came to an end.

For the two important operational tasks represented by my work with Maria and Klara I received no word of commendation from Moscow. I did not expect or require it. Where praise is rare as diamonds and blame swift and severe, it was sufficient comment that I was allowed to continue without reprimand.

XVII

Swedish Spider's Web

MY WIFE has already described the contrast between our first impressions of Sweden and official Soviet teaching about conditions in capitalist countries. No Soviet citizen who visits a Western country can remain deceived on this point. But I had an amusing experience which underlined the true situation.

A Soviet choir, ninety strong, under the baton of the famous Professor Sveshnikov, visited Sweden during our time there and was a huge popular success. The Swedish audiences flocked to hear its resonant, unaccompanied singing and the box office showed a handsome profit after the expenses of the tour had been met. I knew a good deal about the tour, as we had thirteen co-opted agents in the choir, keeping an eye on the other members, and the choir manager, Kambulov, was a permanent N.K.V.D. officer.

I was attached to this choir for a time as guide and interpreter and visited several cities with it. The majority of the choir members were girls and at the conclusion of the tour my wife and I took them shopping in groups of six or seven. Up to this time they had been confined to their hotels and had not had any spending money of their own. It was an extraordinary sight to see our Soviet girls rummaging through huge piles of clothing heaped on the counters—dresses, underwear, stockings—in front of the amazed Swedish shop assistants. The poor girls had only enough money to buy one or two things out of this fantastic treasure and they suffered agonies of indecision which were painful to witness. How we ever got them out of the shop I do not remember.

Even Professor Sveshnikov, the conductor and choirmaster, who came with me to buy two suits, was overcome. The problem of choosing two out of the abundance and variety of suits presented to him was too much. Without some advice from me, as one now more acclimatized to this economy of abundance, I doubt if he would ever have been able to make up his mind.

Sweden's material prosperity could partly be explained by her neutrality in the war. But there were other more fundamental things. We at the Soviet Embassy were constantly astonished at the unpretentiousness of Swedish public men which surprised us all the more when we contrasted it with the wall of pomp, privilege and protection that surrounded every public figure in the Soviet Union. There, a Molotov or a Vyshinsky inhabited a luxurious guarded villa at the end of a constantly patrolled road. There, the population of Moscow saw little of its leaders other than the fleets of armed cars, for whose passage all traffic was cleared from the streets. A fleeting glimpse of the great man, hurrying from car to office entrance, was the most one could expect.

But in prosperous Sweden, where we had been taught to look for a governing class of privileged magnates, the leaders actually put democratic principles into practice. Their salaries were no greater than those paid to rank and file members of our own Embassy and, instead of having official cars, they travelled by public transport or other humble popular means of conveyance. While we were in Sweden, the Swedish Prime Minister, Per Albin Hansson, had a heart attack and died in a tram on his way to a Cabinet meeting. Borman, the Swedish Minister for Foreign Affairs, was a personal friend of our Ambassador, Madame Kollontai. She would ring him and ask for an appointment and he, in deference to her ill-health, would mount his bicycle and ride over to our Embassy to call on her.

We were amazed and mystified. My friend Chernov would say to me, 'Now what do you make of that? Here the Foreign Minister rides round on a bicycle and in Moscow every tin-pot official has a car and two chauffeurs at his disposal!' It gave us much food for thought. But thought is one thing, talk is another. Besides, I had urgent duties.

I had come out to Sweden already charged with an important 's.k.' operation—the investigation of our Ambassador, Madame Kollontai, a distinguished personality and a figure of world-wide renown. The case, for which I was directly responsible, was a good example of the effort which the Soviet Government devotes, quite apart from any espionage against foreign countries, to the secret surveillance of its own emissaries. I studied Madame Kollontai's file in Moscow and was well briefed in the case before I left. The inside story has lain hidden in the secret archives of the M.V.D. until this moment.

Very few Soviet diplomats can claim such a long and devoted career in the service of the Revolution as Madame Kollontai. Her name figured in our prescribed 'History of the Communist Party of the Soviet Union' and my wife and I were both personally curious to see this white-haired old lady of seventy-two, by that time paralysed and restricted to a wheel-chair, but still energetic in mind, who was an old comrade of Lenin, and a legendary figure from the early days of the Revolution.

Born into an intellectual middle-class family, she had thrown herself into the revolutionary movement while still a girl. Under Lenin's rule, when the revolutionary government had seized power, she became Minister for Social Services. Then, when it became necessary to establish diplomatic relations with other countries, she was appointed Soviet Minister to Norway, and later to Sweden. When we arrived she had already served there for eighteen years.

At a celebration in our Russian Club in 1944 she was present with a former Consul, Smirnov, who before 1917 had hidden Lenin in his house from the pursuing Czarist police. Smirnov spoke of Lenin as a man who never considered himself, but gave his whole life to the revolutionary cause. Madame Kollontai described Lenin when he was Chairman of the Council of People's Commissars—firm and decisive as a chairman, but when business was concluded, just one of the comrades. Vividly they conjured up the spirit of an heroic era.

As a Soviet Ambassador Madame Kollontai showed outstanding qualities, both as a leader and a representative. Inside the Embassy she took a human and detailed interest in the welfare of all her subordinates. She interviewed me personally on my first day, asked with solicitude about our hazardous journey and advised me to take full advantage of the ample food supplies in Sweden to build up my health. Her curled white hair and wrinkled face, paralysed on the right side, did not conceal the keen intelligence in her eyes.

'I urge you, Mr Petrov, not to be foolish, as some of our people are, who stint themselves of necessities in order to buy things to take back to the Soviet Union. Health is all important; look after yourselves while you are here.'

Thereafter she always greeted me and remembered my name. She showed an equal concern for the well-being of the lower ranks on the staff, chauffeurs, doorkeepers and their families and she even insisted on food and drink being offered to the Swedish policeman who had to stand duty in front of our Embassy building.

She was always reasonable and polite in her dealings with the staff, even when reproving them. When she was away ill, the rude, hectoring manner of her deputy, Semyonov, made everyone appreciate the Ambassador's courtesy.

With the Swedes, Madame Kollontai, who knew their language and their ways so intimately, was extremely popular. She had friends and contacts in all important sections of Swedish life, including government, business and intellectual and educational circles. These open, friendly contacts were an enormous asset in the discharge of her official responsibility for keeping the Soviet Government informed on Swedish affairs.

It was an education to see how Madame Kollontai went about her work. As soon as she received some specific commission from Moscow —for example, an assessment of Swedish views on neutrality—she would summon her First Secretary, and set the problem before him. Then she would discuss how he could best go about it—perhaps by inviting his friends in the Swedish Foreign Office to lunch and raising the subject, without alarming them by too direct questioning. She would go through the same process with each member of the Embassy diplomatic corps individually. Finally, she would explore the matter herself among her numerous influential friends.

Her aim was to discover the capabilities and contacts of all her diplomatic staff and to encourage them to broaden their touch with the Swedes. This served an immediate practical purpose, and it was also most valuable training for them.

When all the staff had completed their researches, she would collect every scrap of information that had been gleaned and would compile a comprehensive report that could hardly be faulted.

I can testify to this from personal knowledge. Though I was not a diplomat, our N.K.V.D. office had co-opted workers who secretly brought us copies of all the diplomatic cables. Razin and I would read Madame Kollontai's reports to Moscow with admiration and astonishment, and I remember Razin exclaiming in rueful amazement, 'Now where in hell's name does an old woman get information like that?'

It was a revelation of what could be done through friendly contacts and systematic open researches, as against the elaborate conspiratorial secrecy of our own methods.

Madame Kollontai's offence was certainly not inefficiency. It is difficult to see how the Soviet Union could have found a better Ambassador to Sweden. At bottom, it was the length of time which she had spent abroad, and the close and cordial relations which she had established with her Swedish friends, that brought down on her the uneasy suspicions of Moscow. She had a devoted Swedish woman secretary-companion, a Swedish chauffeur and a Russian cook who had lived most of her life in Sweden. These were the immediate causes of Moscow's apprehensions. But once suspicion is aroused, it quickly discovers new reasons for its existence. How far politics at the highest level, in the shape of Stalin's deep jealousy of Lenin, were involved, I cannot say.

But from a study of Madame Kollontai's file in Moscow I had discovered that in her early revolutionary days she had contracted a *de facto* marriage with Dybenko, one of the old Bolsheviks, who was Commanding Officer of the Leningrad Military District, and they had a son. Dybenko, along with almost all the Bolshevik Old Guard, was arrested and shot in 1936 on a charge of Trotskyist activities. In notes for her memoirs, which I later saw, Madame Kollontai recorded her grief at Dybenko's execution, and her incredulity that her late husband and old revolutionary comrade was really a traitor to the Revolution.

Apart from this, Moscow feared that Madame Kollontai was too sympathetic to the Swedes and to Swedish interests and policy. The object was to get her back to Soviet territory where she could be adequately controlled, and at the same time to avoid any action which might produce adverse publicity in the Western countries—a real factor in the case of so famous a personality as Madame Kollontai.

Moscow's first move was a general instruction to stations abroad that all foreign employees, including servants and chauffeurs, were to be dismissed and replaced by Soviet citizens. Madame Kollontai's Swedish chauffeur, Vistrim, who had been with her for many years, had to go. He was devoted to her and wept when he was informed of his dismissal. Another old retainer, her Norwegian housemaid, was also dismissed.

Soon afterwards a new secretary was sent out from Moscow. She was actually a permanent N.K.V.D. officer, whose real task was to keep the Ambassador under observation. Her code name was 'Yelena' and it was intended that she should replace Madame Kollontai's Swedish secretary. But the old lady circumvented this move. She insisted on keeping the latter as her personal private secretary, whom she paid out of her own pocket; she valued her companionship and took her with her whenever she went to the sanatorium at Saltsjö-Baden. With the new secretary she was polite, correct and guarded. Yelena kept us regularly informed of Madame Kollontai's visitors and conversations, but nothing in any way compromising came to light.

The next direction we got from Moscow was to obtain the notes and drafts of Madame Kollontai's memoirs, which it was known she was writing. Razin and I had to plan this operation, which did not involve physical risk, but was delicate, because of the necessity, stressed by Moscow, that Madame Kollontai should get no inkling of it. In the end we managed it successfully, with Yelena's assistance, during the Ambassador's absence. The notes were in a locked chest in her apartment in the Embassy building. The lock offered no difficulty, but the notes were very voluminous and it took us three nights' work to go through them thoroughly and photograph every page before replacing them and locking the chest again. The photographing was done by Vassiliev, whose overt function was Night Duty Officer, but who was a technical expert, and operated a secret radio set from his flat on the top floor of the Embassy. Moscow was very pleased with our success in this operation. It was from these notes that I learnt of Kollontai's feelings about the execution of Dybenko.

She was ill and paralysed by this time and shortly afterwards she was recalled to Moscow and her successor Chernyshev came out. Her Swedish doctor, Fru Nelson, insisted on accompanying her and was granted a visa by Moscow, and Madame Kollontai particularly requested that her Swedish secretary also join her. The secretary was eventually provided with a Soviet passport and followed her to the U.S.S.R.

On arrival in Moscow, Madame Kollontai was given official quarters, was maintained in honourable comfort and acted as consultant to the Government on Swedish affairs. That was her situation when my wife and I left Moscow. She died on 9th March 1952 and was buried with full State honours. She was probably saved by the absence of any real incriminating evidence against her and by her prominence and popularity abroad. Had she been younger, or less distinguished, she might have been imprisoned or relegated to some distant post as a precautionary measure. As things were, the Soviet Government stood to lose more than it would gain by purging her. It is certain that no other consideration mattered a straw with those who had to decide her fate.

The episode of Madame Kollontai's cook provides a small but pathetic postscript to the whole story. Anna Ivanovna was born in Russia, but while still a girl in pre-Revolutionary days she had gone as maid to a Russian family living in Finland. Madame Kollontai found her there and took her into her household. Anna had been her cook for seventeen years when we arrived in Sweden, and a first-rate cook she was. She had won a Swedish award for her professional skill and many foreign guests of the Soviet Ambassador had reason to enjoy the excellent dinners which she provided for her mistress's table.

All the Embassy staff knew Anna Ivanovna, the cook. Whenever anyone went into the kitchen she would come forward beaming with some sample or morsel and say, 'How do you like this?', or 'Try a bit of that'. She was large, fat, kindly and ordinary; not even her best friends claimed that Anna was attractive.

Nevertheless, she longed to have a child, and when one of the Embassy doorkeepers, a single man, began to pay attention to her she was not unresponsive. After a while Anna had her wish and had a child, a daughter. There was no question of marriage. Anna did not blame the father of her child, or try to get alimony from him. She named the child Alexandra after Madame Kollontai, but everyone called her by her pet name 'Lulya'. It was delightful to see Anna's happiness and pride in her daughter Lulya.

Anna had one other great desire, to visit her native country which she had left at such an early age. She was an orphan and her only relative was a sister living in Leningrad. But she was suspect in Moscow's eyes, on account of her long sojourn abroad, and we had her under study along with the rest of Madame Kollontai's entourage. When Madame Kollontai returned to the Soviet Union, Anna stayed on as cook to the new Ambassador and as her child grew she had to consider her future. She had saved quite a sum of money and was considering buying a restaurant in Sweden, where she was comfortable and happy. Moreover, she feared that she would not get a job if she did return to the U.S.S.R., having been so long away.

At this point our N.K.V.D. headquarters decided that it would be safer if Anna Ivanovna did return. A letter arrived in Madame Kollontai's handwriting giving her a rosy picture of conditions, assuring her that she and her daughter would be well looked after, and inviting her to resume her old position as Madame Kollontai's cook. Just how it was done I do not know but there is no doubt that the letter was written under official direction.

That turned the scales, and poor Anna Ivanovna took Lulya and departed for the Soviet Union. I heard later that she had not got the job as Madame Kollontai's cook, and had gone to Leningrad to her sister. She must have found life very hard after the comfort and security which she had enjoyed in Sweden.

Our headquarters suspected that she was an agent of the Swedish Counter-Intelligence. On their instructions we had studied her minutely and had directed some of our co-opted S.K. agents to investigate her; but all our efforts did not produce the slightest evidence of suspicious activities or intentions on the part of Anna Ivanovna. In my opinion she was just a cook.

The most important and productive work which I did in discharge of my 'S.K.' responsibilities for the surveillance of Soviet officials and citizens in Sweden was connected with my agent 'Misha'. I met Misha on an average once a month for a period of three years and I know that Moscow rated him very high as a source of information in his appointed field.

Misha was a Soviet naval officer with the rank of Junior Captain and had been secretly recruited as an N.K.V.D. agent in Kronstadt. He had arrived in Sweden early in the war with a group of Soviet trawlers whose crews were interned for the duration and he had immediately reported to the Soviet Naval Attaché. Since I had the appropriate code-name of 'Moriak' (meaning 'sailor') it was not surprising that Moscow agreed with our Resident's suggestion that I should take over the running of the agent Misha, and I was accordingly introduced to him on his next visit to the Embassy. He impressed me immediately. He was a tall, broad-shouldered, strongly built fellow, well educated and very direct and forthright in his manner. The honesty and thoroughness of his reports were evident from the start. He worked from a sense of duty, and asked for only such money as was required to cover his expenses. Misha kept Moscow admirably informed about Soviet internees in Sweden, who quickly divided into two camps, the pro-Soviet and the anti-Soviet. Misha, on our instructions, joined the anti-Soviet party and made it his business to keep watch on the disaffected personnel.

My first step on taking over Misha was to tighten up the security of our contacting arrangements. I forbade him to meet me at the Embassy. Instead we met at various rendezvous in the city, including a lane off the Kungsgatan and a public lavatory off Humlegardsgatan. In the summer, we met at various places in the woods round Stockholm, usually on Sundays. I often rode to these meetings with rods and fishing gear strapped to my bicycle. At other times we made use of a hiding-place consisting of a simple tin box concealed in a crevice between two rocks. This was useful when, as happened once or twice, I thought I detected surveillance by the Swedish Counter-Intelligence and so did not keep my appointment with Misha.

In due course I learnt the background to Misha's internment in Sweden. As a serving naval officer, Misha had been sent to Dagoe Island, off the coast of Estonia, to take charge of the island's coastal defences. As the German bombing increased in intensity all the larger ships were withdrawn and finally it was decided to evacuate the island. As many men as possible were taken off in the three trawlers that remained. The rest were left behind and were taken prisoner by the Germans.

As the Luftwaffe commanded the Gulf of Finland, the commanding officer of the trawlers, considering that it would be suicidal to try to break through to the Soviet base of Kronstadt, decided to save the ships and men by making for neutral Sweden. But the *Politkom*, the Political Commissar, was fanatically insistent that they must try to get through to a Soviet port. The commanding officer conferred with his lieutenant, while Misha was present, and after some discussion ordered a Petty Officer to shoot the Political Commissar and throw his body overboard, which was promptly done.

On their arrival in Sweden, Misha, whose role was that of an observer during these proceedings, reported the episode to Moscow through our Embassy. Moscow then asked that the three trawler officers should be repatriated to the Soviet Union to answer the charges against them. The Swedish Government refused to send them back against their will, but tried them in a Swedish court. As there were no witnesses, and we could not expose our agent Misha, they were acquitted of the murder of the *Politkom*.

At the end of the war, the Soviet Government launched a great drive to get all internees and P.O.W's back to the Soviet Union. Our new Ambassador, Chernyshev, together with the Naval and Military Attachés, made a tour of the internment camps in Sweden, addressing all the Soviet internees and urging them to return. They were told that their internment was no fault of their own, but was simply the fortune of war; on their return to the U.S.S.R. they would be well treated, would get good jobs and would have nothing to fear. The internees were then lined up and were asked to take one pace forward to indicate that they wished to return to their Soviet homeland. Most of them did, mindful of family ties and their long absence; but in Misha's camp a party of about thirty, led by Basukov, refused.

Then Chernyshev, who was handsome, able and inexperienced, stepped forward and addressed them vehemently.

'Comrades—and I mean you who have just refused the generous offer made by the Soviet Government to restore you to your homeland, our glorious Soviet Union—I warn you now, that if you show yourselves so unpatriotic that you refuse to return of your own free will, you will be compelled to return under much less pleasant circumstances!'

It was a foolish line to take with men who for several years had imbibed the atmosphere of a free country.

At Chernyshev's words, several men who had stepped forward now stepped back and joined the group of non-returners.

The group who decided against returning were the realists. Chernyshev had unintentionally let slip the naked truth that all internees, like all prisoners of war, would be classed as deserters on their return, would be charged with spying, would be suspected of working for foreign intelligence services, and at the very least would be kept under constant watch wherever they went in the Soviet Union. In contrast they had enjoyed a better life as internees in Sweden than many of them had ever known before. They were adequately clothed and fed and were permitted to work and earn money with which to buy extras, and were under few restrictions. The men in Misha's camp had built a dance floor, formed a choir and entertained themselves and guests. Many of them had formed liaisons with Swedish girls, who appreciated the gaiety and prodigality which is an aspect of the Russian temperament, and after the war, when it was legally permissible, a number of the Soviet sailors married Swedish girls and settled down in Sweden.

But the majority chose to return to their country. They believed that they were innocent of any offence, had shown their loyalty by keeping in close touch with the Soviet Embassy during their internment and would therefore be well received in their homeland. In addition, most of them felt the powerful pull of family ties and the land where they were born.

One of the ships' engineers, Bogdanov, who had originally chosen to stay in Sweden, but who had an overpowering longing to see his wife and family again, changed his mind and came to the Embassy the following day, saying that he now wished to go home.

When we returned to Moscow on completion of our service in Sweden I was naturally interested to know what had actually happened to these sailors and other internees who had been repatriated. I got a clue as to their fate when I discovered that the mere notation of having been a P.O.W. on an application form was a bar to any decent employment. The best that ex-P.O.W's could hope for was some arduous, dangerous, or unwanted job. Then I began to piece together case-histories of ex-internees. I found that very few of them had ever seen their families again. Most of them had been sentenced to ten to fifteen years in corrective labour camps in remote frontier regions of the U.S.S.R. as punishment for their sojourn abroad and as a precaution against possible foreign sympathies. Among these deluded sufferers was the unhappy Bogdanov.

Misha's reports were so valued by Moscow that when General Yakovlev, chief of the Scandinavian Department of the N.K.V.D., paid a secret visit to our Swedish Residency, he asked to be introduced to Misha, in order to form a first-hand impression of his quality. It was Yakovlev who had briefed me on my S.K. duties before I left Moscow. After meeting Misha, Yakovlev spoke highly of him, and commended my work with him.

But Moscow's approval of its agents does not run to sentiment. Misha had left a wife and daughter behind in Leningrad and was desperately anxious to get in touch with them, hoping to send them food parcels from Sweden. We instituted inquiries through N.K.V.D. channels, but it was found that Misha's wife, believing him lost at sea, had married an Army doctor and was living at a new address in Leningrad.

Not wishing to upset their valuable agent, Moscow decided to tell Misha that his wife could not be traced and I had to convey this message to him. His distress was painful to see. He did not query the report and concluded that his wife and daughter had probably been killed in the bombing of Leningrad by the Germans. On previous occasions, when he had been pining to get back to the Soviet Union, I had had to tell him that his services in Sweden were more important to the Soviet Union than anything he could do at home. He had accepted the fact courageously, as an order from his superiors, with the attitude that 'duty is duty'.

Eventually Misha married a Swedish girl, with the knowledge and approval of Moscow. After I left Sweden, there was apparently some breakdown in the arrangements for contacting Misha, and in Canberra late in 1951, I received a cable from Moscow which indicated that Moscow was still trying to re-establish contact with him. Whether the failure was purely technical, or whether there were more fundamental reasons, I am quite unable to say.

Never in human history has any government succeeded in throwing such a close, complex and all-embracing network of surveillance over its own subjects as that which is maintained today by the Government of the Soviet Union. Nevertheless its efficiency is constantly coming to grief on the rocks of obstinate human nature and there are added difficulties where foreigners or foreign countries are concerned.

The N.K.V.D. found this during the war with girls whom they trained and directed to become intimate with foreigners, seamen and others, for intelligence purposes. It was asking a lot. The girl would be taken by her foreign friend to a good restaurant and theatre and would have the best that foreign money could buy lavished upon her by an attentive and perhaps interesting companion. Next day, she would have to make a damaging report on her escort of the previous evening to one of our sour and cynical workers in a cold, bleak unfurnished office. It was found that these girls tended to lose interest in their work. Indeed, it used to be reckoned that with the first gift of nylons, fifty per cent of the value of the girl's reports was lost, and the deterioration was swift.

We had such a regrettable case in our S.K. work in Sweden. Pyotr Zavarukhin, a Military Intelligence officer in the Embassy, was young, educated, presentable, single and popular with the ladies. He was of a sociable disposition, spoke Swedish well, and was fond of visiting Swedish clubs and dance halls. It was deemed necessary to keep watch on the 's.k. line' over such a lively young spark, and our choice for the job was our agent 'Jana', whose real identity was Afanasieva, the Ambassador's secretary, who had been recruited to the N.K.V.D. She was an attractive, intelligent girl, with classical features, auburn hair and a nice figure and seemed admirably suited to her task. At first all went well and she supplied a mass of detailed information about Zavarukhin, his activities and associates. But as time went on a change came over her reports. They were as detailed as ever about the associates, but revealed less and less about Zavarukhin himself. In the end she concluded every report with the formula: 'As far as Zavarukhin was concerned, his behaviour and conversation were unexceptionable.'

They were married shortly after we left Sweden.

Finally there was the case of the deserter, Semenchenko. He was a stoker on board the Soviet refrigerator ship *Denis Davidov*, which was refitting at the Swedish port of Goeteborg. When the captain reported Semenchenko's disappearance, the wires between our Embassy and Moscow ran hot. Moscow directed us to report immediately to the Swedish Ministry of Foreign Affairs, accusing Semenchenko of desertion and the theft of 2,000 kroner and demanding that he be handed over. We were to represent him to the Swedes as a criminal.

The Swedish Ministry replied that they would make inquiries of the local police and inform us of the results. Three days later they notified us that Semenchenko was in the hands of the police in Stockholm and I was sent, with our Consul Nikishev, to interview him at the Central Police Station.

We were conducted to a room and after a few minutes Semenchenko was shown in and we were left alone. He was dirty and dishevelled and was still in the working rig which he had been wearing when he broke out of the ship.

I asked him quietly what had made him leave the ship and he told me his story. He said that he was a hard worker and had kept the stokehold spotlessly clean but had had a row with the Political Commissar, who had refused to grant him the ordinary shore-leave accorded to his mates. When Semenchenko protested at the discrimination, the *Politkom* shouted, 'My decision is final.'

Semenchenko lost his temper and swore at him; whereupon the *Politkom* threatened to arrest him, put him in the brig and have him sent back to Russia.

After brooding for more than a day, Semenchenko went ashore, sought out the nearest police station and asked for asylum, saying that he wished to stay and work in Sweden and had no desire to go back to the Soviet Union. The police thereupon took him into custody.

We tried to persuade Semenchenko to return to his ship, saying that the episode was a misunderstanding which could be cleared up without trouble.

'Not likely,' answered Semenchenko. 'I might have gone back if I hadn't been accused of stealing the 2,000 kroner. That's telling the Swedes I'm a criminal. I've never done such a thing in all my life, no, not in all the hard times I've been through. I even left all my pay and gear on board. It's a —— lie about the stealing. No going back for me after that.'

The Swedes refused to hand over Semenchenko against his will and on Moscow's instructions we dropped the matter.

But the story had a sequel.

In 1950, when I was back in Moscow working at State Security headquarters in the Maritime Section, we received an agent's report of an incident which had occurred in the Port of London, when a Soviet merchant ship was lying alongside a Swedish ship. A seaman on board the Swedish ship (his description answered that of Semenchenko) kept shouting across to Soviet sailors on deck such remarks as—'How's your Political Commissar getting on? Do you still get put through the hoops before you go abroad? Is anyone short of foreign dough aboard there, mate?' His Russian was fluent and expressive.

Our Soviet sailors maintained a dignified silence. But they wondered greatly how a Swedish sailor came to be so well-informed about the secret sore spots of the Soviet Merchant Marine.

Neutral Sweden during our time was a rich and productive field for Soviet espionage. Our large and generally well-organized Soviet Embassy was an effective base for operations; there was the reservoir of goodwill towards the Soviet Union which had been built up under Madame Kollontai's enlightened régime, aided by the exploits of the Soviet armies in alliance with the West, and above all there was the anxiety of the Swedes not to offend their great and powerful neighbour, the Soviet Union.

Under these conditions, our espionage systems reaped a rich harvest, despite the valiant and skilful efforts of the Swedish Counter-Intelligence. Apart from my own s.k. work, I gained an insight, in my capacity as n.k.v.d. cypher clerk, into many of the secrets of our intelligence networks and was aware of the existence of many more.

I also gained valuable experience working under such capable and experienced intelligence officers as Razin, whose personality my wife has already described. Razin was particularly expert in winning the friendship and confidence of Westerners. He was a gifted linguist and could talk readily on politics, literature, science, sport and indeed almost any subject. He used to give lectures and much shrewd advice on the right approach to our Swedish hosts. 'Never let your language difficulties embarrass you,' he used to say. 'If you're in trouble, ask the man you're dealing with. Enlist his help; he'll be glad to give it.

'Another thing—never get bothered or confused. You mustn't allow yourself to feel any inferiority; you must show complete confidence in your approach.

'Finally, take a sympathetic interest in the views of the man you are cultivating. That's the first essential in winning his confidence.'

Razin was a good example of his own preaching. Apart from anything else, he won the liking and respect of his subordinates, in marked contrast to his predecessors, Yartsev and Mrs Yartsev, who were energetic but woefully lacking in caution and judgment.

Razin had a sense of proportion and gave me sensible advice on my s.k. work.

'Volodya, don't you waste your time on investigating why Ivan Ivanovich, the chauffeur, had a drink too many at the Soviet Club last Tuesday. Let the Party Secretary or the Ambassador deal with that. Our job is to concentrate on knowing all about the organization and personnel of the Swedish Counter-Intelligence. We must find out whom of our Embassy they are studying and their methods and tactics.'

He decided that we should concentrate on foreign language teachers and on foreigners employed in our Tass News Agency and in the Soviet Trade Representative's office.

A Swedish woman teacher, who had been employed for a long time by our Embassy, and who taught me and several others, aroused our suspicions. She asked questions that seemed unconnected with her teaching work, such as the duties of a number of Embassy staff. Later we learned that she had a sister who was married to someone in the Swedish Counter-Intelligence. Our suspicions were confirmed by the following device. We wrote a long letter addressed to a trusted but open contact of our Embassy, a German resident in Sweden, and carefully inserted some inconspicuous material, including human hairs, between the pages. We gave this letter to our teacher to post, having previously arranged for it to be returned unopened by our friend. Sure enough, when we examined it we found that the hair was missing, proving that it had been surreptitiously opened in transit.

We did not show our hand, but simply informed the language teacher that her services were no longer required.

I had some personal brushes with the Swedish Counter-Intelligence.

Once I was riding my motor-cycle to a rendezvous in the woods with my agent Misha, when I suspected that a car was following me. I stopped, and pretended to be making some adjustments to my machine and when the car passed me I noted its appearance and number-plate. Then I turned left, down a cul-de-sac that led to a jetty, where I got out my tackle and began to fish. Before long the same car drove up, stayed a short time and drove off. I missed my meeting with Misha, but I caught six or seven tasty perch.

On another occasion, when an Embassy colleague and I were out fishing near Stockholm, I recognized the make and number-plate of a car which had been reported to us as belonging to the Counter-Intelligence. When we stopped, the car pulled in a little distance away and two young men got out and began unpacking fishing-rods and a picnic basket.

I decided to take the bull by the horns and walked over towards their car. Their obvious unease and discomfort as they saw me approaching, confirmed my suspicions. The best value of a shadower is gone once his description is known to the enemy. I lost nothing, as they evidently knew me by sight already. 'Would you be so good as to lend me some matches, please?'

'Matches? Oh . . . yes . . . certainly.'

They fumbled and produced the matches. I thanked them and walked back to our picnic spot. Soon afterwards they packed up their basket and fishing tackle and drove off.

But often the boot was on the other foot.

Our Embassy Accountant, Leonid Schiokin, was secretly a Military Intelligence officer. I met him afterwards in Moscow in the Committee of Information, and he told me this incident himself. He had an agent whom he used to meet at night in a forest overlooking a stretch of water. One night he cycled out to his rendezvous, taking his usual elaborate precautions against being 'tailed', for he was able and experienced in conspiratorial technique. But the Swedes were better this time. As he sat in the darkness of the forest in quiet conversation with his agent, there was the blinding flash of a photographer's bulb; the Swedes had photographed Schiokin with his agent.

What happened to the agent I don't know, but Schiokin was hastily recalled to the Soviet Union for fear of arrest, as he had no diplomatic immunity.

This was a more frequent occurrence in Sweden than was ever reported in the Swedish Press or known to the Swedish people. While in Sweden I knew of at least five other Soviet intelligence men who were caught in compromising illegal activity by the Swedish authorities. As they enjoyed diplomatic immunity, they could not be charged, as their agents could, in the Swedish courts. Each was simply declared *persona non grata* by the Swedish Government in a note to our Ambassador and was sent back to Moscow. They would not suffer on their return, unless it was clear that they had been caught through their own stupidity or negligence. Someone else stepped into their shoes and the vast machine of Soviet espionage pursued its course uninterrupted.

The standard of professional skill shown by our workers was far from uniform. The Yartsevs, husband and wife, who preceded Razin as N.K.V.D. Residents, were second-rate operators, lacking both his skill and discrimination.

Mrs Yartsev worked furiously, with a nervous energy and tremendous conscientiousness. But her work was superficial. Quantity, not quality, was her obsession. She would study all the Swedish newspaper clippings that the Tass news agency regularly sent back to Moscow. If she came across the name of someone she had met, she would immediately sit down and write a report to Moscow, describing her meeting with the person in question and then retailing as Top Secret Intelligence the very material which had already been culled from Swedish papers and sent back to Moscow by Tass. I pointed out the futility of this procedure, which greatly incensed her (she once tried to hit me with a typewriter) and Moscow repeatedly came back with reproofs for cables which contained nothing of value. But there was no stopping Mrs Yartsev. When General Yakovlev, Head of the N.K.V.D. Second Department, visited us in Sweden, he made some caustic comments on the subject and told us flatly, 'Ninety per cent of the information which we receive from you by cable in secret cypher is of no interest whatever, and has already appeared in the press.'

Perhaps General Yakovlev spoke with some exaggeration to impress his point. But if not, and ninety per cent of the total espionage effort was in fact wasted, the other ten per cent brought in a harvest of secret military and political intelligence which was of immense strategic importance to the Soviet Union.

It is only in the last year or two that the extent of this espionage has been revealed and the Swedish public aroused to the true aims, methods and attitude of their powerful neighbour, the U.S.S.R.

On the 21st September 1950, Swedish police arrested Ernst Hilding

Andersson, the Swedish naval petty officer who, in less than a year of active and daring espionage had given the Soviet Government an accurate, detailed, up-to-date picture of numerous Swedish naval secrets. Andersson furnished regular reports on the Stockholm naval base, and the Swedish Baltic Fleet. He mapped and described Karlskrona, the big naval base in the south of Sweden; he reported on a visiting British flotilla. In response to a specific Soviet request, he supplied details and photographs of Swedish defences in the northern area, which, he was told, the Russians must occupy 'before the Americans drop tens of thousands of men there', including the pivot of Sweden's defences there, the Boden fortress.

Andersson's active espionage took place after I left Sweden, but I knew Vinogradov, the Soviet Naval Intelligence officer who first sowed in Andersson's mind the idea that he should spy for the Soviet. He was First Secretary at the Embassy in our time. His wife had travelled to Sweden with us. I also knew Anissimov, the Tass agent, who was secretly another Naval Intelligence officer, and who took Andersson over from Vinogradov and ran this important Soviet agent.

Naval and Military Intelligence workers keep their activities strictly secret from N.K.V.D. personnel. Nevertheless, I picked both Vinogradov and Anissimov as sailors before I learned officially about them and I guessed that they were Naval Intelligence representatives.

The other sensational Swedish spy case which only recently came to light was that of Fritiof Enbom, who was arrested in February 1952. Enbom, like Andersson, was a Swedish Communist. Unlike Andersson, who was defiant and unrepentant to the last, Enbom suffered great mental conflict, and himself made the first moves which led to his arrest. He said that he had become disillusioned about the policy of the Soviet Union, especially after the Communist seizure of Czechoslovakia.

Enbom, unlike Andersson, was recruited as an N.K.V.D. agent. He was not handed over to Military Intelligence, in the person of our friend Zavarukhin, until 1946, after he had been operating for the N.K.V.D. for three years, even though the material he supplied was of military interest. As cypher clerk to the N.K.V.D. office, I was in touch with the Enbom case from the time of our arrival in Sweden and myself handled the cypher messages which passed between our office and Moscow, including Enbom's reports. His code-name was 'Nabludatel' meaning 'Observer'.

Enbom's first assignment, which he received through a leading Swedish Communist, was a straightforward one. Between July 1940 and August 1943 the Swedish Government, under heavy German pressure, permitted the transit of German troops through Sweden on their way to Finland. Enbom, as a railway linesman, was asked to report on this traffic to his Swedish Communist friend, knowing that it would be transmitted to the Soviet Government.

In February 1943 the Swedish Communist introduced Enbom to a Russian at Karleksudden Point, on Djurgoerden Island. Enbom never learnt the name of his Russian contact, but described him as a short, dark, sturdy man, between forty and forty-five years old, who spoke good Swedish with no noticeable accent. The Russian made contacting arrangements and promised to supply him with a wireless set.

That Russian was my colleague Vassiliev, who operated the secret wireless set from a room at the top of our Embassy. Vassiliev told me about his secret meetings with 'Observer' and the careful precautions which he invariably took. 'Observer's' reports were transmitted by Chernov, after which I encyphered them for transmission to Moscow. I can remember a number of such reports in this sort of form: 'On this date a train of twelve carriages, carrying approximately 1,000 German troops, equipped with the following arms, passed through . . .'

In October of the same year the running of 'Observer' was taken over by Fedor Gregorievich Chernov, whom I got to know well. I succeeded in interesting him in the delights of fishing and our families shared a summer house in the country outside Stockholm one summer.

Chernov was tall and slim, with a broad face and close-cropped light brown hair. He was an experienced, painstaking and highly efficient intelligence officer who omitted no detail in his preparations. The precautions surrounding his contact with Enbom and the device of the bent hairpin stuck in the fence of the Oestermalm Sports Ground as a signal to his agent, were typical of his careful work.

Chernov used to come into the secret cypher room, where all such discussions took place, fuming at the slackness of the Yartsevs, for whose professional skill he had the greatest contempt.

'Listen to the latest about those silly b——s!' he would exclaim. 'They don't know the first principles of conspiratorial work! How can we work with such dumbbells?'

Once he described irately how the Yartsevs, Spichkin, Panin (an engineer in the Trade Representative's office) and the chauffeur Troitsky (who was an N.K.V.D. worker) had all gone off in the same car to meet their different agents, dropping one conspirator off here, another there.

'They went off like a battalion!' stormed Chernov. 'Stand back there! General Yartsev and staff are going out to meet the agents!'

Chernov had a high opinion of himself, but he had one great virtue in an intelligence officer. He never boasted of his achievements and was as reticent about his own successes as he was eloquent about others' shortcomings. His reports to Moscow were always meticulous.

Chernov's departure from Sweden resulted from an interesting case of which I had some knowledge. Some time in 1946 a certain Swedish journalist approached our Embassy with an offer of information. Because of his initiative, Moscow gave him the code name of Dobrovolets, meaning 'Volunteer'.

'Volunteer' explained that he had a highly placed friend in a Swedish Government department who was being blackmailed by a girl and was in desperate need of money. However, because of his position he was unwilling to risk direct contact with our Soviet Embassy and had asked his journalist friend to act as his intermediary in the matter.

'Volunteer' brought samples of the information which he could supply, and Moscow were so impressed with it that they authorized the payment of the large sum of 11,000 kroner to 'Volunteer', followed by payments of 500 kroner a month. Chernov took over the case and had a number of meetings with the journalist at which he tried very hard, on Moscow's instructions, to discover the identity of the alleged high official. This 'Volunteer' steadfastly refused to disclose. However, I believe that in the end he agreed, under this continuous pressure, to produce his friend, and persuaded a fellow-journalist (on the ground that it was in the national interest) to pose as the important Swedish official. His hoax must have been skilfully carried out, for Chernov continued to meet and pay 'Volunteer'. Altogether, the case ran on for about six months.

Then, one night after a meeting with Chernov as he left the house which they used for their secret meetings, 'Volunteer' was arrested by the Swedish police. He confessed and was charged, and the Swedish authorities sent a protest to our Ambassador which resulted in Chernov's recall from Sweden on the grounds of his being *persona non grata*.

While the case was running we had many discussions in the N.K.V.D. office as to the authenticity of 'Volunteer's' story. Moscow rated his information highly and we wondered whether he could be a 'plant' by the Swedish Counter-Intelligence. I believe the truth is that he was an impostor who cleverly fabricated the information himself, and that his detection resulted from skilful shadowing of Chernov by the Swedish Counter-Intelligence.

Chernov's recall was a real loss to Soviet Intelligence, which had scored major successes with agents run by him, Enbom in particular.

A full account of the secret information acquired by Enbom, either in person or through sub-agents, and transmitted to the Soviet Government, has never been published, but it has been revealed that he furnished a mass of material on Sweden's military defence lines in the north, hinging on the fortress of Boden, and it is clear that the Swedish Government viewed the leakage as very serious indeed. I remember myself encyphering reports from him which gave numerous details of gun emplacements, types and calibres of guns, fortifications in various fjords, jetties, landing facilities and the whole range of Sweden's border defences.

I am not surprised to learn that when the story was revealed, following earlier publication of the Andersson case, Swedish public opinion was deeply shocked and alarmed, and that the Swedish Government made a sharp protest to the Soviet Union.

The Soviet Government's reply was characteristic in its unconvincing denial, accompanied by a thinly veiled threat. It asserted that the Swedish Government's protest was 'based on false statements made by provocateurs whose object it is to slander members of the Soviet Embassy staff and to impair good-neighbour relations between Sweden and the Soviet Union.'

My four years' service in Sweden left an abiding impression in my mind of the prosperity and truly democratic atmosphere of this small capitalist country. It brought home to me in a hundred ways the falseness and futility of Soviet propaganda and the stupidity and inhumanity of the system I served. I pondered over these things. But the same system had opened up for me a career in which I was successful, privileged and trusted. I had no personal grievance to goad me into action. That was to be provided later, under very different circumstances, in our Embassy at Canberra.

XVIII

The Eye of the Sphinx

I BEGIN with a remarkable fact.

In all my twenty-one years as a professional State Security Officer, I never came across one authentic case of foreign espionage in the Soviet Union in peace-time. Thousands were accused of espionage and shot. Public scapegoats like Zinoviev, Yagoda and Beria were invariably accused of being agents of British, American or German Intelligence without a shred of evidence being produced. During the war there were certainly cases of Soviet citizens captured by the Germans who were parachuted back into Soviet territory as spies. But I never heard of a case in Russia comparable to those of Fuchs and Nunn May in Britain, Greenglass or Golos in America, Andersson and Enbom in Sweden, or Richard Sorge in Japan.

Yet, according to the ceaseless warnings of the Soviet authorities, Russia is so riddled from top to bottom with the agents of foreign intelligence that only perpetual and relentless vigilance saves it from destruction.

What is the explanation of this paradox? The answer is simple. The vast machinery of State Security in the Soviet Union is chiefly employed not against foreign espionage (which would be extraordinarily difficult in face of the precautions maintained on Soviet territory) but against the Soviet people themselves. Its special tasks are to prevent Soviet citizens from developing sympathy or admiration for foreign countries and to suppress all criticism and protest against the Government.

Among the books which I left behind in my flat in Moscow were the complete works of the Russian poet Alexander Blok, whose poems are very popular in the Soviet Union today. Blok in his poem *The Scythians* describes Russia as 'a Sphinx who peers, peers, peers at thee, with hatred and with love'. The love of the Soviet Government for its subjects is jealous and watchful; the hatred against a suspected waverer is quick and ruthless. I speak from long and intimate experience as an executive of this official vigilance.

I have already described my 's.k.' work in Sweden, where I was responsible for keeping security watch over the members of the 'Soviet

Colony'; that is, over all special representatives in Sweden, including Embassy personnel, trade delegations, Tass news agency and all holders of Soviet passports, including the servicemen interned in Sweden for the duration of war.

From our return to Moscow in the autumn of 1947 until our departure for Australia in January 1951, I was wholly employed on this 's.k.' work; my responsibility was the loyalty, conduct and morale of Soviet seamen in ships visiting foreign ports. In practice, this amounted to considering cases of reported offences and organizing the proper handling of offenders.

Merchant seamen, of course, were in a particularly sensitive occupation from the Government's point of view, for their business compelled them to see foreign countries and peoples with their own eyes, and invited them to compare what they saw with what their Government told them. It was a dangerous process. Such contrasts are powerful and vivid. I remember my own impressions after the cold voyage back from Sweden, as our ship, the *Byelo-Ostrov*, entered Soviet waters. There was Kronstadt, scene of my naval apprenticeship, but somehow looking much less gay and lively than it used to appear from the deck of the *Volodarsky*. And then Leningrad, so desirable when we had a few days' leave—how dilapidated the wharf was now, with its neglected-looking equipment! How grey Leningrad itself seemed, with its shabbily dressed people and poorly lit streets, after gracious Stockholm. Already it was two years since the war had ended. There had been time for recovery and cleaning up, if there had been the will and incentive. Then the Soviet customs officers arrived on board. Any foreign literature, gramophone records, chocolate? We had some chocolate?

'Then I suggest that you give several blocks to the Border Officer, his daughter is ill and he would appreciate it very much.'

I handed over five or six blocks. It was a cheap price for avoiding endless difficulty and delay with our luggage. Customs men and Border Guards considered it no more than a justifiable toll which they levied on persons coming back to the Soviet Union from the abundant West.

It was no great matter, but it was a reminder that we were returning to the land of hardship and scarcity for all but the privileged few.

I felt a stab of apprehension as I caught myself in the act of such reflections. Automatically I began to reckon up possibilities when we reached Moscow. On the surface we had nothing whatever to fear. We had both done well in our work in Sweden and I was not aware of any grounds for accusations against us on our return. But I knew the Soviet system too well to feel secure on that score. There might have been some adverse reports of which I knew nothing; moreover, there had been many high level changes in the State Security Service in our absence. How would we fare? I well remembered how the mere fact of having served abroad had been enough to damn men in 1937 and 1938.

My fears proved to be unnecessary. I reported for duty and was appointed to the newly-constituted Committee of Information (known by the initials K.I.).

This Committee of Information is worth describing as an example of the continuous reorganization that goes on in all Soviet institutions. The K.I. was a promising idea that failed in practice. The plan may have originated with Molotov, first head of the K.I., who was succeeded by eminent figures, including Malik, Vyshinsky and Zorin. The idea was to get together in one building, under the direct control of the Soviet Government, all Departments and Sections dealing with secret foreign intelligence. Hence the K.I. combined G.R.U. (Naval and Military Intelligence) with the Foreign Intelligence Departments of the old N.K.V.D., while all the other functions of the N.K.V.D.—internal security, border guards, labour camps, etc.—were divided between the Ministry of State Security (M.G.B.) and the Ministry of Internal Affairs (M.V.D.). In other words the Foreign section of the N.K.V.D. was removed, and put in the same box with its only competitor, Military Intelligence.

This Committee of Information, where Doosia and I now both went to work, was housed in two imposing buildings which had been the headquarters of the Comintern, in the old suburb of Rostokino, near the Agricultural Fair on the outskirts of Moscow. This situation was something of a bugbear, for it meant an hour and a half's bus journey each way (unless you were in the official car class). The hours we worked were 10.30 a.m. till 7.30 p.m., six days a week. As all classes, Party work and special tasks had to be done outside these hours, it meant many late nights, when travelling time was included. In these two large office blocks were accommodated several thousand workers divided between a multitude of Departments covering every area of the non-Soviet world, and dealing with such subjects as Illegal Agents, Misinformation, Emigrés, Delegations, Scientific Intelligence, Cyphers, Wireless, Technical Equipment, Archives, Library and Foreign Language Courses. There was also a clinic and a dining-room.

The K.I. broke down for two reasons. The Ministers who were its nominal heads were too busy with other matters, and control by a

Committee was cumbersome and clogging. Moreover, the Military Intelligence men resented the dominance of the State Security men, who headed all the K.I. departments.

In the middle of 1948, at the insistence of Marshal Bulganin, the Military Intelligence Sections withdrew from the K.I. and were set up again under their own independent command. And at the end of the same year our S.K. and E.M. Sections also withdrew and returned to their natural niche in the Ministry of State Security. I was glad to shift our office back to No. 2 Dzerjinsky Square, which saved the tedious bus journey.

However, what was left of the K.I. after these amputations, continued to function throughout the rest of our time in Moscow. Doosia remained in it, in the Swedish Intelligence Department, and it was not finally disbanded till the end of 1951, after we had been nearly a year in Australia.

Whether my umbrella was the K.I. or the M.G.B. made little difference to the job. The jealous eye of the Sphinx does not shut and the rule of suspicion and fear is not affected by any number of changes on the surface.

However, S.K. work had acquired a new priority. Before the war it had been merely a sideline, carried out by N.K.V.D. Residents in Embassies abroad in addition to their other duties. Now I found a number of sections devoted solely to S.K. work in different areas of the world. When I was briefed in Moscow for my S.K. job in Sweden, I was handed a single bulky file to read, containing correspondence, staff lists and miscellaneous reports all under one cover. But before I left for Australia I read orderly S.K. files on every member of the Canberra Embassy. The difference was symptomatic.

Why this increased emphasis on supervision of Soviet citizens abroad? At the end of the war the Soviet authorities received a shock. They found that three million Soviet P.O.W's and displaced persons wanted to remain in war-ravaged Europe rather than return to life in the Soviet Union. These Soviet citizens, civilians and P.O.W's, had seen at first hand the much higher standard of living enjoyed even by peasants and workers in the capitalist West.

At Yalta the Allied Governments unwisely agreed to repatriate these 'non-returners' by force to the Soviet Union. Nevertheless, thousands of them managed to escape the loving embrace of their country, which conveyed the unhappy victims straight to labour camps as suspects and traitors. The extent of this reluctance to return had alarmed the Soviet Government.

In addition, there had been the disturbing cases of officials who had fled from the Soviet service and had sought refuge in Western countries—Kravchenko and Mrs Kasenkina in America, Gouzenko in Canada, Tokaev in Britain, and a number of others.

Sterner supervision was the Soviet answer. Soviet delegations going abroad were a responsibility of the s.k. Section where I worked. For example, we covered a delegation of Soviet firemen invited to England by the London Fire Brigade. We watched the Soviet delegation to the United Nations and the delegation of about eighty to the World Peace Conference which was to have been held in London but which was transferred to Warsaw when the British authorities made difficulties. We even covered a Soviet film unit which visited Communist China to make a film.

For all these we appointed a chief s.k. representative to travel with the delegation and recruited agents, in the proportion of about one in ten, whose task was to render regular reports on their companions. As each delegation was already meticulously screened before leaving the Soviet Union, it is not surprising that most of the reports were innocuous, but that would not be held to justify any relaxation of s.k. vigilance.

Important persons who were known outside the Soviet Union presented a special problem. Though subjected to the same careful examination, serious reports against them were often overruled by higher authority for policy reasons. There was the attractive actress, Serova. She had been seen talking to an American officer; it was said that she had even visited his flat. Yet she was allowed to go on tour abroad. Then there was the case of the world-famous Soviet writer, Ilya Ehrenburg, who was included in the Peace Delegation which I have mentioned. He contributed numerous articles to *Izvestia* and *Pravda* during the war, appealing to the patriotism of the Soviet people and urging a total effort against the Germans. But when we applied the normal s.k. process of summarizing his file, our report on Ehrenburg was pages long, and was crammed with 'compromising material'. His house was frequently visited by foreigners, his daughter was said to have visited the American Embassy, he himself had been to the United States. Ehrenburg's dossier bristled with suspicions and allegations. A simple m.g.b. worker, full of conscientious zeal, would have cried, 'Arrest him on the spot!' But the Central Committee of the Party, who had the final decision, allowed Ehrenburg to go abroad. He was a world personality. To prevent him might have brought adverse publicity, to which the Soviet Government is by no means insensitive. Besides, when Ehrenburg travelled abroad, he always left his family behind in the Soviet Union.

Foreign delegations visiting the Soviet Union were the responsibility of another Department altogether. However, I know that in such cases lists, with full personal particulars of delegates, were supplied by our M.G.B. Residents abroad and that the Department in question studied the background, opinions and weaknesses of all foreign visitors, with a view to recruiting them by appeal or pressure if conditions seemed favourable.

My own special task was supervision of Soviet merchant seamen in ships plying on the lower Danube, where that great waterway passes through Austria, Czechoslovakia, Hungary, Yugoslavia, Bulgaria and Rumania. It may surprise some readers to know that Moscow regarded these 'Peoples' Democracies' with suspicion almost as deep as that with which they regarded Western countries. They were supposed to be honeycombed with Foreign Intelligence agents, and close association between our sailors and their nationals was sternly discouraged.

We exercised our control through maritime agencies in all these countries and through permanent M.G.B. representatives in Bucharest and Budapest. On every ship we had S.K. agents covering officers and crew. These agents were mostly recruited while on Soviet territory; they were generally unpaid, but were flattered and gratified to be the trusted assistants of the powerful and authoritative M.G.B.

Through them we received a volume of reports about the suspicious contacts and bad behaviour of our sailors at Danube ports. I always strove to evaluate these reports for what they were worth. I had seen too much flagrant injustice, too many baseless charges, too many condemnations on mere suspicion. I had known men convicted and punished on bare notations such as: 'was seen lingering in the vicinity of the U.S. Legation', or 'judging by the look on his face, he harbours something which is anti-Soviet'. Once in Sweden I had received an urgent cable from Moscow, saying that the captain of a Soviet ship then on its way to Sweden was planning to desert there. Four of us from the Embassy drove at once to the port of Karlskrona and met the ship when it docked at dawn. We went straight on board and greeted the captain, who was astonished at such a delegation to meet him. While the others were having a drink with him, I went to the cabin of the Political Commissar and I introduced myself. He embraced me with tears in his eyes.

'Thank goodness you're here, Comrade! You're only just in time! This is where he planned to do it!'

I got him to tell me what he knew and I found that it was the *Politkom* who had warned Moscow about the captain and had prompted Moscow's cable to me.

'How did you find out about this, Comrade?' I asked.

'I observed his behaviour in Finland, how friendly he was with the ship's chandler there. . . .'

'Did he say anything about his plan to desert?'

'No, he was too cunning and cautious, but I put two and two together. I beg you, take no chances!'

I left him and questioned our s.k. agents in the ship's company, establishing contact with them by means of their code-names. They were not known to the *Politkom* and gave independent views. None of them had the slightest suspicion about their captain, whom they all highly commended, but from several I learned that the captain and the *Politkom* were on bad terms. We kept an eye on things till the ship sailed, but it was clear to me that the charge against the captain had been fabricated by the *Politkom* out of personal enmity and spite.

Nevertheless, at another port, the captain was arrested and taken to Moscow for interrogation. After a couple of weeks he was released, completely exonerated of the charge. In Soviet terms that means that there cannot have been even a breath of legitimate suspicion against him.

With this sort of thing in mind, I always asked for confirmation of the charges against the sailors from more than one source. This made me unpopular with the M.G.B. Residents in the Danube ports, who did not want the trouble of pursuing cases further, and with my section chief Denisov. Denisov was a little peppery man with a foul tongue and a consuming ambition. A careerist through and through, he wanted to demonstrate his severity and vigilance to his superiors. In spite of Denisov's impatience, I objected to condemning men on the basis of a single unconfirmed agent's report—often malicious or exaggerated.

'These lads are young and silly,' I would argue, 'but that does not mean they are dangerous or anti-Soviet. We ought to check each case thoroughly.'

'Quite unnecessary! We've no time, anyway,' snapped Denisov. He would send every report up to the Central Committee and usually the man would be debarred from further foreign service or dismissed from his job for some trifling or harmless slip. Often it was simply because he had been seen at a cinema with a Rumanian or a Czech girl.

One old bargeman, who had lived for years aboard his barge with his wife, son and daughter, lost his job, his home and his livelihood because in Yugoslavia his children went to a party with some Yugo-slavs.

Denisov was my senior, but we had many angry differences over this issue. Perhaps my background had something to do with it—the com-munity life of village and mess deck, which made me want to give these misguided sailors a second chance. Sometimes I won my point, but often my objections were swept aside.

My duties were laid down. To refuse to carry them out would have been the end of me. But they never destroyed my lifelong dislike of callousness and injustice towards simple and innocent people. My feel-ings, I know, are shared by millions of my countrymen, now silent and helpless under the empire of fear.

★ ★ ★

In the course of my s.k. work in Moscow I came across the tracks of two major events, both of which are outstanding landmarks in the history of Soviet Communism—Tito's break with Moscow and the assassination of Leon Trotsky. The phenomenon of Tito's Yugoslavia remains world news. As I write, Krushchev and Bulganin have just paid their visit to Tito and seem to have gone to enormous lengths to heal or at least lessen the breach between the two countries. As far back as 1953, when I was in Canberra, we received instructions from Moscow not to decline invitations from Yugoslavian representatives in Australia and to invite them back to our Soviet receptions.

The reason for this anxiety on the part of the Soviet Union to win back Yugoslavia to the Soviet orbit is obvious. That a country which, after the war, was hailed as a model of a young 'Peoples' Democracy', based firmly on Communist principles and practice, should declare its national independence, and should enter into close relations with Western countries, is an ominous spectre for the rulers of the Soviet Empire. Will Tito's example spread to other 'Peoples' Democracies'? Will Communist China follow a similar road? Will the Soviet Govern-ment be able to anticipate and counter such revolts in the future? The Sphinx in the Kremlin is obviously doing some very hard thinking on these questions.

Tito's break in 1948 came as a rude and severe shock. A few months earlier Stalin had been entertaining Tito and his Foreign Minister Kar-delj, a brilliant Marxist theoretician, in Moscow, and Tito had visited m.g.b. schools where Yugoslavian intelligence officers were being trained. I remember the wave of dismay that passed through the m.g.b.

ranks when the Yugoslavians broke away. Our reaction was, 'We've told them all our secrets and now they've deserted us!'

Most of the students went back to Yugoslavia (Yugoslavia held plenty of Soviet hostages for them) but some refused to return and published a declaration in the Soviet papers accusing Tito of being a traitor to his country and the cause of Communism. Throughout the Soviet Union all pictures of Tito were burnt.

But Tito took a different line. In Yugoslavia the portraits of Lenin and Stalin were not immediately removed; there were no attacks on the Soviet leaders. Tito insisted that he was still a strict orthodox Marxist and Communist. He took his stand on national independence and the right of Yugoslavia to decide the pace and direction of socialism within her borders, for herself.

His biographer, Dedijer,[1] expresses Tito's attitude as follows:

'Moscow refused to tolerate any movement independent of itself, any movement that had primarily the interest of its own country or its own people in view; it wanted a movement which would be blindly obedient and in fact a weapon of Russian foreign policy.'

Tito led a successful secession movement within the Communist camp, the defection of a whole Communist country from Moscow's control.

The irony of the situation was that Tito originally owed everything to Moscow's support. A cypher clerk called Zhukov, who worked in my section, later served with Tito in the partisans during the war, harassing the Germans in the mountains of Yugoslavia. On his return he told me that Tito was timid and a defeatist under fire and walked with a stoop, in constant fear of attack. But after the defeat of the Germans, he was a different man. With his bodyguard round him and the Red Army troops supporting him, Tito marched into Belgrade with his chest out and the air of a conquering hero. Such at least was Zhukov's description.

Inevitably security and intelligence matters played a large part in Moscow's attempted domination of Yugoslavia.

Today Moscow maintains its hold over the satellite states of the 'Peoples' Democracies' by means of Soviet 'Counsellors' attached to all the important Ministries of these countries, but superior to all the others is the Counsellor on Security matters. He is always a high-ranking M.V.D. officer. The Security Chiefs of the satellite countries always act on the advice of this Soviet Counsellor; most of them have been

[1] *Tito Speaks*, by Vladimir Dedijer, Weidenfeld and Nicolson, London, 1953.

through M.V.D. schools themselves. Under the Counsellor is the M.V.D. Resident in the Soviet Embassy or Consulate.

Tito did not object to this system in principle, but he insisted in a letter to Stalin on 1st March 1948, that the Soviet Union must obtain its information only from top-level official sources in Yugoslavia, not from other unauthorized Yugoslav sources.

This did not suit Moscow's book at all. From the very beginning, our Soviet missions had busily recruited Yugoslavs to work directly for Soviet intelligence. The Soviet authorities wanted to have their own men planted in the Yugoslav Communist Party and State machine. This represented an important principle of Soviet intelligence work, but was not likely to appeal to the Government of a country which wanted to run its own affairs.

Stalin and Molotov, in reply to Tito's letter, demanded recognition of the right of Soviet officials and technical specialists in Yugoslavia to obtain information from any Yugoslav official.

The letter ended with a threat which links Tito's case with my other study of a Communist Opposition leader.

'We think Trotsky's political career is sufficiently instructive. V. M. Molotov. J. V. Stalin.'

From an M.G.B. colleague, Ivan Inkov, who was working in our Soviet Consulate in Yugoslavia at the time when Tito and Kardelj were planning their break with Moscow, I learned the inside story. Inkov ran a group of Soviet agents in Tito's and Kardelj's intimate circle and from their reports he became convinced that Tito and Kardelj were planning a 'deviation'. He repeatedly put this up to his boss, Kozhevnikov, the M.G.B. Resident, but Kozhevnikov pooh-poohed the idea. He was himself in close personal touch with Tito and was convinced of Tito's unswerving ideological loyalty to Moscow. In Inkov's opinion, Kozhevnikov was lulled by Tito's personality and by the pleasures of high life in Yugoslavia. According to Inkov, Kozhevnikov lived in great luxury and was a hard man to contact on matters of business.

Inkov was recalled to Moscow and reported in person to various M.G.B. chiefs his suspicions about Tito and Kardelj. As a result, a Special Commission headed by Colonel Pudin was sent to Yugoslavia. But once again Yugoslavian hospitality overpowered suspicion and the Commission found nothing to cause alarm.

If Inkov's warnings had been heeded, Tito might have been lured to Moscow under some pretext and disposed of and the course of history might have been changed.

But they were not.

The shock of Tito's break precipitated fresh investigations. I was present at a departmental meeting in the Committee of Information when Inkov roundly accused Pudin of spending his time in Yugoslavia hunting and drinking instead of pressing forward his inquiries. Pudin, in a blustering bull-like voice, denied the charge.

A second Commission was set up to investigate all the reports received on Tito before his break; Inkov was called before it to give evidence many times.

Who finally paid for the stupendous failure of Soviet intelligence and Soviet policy represented by Tito's break? The answer is—no one. As the investigation progressed it was found that all reports on Tito had been faithfully sent up to the Central Committee of the Communist Party. Too many important people were too deeply involved for a scapegoat to be selected, and so the whole business was shelved and hushed up. It was impossible to isolate a suitable victim.

The second historic figure about whom I gained authentic inside information was Leon Trotsky. I myself never saw Trotsky, the energetic professorial leader of the Left Opposition whom, under Stalin's rule, we were taught to regard as the most diabolical enemy of the Soviet people who had ever lived. But I saw a volume of Trotsky's massive file, in the archives of the Committee of Information, and I can settle a question which has remained a matter of speculation up till now, concerning Trotsky's assassination in 1940.

I saw Trotsky's file by accident and through a defect in our Soviet records system. It happened in 1948, as follows:

At that time there were two main Intelligence Registries, or Archives as they are called, in the Soviet Union. The first was in the basement of No. 2 Dzerjinsky Square and was the Registry of the First Special Department. There, on shelf after packed shelf, were housed the records of every person accused or suspected of political offences inside the Soviet Union since the Revolution of 1917. These files numbered many millions; some were feet thick, others no more than a brief note on a single sheet of paper. A friend who worked there told me of the gigantic task of reviewing all these files, the majority of which consisted of old, useless, or unreliable reports. But all were graded Top Secret. Each time I visited the Registry I had to produce my Identity Card, and hand in my request slip through a window on the right-hand side of the stairs that led down from the street. All files had to be studied on the spot, in a special reading room. No files might be taken out of the building. Of course, authorized M.G.B. officers like myself, were permitted to keep working files, consisting of notes and summaries, in our various M.G.B. departments and sections.

The other registry belonged to the K.I. and contained all the foreign files. It occupied three floors in a section of one of the Committee of Information buildings. This registry covered the whole field of foreign intelligence—Soviet agents abroad, Counter-Revolutionary organizations in foreign countries, dossiers of foreign politicians, scientific and technical intelligence. At that time the records of Soviet atomic espionage were kept there, including the whole story of the celebrated Canadian case laid bare by the flight of Gouzenko from the Soviet service. If the K.I. were still in existence, that is where the file of V. M. and E. A. Petrov would be kept. But the two registries were later amalgamated, so our files should now be housed at No. 2 Dzerjinsky Square.

I often went to this K.I. registry to check the records of sailors; the staff knew me well. But our filing system was cumbersome. The files consisted of grey cardboard covers, containing papers which were permanently fastened together; as each new report came in, it was stitched on to the preceding papers with thread. Thus each file came to contain a mass of material, much of it irrelevant. When the Soviet armies invaded Germany and reached Berlin, we discovered the superiority of the German filing system in which pages which were required for reference could be detached from a file, and later reincorporated without difficulty. This made it possible to limit the access of any one person to secret material much more effectively than could be done under our system.

But to reorganize our filing system would have been a mammoth task. Therefore, when I came across a reference to Trotsky on a seaman's dossier and wanted to check it, I was handed the whole volume of Trotsky's file.

It did not take me long to clear up the point I was looking for and I should have returned the file, but curiosity was too strong. Though it was four or five inches thick I skimmed right through it. After all, Trotsky, though damned, was a legendary figure of Soviet history. Trotsky in the early days, stood second only to Lenin as the organizer of the Bolshevik Revolution and as the prophet of the new Russia. He was Lenin's Commissar for Foreign Affairs, then Minister for War when the Red Army defeated the Whites; later he organized the troops as 'labour armies' to restore vital railway communications within the Soviet Union.

Lenin's death seemed to leave him the natural successor, but that was where he clashed with the rising star of Stalin. As leader of the Left Wing of the Opposition, Trotsky was first expelled from the Communist Party and in 1929 banished from the Soviet Union. He lived in Turkey, France, and Norway, went to Mexico in 1937 and was assassinated there on the 20th August 1940.

Trotsky is the example *par excellence* of that phenomenon for which the Soviet system provides no place—the Opposition leader. Apart from the naked struggle for supremacy, Trotsky differed from Stalin on important points of policy. He stood for an immediate all-out policy of industrialization in the Soviet Union, to be pushed through regardless of other factors, and he insisted that the Revolution in Russia could not proceed without simultaneous revolutions in other countries, whereas Stalin proposed to achieve 'socialism in one country' first.

On both these points it is my opinion that Stalin was the realist and Trotsky the mistaken visionary. Certainly if the Soviet Union had waited until she had succeeded in fostering similar revolutions in the other countries of the world, she would have waited a long time.

But to disagree with your opponent is one thing; how you deal with him is another.

Trotsky's file was interesting, both for its disclosures and its omissions. It contained a mass of published articles by Trotsky in which he attacked and criticized Stalin's policy, and a series of letters between Trotsky and his son Sedov. One piece of evidence was conspicuous by its absence. According to Soviet official statements, Trotsky carried on a persistent correspondence with dissident groups inside the Soviet Union, inciting them to violent revolt against their Government. If so, some of these letters would certainly have been intercepted and put on the file, along with Trotsky's other correspondence. In fact, I did not see one such letter.

However, there were detailed descriptions of Trotsky's life as an exile in Norway and this reminded me that soon after I joined the O.G.P.U. in 1933 we used to get cypher telegrams from the O.G.P.U. Resident in Norway giving a very full account of Trotsky's life and behaviour and reporting the progress that had been made in getting O.G.P.U. agents into his circle of intimate friends and admirers.

The facts of Trotsky's actual assassination are well known; indeed, the assassin, Jacques Mornard, readily re-enacted the whole crime for the Mexican police. I have recently read several newspaper reports speculating on whether Mornard will claim the parole to which he is now entitled, or whether he will be too afraid to come out of the security of his quarters in the Lecumberri prison, where he enjoys considerable comfort and affluence.

Investigations into the background of the crime have revealed that Mornard won the affections in Paris of a New York girl on holiday, Sylvia Ageloff, who was introduced to him by her travelling companion Julia Weill. Julia was then secretary to Louis Budenz, an American Communist who broke with the Party in 1948. In August 1939, Mornard followed Sylvia back to the United States, travelling on a Canadian passport as 'Frank Jacson'. It was found that this passport had been originally issued to a Yugoslav who was killed fighting in Spain with the International Brigade. All members of the International Brigade had to turn in their passports and the passports of the men who died were sent to Moscow. In this way the Soviet authorities obtained a fund of genuine foreign passports for the use of secret agents.

Mornard went to Mexico and through Sylvia's sister, a member of Trotsky's circle, was introduced to Trotsky's friends and gained access to the fortress-villa where Trotsky lived under constant guard. Finally, posing as a devout disciple, he was introduced to the great man himself.

At 5.30 p.m. on 20th August, Mornard walked past the guards, carrying a coat over his arm, though it was warm weather. Under the coat, slung from his wrist, he carried an ice-axe. He also had with him a dagger and a revolver. Trotsky's wife met him, conducted him to Trotsky's study and left them alone. As Trotsky bent over the table, studying a paper on French Trotskyists which Mornard had written, Mornard struck him with the ice-axe, but the first blow did not silence him. His screams brought his wife and the bodyguard, who battered Mornard until Trotsky cried, 'Let him live! He must tell his story.' Trotsky died twenty-five hours later without regaining consciousness.

It is also said that, when the guards attacked him, Mornard cried, 'They made me do it—they imprisoned my mother!' But from that day to this he has steadfastly refused to reveal his identity, his history and his associates. He insists that he committed the crime from purely personal motives, as a Trotskyist who became disillusioned with his leader.

That the crime was really a political assassination directed by Stalin has remained a speculation, in spite of exhaustive police inquiries in many countries. I read a recent article[1] on the case which concluded: 'Despite what seem well-founded suspicions, the direct association [of Moscow with the crime] has never been established.'

[1] *The People*, 7th November 1954.

I can confirm those suspicions from the evidence of my own eyes. Trotsky's file, which I read in the K.I. Registry in 1948, contained the detailed planning by N.K.V.D. experts over a period of years, which led up to the successful assassination.

Though I read the file quickly, with a certain apprehensive speed, I remember clearly these planning papers. One of them had a footnote comment by a senior N.K.V.D. officer that Trotsky should never have been allowed to leave the U.S.S.R.

There were also copies of instructions sent out from N.K.V.D. Headquarters in Moscow to the N.K.V.D. Residents in all the countries where Trotsky had lived at various times, including instructions to the N.K.V.D. Resident in the Soviet Consulate-General in New York, who directed the assassination operation on the American continent. There was complete photographic documentation of Trotsky's life, from the first days in the Soviet Union, before his banishment in 1928, right up to his last days in Mexico, after he had grown the pointed beard which features in his later pictures. There were numerous photographs taken inside his fortified villa, perhaps by Mornard himself, showing the guards, fences and courtyards, photos of Trotsky with his wife, Trotsky having tea with his friends, Trotsky's dog.

I recall that the description of the actual killing said that the broad end, not the pointed end, of the ice-axe had been used.

The crudeness of the instrument may seem strange, but if Mornard had been as skilful as my colleague Bokov, who killed the Soviet Ambassador with a single blow from an iron bar, he would have fulfilled his task with very little noise and might have walked out of the gate of Trotsky's villa quietly and unmolested.

The secret department which organizes such operations outside the Soviet Union was at that time headed by Colonel Serebriansky, a quiet, stooping man with a brilliant planning brain. Later it was directed by Sudoplatov. Now it may be under the direction of Leonid Studnikov, the man who last year sent out Captain Khokhlov (who gave himself up to the Americans) with his poisoned bullets and noiseless camouflaged revolvers, to assassinate the leader of an anti-Soviet organization in Berlin. Khokhlov has reported that the direction of Trotsky's assassination, and the training of Mornard, was actually carried out by Serebriansky's deputy, Eitington, whom I remember seeing at N.K.V.D. Headquarters in Moscow.

One thing is certain—the work of the assassination department goes on, whoever may be running it. Changes among State Security personnel are frequent and I cannot tell who may be sitting in the Top

Secret Registry in Number 2 Dzerjinsky Square studying my file at this moment.

But one thing at least I may hope: that if a similar fate overtakes me or my wife, there will no longer be any doubts as to who is responsible, and that the whole world will know that our death was deliberately planned by a Government which regards political murder as a normal way of dealing with those who differ from it.

XIX

Moscow Farewell

HOME to Moscow! All the luxuries and excitements of our four and a half years in Sweden could not alter the fact that for me Moscow meant home. Especially, it meant my family.

As the train from Leningrad made its way through the outskirts of Moscow, the weather was bitterly cold and snow was falling. Volodya sat quietly. He had no family to greet him; his father and his two brothers were dead and his old mother was far away in Siberia, in his native village of Larikha.

But my family, I knew, would be at the station to meet us, and as we drew in to the platform, I peered along it anxiously and excitedly.

Yes, there they were! Mother, Father, my brother Valentin, my young sister Tamara, they were all there. How we hugged and kissed one another with tears of joy, after the four long years of separation in which so much had happened. Tamara I could hardly recognize. She had been five when we left for Sweden and now she was nearly ten. At first I made serious mistakes and talked to her as though she were the little girl I remembered, but presently I got used to the change and she was soon chattering about her school and her favourite books.

Our friend Chernov had come to meet us with an M.G.B. car. We had said goodbye to him in Sweden when he was recalled to Moscow following the arrest of our agent 'Volunteer' and the protest from the Swedish Government declaring Chernov *persona non grata*.

He seemed none the worse for that episode and we appreciated his thoughtfulness in coming with the car. We all packed into it and drove off to our flat, which Mother had been looking after in our absence. When we opened the door and walked in I was taken aback.

'Mother, whatever is this? All these boxes and crates—it's like a warehouse!'

'These are all your things, Doosenka, just as they arrived from Sweden. I haven't opened anything, or placed a single chair. I knew you would want to arrange everything yourself, to your own liking, so I left everything till you got back.'

We laughed and made ourselves comfortable among all our belongings. Mother had lunch ready and soon we were busy, eating, drinking and exchanging all our news. I told Mother all about Sweden and my illnesses there and Tamara wandered about looking at things, or sat down and strummed at the piano (later she came regularly for music lessons). For the first ten days she and Mother stayed with us at our flat —I wanted Mother with me—then they went home and we resumed ordinary life, with frequent visits between us.

Family and home—these anchorages mean more, not less, in a country like the u.s.s.r. where the ordinary citizen lives so much at the mercy of unpredictable forces and where all other securities are so tenuous and uncertain. That is why, as I know now only too well, these very bonds of family affection are a vulnerable area, a weak spot in the individual's defences and are used by the Soviet State to intimidate, punish and control its subjects.

But Volodya and I seemed, for the present, about as safe and secure as it is possible for Soviet officials to be. It was clear that nothing in our record in Sweden stood to our discredit. Volodya was appointed to the 'Soviet Colony' department of the Committee of Information; he has described his task of keeping watch on the crews of Soviet ships plying on the Danube.

I, too, was first appointed to s.k. work in the k.i. in a section concerned with Spitzbergen, where a riff-raff collection of Soviet nationals were employed in the coal mines. I had to study the security reports sent back by our agents there.

One case, I remember, revolved round a piece of wood which had been found in one of the latrines inscribed with abusive references to Stalin. The bad living conditions in Spitzbergen were a more potent cause of discontent than any real political disaffection. However, the Soviet Government does not, in practice, differentiate very much when criticism of its policy or administration is concerned.

Presently I was transferred to a section dealing with Sweden. It was routine work, but it was a good job. With our combined salaries, and since, to our regret, we had no children, Volodya and I were able to live in a comfort that aroused the envy of our colleagues in Moscow. Moreover, back in Moscow I was able to resume my career as a. Communist. My years in Sweden had been time lost in this regard, since membership of the Party cannot be granted abroad, but only within the u.s.s.r. I worked hard for the privilege, studying and carrying out the duties of Komsomol Secretary of my department during the required probation period. In 1949 I was admitted as a Candidate Member and in 1950 as a Full Member of the Communist Party of the Soviet Union. It had been a long, hard climb, but it seemed that at last the cloud which had hung over me ever since the arrest of my first husband, Roman Krivosh, thirteen years before, was now finally dispelled. I little guessed what fate had in store for me as I settled back to work and life as a member of Moscow's privileged bureaucracy.

We had jobs, we had a home. Our two-roomed flat on the fifth floor of an apartment in Furmanny Lane was spacious and well-appointed. We had a lift, electric light, gas and telephone and we shared a bathroom and kitchen with only one neighbour. When I had unpacked all our things and arranged them to my liking, I felt a satisfaction known to all too few in desperately overcrowded Moscow; I felt I had my own place where I could really rest, relax and be at home.

I appreciated my own good luck as I heard story after story of families disrupted through congested living conditions. Our neighbour Anna had been evacuated with her son during the war after seventeen years of happy marriage, leaving her husband in Moscow. On her return she found that he had formed a liaison with a girl, who was expecting a baby. Eventually Anna agreed to a divorce, though she still loved her husband dearly. But for a long time, owing to accommodation difficulties, they had to live in neighbouring rooms and Anna had to see the girl who had supplanted her taking her new baby out for a walk, while her own son was neglected by his father.

Our predecessors in the flat were an even worse case. The husband and wife were separated, but could find nowhere separate to live. The wife accordingly occupied one room, where she had drinking parties and entertained men; the husband (whose room formed a passageway to hers) behaved similarly with women friends in retaliation, and their seventeen-year-old daughter followed the example of her mother and father. As a result of this sort of life, the daughter got tuberculosis and had to go to a sanatorium. This brought the parents to their senses and they decided to move at all costs. The mother then moved to Volodya's old room, while the father took over the room that I had occupied. I was relieved to hear that the father reformed his ways and eventually nursed his daughter back to health.

Such stories often came to my mind when I gazed at one of the new imposing public works, requiring armies of men and huge quantities of material, such as the famous Moscow underground, the Metro. Though splendid, it seemed to me unnecessarily lavish and ornate. I knew the reason, of course—to impress foreign visitors, and the Soviet people themselves, with Soviet achievements. But I would ask myself—should not some of this money and effort have gone to building homes for the hard-pressed ordinary people? Of course, I kept these thoughts to myself. At our Embassy in Canberra, when strangers asked me about the Metro, I would counter their questions by asking, 'Have you seen pictures of it?'

'Yes.'

'Don't you think it is fine and impressive-looking?'

'Oh, yes.'

'Well, if it has a fine appearance it has justified its purpose.'

The housing shortage in Moscow was worse in 1950 than before the war, as the expanding bureaucracy swelled the population of the capital. The story of Katya, a simple peasant girl whom I knew well in Moscow, is typical of this influx, which is unmatched by any adequate housing programme. It also shows what ordinary women in the Soviet Union have to endure.

Katya's mother died when she was a year old and her father married again. He was a peasant worker on a collective farm which was extremely poor. To survive between harvests, after the Government levy had been collected, Katya's family had to eat potato-tops and cabbage which they grew in their own vegetable garden.

There was a grimly expressive saying among the peasants at the time, 'The bear takes the top of the crop and only the roots are left.'

With the outbreak of war, Katya's father was called up to the Army and an order came from Moscow that their collective farm was to provide fourteen women for forestry work. Katya was then only fourteen years old and was under the required age, but, because she was a sturdy well-grown girl, the head of the Collective, in the face of her stepmother's protests, decided that she should go. There was no appeal, his word was law. For the next fourteen years of her life Katya did manual work that would have exhausted many men; tree-felling, sawing, stacking timber in the forests near Ryazan. She was constantly wet through and was so wretchedly fed that she had to forage for enough to keep herself alive. She developed chronic trouble with her feet and suffered severe skull injuries when another woman accidentally struck her on the head with an axe. She never completely recovered from this. Even when I knew her, Katya could not sleep in the dark; she had to have a light, or else she felt as though she were being choked. Early in the war her father was killed, and her stepmother received the pension of 120 roubles a month—enough to live on for five or six days at most. After the war, on her release from forestry service, Katya brought her stepmother to Moscow and got work in a factory. There Katya met Andrei, a fellow-worker who fell in love with her and asked her to marry him.

Andrei was kind and devoted but he had nowhere for them to live. It may be of interest to Western readers to know how Katya and Andrei started married life together.

As a bride Katya came home to a single room in which lived Andrei, his mother and father and six grown-up elder brothers. Katya told me that, in addition, her mother-in-law resented and oppressed her and demanded that she hand over the whole of her small pay packet. Eventually Katya and Andrei escaped from these intolerable conditions to a room of their own—the most that a bride can dream of, or the average family expect, in Moscow today.

Three different classes existed in Moscow as we knew it. At the top were the notables, the great ones, a limited, privileged circle, who, so long as they maintained their position, lived in luxury, with town and country houses, servants, cars and chauffeurs and the best of everything. Such were Government Ministers, Department heads, Service chiefs and outstanding literary or theatrical figures. Apart from official occasions in the Red Square or at the Bolshoi Theatre, these great ones are never seen by the ordinary populace, except in fleeting glimpses as they sweep through cleared streets in guarded and escorted cars, or hurry from car to office and office to car.

In this orbit circulate ballerinas and actresses who have protectors among the great. Such was the singer A—— B——, rumoured to be the mistress of a very prominent official, who disappeared from radio programmes after his death. And such was the dancer G—— D——, whose husband was a senior official. In consequence she went on tours abroad and received the best ballet parts, while greater artists had to take second place.

G—— D—— was a byword for her ostentatious bad taste. She drove in a super-luxurious car and wore clothes that, though sumptuous, generally managed to be discordant or unsuitable. They earned her much ridicule behind her back.

I saw her once in Kuibyshev when the Bolshoi Theatre was evacuated there. She was wearing a very beautiful fur coat, and was parading up and down the street by her car, waiting for her important husband. It was an amusing spectacle to me, but it roused bitter feelings in half-starved needy onlookers. I saw one poor woman dressed in rags, gazing with envy and hatred at this display of wealth and privilege by one of the new ruling aristocracy.

Below this upper crust was a large but still privileged middle class of persons like ourselves, outside the ruling clique, but distinguished by Party membership and possession of good Government jobs, which enabled us to live comfortably so long as we made no slip which might enable jealous rivals to displace us. There were plenty of people anxious to do this, as we knew well enough.

Volodya and I both worked hard to maintain our position. He often had to stay on at his office in the evenings. I had the studies and duties I have mentioned as Party Candidate and Komsomol Secretary for my department. Membership of the Communist Party and of the State Security Service is very far from a sinecure.

Party membership in particular, which is the key to advancement in the Soviet Service, carries heavy obligations and real restrictions. Divorce, for example, remains a simple matter for an ordinary citizen, if he can pay the stipulated alimony. It is a different matter for a Party member. The Party unit to which he belongs will examine the case thoroughly and investigate both sides of the question. It is common for wives of Party members to write in and complain about their husbands' behaviour. This happened in my own section. The wife of an M.G.B. colonel wrote in to the Party complaining that her husband was unfaithful to her with another woman; she considered him a disgrace to the M.G.B. Service and concluded, 'I refuse to live with him any more, but I want the Party to help him to take himself in hand, and prevent him spoiling any other women's lives.' Our Party group discussed the wife's plea, heard the husband's case and, after investigation, reprimanded him severely. He had to work very hard to get the reprimand revoked.

Life in the Soviet Union does not encourage sentimentality.

A practice strictly forbidden, but still carried out in secret, was for M.G.B. workers who were contemplating marriage to check the dossier of their future wife or husband to discover in advance if there were any 'compromising material' recorded on the file.

From my own bitter experience I was able to appreciate their desire for this unromantic but understandable precaution before choosing a life's partner and contracting an alliance which could ruin their life.

But the mass of the Moscow people live without the privileges or obligations of Party membership. They are the nameless, passive subjects in the Empire of Fear who stand for hours and days in queues and struggle for the basic necessities of food and clothing.

Foreign visitors often wonder what goes on in the minds of these multitudes as they journey to and from their work, or file in silence past the embalmed body of Lenin (with Stalin now beside him) in his tomb in the Red Square.

It is very hard to say what the Soviet people think. Even the lowliest
Soviet citizen knows that silence is safety and speech dangerous; that in
every building and staircase there are people anxious to advance themselves by reporting criticisms and complaints to the authorities.

There was one such woman in our own block of flats. Her husband
was an M.G.B. worker and she systematically collected gossip from all
the other wives in a more-than-casual way. Volodya warned me, 'Be
careful of her; she's a dangerous woman.' The Soviet Government is
well aware of the general discontent, the weariness with shortages and
the hunger for better conditions. But it relies on suppression to deal
with the problem. This is facilitated by the permanent atmosphere of
crisis and preparation for 'defensive' war, which is maintained in the
Soviet Union. From time to time gestures towards a better deal for the
masses are made. Malenkov sponsored one such move. But Krushchev
has evidently reverted openly to the old austerity policy, giving
priority to heavy industries to safeguard the Soviet Union against
foreign foes. Farewell hopes of relief for the Soviet people!

The scarcity of commodities is illustrated by the story of my watch.
Watches were very hard to get in the U.S.S.R. and Soviet-made watches
were bulky and clumsy. Just before our appointment to Sweden, a
friend of Volodya sent me a delectable stainless steel wrist-watch from
Japan. It was so small and dainty that when I first put it on, my arm
seemed of its own accord to display my watch to best advantage. It was
a rare prize indeed. I thought myself the luckiest woman in the world.
But after a time my watch developed the habit of stopping and unwisely I took it to a Moscow watchmaker. He had a look at it and said
loudly, 'The minute hand is too long, it's touching the rim.' Before I
knew what he was doing he took a pair of scissors and cut off the
minute hand to almost the same length as the hour hand, completely
ruining the watch's appearance. I was so furious and dismayed that I
broke down and wept, though the shop was full of people. 'Look what
you've done!' I cried. 'You've ruined my watch!'

But the watchmaker made no apology, he simply asked for his money
and turned to the next customer.

I went home in tears.

When I got there I told Volodya the whole tragic story, but he
answered, 'Don't cry, we're going to Sweden. I'll get you a better
watch—perhaps even a gold one.'

'I don't want a gold watch,' I sobbed, 'I want this one.'

A few evenings later Volodya came back from work and said, 'I've
found a buyer for your watch. You won't want it in Sweden.' I thought

he was joking, but he was quite serious and went on to explain. A friend of ours had recently been presented with his first child and had promised his wife a wrist-watch to mark the event.

But he had completely failed to find a suitable watch, and had told Volodya of his predicament. Volodya had listened sympathetically, adding kindly, 'Perhaps my wife will sell you hers.'

Next day this man came up to me in the office and asked politely if I could tell him the time. I obliged. 'Thank you, Doosia,' he said. 'By the way, I'm getting congratulations on all sides on the birth of my son and heir.'

'Oh, I congratulate you, too, most sincerely.'

'Yes, indeed, thank you. But, alas, I'm in an awkward position now. I promised my wife a watch and I don't know how on earth I'm going to get her one. Listen, Doosia; you are going abroad; you have always been my good friend. Will you sell me your watch?'

I answered, 'Are you mad? I'd sooner die! Why, I've dreamed all my life of having a watch.'

This conversation took place some six weeks before we were due to leave for Sweden. From then on the embarrassed husband kept at me, gently but persistently returning to the idea that I might be willing to sell him my watch, and describing with a wealth of detail the wonderful watches which I would be able to get abroad.

But to every suggestion I replied, 'No, never; I wouldn't dream of selling my watch.'

On the last day he called at the flat to say good-bye and wish us good luck. Once again he made a last pathetic appeal to me to help him out of his difficulty. Volodya supported his plea.

It was too much. The car was already waiting for us at the door. I took off my watch, gave it to him and said with tears in my eyes:

'Take it, as a present from me. You deserve it.'

He later proved a friend indeed to us. While we were away in Sweden he helped my mother to recover her room, which had been occupied by another family when she was evacuated from Moscow.

When we at last reached Sweden, the first thing I did was to get another watch. We went straight to a jeweller's and I chose it myself— a beautiful, small, oblong, gold Omega. I have it still and it is still a joy, even though the glass has become rather chipped along the edges from knocking against the hard steel of safes.

But a watch is a possession undreamt of by the ordinary Soviet worker whose mind and body are fully engaged in the struggle for existence. He has little time for individuality. Five-year plans and increasing production quotas press on him. After work he arrives back to a crowded room, without facilities for washing, rest or recreation. He has to spend so much of his earnings on food that there is little left for clothing, let alone other luxuries. Only the *élite* in Russia have pyjamas; men sleep in their underwear, women in their slips.

The women suffer most. Practically every housewife must have a job as well as her husband. Almost none can afford to concentrate on their homes and families. Shopping, housekeeping, washing, mending and ironing must be fitted into non-working hours, under the most difficult conditions.

Queues may form a day or more before a shop opens, especially when there is to be an extra release of flour, which the Government used to grant before holidays. As these queues are constantly dispersed by Militiamen (the Soviet police) some unofficial organizing goes on. An organizer goes along the queue writing each woman's number in black pencil in the palm of her hand. She goes off and comes back when her turn is due.

There are no laundering soaps available, like Lux or Persil, only ordinary soap. Here is an official advice for washing day which I read in a Soviet woman's magazine: 'First soak the linen for some hours in tepid water; next rub each article all over with soap; and put into a large metal container. Then dissolve two or three tablespoons of washing soda in a bucket of water and pour into the container; then boil for about two hours. Rinse several times, then dry.'

Imagine the work involved, even under the best conditions! But the average Soviet housewife has to do her washing in a shared kitchen and dry the washed things in the same kitchen, or in her room, or in a corridor. Otherwise, there is a communal yard, where she can hang out her clothes to dry, provided she has time to watch them continuously against the perils of children's dirty hands or light-fingered neighbours. The ordinary Soviet woman does her washing at night, after the day's work.

Where goods of any sort are so scarce, thieving is widespread. Nothing can be left unwatched for a moment. One acquaintance of ours refused ever to leave his room unoccupied; he or his wife had to be there all the time. They even took their holidays at different times. 'Otherwise, who will watch our things?' he asked.

When, after my return from Sweden, I gave some clothes to a Moscow dry-cleaner, I was warned to cut off all the buttons or I would lose them. I removed the buttons, but left a zip-fastener in place. It was gone when the clothes were returned to me.

There is a story about Vertinsky, the famous White Russian singer, who, after years abroad, developed a great longing to return to his native land. After prolonged negotiations and investigations the Soviet Government agreed to allow him in. He arrived by sea and stepped once more on to Russian territory at Vladivostok.

Vertinsky knew what was expected of him. He put down his baggage, crammed with foreign luxuries, on the quay, and gazed in admiration at the new buildings and port works which had sprung up in his absence.

'Oh, my country!' he exclaimed admiringly. 'I do not recognize you!' He looked down and saw that his bags had disappeared. 'Ah, my country,' he said sadly, 'I recognize you!'

Like everyone else in the Soviet Union, Volodya and I worked six days a week, but Sunday was a holiday, when we would go for a picnic or visit a park or a theatre. The Bolshoi Theatre is inaccessible to most Moscow citizens without some special pull. It is the preserve of foreign visitors and high Soviet officials. But we often visited the Red Army Theatre, the Gorky Art Theatre and others. Modern Soviet plays and films are mostly confined to approved themes, such as vigilance against foreign intrigues, Komsomol achievements in the war, what the Soviet citizen can do for his country. However, they are generally free from the unreality and sentimentality of many foreign films. A certain number of foreign films used to be shown in Moscow cinemas, provided that they portrayed the poverty or decadence of life in non-communist countries. But the undoubted favourites with Moscow audiences were dramatized versions of the old Russian classical authors, Dostoievsky, Gogol, Tolstoy, Turgenev. These have a never-failing appeal.

The Kremlin, itself a symbol for sinister mysterious power to the outside world, shows other aspects to the Moscow crowds who visit it, as Volodya and I did with a party from the office. Entering from the side of the Alexandra Park, we passed trees, neat flower-beds, well-kept lawns and many old buildings. It was as clean, tidy and official as Buckingham Palace. Inside, we were conducted through the Museum of Ancient Arms, housing historical relics of the whole Czarist epoch, especially those of Peter the Great, who opened a window to Europe, founded the Russian Fleet and built Petrograd (now Leningrad), to be the equal of any European city. I was always stirred and fascinated by these records of my country's history. The Soviet Government understands the importance of these memorials of the past and tries to enlist the feelings they evoke. During the war, for example, the Soviet people were rallied by reminders of the parallel between our struggle against the German invaders and Russia's defeat of Napoleon's Grand Army in 1812.

Even so, the friendly reception which the advancing Germans at first received in many districts of Russia showed how deep and widespread was the discontent of the Soviet people with their Government. German atrocities did more than spontaneous patriotism to create solidarity between the rulers and the people of the Soviet Union.

Perhaps because their everyday lives are now so drab and strenuous, Moscow people tend to let themselves go on occasions of public holiday —1st May (International Day); 7th October (the Soviet National Day); 5th December (Day of the Stalin Constitution) and the New Year holiday.

Swedish and Australian cities are deserted on holidays; people are in their homes or elsewhere. But in Moscow the streets are crowded with people celebrating in any way that takes their fancy, singing, dancing, playing games. There is music everywhere, from radios, gramophones, pianos, accordions, balalaikas. People don't try to dress up; for most of them it would be impossible; they just come out in whatever clothes they have.

For two or three days before May Day all public buildings are illuminated with many-coloured lights; the Red Square is decorated; the flags of all the Republics of the u.s.s.r. are displayed, vast portraits of the Politburo members appear and great banners are shown, greeting the delegates from the countries of the world with slogans like 'Proletarians of the World Unite', 'We greet the Communist Parties of the World', and 'Workers of Capitalist Countries Struggle on for the Improvement of Living Conditions'. Only those Soviet citizens who have visited foreign countries can fully appreciate the irony of this last appeal.

On May Day morning everyone wakes early, for there are strenuous preparations ahead and the midday feast must be got ready before guests and friends begin to wander in. Each household prepares whatever it can afford. In the average family this is probably not very much —perhaps *piroshki* or meat pies, and a little more meat than usual in the soup. However, whatever can be mustered is spread out on the table. It is part of the Russian temperament on a holiday to be prodigal of the good things while they last. The usual thing is for a dozen or so friends to club together to buy food and drink for the occasion.

For the privileged households there may be a variety of other Russian delicacies, such as carrot, cabbage, or mushroom pies, rice and egg pies, sweet mince pies, turkey, pork, salt fish, stuffed fish, fish in jelly, brawn, ham, cheese, butter and caviare. Drinks include vodka, beer and wines, again governed by the taste and the purse of the particular family. Vodka is usually drunk only by men. Mother and I always preferred wine.

In the afternoon and evening guests will arrive and visits be paid to friends, with much talk, singing and laughter. It is all very gay and very Russian in its wholehearted abandon to the mood of the moment.

I last saw Moscow amid the New Year Festivities of January 1951. But my own mood was tinged with queries and anxieties which kept breaking in on the spirit of the holiday. Not five days before we had been notified that our Australian visas were ready, and that we must leave on 2nd January. The bustle of New Year preparations was already upon us; it was unthinkable that they should be neglected. New Year is the supreme Soviet holiday.

In the end I packed for Australia in fifteen minutes. It was not quite so drastic as it sounds. I took only the minimum, knowing that in a foreign land of abundance I would be able to buy all that I needed.

We moved in a whirl of guests and celebrations right up to the time of our departure. On the first day we had close family friends, on the second our colleagues and friends from the office. My family stayed with us all the time; inevitably our gaiety was restrained and overshadowed by our coming separation. We ate and drank, sang, chatted, danced and listened to operatic music (my father's favourite choice) and I wore my best dress, a rose coloured crepe with tiny pleats which I had bought in Sweden for the Victory celebrations. But Mother especially was sorrowful and heavy-hearted, almost as though she had some premonition that she would never see me again.

When we showed her Australia on the map of the world which hung above Tamara's bed, she sighed and said, 'It is such a long way. Why weren't you sent to some nearer place?'

I always answered, 'What difference does it make? It should be an interesting country to see; the countryside is green all the year round—there's no winter there!'

'No winter?' It was beyond Mother's comprehension. 'How is there no winter?'

Then Tamara would give her a lecture on Australia, drawn from her geography lessons at school and from what she had read in the Soviet *Encyclopaedia*.

Tamara was fascinated by the description of a koala bear, so different from the European brown bears we knew. She implored me to bring her back a live one as a pet, or even a toy one if that was too difficult, and I promised that I would do what I could.

Dear Tamara, wherever you are, I could not fulfil your request. But if you knew the full story you would understand why I could not do it, why it was impossible for me to do anything other than I did, and you would forgive me.

On the night before our departure our guests stayed with us talking into the small hours, almost until we had to leave. But Mother was worn out and went to bed in our flat and Tamara also. When it was time to go I woke them and said good-bye, then left them there to sleep.

The official car was at the door. I threw my last belongings into the case, squeezed the lid shut and we were off to the airport. Our baggage was weighed, Customs officials examined and cleared it and, in the early pre-dawn light, our plane took off and headed for Prague, the first step of our journey to London and Australia.

Farewell, Moscow, farewell for ever.

XX

Moscow by the Molonglo

MOSCOW takes its name from the Moscow river, which snakes through the centre of the great city, and at one point flows close by the ancient walls of the Kremlin. The Molonglo is the quiet, willow-lined stream that winds through the rural centre of Canberra, Australia's federal capital. The title of my chapter is no exaggeration. Volodya and I had said good-bye to Moscow only to find Moscow waiting for us 'down under'. The Soviet Embassy in Canberra, whose doors we entered for the first time on 5th February 1951, was, to a unique degree among foreign embassies, a microcosm of its parent. It was a Soviet fortress on alien territory, a little Moscow on Australian soil.

The Embassy itself, a long two-storied brick building originally designed as a guest house, looked anything but a fortress, even though its high hedge protected most of our windows from prying eyes. It fitted in well enough with the amiable semi-provincial atmosphere of the rest of Canberra. The gates stood open during the day; postmen, telegraph boys, tradesmen and visitors came and went by the front entrance. But behind this undramatic façade was a mentality that was constantly on the defensive, and maintained a barrier between ourselves and the town and people around us. There was no need for special inculcation of this attitude in Soviet citizens appointed abroad; it is habitual, and is well understood by high and low in the Soviet Union as a rule to be observed in all dealings with foreigners and foreign countries.

The reserve was certainly not on the side of the good-natured, easy-going Australians. Throughout our stay in Canberra we met with nothing but friendly treatment. The shop-people did not become less obliging when they recognized me as a Soviet Embassy official. Informality and cordiality marked any parties or meals to which we were invited in Australian homes.

Volodya said that if ever he got into difficulties with the car, some stranger was sure to come up and ask, 'Can I give you a hand there, mate?' Once in the country two farmers towed the car ten miles behind their truck without expecting any reward. I soon became warm friends with the Australian woman who came to the Embassy to teach me English; she asked me to her home and introduced me to her family.

But at the same time, in accordance with standard instructions, I acted on the assumption that she was an agent of Australian Security, whose job was to report on me. (In Moscow a person in her position would inevitably have been an M.V.D.[1] agent.) Even if I had known then, as I know now, that this suspicion was wrong, I would still have had to maintain the vigilance required of all Soviet representatives abroad, and especially of a 'Captain of State Security'.

'The Soviet Union is a fortress besieged by world capital.' Lenin's phrase applied with added force to a Soviet outpost in a capitalist country. We were taught to look for an anti-Soviet or a counter-intelligence purpose behind all apparently innocent approaches. On the voyage out in the *Orcades*, for instance, an elderly Russian-speaking woman had sought my company on deck, but when she began to ask a number of personal questions about our Soviet people on board, I politely excused myself. It might have been simple curiosity, but I was taking no chances. The Kislytsins, who came out later, became friendly on the voyage with a Russian woman who had settled in Australia and who gave them her name and address in Sydney. On arrival here, Kislytsin checked on her with Moscow and asked permission for his wife to correspond with her. Moscow found nothing about her in their records; their reply was—'As this woman is of no interest to us, your wife should cease corresponding with her.'

So the woman's letters to Mrs Kislytsin went unanswered.

This story illustrates better than any generality the terms under which we Soviet representatives abroad had to conduct all relations with foreigners. Such contacts are permissible on two grounds only—business, and cultivation of the person for a purpose approved by Moscow. Otherwise, avoid contact. We were particularly instructed to avoid all interviews with foreign press reporters and photographers, on the assumption that these were all, to a man, agents of the counter-intelligence. They certainly would have been in the Soviet Union.

Of course, diplomatic staffs are expected to mix with other diplomats and with officials of the country to which they are posted, but all such contacts must be reported and justified by their usefulness to Moscow.

The policy is to make the Soviet Embassy a self-contained unit, forti-

[1]For simplicity, we use 'M.V.D.' throughout our Australian chapters, even where M.G.B. or K.I. would be the correct designations.

fied against the attacks and enticements of the capitalist society round about. Social and official life is confined as much as possible to the Embassy community. In Canberra we had two or three meetings a year of the whole staff when we met as members of the Trade Union of Soviet Trade Employees, but we had a meeting every month of the Communist Party members, the inner group, the responsible 'cadres'. Once a month we, the *élite* representatives of the Communist Party of the U.S.S.R., had to assemble in the front hall of the Embassy and the doors would be closed. The Secretary would then say, 'I declare this meeting open. Present your candidates for the Presidium for tonight's meeting.' Voting, by show of hands, we would elect a Presidium of three, who would in turn elect their chairman for the evening. The Chairman would then take charge of the agenda and would call the speakers to the special rostrum with some such introduction as, 'Comrade X will now give a talk on moral and political training in the Embassy'; after this there would be comments and discussion by the others present. Sometimes there would be nothing but innocuous discussion of non-controversial topics, but at other times personal enmities and bitterness flared up fiercely, though always clothed in the language of official duty and zeal for the Party. Everyone knew that the Minutes of these meetings went back to the Central Committee in Moscow, who were the ultimate arbiters of the fate of every one of us present. This knowledge did not help people to relax at Party meetings.

According to the Constitution of the Communist Party of the Soviet Union, all Party members, whatever their status or position, have an equal right to free speech and criticism within the Party. Malenkov, in his speech to the Party Congress in Moscow in the autumn of 1952, had re-emphasized this excellent principle, when he said, 'Criticism and self-criticism from below is an absolute necessity and conditions must be created to assure that everyone in the lower ranks can come forward fearlessly with his criticism.'

So much for the theory. In practice we found things rather different. But I will come to that.

As for social life, we had our own film shows, social evenings, picnics and private parties. Volodya and I were among the few members of the staff capable of carrying on a conversation in English. This ignorance of the language increased the isolation of ordinary staff members from their foreign hosts. Language difficulties were a major barrier. At Melbourne, on the voyage out, Third Secretary Kharkovetz and his wife visited the city and got lost. Although he knew some English he was too shy to ask the way back, and they wandered about for two hours before they spotted another passenger from the *Orcades* and followed him back on board.

Kislytsin, though he had spent three years in London, showed himself acutely shy at our receptions in Canberra, and Antonov, the Tass agent, allowed his language difficulties to undermine his confidence so much that Moscow wrote admonishing him not to be so dismayed about them. But this undermining of confidence in dealing with foreigners is one inevitable result of the Soviet Government's own deep-rooted policy of isolation and suspicion. How can confidence be encouraged under a régime of fear?

Social evenings, for our Soviet people only, were held at the Embassy on the eve of all Soviet public holidays. A committee of two or three would be appointed at a general meeting with the duty of buying food. We women took it in turns in alphabetical order, to assist the cook, arrange and set tables, serve the food and drink and clear away and wash up afterwards. Before the meal there would be a lecture to remind us of the significance of the occasion. Then at half-past eight or nine we would sit down in the main reception room of the Embassy to a typically Russian feast—all the food piled high on the tables, everyone talking and helping themselves without ceremony. At a separate table in another room the Embassy children had their feast, with glasses of lemonade. We grown-ups drank wine, whisky, gin, brandy or beer, according to taste.

Two items were always conspicuous by their absence—vodka and Russian caviare. Moscow always kept us so short of these that our stocks had to be conserved for foreign guests who wanted to feel that they were being entertained in truly Russian style.

We would drink toasts to our Soviet leaders, to the Communist Party, and to one another; there would be music, singing and Russian dances. Presently the children would rush in, screaming, shouting, rolling on the floor and wrestling with each other. The women usually danced with each other, while the men sat at the table, talking and drinking. However, the Ambassador, Lifanov, was a man transformed on these occasions. He would dance, sing Russian folk-songs (he had a good voice) and be the life and soul of the party.

Official receptions, when we entertained foreigners, were an entirely different matter. Apart from the Lifanovs and ourselves, I doubt if any other members of our staff felt at ease or enjoyed these occasions. Strenuous preparations began early in the morning, with the Ambassador in personal charge. The dilapidated furniture was moved out of the reception hall, the tables were covered with cloths down to the floor to conceal their battered legs, vacuum cleaners buzzed all day, someone was sent post-haste to buy more glasses (we never seemed to have enough). When this crisis occurred, as it did before every reception, I used to recall a proverb which pokes fun at Russian improvidence and our national tendency to leave things to the last moment, 'When we are about to go hunting, then we feed the dogs.'

The Ambassador always ordered all members of our diplomatic staff and their wives to be present. For most it was an excruciating torture. Uneasy, unable to converse with the visitors, they stood like dummies. Then, when the last guest had departed, they would heave a heavy sigh and exclaim, 'Thank the Lord, *that's* over!' (That is the exact Russian phrase. A generation of anti-religious propaganda has not eliminated such expressions from common Russian speech.)

Then we would rearrange the tables and sit there amid the remains of the party while the Ambassador asked for comments.

There was always one: 'Not enough vodka!'

He would reply, 'We couldn't help that; Moscow didn't send us enough.'

Moscow's requirement was that every conversation of any significance should be reported, together with comments on persons of interest who had attended. These receptions were fishing grounds for useful contacts, which might ultimately produce recruits for our espionage networks.

The non-diplomatic members of the Embassy staff did not attend such receptions, but the Tass representative always came. The distinction of 'diplomat' was highly prized within our own ranks. When we travelled out to Australia in the *Orcades* Volodya was classified merely as a 'clerk'. He was promoted to Third Secretary, with diplomatic rank, soon after our arrival. This device was intended to prevent the Australian Counter-Intelligence from assessing his true importance on the Embassy staff. But on the voyage, because of this difference in status, the ranking Third Secretary, Kharkovetz, who travelled with us, arranged to have his meals at a different sitting, rather than share our table in the dining saloon. We ate with the chauffeur, Koukharenko, and his wife Valya.

Since all foreign Embassies in Moscow are obliged to employ Russian domestic staff, cooks, cleaners, etc., who are in fact all M.V.D. agents, Moscow naturally insists that all such humble jobs in Soviet posts abroad must be filled by our own people. The employment of locals was forbidden. Among this lower order of Embassy employees at Canberra were Masha Golovanov and her husband, who was a

Night Duty Officer, and Koukharenko, the chauffeur. These simple folk were our friends whom we trusted and who had no part in the intrigues which eventually drove Volodya to seek the desperate remedy of flight.

Fedya Koukharenko was a good husband to his young wife Valya and was devoted to his little boy Lyosha. She was grateful for this, loyally supported her husband, and got him out of a number of scrapes into which his fondness for the bottle landed him. Once she heard that the Ambassador was refusing to allow Fedya to drive him home, on account of his drunken state. She hurried to the Embassy and found Lifanov in a quandary. 'What do you think?' he asked her. 'Is he too drunk to drive me?'

Valya looked at her husband.

'He is drunk, but not too drunk to drive,' she replied stoutly.

'Are you sure of that?'

'If he does not get you home safely, you can cut my head off.'

The Ambassador got into his car, Fedya drove him to his home without mishap, drove back to his own house, stopped the car at his front gate, fell asleep, and slept at the wheel till dawn.

Valya saw the Ambassador at the Embassy the following morning and asked pertly, 'Well, Nikolai Mikhailovich, are you going to cut my head off?'

Lifanov could be very genial when it suited him. He laughed. 'No, Valya, it would be a pity to cut off such a clever head as yours.'

The Koukharenkos were a happy family. Fedya used to talk confidentially to the five-year-old Lyosha, who was very proud of his 'r's'. When anyone asked him, 'What does your father drink, Lyosha?' he was delighted to be able to answer, 'Rrrrum!'

Because he got bullied by the other Embassy children, Lyosha played with the Australian children in Lockyer Street, where they, and we, lived. He became a favourite with them, especially as he always shared his sweets with them and reminded his mother to get a present when any of them had a birthday. Once when young Lyosha was missing, Valya went along the street asking his playmates if they had seen him. The children thereupon organized a search-party and found Lyosha at a nearby shopping centre.

I tell this story to show that Soviet people are fundamentally the same as other people, and are natural friendly neighbours when the pressure of fear does not compel them to be hostile and suspicious.

When Volodya and I were first shown into the Canberra Embassy, and were confronted with our future colleagues, ranged to receive us, my heart sank. The women especially looked a dreadfully unprepossessing lot, dumpy, drab and stolid. I was to find both enemies and friends among them in the days ahead.

However, a tall, well-groomed man, who looked quite a dandy by Moscow standards of dressing, advanced and said with aplomb, 'Greetings and welcome to our Embassy; my name is Prudnikov.' We responded with our names, shook hands with him and were introduced round the assembly.

Prudnikov, whose name had been mentioned to us by a friend at M.V.D. Headquarters in Moscow, was the Chief Cypher Clerk at the Embassy; we had been advised to keep on good terms with him. Prudnikov was secretly a co-opted (not a regular) M.V.D. worker. He was in charge of the secret section of the Embassy, at the southern end of the top floor, where all the cyphering and secret correspondence was handled, and only specially nominated persons were admitted. Prudnikov was very friendly and helpful to us at first, until it began to look dangerous, when he changed sides. His wife was a nice woman, who brought up their son to be obedient and polite, but her husband called the tune. They occupied two rooms on the top floor of the Embassy building. It is a rule that Chief Cypher Clerks must live on the premises.

We soon met the other members of the relatively small Canberra Embassy.

Lifanov, the Ambassador, who in his nine years in Australia became a familiar figure to many diplomats and Australian officials, appeared to most of them as a genial host and acquaintance, with a kind, almost fatherly manner, who talked of his apprenticeship as a fitter in a Moscow factory, and of all that he owed to the Revolution. There was another side to his character, which I will describe presently, and it is likely that his family were at least prosperous influential folk in the village where he was brought up. I judge this from his education, and from his family's influence with the priest. In old Russia before the Revolution it was the priest, not the parents, who chose a child's name at baptism. But Lifanov told us that his family had been allowed to choose his names themselves.

Mrs Lifanov had a difficult position to fill. She was Lifanov's second wife. His first wife, a beautiful woman, had left him, leaving him with a daughter who was the apple of his eye. His second wife had been a tutor to this girl in Moscow. She had a good brain, and became fluent in English in Australia. But she had no clothes-sense and did not seem to care how she looked. It may have gone deeper than that. Brought up in a very poor family in Moscow, she regarded her time abroad, as so many

Russians do, as a golden chance to amass possessions unheard of in the Soviet Union. She skimped on the housekeeping money to buy materials; and had a special room where she accumulated odds and ends, like the miser Plushkin in Gogol's satire, *Dead Souls*. Her clothes were the laughing-stock of the Embassy staff. Even doorkeepers' wives, on a quarter the salary, dressed better, and people used to ask concerning the old brown coat which she wore at all seasons, year in, year out, 'Is there any lining left i n it?' In her nine years in Australia she bought one pair of nylons; after that, declaring them too expensive, she wore patched cotton stockings. Once when our whole staff were going to see some sheepdog trials, she appeared in stockings so stained and dirty that her husband clapped his hands in front of us all and cried, 'Come, Mother, you can't go out like that! Look at your stockings!'

'No one else would have noticed it!' she answered, ran back to the Embassy and refused to appear again. My last picture of her is when the Lifanovs left for Moscow. She was wearing a silver fox fur over a raincoat.

Poor woman, she had a lot to put up with. Though she was thin, she tried to indulge her husband's preference for plump women by wearing several petticoats and thick underwear, even in hot weather. But he would call her a *mujik* (peasant) and say she was hopeless. Once when Volodya returned from a trip to Sydney with Lifanov, he told me that Lifanov had bought his wife a nice dress. Afterwards, at her house, I asked her to show me her nice new frock. She showed it to me, but said, 'It's not for me, you know, it's for his daughter Galina.' Such incidents cannot have helped her to feel confident and happy in her position as Ambassador's wife.

Towards me, her husband's new secretary, she was suspicious and hostile. There was a background to this. My predecessor, a single girl, had been on extremely friendly terms with the Ambassador, and his wife thought that I might follow her example. So, I discovered, did the Ambassador. They were both wrong. I was correct and official in my dealings with him. But neither of them liked me any the better for it.

Of the diplomats' wives I liked Mrs Zaryezov, wife of the Second Secretary, the best. She was moderately tall, plump, and wore a typically Russian hair-do, a bun at the back of her head. She was well-educated, had been a teacher and played the piano for our social evenings at the Embassy. She was a good mother, too. Her son, Misha, though only three, used to greet people politely and, if asked in English, 'How are you?' would reply 'Very well, thank you.' If other children called him out to play, he would say, 'Excuse me.' This was in marked contrast to the rowdy, undisciplined children of Kovaliev, the Commercial Attaché. However, as he was frequently drunk at social occasions when the children were present, they can hardly be blamed.

But Mrs Zaryezov often seemed melancholy and I came to the conclusion that it was because her husband was extremely niggardly over her clothes. In the two years I knew her I only saw her wear two bought dresses, both two-piece frocks. Normally she wore unbecoming clothes which she made herself. She had very few shoes, though what she had were in good taste and she had only one suit, which fitted her, as we say in Russian, 'like a saddle on a cow.' Her husband had probably had it made to order in Sydney without any fittings. Poor thing, she knew it well enough, but could never do anything about it, because of her husband's meanness. It was all the more distressing because she was, for the time being, in a country where, if you had money, there were good clothes to buy. Back in Moscow, most of these things would be unobtainable at any price.

Altogether, Mrs Zaryezov was a nice woman who was pleasant to everyone and bore her affliction with considerable resignation.

XXI

Gathering Storm

Now I come to the story of the campaign against us in the Embassy, first under Lifanov, then under his successor, Generalov, which in the end drove Volodya to desperation and changed the course of both our lives. It is a story that reveals at every point the special characteristics of the Soviet system. It is a documentary of the empire of fear. By chance, Zaryezov's meanness marks a first move in the game.

Both Volodya and I had been posted to Australia as Intelligence Officers, I as a Captain of State Security, he as Lieutenant-Colonel. (Later he was promoted to full Colonel.) We were sent out to organize Soviet espionage under cover of our official Embassy appointments. But this cover was vital; it had to be effective not only against the enemy counter-intelligence, but against our Embassy colleagues, apart from those authorized by Moscow to be 'in the know'. Hence the complex web of security precautions within our own ranks.

As soon as we received our foreign appointments, we severed all apparent connection with the M.V.D. in Moscow and behaved as ordinary employees of the Ministry of Foreign Affairs. We went to work at that Ministry and we each did courses to fit us for our cover roles—Volodya as Consul, I as Secretary-Accountant (I knew nothing of accountancy when I started). We each had to learn sufficient details of our pretended careers in the Ministry of Foreign Affairs to deceive any inquisitive colleagues as to our real background as permanent M.V.D. officers.

This procedure illustrates how, in Moscow's eyes, the open functions of an Embassy are subsidiary to the main business of espionage.

At Canberra my job as Accountant brought swift complications. It appeared that thirty-four years of socialism in the Soviet Union had not abolished the interest of Soviet citizens in money. Because of that, I was the cause of our first collision with Lifanov.

I might have been warned by the experiences of a woman friend of mine who had been Accountant at the Soviet Consulate-General in Pretoria, and who had objected to her boss's wife booking up her private laundry as public expenditure. 'If you let your chief have his way,' she told me, 'you are in Moscow's bad books. On the other hand, if you stick strictly to Moscow's rules you will be unpopular with your chief. Choose for yourself.'

I chose to obey my written instructions from Moscow. They were quite clear and my own reputation was at stake. In fact my predecessor had been reprimanded and fined for irregularities. When I took over I insisted on all the staff paying the regulation rent for their furniture (it was Embassy property, not their own). Zaryezov led the protests and the Ambassador tried to override the regulations, saying, 'I'll attend to that; your job is simply to pay out money as I direct.'

But I was not prepared to contravene Moscow's instructions. I refused. When the Moscow Auditor in due course visited Canberra, he approved my accounts and confirmed my action.

But Lifanov was now my enemy. Instead of an amenable young girl, he had now a correct but official secretary and an accountant whom he could not dictate to.

That, briefly, was how it all began.

Zaryezov now returned to the attack. At a Party members' meeting he raised 'the matter of Petrova's table'.

'What is that?' I asked in bewilderment. Then he explained. Before my arrival someone had put a large portrait of Stalin in the centre of the table where I worked, underthe glass top. Without touching Stalin's portrait, I had added, near the bottom corner, two magazine pictures; the first of a Hollywood actress with an eccentric hair-do, the second of a dog playing the piano. Both these pictures had amused me and I had put them under my table-top without another thought.

'Comrade Petrova,' announced Zaryezov severely, 'keeps pictures of a girl and a dog close to the portrait of Stalin.'

'What nonsense!' I answered, 'they are not close together at all. I certainly never intended a jibe at Stalin; you know that, Comrade Zaryezov. If you are trying to prove your vigilance, this only shows up your malice!'

But I was very upset. The consequences of such a petty incident can be very serious in the fear-ridden whispering gallery of Soviet official circles. I knew very well that the minutes of every Party meeting went to the Central Committee of the Party in Moscow. In most countries such a charge would have been laughed out of court. But I did not take it lightly. I wrote to the Central Committee, insisting on the baselessness of the charge. I even enclosed a sketch of the lay-out of the top of my table. I knew only too well what a breath of suspicion, however baseless, can do on the file of a Soviet citizen.

It was Zaryezov who later brought an equally ludicrous charge against Volodya. When Volodya was sitting in his Consular office on the ground floor of the Embassy, our dog Jack jumped through the window, and ran up and down in the corridor before he was caught and taken home. Zaryezov moved a censure motion about this occurrence which was recorded and sent to Moscow with the minutes of the meeting. That was in Lifanov's time.

When the new Ambassador, Generalov, arrived with all the authority and importance of an emissary fresh from Moscow, one of his first actions was to send for Volodya. With the utmost solemnity he said, 'Vladimir Mikhailovich, the Central Committee of the Communist Party of the Soviet Union has ordered that you are not to bring your dog into the precincts of our Embassy.'

To Western readers these incidents may seem too trifling and petty to be considered, the commonplace frictions that occur in any office or station, like our Canberra Embassy. But, in a small Soviet community like ours, living under the remote yet menacing shadow of Moscow's authority, these small incidents could be, and were, magnified to alarming proportions. They were like the first warning pebbles of an avalanche.

What was at the root of the hostility and intrigue against us which began almost from the time of our arrival in Canberra?

Envy played a big part. Volodya and I had no children and were both in good jobs. We computed our combined annual salary at about £A8,000. Its actual purchasing power in Moscow (where half of it was deposited) was nothing like that value. Nevertheless we were quite the most prosperous couple in the Canberra Embassy. Lifanov never failed to raise his eyebrows and make some pointed comment on our prosperity when I brought him the staff salary lists to sign. We had our own house, 7 Lockyer Street, in the suburb of Griffith and we had a minimum quantity of furniture which was M.V.D. property.

I am sure that many of the other Embassy women were jealous of my liking for nice clothes and my good fortune in being able to buy them. But the root cause of the trouble, it seems to me now, was deeper than any of these issues. It was a conflict inherent in the whole Soviet system of suspicion, check and counter-check. Lifanov knew that Volodya and I were M.V.D. officers and therefore represented a separate arm of authority which was never safely under his control. We had our separate channels of communication, our own Headquarters in Moscow.

It was, in fact, quite common for Soviet Ambassadors abroad to attempt to discredit the M.V.D. Residents, and to bring about a quick shuffle of replacements, lest the Resident should acquire too much in-

fluence and become a threat to the Ambassador himself. It was an
understandable reaction in the circumstances.

After Beria's arrest, Lifanov told us of a particular personal reason
which he had for hating the M.V.D. In 1938, the worst year of the
purges, his brother had been arrested and kept in prison for six months;
on his release he would not tell anyone the reason for his arrest; he had
promised to keep silence.

For all these reasons Lifanov encouraged a campaign to discredit and
isolate us among the Embassy staff. Mrs Lifanov spread hostile gossip
against us among the Embassy wives. Under the Soviet system gossip
has exceptional power to harm.

Lifanov also enlisted the Party Secretary, Kovaliev, against us. The
power of a Soviet Ambassador over his staff lies in the fact that a period
of foreign service means extra pay and an opportunity to acquire commodities unprocurable in the Soviet Union. It is a chance that may only
come once in a lifetime. Each staff member goes in fear of the Ambassador's power to have him recalled at short notice to the Soviet Union,
as well as to make a damaging report on his behaviour abroad. I heard
Lifanov threaten Koukharenko once, 'I'll have you sent back to Moscow if you don't behave!' What a mockery of the myth that Soviet
citizens abroad are always longing to get back home!

The Ambassador calls the tune. The Kleshovs, for example, were
friendly to us at first. Then their attitude became reserved and distant.
On the eve of their return to Moscow I asked Mrs Kleshov directly
about it.

'Why do you avoid my company? Why do you dislike me?' She
relented. 'Doosia, I don't dislike you at all. Now that we are going
back, I can tell you that we are your friends. But we dared not ignore
the Ambassador's lead.'

I understood. There is an apt Russian proverb: 'The fish goes bad,
beginning at the head.'

Gradually the whole staff began to take their cue from the Lifanovs
and to adopt the same guarded reserve, though most of them had no
feelings of personal ill-will towards us. It was the old scramble to avoid
being linked with anyone under the cloud of official disfavour. Prudnikov was in a key position to keep himself informed on the progress
of these intrigues. As Chief Cypher Clerk, he saw all the secret communications of the Embassy except the correspondence between our
M.V.D. office and Headquarters, which we handled separately, using our
own codes. Prudnikov had been secretly co-opted in Moscow as an
M.V.D. agent. Moreover, a feud arose between him and our Party

secretary Kovaliev, after Kovaliev succeeded him in that position. Therefore, Prudnikov decided to show us two signals which vitally concerned us.

But first, a glance at world events.

On the 6th March 1953 we heard the news of Stalin's death. It came to us as a bombshell. At first we did not believe it. We had had no prior notification from Moscow. The first we knew was when Australian pressmen began to besiege the Embassy with telephone calls asking for confirmation of the report. I should explain that the decrepit radio on which we struggled to hear the Moscow news was not functioning properly. (After this experience a good set was bought.) The Ambassador could tell the pressmen nothing. At his direction Volodya booked a trunk call to our Soviet Legation in New Zealand, to see whether they could shed any light on the matter. While waiting for the call, our radio picked up Moscow, and we heard the momentous news confirmed.

Thereafter everyone went about the Embassy with ostentatious grief, in deference to the fiction that Stalin was a figure revered and loved as Lenin, Kirov and other old Bolsheviks had been loved by their people. Crocodile tears coursed down official cheeks. Lifanov appeared in his shirt-sleeves, as though too distracted to bother about his appearance. We stood round reverently, listening to the interminable description by Moscow Radio. Wearily and absent-mindedly I sat down in a chair. Somebody turned on me indignantly and exclaimed, 'Doosia! How could you? At a time like this!'

But there were no incurable cases. In time everyone recovered from their grief for Stalin.

Then came still more dramatic and startling news. On the 10th July the arrest of Beria was announced to the world. He was our supreme chief. Immediately after Stalin's death, Beria had united under his own control the two key Ministries of State Security and Internal Affairs under the all-embracing title of M.V.D.

Three months later Beria fell, brought down by the outmanœuvrings of Malenkov and other rivals jealous of his immense power.

These climacteric changes at the top did not immediately affect the operations of the State Security machine at the level where Volodya and I worked. We made no comment to anyone, and continued with our jobs.

Soon afterwards a Party meeting was called to hear the charges against the traitor Beria, which Moscow had sent out in detail. The Party Secretary read them out to us. There was nothing original in them to anyone who remembered the great Moscow trials of the 'thirties. We were told that Beria had sabotaged Soviet industry and agriculture, had been a long-term agent of British and American Intelligence, had conspired with foreign countries to restore capitalism in the Soviet Union. Furthermore it was charged that Beria had tried to place the M.V.D. above the Government and the Communist Party of the Soviet Union; from the first moment when he took over control, he had begun a widespread replacement of staff with this object in mind. Therefore, every Soviet citizen must be on his guard against the enemy; in particular, added Kovaliev, every member of the Embassy staff must beware of efforts by agénts or followers of Beria to insinuate themselves into important positions and recruit further adherents to this cause.

That was a very quiet meeting. We listened to the charges with wooden faces; nobody had anything to say. Then we all went home.

But certain persons' minds had been busy and had hit on a new way to discredit us.

Some time after this meeting Prudnikov showed us the signals to Moscow which really frightened us. There were two—one from the Ambassador to the Ministry of Foreign Affairs, the other from the Party Secretary to the Central Committee. In identical terms they charged (1) that I was causing division in the ranks and (2) that, together, we were plotting to form a Beria faction in the Embassy.

The first charge was almost a matter of routine in Soviet campaigns of defamation. We could hope that Moscow would take it with a grain of salt. Indeed, this had happened once before. Volodya, as Acting-Resident, had received from M.V.D. headquarters a mildly-worded letter which read, 'According to information in our possession, Mrs Petrov occasionally shows a lack of tact in her relations with the employees of the Embassy, including the Ambassador, which cannot fail to have an adverse effect on her work. In this connection we request you to administer an appropriate reprimand to her.'

Volodya showed me this letter. I quote from the transcript of the Royal Commission's proceedings:

Windeyer: The headquarters in Moscow having directed you to reprimand Mrs Petrov, did you reprimand her?
Petrov: Yes, I did.
The Chairman: What did she reply?
Petrov: She only laughed.

It was clear that the letter had been sent in response to representations made by Lifanov through the Ministry of Foreign Affairs. We heard no more about the matter from Moscow and the episode seemed to have blown over.

But neither of us felt like laughing over this Beria charge. Its falseness made little difference to its menacing implications. It was a political charge of the gravest kind. Both of us had seen people's lives blighted by far less serious accusations. Rage mingled with my alarm. My fight for life after Krivosh's arrest, my thirteen years' toil and struggle to prove myself and to clear my name, came over me afresh. Now it was on again in deadly earnest. This time I was not simply the victim of my husband's fate; Volodya and I were both equally threatened.

The 'Beria group' charge was utterly baseless. It was merely an attempt to link us with the latest victim of the struggle for supreme power in Moscow. Although Beria had been head of the m.v.d. we were in no sense his personal followers. We would certainly have been arrested at the time of his fall if that had been the case. As for 'splitting the collective', it was true that I had refused to be as subservient to the Ambassador as he wished, but I felt that I had right and Moscow's directive on my side. Our isolation from some members of the staff had been Lifanov's doing, not ours.

As soon as Prudnikov showed us the signals from Lifanov and Kovaliev, we at once sent off our own account of the business to m.v.d. Headquarters. Neither we nor our attackers received any immediate reply; Moscow reserved its judgment for the time being. Up to the very last moment Volodya and I hoped that the slanders against us would be exposed and discredited in Moscow.

Then Lifanov was recalled. But before his departure, in September 1953, he brought his charges into the open at one of the Party meetings which were the battleground for the open part of the campaign.

'Comrade Petrova,' he accused, addressing the worried faces of his intimidated staff, 'has been a harmful influence here ever since her arrival. She has caused division and dissension in our Embassy, and she has used her husband as a mouthpiece for her schemes! This pair have presumed too far; they have tried to set themselves above the Party Secretary here and above myself, as Ambassador.

'I charge them with plotting to form a Beria faction in our Embassy!'

Kovaliev backed him up. In spite of our indignant denials, the writing was on the wall. From that point it was either them or us.

Lifanov's object was obvious. He wanted the minutes of the meeting, endorsing what he had said, to reach the Central Committee, to convince Moscow that his quarrel with us was not a personal feud, but had the backing of the Party comrades in the Embassy. Obediently they followed his lead.

But not all. It was at this meeting that blunt, honest Ivan Golovanov rose and exclaimed to Volodya, 'Vladimir Mikhailovich, you have denied all the slanders and lies that have been spoken against you. They can be refuted and you yourself are in a position to refute them.'

Volodya answered him wearily from his seat:

'Ivan Ivanovich, you are still young, and there are many things you do not know.'

After this meeting Prudnikov became extremely careful where we were concerned. Though remaining outwardly friendly, he avoided us and never again came to our home. He had a delicate path to tread. On the one hand he wanted to keep in our good graces since we represented the M.V.D.; on the other, the good opinion of the Ambassador was all-important to him for his future. He watched to see which way the cat would jump.

Lifanov's departure gave us fresh hope. Perhaps his successor would usher in a new era and improve the poisoned atmosphere in the Embassy.

But Lifanov had made his plans where we were concerned. The copy of his telegram to Moscow had been destroyed according to regulations. But a copy of Kovaliev's telegram was left on the files, and on it Lifanov wrote, 'Comrade Prudnikov, please inform Generalov of the contents of my telegram concerning the Petrovs.'

Prudnikov showed us this, in his effort to keep in with both sides. But just what he said to the new Ambassador, we, of course, never knew.

The new Ambassador, Generalov, arrived in October 1953, and our hopes of a better deal were dashed at once. He greeted the other members of the staff, but patently avoided us as long as he could. His first words to Volodya were the warning about our dog Jack, which showed that he had studied the reports on us before he left Moscow and had evidently received some directions. Our best hope now was that M.V.D. headquarters would step in firmly on our behalf. They had not yet spoken.

Generalov's wife originated the pie-throwing story. She was prejudiced against me from the start. The truth of that episode was as follows. When preparations for receptions were required, we women took our turn in alphabetical order. But Mrs Generalov omitted her obsequious satellite, Mrs Pipniakov, and told me to take her place. I refused, as a meeting of the women had fixed the roster system, but in the end I gave way. While we were making meat pies in the kitchen, Mrs Generalov came and stood beside me. As I put a pie down she would pick it up and remake it in the most ostentatious way. At last I turned my back on her and walked away. Then she concocted the story that I had thrown a pie at her. Generalov accused me of this at the next Party meeting, but not one of the other women who had been present was prepared to support the story.

Generalov's next move was to dismiss me from my job as Ambassador's secretary. This was strictly against regulations. As I had been appointed to the job in Moscow, I could not properly be removed locally. I protested, but got no support from our colleagues. They were afraid to speak. The odds were mounting against us.

Prudnikov was silent also. He was due for recall to Moscow, and was in such terror about his future that he became actually ill. When Generalov wrote him a strong commendation to take back, he became flushed with delight and recovered his health overnight. Naturally, when local tyrants get such a sense of their own power, they resent the presence of anyone who questions their dictatorship. That was at the root of all our troubles in Canberra.

Meanwhile, apart from the strain imposed by this campaign against us in our own Embassy, we had exacting duties to perform on behalf of Soviet Intelligence in Australia.

The situation which I found in our small M.V.D. Residency in Australia was very different from that in Stockholm.

We were desperately short-staffed. In our four years' stay, I only left Canberra three times, for brief trips to Sydney. Soon I asked to be relieved of all outside operational tasks, which Moscow agreed to. I had, indeed, a strenuous enough programme inside the Embassy. Apart from running my own house, I did duty as Embassy Accountant and Ambassador's secretary, with an office on the ground floor, and as cypher clerk to the M.V.D. Resident, with an office in the secret Cypher Section upstairs.

One amusing incident arose from my dual functions as Ambassador's secretary and M.V.D. officer. For some reason much of the Australian mail for our Soviet people, even though addressed to their homes, was delivered by the Canberra postal authorities to the Embassy itself. Lifanov directed me to open all such mail. His reason was that a number of anti-Soviet Russians in Australia had begun to write provocative letters to Embassy workers, enclosing anti-Soviet pamphlets. It was my job to intercept these pamphlets, which I handed over to Volodya. He destroyed them, and we sent a few copies to M.V.D. Headquarters for record purposes.

One day, just before Lifanov left for Moscow, I opened a letter addressed to him at his home, but delivered to the Embassy. The letter itself was typed, but Lifanov was addressed in handwriting by his first two names. The writer, who signed his name, urged Lifanov to stay in Australia instead of returning to the Soviet Union; he had been popular during his long stay here; he ought to think of the future of his wife and son as well as his own. A Post Office box number was given for contact. I kept this letter from Lifanov and showed it to Volodya. The diplomatic couriers were just leaving for Moscow, so we added a paragraph to our periodical report and sent the letter off to M.V.D. Headquarters.

The effect was electric. Within a few days we were bombarded by Top Secret signals from Moscow, urgently demanding all details— How was the letter addressed? How was it delivered? Who had seen it? What further action had been taken? It was clear that Moscow was thoroughly alarmed and was anxious to forestall any possible attempt at defection by Lifanov on the journey, should the letter have sown any dangerous ideas in his mind. We assured Moscow that we had protected Lifanov from the letter and that he had not seen it.

In the event, it is unlikely that he ever did see it, or learn of its existence; it would remain on his personal dossier in the secret files of the M.V.D. There it will stay till his death. It is equally unlikely that he will read the pages of this book; inside the Soviet Union that privilege will be reserved for a very select number of high M.V.D. officers and Government officials.

This episode of the letter has an ironical twist in the light of our own subsequent fate. My various duties certainly kept me busy.

Pakhomov, who became M.V.D. Resident soon after our arrival in Australia, was also the Soviet's Tass agent and lived in Sydney, two hundred miles away. Therefore, I had to cope single-handed with all M.V.D. correspondence between ourselves and Moscow. Later, when Pakhomov was recalled and Volodya was made Acting Resident in his place, it was easier from the point of view of communications.

But by that time the Embassy campaign against us had become intense and relentless. We had the task of organizing Soviet espionage against Australia, while defending ourselves against the attacks of our jealous colleagues on our doorstep. The Embassy, which should have been a strong home base, had become more menacingly hostile than the alien society whose secrets we had to steal. I remembered the 'Second Front' which Stalin had called for so vehemently when the Germans were pressing the Soviet armies hard. Volodya and I had to fight a war on two fronts with a vengeance.

The campaign undermined Volodya completely. After the Beria accusation he was hardly recognizable as the same man. Instead of his normal placid self he became nervous and haggard and distraught. He knew too much, had seen too many tragedies which had their origin in the sort of lies and calumnies that were now being directed at us.

It is time for him to tell the story of his work in Australia, and of the stages that led remorselessly to his fateful step on the 3rd April 1954.

XXII

Consul—Conspirator—Spy Chief

'In australia, Comrade Petrov, you will have a most important task.' Small, dapper General Utekhin spoke politely and precisely as he briefed me at m.v.d. headquarters in Moscow. 'Anti-Soviet elements are strong there. The Australian immigration policy has opened the door to anti-Soviet Balts and to renegades among Soviet citizens who refused to return home from Germany. You must detect these individuals and organizations, and recruit agents to report their plans and activities.'

That was my commission from the 'em' Department of the m.v.d., which watched 'Emigré' populations in every country where anti-Soviet forces might gather strength. The case of Khoklov, who was sent to assassinate the leader of an anti-Soviet emigré organization in Frankfurt, shows the degree of Soviet concern with this problem.

My other secret assignment was the 's.k. line', which meant that I was responsible for keeping security watch over all the Soviet colony in Australia, namely, the members of our Embassy, and the two hundred miscellaneous holders of Soviet passports. I knew the principles of this job pretty thoroughly, having worked on it for the previous three years in Moscow, and before that in Sweden. Before leaving for Australia I examined the s.k. files on the Canberra Embassy, to put myself fully in the picture. I was interested to see that Ambassador Lifanov himself featured in them. Lifanov's file recorded that two arrested students declared him to have been a member of a Trotskyite group in his student days. However, just before they were shot, the students had retracted. Perhaps they had merely hoped to save their own lives by denouncing someone else. I did not attach much importance to the story. When I got to Australia I told Lifanov, on Moscow's instructions, that I was charged with s.k. work in the Embassy, but naturally kept to myself my knowledge of his own file in Moscow. He made no comment on my disclosure, and promised his assistance with this important task; but I doubt whether it increased my popularity with him to know that I was the m.v.d.'s secret overseer. Also on the files was the scandal of Mrs Nina Smirnov, wife of a previous Embassy Accountant, who had tried to escape and settle in Australia. She had made arrangements to get a job in Sydney and had actually taken trunks and travelling cases to the home of a woman friend in Canberra when her plan was discovered, and she was arrested and sent back to the Soviet Union. The file recorded that her husband, who assisted the Soviet authorities, had not been punished but that Mrs Smirnov herself had been sentenced to ten years as a political offender. My s.k. job was to detect and prevent any other attempts of this kind. I recruited half a dozen 'collaborators', and directed the investigation of one or two suspected cases; but no compromising material came to light, and I can justly claim that no defections occurred while I remained in the Soviet Embassy at Canberra.

What greater irony could there be than the fact that the first person to escape from the Soviet Embassy to refuge in Australia was myself, the specialist in preventing such occurrences! But it is more than ironical, it is an exposure of the whole system of loyalty ensured by supervision. I was entrusted with this very confidential work because of my struggle up from proletarian origins and my unblemished record as a sound, unambitious Party worker and m.v.d. officer.

And, indeed, when I arrived in Australia I had no thought of defection in my mind. I fully intended to carry out the tasks assigned to me by Moscow to the best of my ability during my term in Australia. I will describe presently the shocks and intrigues that drove me to become a refugee (my enemies will say a traitor) from my service and my country. Fear drove me to do what I did. Fear is a potent weapon; but it often turns back on those who use it.

But first, something about my life and work in Australia. The country impressed us at once. At Melbourne, our first port of call, we were delighted by the beautiful Botanical Gardens, the black swans—a marvel I had read about—and the shops crammed with an abundance of goods. At Station Pier, where we berthed, the bronzed and burly wharf labourers were in marked contrast to the pallid and undernourished dock workers one sees at Russian ports. Sydney made an equally favourable first impression, from the moment we passed the Heads. Pakhomov, the Tass representative, met us along with Sadovnikov, the m.v.d. Resident, and took us to lunch at his flat and then shop-gazing. In Sydney there was the same sense of prosperity-full shops, everyone in the street well and fashionably dressed. One thing that struck me was the attentiveness of the salespeople. In the Soviet Union, scarcity and strict controls put the buyer in the position of a suppliant. In Moscow I often had to go up to a salesman lounging against a wall and practically force him to serve me. There are too many buyers and too few things to buy.

In Canberra, though it seemed more like a pleasant country town than a capital city, we had our own house and garden; we appreciated the trees, parks, and houses, each with their own gardens, and the fine dry climate. Some of my happiest interludes there were fishing and shooting trips in the country round Canberra. There seemed every reason why we should enjoy our tour of duty here no less than our pleasant years in Sweden. It was not Australia's fault that things were so different for us.

As well as those of Consul, my open official duties included that of representative of VOKS, the Soviet cultural organization. In this way I had a chance which my jealous colleagues greatly envied, to travel about, meet the local population, and see the country.

The Australia-Russia societies in the various states were my channels for the distribution of VOKS material. I sent these societies quantities of Soviet literature, gramophone records and films which we supplied free of charge. The profits which they made in this way helped to finance their activities.

On a visit to Brisbane, my hosts drove me round the city and its out-skirts, showing me the beautiful orchards and flower nurseries, and a pig farm run by a Czech member of the Society (now naturalized) who spoke with enthusiasm on the topic of pig-culture. The blood of my peasant forebears was greatly stirred. I also had another rare treat. Asked what special dish I would like, I answered without hesitation, 'Siberian *pelmeni*'. The Russian wife of a member of the Society cooked a quantity of these tasty meat dumplings, which I had not seen since I left Russia; I think I must have eaten at least fifty. Devouring the favourite delicacy of my boyhood days, among Russian folk who had fared so well in this new country, I could not help contrasting their situation with the collective farm of my native Larikha, where my own brother had toiled and endured such hardships, for such a meagre re-turn; I pictured in my mind the collective farms across the length and breadth of Russia, and the suffering millions of Russian peasants who had little beyond mere existence, yet dared not complain lest they lose even that.

I pictured this contrast again when I read the speech of Lance Sharkey, the General Secretary of the Communist Party of Australia, at the Nineteenth Congress of the Communist Party of the Soviet Union in Moscow in 1952. Sharkey said: 'The mighty Fifth Five-Year Plan opens up perspectives for the still more brilliant future of the peoples of the glorious Soviet Union. I have listened with keenest attention to the reports on the upsurge of Soviet agriculture. In startling contrast, in our country, fierce capitalist exploitation of the soil, the ups and downs of the market, the unchecked ravages of floods, fires and droughts, the consequent ruin of the farmers, have created a situation where 8,000,000 inhabitants of an entire continent are no longer assured of adequate food supplies. Such is capitalism!'

Of course I did not voice my thoughts to my kind hosts. The function of VOKS was to promote 'cultural relations'; that meant, in practice, to present a glowing picture of the Soviet Union. That was my job, not the dispelling of illusions. Even so, I was a moderate, rather than a fanatic. I did not appear outraged when an Australian visitor to Russia was heard expressing a distaste for Russian beer. I did not agree with my colleague Zaryezov who snorted—'Hm! If she doesn't like Soviet beer, she doesn't like the Soviet Union!'

The two main centres of VOKS work were the big cities of Sydney and Melbourne. In Melbourne, I dealt with John Rodgers, Director of Australia-Soviet House, 330 Flinders Lane. I did not approach him in my M.V.D. capacity for espionage purposes, or tell him that I was an M.V.D. officer. During my visits to Melbourne he would discuss the work of Australia-Soviet House, and ask me for the latest Soviet films, music and literature. On his side he was required to supply me with a half-yearly progress report which the Ambassador and I forwarded to the Ministry of Foreign Affairs in Moscow. From our point of view the Society was an important vehicle for Soviet propaganda. Personally, Rodgers showed me the same open-handed hospitality that I had met elsewhere in Australia. If we had a meal or a drink together he would insist, 'No, no! While in Melbourne you are my guest! I'll be yours in Canberra.' I visited his home, and took presents for his little boy (not paid for out of any VOKS, M.V.D. or official funds); and he and his family dined with Doosia and myself at our house in Canberra. We were both impressed with Rodgers as a man; he was intelligent, forceful and assured, in business matters and in social life, and seemed to us a very good husband and father. Rodgers had paid a short visit to the Soviet Union and whenever he spoke enthusiastically about the achievements and the spirit of the Soviet people in their socialist homeland I did not contradict him. It was not my business to tell him about the real Russia, behind the façade shown to visitors, the Soviet Russia that I knew and had grown up with. The real Russia is not the shop-window selection of 'samples' shown to foreign visitors on their planned and conducted tours. It is not the picked features of Moscow, Kharkov, Stalingrad and other show places. It is the grim severity of towns like Sverdlovsk, Omsk, Novo-Sibirsk; the drab factory workers, driven remorselessly by an imposed production quota; the millions of peasants in the 300,000 collectivized villages of Russia; and the ten or fifteen million slave labourers in the camps which I knew of when I handled the N.K.V.D. telegrams between Moscow and the camp commandants. Nobody can deny the immense technical and industrial achievements of the Soviet Union. But anyone who talks about them needs to know the truth about the vast mountain of human misery on which those achievements are built. Of this my Australian friends had not an inkling, and it was not my business then to enlighten them.

For me in my open capacity as VOKS representative and my secret assignment against anti-Soviet emigrés in Australia, the Russian Social Club at 727 George Street, Sydney, provided a natural base for operations. The members of the Russian Social Club were a mixed and varied assortment. The Club had been founded during the war in the cordial era when the Soviet Union and the Western powers were allies in arms against Hitler. We considered it to be still pro-Soviet in complexion and a useful centre for the distribution of Soviet literature, records and films. The Club occupied three rooms, provided an excellent restaurant service and attracted a number of non-political members, who came for the Russian food, music and conversation. It provided just the kind of social circle which a Soviet official needed to get acquainted with emigrés in a foreign country.

Over this Club presided the well-known figures of Mr and Mrs Klodnitsky. This middle-aged pair were Russian-born, but had married in Paris and had lived outside Russia ever since the Revolution. Mrs Klodnitsky was President of the Club and her husband was a committee member. Mr Klodnitsky, who really belonged to the old Russia, amazed me by his knowledge of Russian classical writers, novelists and poets alike; his recitation of passages from Tolstoy, Gogol, Dostoievsky, Lermontov and Pushkin, surpassed anything I had ever heard. In the Soviet Union today even the best students of literature are so overburdened with outside duties and responsibilities that they can never make the works of the great Russian writers a part of themselves as Mr Klodnitsky had done.

One of my duties was to arrange the repatriation of Soviet emigrés to the U.S.S.R. In 1952, the Soviet Government declared an amnesty towards all the 'non-returners', namely those Soviet citizens who had been in foreign countries at the end of the war and had refused the summons to return to their native land. The punitive policy towards these people was renounced and a vigorous repatriation campaign was launched. Two special employees joined our Embassy, Gordeyev and Pavlov, whom I knew to be colonels of Military Intelligence but who were Repatriation Officers as well. As Consul I had to arrange the travel documents for all Russian repatriates from Australia and I interviewed most of them personally. There were some poignant stories. Often the indecision and mental anguish of these people was heartrending. On the one hand they were fortunate immigrants to a land of plenty and opportunity; most of them were enjoying a material prosperity such as they had never known before. On the other hand there was the natural yearning of any migrant towards his own home and country, a yearning skilfully exploited in an illustrated pamphlet issued by the Soviet Government entitled *We returned to our own land*. This showed pictures of returners who were happily settled in good jobs back in their native towns and villages. Most of the repatriates were moved by a deep longing to see some parent or relative whom they had left behind.

There was Kapustin, for example, whose background was known to me. During the collectivization he and his father and mother had been exiled to North Siberia as a Kulak family. He was released before the outbreak of war and was working as an engineer in an agricultural implement factory in Kharkov when the Germans captured the city. Kapustin then consented to go to Germany to work, taking his wife and his wife's mother. The end of the war found him in the American Zone. Refusing repatriation to the u.s.s.r., he and his household, including two children, migrated to Australia. He and his wife both got good jobs in Sydney and seemed happily established. But Mrs Kapustin's mother pined to return, to die in her native village, and Kapustin also longed to see his own parents. When the amnesty was announced he had lengthy discussions with Pakhomov and then with me, on the question that tormented him; would he suffer punishment if he returned? I could only point to the Government's assurance of pardon and employment. In the end they went back. I got a cable from the m.v.d. in the transit camp where they were held while their case was re-examined; in reply I gave Kapustin the best clearance I could of any anti-Soviet tendencies. I never heard their ultimate fate.

One repatriate, Peter Bronski, had no sooner reached Soviet territory than he began to write numerous letters to his friends in Australia, saying how happy he was to be back and extolling conditions in the u.s.s.r. However, as these letters were not sent through ordinary postal channels, but came in the diplomatic bag and were delivered by our repatriation staff, the recipients viewed them with understandable suspicion. None of Bronski's friends applied to return. As a fisherman, I would say that the fish did not bite because the water was muddy.

The case of Yalinichev had come to my notice in Moscow, before ever I thought of coming to Australia. He was a seaman who deserted from a Soviet ship in Egypt, and later made his way to Australia. There we lost track of him, and did not expect to hear of him again. I was therefore astonished when a presentable well-built young man walked into my Consular office at Canberra, introduced himself as Yalinichev and said that he wanted to go home to the Soviet Union. He told me his story. During heavy weather at sea when all the crew were struggling on deck he had abused the Political Commissar for not lending a hand. He had later deserted the ship for fear of the consequences of this outburst. In Australia he had found a good job, had made good friends and had fallen in love with an Australian girl. However, his hopes in that direction came to nothing. Disappointed, and longing to see his own country and his father and mother again, Yalinichev asked to be sent home. He was still progressive and pro-Soviet, he told me, and was willing to take the consequences of his desertion.

I arranged his return. M.V.D. were interested in the case and asked particularly for his ship and cabin number. I heard that in London he was met and escorted direct to the Soviet Embassy, then flown to Moscow. What I knew but was strictly forbidden to tell Yalinichev was that the Soviet penalty for desertion is not less than ten years in a labour camp.

Why was the Soviet Government ready to pay the fares of these people and to take so much trouble to get them back? Chiefly, I think, for propaganda reasons, to show the Soviet Government's paternal interest in Soviet nationals everywhere, and also to reduce the number of former Soviet citizens abroad who might form an opposition party on foreign soil. The Soviet Government finds its subjects much more docile when they are safely within the confines of the U.S.S.R.

In February 1952, when I had been just a year in Australia, I was instructed to take over the job of M.V.D. chief in Australia from Pakhomov, who was being recalled to Moscow. I do not know the reason for his recall, but he had reported being under observation in Melbourne. I was now responsible for directing all M.V.D. espionage in Australia. And I had to do this in addition to my overt duties as Consul and Third Secretary.

Though the change meant promotion for me, I was sorry to lose

Pakhomov. We had worked well together and had had many talks about the problems and possibilities of our job.

I was originally posted to Canberra with a limited 'EM' and S.K. brief, but Pakhomov had been given a wider picture of espionage tasks in Australia. 'Our chiefs in Moscow think a lot of Australia,' he told me. 'They consider it an important country for our work because of its size and resources, its use as an American base in the last war, and its strategic position near the countries of Asia. There's a big field of work here.'

Pakhomov, though he had been secretary of the Communist Party in Moscow University, and had been through the Diplomatic School, was not a particularly diplomatic personality. His appearance was against him—a wide face with silver-grey hair over a balding pate—and he was apt to abuse and browbeat people. His manner aroused great resentment among members of the Russian Social Club.

But Pakhomov, despite his faults, was courageous and energetic. As Tass man he established wide contacts among journalists in Sydney and in the parliamentary press gallery at Canberra. Among his contacts was 'Zemliak', a young Sydney journalist who supplied him with detailed personal particulars about a large number of Australian journalists in a report which achieved fame during the Royal Commission as 'Document H'. The original typewritten report was among the documents which I handed over to the Australian Security organization. These personality reports included such items as 'heavy drinker' and other weaknesses and characteristics which could be used as pressure points with a view to recruiting the subject as a Soviet agent, either by inducement or blackmail. Moscow commented that this information was very valuable, and gave Pakhomov's successor, Antonov, the special task of further developing 'Zemliak'. We hoped to recruit him as a regular agent, especially when he obtained a semi-official post as Press Secretary to Dr Evatt, Leader of the Opposition in the Australian Parliament, but we had not succeeded in doing so when I left the Embassy.

When I heard of Pakhomov's pending recall, I appealed to Moscow to allow him to stay and to give him some cover appointment at the Embassy. The two hundred miles between Canberra and Sydney had made co-ordination difficult and I thought that in Canberra, Pakhomov could do effective work in spheres which were important espionage targets, the Parliamentary press gallery, the Diplomatic Corps, Government departments. But Moscow did not approve, so back to Moscow he went.

By contrast, his successor Antonov was a timid operator. Perhaps the best indication of his character is the following paragraph in a Moscow letter concerning a car. (Officially it was a Tass car, but actually M.V.D. property. Antonov, incidentally, was terrified of driving, especially in traffic.)

'Taking into consideration Ignat's [Antonov's] statement that he refuses to take the motor-car because he is afraid to drive it in Sydney, we recommend to Ignat, before making a final decision, to take motor-car driving lessons for which purpose he may use fifteen units out of M.V.D. Section funds.'

Kislytsin also, who joined our M.V.D. staff about this time, was timid and apprehensive in his outside work, and was unduly worried about his lack of proficiency in the local language. Antonov, as a Tass man, did not have diplomatic standing, and so was liable to arrest by the Australian police. That did not apply to me or to Kislytsin, however, who enjoyed diplomatic status.

I think it was dread of committing a blunder that destroyed their confidence.

Soon after I became M.V.D. Chief I got instructions from Moscow about organizing 'illegal work' in Australia. The Soviet term 'illegal' bears little relation to the technicalities of law in the countries concerned; for the work of a so-called 'legal' M.V.D. Resident in a Soviet Embassy is certainly aimed at inducing espionage agents to commit criminal acts contrary to the law of their country. The term 'illegal' simply indicates that the spy-master or agent works without the 'legal' cover of an official Soviet representative and must operate independently of any Soviet Embassy, Legation or Consulate. The two systems are designed to work concurrently but separately; each has its own advantages and drawbacks. The vital importance of the 'illegal' system is that it can continue to operate in time of war, after diplomatic representatives have been withdrawn.

Moscow's letter on 'illegal work' read:

'The aggravation of the international situation and the pressing necessity for the timely exposure and prevention of cunning designs of the enemy, demands a fundamental reorganization of the whole of our intelligence work and the creation in Australia of an illegal apparatus which could uninterruptedly and effectively operate under any conditions.'

At the same time Moscow warned us that we must discuss this matter with our agents delicately, and in such a way that 'no panic is caused among them, and so that they would not interpret our preparations as a sign of inevitable war'.

Whenever we received letters in this strain I could not help reflecting how easy it was to draw up flawless plans and pen excellent advice to us in the field from the safe eminence of a desk in Moscow headquarters.

For example, the crack in the boards of a railway bridge near Canberra, which I proposed as a 'Bank' or safe hiding place for secret material deposited by agents. In vetoing my suggestions, some M.V.D. bureaucrat in Moscow, who had never been within 10,000 miles of the peaceful countryside round Canberra, took the opportunity to write fifteen pompous paragraphs of general principles about secret hiding places. He even warned me to beware lest the material be destroyed by rodents. No doubt he ate a good lunch at the M.V.D. restaurant and thought that he had written a masterly directive which would remain as a model treatise on the subject.

To help me start the plan for 'illegal' work I had Antonov and Kislytsin. Our task was to assist the entry and establishment of 'illegal' agents, who would thereafter sever their connections with the Embassy, and operate independently with their own lines of communication to Moscow.

Two examples illustrate our preparations for 'illegal' work in Australia.

Pechek (whose real name was Vincenc Divisek) was a Czech who, during the war, was conscripted into the German army, deserted to the Russians, and, after training, was parachuted back into Czechoslovakia with a wireless set. He proved an extremely good Soviet agent, and worked with the Czech underground. After the war he was manager of an hotel which was taken over by the Communist Government when it seized power in Czechoslovakia. Pechek then applied for permission to migrate to Australia, where his wife had relatives. But his former Russian Intelligence Chief, Captain Medvedyev, got in touch with him in Prague. As the price of his exit permit, Pechek agreed to act as a Soviet agent in Australia. Rendezvous arrangements were noted by Pechek in his diary. The agreed place, chosen at random from a travel leaflet, was Governor Phillip's statue in the Botanic Gardens, Sydney. Pechek was to wear a brown hat and carry a black brief-case; his contact man would ask, 'Can you direct me to Hyde Park?' and Pechek was to reply, 'I don't know; I just arrive from Prague.' Moscow made several unsuccessful attempts to regain contact with Pechek in Australia. What none of us knew was that when Pechek arrived in Australia in 1949 he went straight to the Australian Security authorities, told them the whole story and kept a number of appointments under their direction. For some reason (fortunately from the Soviet point of view) his Soviet contact men did not appear. I myself was directed to one rendezvous, though this was contrary to normal 'illegal' practice. Moscow told me that Pechek had been informed by separate letter of the arrangements, but he did not show up. I was probably saved simply by a breakdown in our staff work. If Moscow had entertained any suspicions about Pechek they would not have been pressing us to reactivate him after five years' quiescence in Australia, as they were when I left the Embassy.

One day in November 1952, I stood by the bedside of Mrs K——, an old Siberian woman who lay ill and paralysed in a room in her unpretentious house in a poor suburb of Sydney, not far from Central Railway Station. Long an invalid, she had been struck by paralysis when someone poisoned her Alsatian dog, to which she was devoted. With me was Dr Bialoguski, who was giving her medical attention. She was showing me a photograph of her only son, who was living at Okhmolinsk in Siberia.

'That's him,' she said, 'I wouldn't mistake my own son even after all these years. If he walked in that door now I'd know him at once.'

'And what about your grandchildren?' I asked her. 'Would you know them by sight?'

'Oh dear, no,' she answered, 'I've never seen them. I wouldn't know one of them, I'm afraid. But I'd give anything to set eyes on them, on my own flesh and blood.'

As she lay there, frail and forlorn, she reminded me of my own mother, just such another Siberian peasant woman, when I said goodbye to her for the last time in Larikha, just before she died. Like my mother, Mrs K—— longed to die in her native village, but there seemed no hope of that now.

Her name had come on to the books of the M.V.D. in a curious way. She and her husband, a plumber, had migrated to Australia by way of China in 1912, and had prospered in Australia. Some time before my arrival she had approached our Embassy in Canberra. Her husband was dead, she was too ill to travel, and she wanted to bequeath her house and furniture to her only son in the Soviet Union. Could we arrange it? My M.V.D. predecessor Sadovnikov handled the case. He found a lawyer for her, arranged the business and forwarded her will and all details to the Soviet Union.

Now, seriously ill, she had appealed to the Embassy again. I was able to reassure her that her will was intact, and to arrange a small mortgage on her property to eke out her pension. I gave her this help as Soviet Consul. But I had a further task with Mrs K——. My questions about her family were not casual; they had been dictated by M.V.D. Headquarters in Moscow, who are always interested in such human stories. Moscow proposed to send out a regular M.V.D. worker for 'illegal' duties in Australia in the guise of one of Mrs K——'s relatives.

After this visit I reported that the plan would be feasible if the worker posed as one of her grandchildren, and if the connivance of her son were secured. That detail was probably not beyond the capacity of the M.V.D. in the Soviet Union.

I heard no more from Moscow. That is all I know of the story.

The important facts of my work as M.V.D. chief in Australia have been told in the Report of the Royal Commission on Espionage. Here I offer some general comments. My evidence before the Commission, and that of my wife, made clear what careful planning and elaborate machinery were employed by the M.V.D. in Australia, as in other countries, for the purpose of espionage. Espionage is a distinct and principal Soviet industry. This must be so; because the Soviet Union, alone of all the great powers, regards itself as being in a continuous and chronic state of covert warfare with the whole world outside the borders of the Communist empire. And conspiratorial techniques are natural to a régime that seized power and maintains power by conspiratorial methods. Soviet espionage has reaped a rich harvest by such methods, especially against friendly and unsuspecting countries.

Our aim in Australia was the same as elsewhere—to recruit and develop top-level agents, capable of supplying the Soviet Union with top secret political and strategic information. But the problems in my time were considerable.

'Intelligence work in Australia in 1951–52 was actually at a standstill, and has not produced any noticeable results.' So began the Moscow letter of 6th June 1952, which instituted a new attack on the problem and promised reinforcements (represented by Antonov and Kislytsin). Moscow considered them trained and qualified officers; but, as I have explained, neither of them was well prepared or suitable for field work abroad.

We increased our efforts and achieved minor successes. But times were not what they had been for Soviet espionage in Australia. In line with Moscow's general policy I was never given full details of earlier achievements in this field, and only knew what colleagues passed on to me or what Moscow chose to impart as background to my own efforts.

But it was plain that there had been major Soviet successes in Australia. When Kislytsin arrived fresh from M.V.D. Headquarters in Moscow, I got some positive light on this matter. He told me that in the years after the war a situation very gratifying to the Soviet Union and very serious for Australia had existed. A group of well-placed agents had obtained official secret documents which found their way to the hands of Makarov, Sadovnikov's predecessor as M.V.D. chief in Australia, and thence to Moscow.

Moscow was naturally keen that we should recover this advantageous position and should develop such strategically placed sources again. But it was not easy to do.

New factors made the task of Soviet espionage immensely more difficult than it had been in the halcyon post-war years. It was partly a change in the climate of world opinion, following the disclosures of the Canadian case, the Fuchs case, the disappearance of Burgess and Maclean, and other startling revelations of Soviet espionage. No longer were we able to exploit the friendly, unsuspecting attitude which the wartime alliance had created in Western countries towards their Soviet allies.

Yet the change of mood among the general public was not decisive. In Australia we found ordinary acquaintances friendly, casual, unsuspicious. The official attitude was also tolerant. In March 1952, when the British and American Governments imposed travel restrictions on Soviet diplomats, in reciprocation of the strict travel control imposed on all foreign representatives in the Soviet Union, we expected a similar blow to fall on us. Lifanov and I discussed the possibility and prepared for it. But nothing happened, and we continued to move round Australia at will and without notifying anybody. This unrestricted freedom of movement was a great help to us in carrying out conspiratorial work undetected and in eluding Security surveillance.

The difference in Australia was due much more to the fact that the reorganized Australian Security Intelligence organization had embarked upon an active counter-espionage programme, and had taken the initiative in investigating the activities of the Australian Communist Party and our Soviet Embassy. We had various indications of this.

Platkais was observed on his way to a secret rendezvous. Pakhomov had reported being photographed in a park in Canberra. I myself identified one observer in a bar (correctly, as I later found, though I failed to detect a number of others who had been close to me). We expected this attention, but it limited both us and our agents. Soviet espionage thrives best in a climate of tolerant apathy and ignorance about Soviet aims and methods.

This new initiative by Australian Security had its effect on many aspects of the work of our Embassy, but nowhere so directly and decisively as in my own particular case. It meant that when I had reached a point of desperation as a result of the campaign of slander and persecution by my fellow-countrymen, a door of escape opened.

But before telling that story, I supply the key to the mystery of Burgess and Maclean.

XXIII

Maclean and Burgess

'SO IT has come off at last!' It was our colleague Kislytsin who spoke and there was a smile of pride and satisfaction on his face as he walked into the M.V.D. office at Canberra. In his hand he carried a newspaper report of the disappearance from Switzerland of Mrs Donald Maclean with her three children on 11th September 1953.

'I knew about this business,' he said. 'It has happened just as we planned it. I must cable Moscow and ask whether they want the Australian press reports about it.'

My wife, as M.V.D. cypher clerk, sent off the cable and presently received Moscow's reply asking for all important press references.

When we arrived in Australia in February 1951, we had never heard the name of either Burgess or Maclean; indeed, we had no knowledge of their existence. When the Australian press published reports of their disappearance on 25th May of that year, we knew no more about the matter than any other baffled newspaper reader, and Moscow naturally saw no reason to inform us of secrets which had no bearing on our own special sphere of duties. But now the situation was different. And as I was Kislytsin's M.V.D. chief in Australia, I insisted on knowing the background to the correspondence.

Kislytsin told me that both Burgess and Maclean were long-term agents who had each been independently recruited to work for Soviet Intelligence in their student days at Cambridge. Their flight was planned and directed from Moscow; Kislytsin was present during the planning of the escape operation. The reason for their flight was simple and drastic; they had discovered that they were under investigation by the British Security Service.

Kislytsin was in personal touch with the work of these two important agents over a period of years. At the end of the war he was posted to the Soviet Embassy in London as M.V.D. cypher clerk, and himself handled the material supplied by Burgess. At this time Burgess was bringing out brief-cases full of Foreign Office documents, which were photographed in the Soviet Embassy and quickly returned to him. Kislytsin used to encypher the more urgent information and send it to Moscow by cable; the rest he prepared for dispatch by courier in the diplomatic bag.

While he was in England Kislytsin never saw either Burgess or Maclean; but he knew the Soviet official who was in contact with Burgess and who used to return to the Embassy with muddy clothes after his meetings, which evidently took place at some obscure and dirty rendezvous.

Kislytsin was in London from 1945 until 1948, when he was recalled to Moscow. There, after a year on an intelligence training course, in which he specialized in English, he was appointed to the First Directorate of the Committee of Information, where he was put in charge of a special one-man section of the top secret archives. This section was devoted solely to the great quantity of material supplied by Maclean and Burgess. Much of it had not even been translated or distributed to the Ministries concerned; but Kislytsin used to show particular files and documents to high-ranking officials who visited his section for the purpose.

When Burgess and Maclean discovered that they were under investigation by the British security authorities, they reported the matter to their Soviet contact in the utmost alarm. Kislytsin was then in Moscow and attended the conference of senior M.V.D. officers summoned to discuss the possibility of getting these important agents out of danger to the safety of Soviet territory. Among those present were Colonel Raina, Chief of the First Directorate (dealing with Anglo-American territories) in the Committee of Information, and Gorsky, who succeeded Raina in that post. I myself knew both these officers by sight. I once saw Raina in a boat with his young son fishing in the Uchinskoya Reservoir, a fishing area near Moscow reserved for senior Government officials. And I remember seeing Gorsky, a tall man of Jewish origin, in the M.V.D. dining-room. When my successor Kovalenok arrived in Australia he told Doosia that Gorsky had been dismissed from his post for concealing some compromising political facts about his relatives; his Jewish connections may also have had something to do with his downfall.

At this conference, the perils of the proposed operation caused much misgiving and many plans were put forward and rejected. Kislytsin mentioned that the route finally selected included an air passage over the border into Czechoslovakia; presumably Burgess and Maclean travelled from Paris by Czech or Soviet plane to Prague and then on to Moscow.

Kislytsin met them personally for the first time on their arrival in

Moscow from London. He frequently visited them at the comfortable house on the outskirts of Moscow where they were accommodated, and he was the officer responsible for their maintenance and welfare. He signed the requisitions for their material needs and prepared plans for the best exploitation of their services. He told us that when he last saw them, Burgess and Maclean were supplied with the best of everything, were in good health, but were missing their families. They were then acting as advisers to the Soviet Ministry of Foreign Affairs on Anglo-American matters.[1]

Kislytsin was aware of the second plan, to bring out Mrs Maclean, and recognized some of the details when he read in the Australian papers the reports of its successful execution. My belief is that Maclean told his wife of his destination before he left, but I cannot be sure of this. At any rate she participated fully at a later stage of the escape plan. Kislytsin said that it had been intended that Soviet officials in London should get in touch with her on the matter, but that they became too apprehensive about British security measures to risk making contact. Later, after she went with her mother and her three children to live in Switzerland, she was in touch with an M.V.D. representative, who undoubtedly arranged her flight.

When Kislytsin left Moscow to come to Australia at the end of 1952, he handed over his special section to Sadovnikov, who had previously been the M.V.D. Resident in Canberra. (It was Sadovnikov, who, with Pakhomov, came to meet me when I first arrived in Australia, and his handwritten notes were amongst the documents which I gave to the Australian authorities when I fled from the Soviet Embassy in Canberra.)

Since my wife and I left the Soviet service and sought refuge in Australia, we have read two books,[2] which provide an interesting background to Kislytsin's account. Mr Geoffrey Hoare gives much detail about the escape of Burgess and Maclean from London and across the Channel to France on the night of Friday, 25th May 1951. There he loses track of them. (Kislytsin's story suggests that arrangements had been made for them to be taken aboard a plane in Paris and to continue their journey to Moscow by air.)

[1] A recent writer, Mr Geoffrey Hoare, quotes a British expert on Russian affairs, as saying that, at this time, 'passages in pure Foreign Office terminology' were beginning to appear in Soviet notes.

[2] *The Missing Diplomats*, by Cyril Connolly, Queen Anne Press, 1952.
The Missing Macleans, by Geoffrey Hoare, Cassells, London, 1955.

Mrs Maclean reported her husband's absence to the Foreign Office on the following Monday morning and the search began. She had been left with the two boys, Fergus, aged seven, and Donald, aged five; soon afterwards she went into hospital where their third child, a daughter, was born.

On 3rd August, Mrs Maclean's mother received £2,000, sent to her through two Swiss banks. Two days later Mrs Maclean herself received a letter from her husband which had been posted in Surrey, quite close to her home. This was probably arranged by the m.v.d. Resident in London. In his letter Maclean gave no address or sign of where he was or what he was doing, but explained that the £2,000 was for her and the children and said that she must know in her heart that he had to do what he had done. Mrs Maclean (who showed the letter to the authorities) could offer no explanation of what this meant and in the following months she spoke to friends of her intention to divorce Donald and to end the 'façade' of their marriage. I have no doubt that this was part of a 'cover' plan in which she co-operated.

In September 1951 she and her mother went to live in Geneva, where the boys were sent to school. It was on Friday afternoon, 11th September 1953, two years and three months after her husband's disappearance, that Mrs Maclean drove off with her children in her black Chevrolet car, ostensibly for a week-end visit to friends, and disappeared also. Their movements were traced as far as the Austrian border, and there the trail ended.

How valuable were the services of Maclean and Burgess to the Soviet Union?

Both were brilliant students, who made their way to important positions in their country's service. Burgess in 1939 did highly confidential work for the British War Office, worked in the European Propaganda Department of the b.b.c., and joined the Foreign Office in 1944, where he was first appointed to the Far Eastern Department, and later to the British Embassy in Washington.

Maclean seemed to his friends a more stable and reliable character. He joined the Foreign Office in 1935, worked in London until 1944, when he was appointed to Washington, and, at the time of his disappearance, was back in London as Head of the American Department.

The quantity and quality of the secret information which these two men were able to supply to Moscow in the course of their official careers can well be imagined.

What was the motive that induced two men in such responsible positions to act as Soviet agents? They were both members of Left Wing groups at Cambridge and, according to Kislytsin, both were recruited for ideological reasons.

'Around 1933,' writes Mr Hoare, 'so disgusted was he [Maclean] by the spinelessness of the Western democracies in general and of his own country in particular, he had seriously considered giving up his planned career and going to work in Russia. But, quite suddenly, he reverted to his original plan, and, after taking his First in Modern Languages . . . was accepted into the Foreign Service.'

This fits Kislytsin's account. I guess that this was the point at which Maclean was recruited to work for the Soviet Union, and that he was advised that he could do more to help the cause by going forward with his career than by going to Russia.

Maclean knew Burgess, who was two years his senior, at the University; but they do not seem to have been close friends, and during their official careers were seldom in the same country at the same time. I got the impression, from Kislytsin, that they did not know each other as Soviet agents until the emergency of their flight together. I do not know on what terms they worked at a later stage. But it is the fixed policy of Soviet Intelligence to secure agents who are ideologically indoctrinated, and then to employ every other means—payment, blackmail, flattery or whatever else will serve—to strengthen the Soviet's hold over them. In the years when these two were recruited, the true nature of Soviet Communism was concealed from many people in Western countries; even in the Soviet Union its worst horrors had not then been demonstrated. But how could the deceptions of Soviet propaganda maintain their hold for so many years over a man with the knowledge and intelligence of Maclean?

Mr Connolly describes how he lunched with Maclean at the end of 1950, a few months before his disappearance. Maclean talked about the war in Korea: 'His argument was that what mattered most in the world was people. The Koreans were people, but in the stage which the war had reached, both sides had entirely forgotten this and were exploiting them for their own prestige. It was essential at all costs to stop the war and get them established as people again.'

If there is one fact above all others which needs to be understood about the Soviet system, it is that, under it, people do *not* matter. If our story has not made that plain, it has failed completely to convey the true picture. A system where people mattered would be a radically different régime from that which we have known. It would mean a freedom which, in our experience, the Soviet Government cannot and dare not allow.

From the inside we know this to be the truth. Were Burgess and
Maclean blind to this fact to the very end? Or had they gone too far to
turn back? And how much have they been allowed to see, how much
have they allowed themselves to see, in the empire of fear that reached
out and pulled them in to itself?

XXIV

Escape Route

A SOVIET official who escapes from the Soviet service to refuge in a Western democratic country passes from one world to another. It is difficult for people who have lived all their lives in the free world to understand how formidable that step looks from the other side of the Iron Curtain. So many fears hedge it round that it is rarely taken, except under the impact of an even greater fear.

But I can hope that more people in the non-communist world will understand what it means when they have heard our story. They will understand how such a step, for Soviet officials, even though, like ourselves, they have served for years in foreign countries, remains a huge leap in the dark, a launching into the unknown, a hazard whose end cannot be foreseen. This uncertainty is perhaps the greatest barrier of all to those who contemplate crossing this dangerous frontier. It is a barrier the Soviet Government strives desperately to maintain. It was a major obstacle in my own case.

Others before me had dared to cross this frontier. Though the names of such people are never publicly mentioned inside the U.S.S.R., I knew some of their stories. While in Sweden, I had read in English newspapers about the flight of Igor Gouzenko from the Soviet Embassy in Ottawa. In Canberra I saw Kravchenko's book *I Chose Freedom*,[1] a copy of which had been left by some curious chance in our secret M.V.D. office in the Embassy. And on 2nd February 1954, when my own crisis was reaching its climax, the Australian press carried an account of the flight from the Soviet Embassy in Japan, of Yuri Rastvorov (whom my wife and I had known as an M.V.D. officer in Moscow) to refuge with the Americans.

Knowledge of the existence of this way of escape lies in the background thoughts of every Soviet official, and remains a permanent spectre to the Soviet Government wherever contact between Soviet citizens and the outside world is concerned.

How was my own decision conceived and born? The Ambassadors

[1] Robert Hale, London, 1949.

277

in Canberra were its parents. The Australian Security Organization played the part of midwife.

Gouzenko's experience was very different from my own. When he walked out of the Soviet Embassy in Ottawa with his bundle of documents, he threw himself on a society that was busy with other problems and had hardly heard of Soviet espionage. He has described how, for two anxious days, he trudged round newspaper offices trying to get someone to take an interest in him before it was too late. That was the world of September 1945, when the U.S.S.R. and the West had just emerged as victors and allies in the struggle against Fascism. But, on the 3rd of April 1954, when I stepped into Mr Richards' car in Sydney and drove away to political asylum in Australia, the Australian Security authorities had been able to prepare in detail for the possibility of my defection. Once I had made up my mind to stay in Australia, everything went, to a surprising degree, according to plan. The agonies of fear, doubt and conflict which led up to my decision are another story.

I suppose it really began far back in my native Siberia, when, as I have described, I saw the sufferings of my own peasant folk under collectivization, and the ruin of my native village of Larikha. After that, the horrors of the purges, the victimization of innocent people, the desperate poverty of the Soviet masses, followed by the striking contrast of conditions in other countries—all these had destroyed my faith in the professions of our régime, long before I came near the point of action. I had reached a disillusionment, even cynicism, which today is general, though concealed, among Soviet officials who have seen the outside world and allow themselves to think honestly.

Whenever I travelled from Canberra to Sydney to meet the diplomatic couriers or other new arrivals from Moscow, I was reminded of the true state of affairs. These couriers always asked me to take them around the shops to spend their precious foreign currency on articles unobtainable in the Soviet Union.

Once I asked one of these visitors how things were at home. This man knew me well and, carried away by his feelings, threw discretion to the winds.

'Oh, —— awful!' he exclaimed. 'High prices and poor quality.'

The persistence of shortages down to the present moment is confirmed by the American journalist, Stewart Alsop, who took up Krushchev's invitation to foreign journalists to visit the U.S.S.R. and wrote from Moscow (5th July 1955) that 'all consumer goods are snapped up almost regardless of price, as soon as they appear in the shops'.

But for myself and my wife personally this difference was immaterial to our decision to stay in Australia. We left behind us in Moscow a comfortable flat, clothes, furniture, a bank balance equal to £A13,000, excellent jobs and a position among the privileged bureaucracy. Money was not our motive.

Fear drove and a way of escape was offered.

I will begin at the beginning.

'Dr Bialoguski, let me present our new Third Secretary, Mr Petrov.' It was Pakhomov who spoke, at the Russian Social Club in Sydney, soon after my arrival in Australia.

The dark, bearded man in his middle thirties shook hands, bowing slightly as he did so, and answered in Russian with a noticeable foreign accent.

'I am very glad to meet you.'

So began an acquaintanceship which played a part, though a much less important part than he represents, in my decision to stay in Australia.

Dr Bialoguski was born in Kiev, Russia, but had lived most of his life in Poland. In 1941, a few months before the Germans launched their attack on Russia, he obtained permission from the occupying Soviet authorities to leave Poland. He travelled by way of the Trans-Siberian railway to the Far East, and emigrated to Australia. There, after a short period in the Australian Army, he had obtained his medical degree under a Commonwealth scheme for ex-servicemen. When I met him he was a naturalized Australian citizen, was married to an Australian wife, though they were separated, had his doctor's plate up in Sydney's dignified Macquarie Street, and had a practice consisting largely of migrants from Slav-speaking countries, who were glad to find a doctor who spoke their own language.

Dr Michael Bialoguski, I discovered, was on the Committee of the Russian Social Club and was a frequenter of 'Progressive' circles; he was assured and knowledgeable about Australians and Australian life and was an ambitious musician who, for a time, was a first violin in the Sydney Symphony Orchestra.

What better helper could I hope to find in my 'EM' work among the migrants? Through his surgery alone he had wide contacts among them. I began to cultivate him carefully for this purpose. It was a gradual process; but in the end, hardly a visit to Sydney passed without my ringing him from the airport, calling at his rooms, or dining with him at the Adria restaurant at King's Cross, where good continental food was to be had. He, on his side, responded readily; he sometimes saw me off to Canberra at the airport, or drove me in his car to addresses which I had to visit in Sydney. Very soon we were on terms of 'Mikhail' and 'Volodya'. Before the end of that year I had allotted him the code name of 'Grigorii', and with Moscow's approval, had entered on a programme of development aimed at his recruitment as a regular, conscious Soviet agent.

Of course I first checked back on him to Moscow (Poland being a 'Peoples' Democracy' under Soviet control) who investigated his background and authorized me to go ahead.

Moscow's knowledge and approval of this plan was a vital factor in the story. Without that our association over the years would have been impossible, for, as I have explained many times, Soviet officials do not maintain such friendships with foreigners unless they are officially sanctioned for a purpose advantageous to Moscow. It also meant that as M.V.D. chief I could warn off any over-zealous colleagues, from the Ambassador down, who began to ask questions about my friendship with Dr Bialoguski.

In pursuance of my plan I encouraged Bialoguski to assist me in matters of gradually increasing importance. At my request, he provided me with an assortment of official forms which he obtained from the Immigration Department in Sydney. Moscow was anxious to obtain any forms which might assist them in smuggling illegal immigrants into Australia. However, I have since discovered that these forms were available to the public and that Bialoguski obtained them from the inquiry desk. I have mentioned that it was Bialoguski who came with me on my visit to old Mrs K——, whom Moscow planned to use by slipping an illegal worker into Australia in the guise of one of her grandchildren. Moscow instructed me to continue the cultivation of Grigorii.

But in all our conversations at his flat, or over a drink or a meal, I never disclosed to Bialoguski my secret M.V.D. role. Even at the end, when he and I met Mr Richards of the Australian Security Service, I never gave Bialoguski any grounds to know me as anything more than Consul and Third Secretary. As to any other functions of mine, he was guessing up to the end. I am quite sure that he did not know I was an M.V.D. officer until I had placed myself in the hands of the Australian authorities and the fact became public knowledge. On the surface the friendship between Bialoguski and myself was casual, cordial and natural, as between a Soviet official and a Russian-born Soviet sympathizer. We drove about together, went to parties together; in the latter stages, from the middle of 1953 onwards, I even stayed overnight at his flat in fashionable Wolseley Road, Point Piper. But there were careful reserves on both sides.

Why, it may be asked, did I not become suspicious of such a cordial companion and generous host, who spent so much time in my company? The answer is, that I did develop such suspicions. My wife warned me once, after Bialoguski had visited us in Canberra, that we needed to be careful of him, in spite of his assistance to us. Moreover, as a result of observing him at social gatherings, at the Russian Social Club, at parties given by the Czechoslovakian Consul-General, and at various meetings held under the 'Peace' slogan, I came to the conclusion that Bialoguski was very far from being a fanatic for the Communist cause. On the contrary, I put him down as a sceptic, with some qualifications as an actor. The irony of it was that Bialoguski was probably greatly helped in his efforts to gain acceptance in those circles by the fact that he was seen frequently in the company of Third Secretary Petrov of the Soviet Embassy.

Later, to Mr Richards, I described Bialoguski satirically as 'a great fighter for peace'. By that time I knew that Bialoguski had no more illusions about the 'Peace' movements in which he took part than I had myself, and recognized them realistically for what they were and are— an instrument of Soviet foreign policy.

But my suspicions about Bialoguski's true role had to be balanced against other factors. He was an energetic and able helper in the migrant field; he had a good position in Australian life; I found his assistance very useful.

I decided to avoid dramatics, to 'play along' with Bialoguski, and to continue cultivating his friendship, while making use of his services and telling him nothing about my secret M.V.D. work. So I continued to meet and associate with him openly without any cloak of conspiratorial secrecy.

It is impossible to say how this strange, complex association between Bialoguski and myself would have developed had not the campaign of intrigue in the Embassy brought matters to a head. My wife has described its beginnings under Lifanov and Kovaliev, its crude intensification by Generalov. In its early stages we found this campaign irritating and distressing, but when the 'Beria group' charge was introduced and when Generalov, fresh from Moscow, resumed Lifanov's attacks with such blatant confidence, our resentment became mingled with very real fear.

Most alarming of all, M.V.D. Headquarters in Moscow, to whom we looked for support against the Ambassadors, seemed unwilling or unable to give us the reassurance we were looking for. This in turn encouraged the Ambassadors to further assaults.

As the attacks of our local Embassy tyrants became more intense and ominous, I tended to let off more steam to Bialoguski when I met him in Sydney. It was 'any port in a storm'. In the Embassy Doosia and I were isolated and friendless, beset by intrigues and slanders. Sydney was a welcome relief from the poisoned atmosphere among my nominal allies in Canberra and, at various times, I told Bialoguski of the persecution we were suffering.

Sometimes my pent-up feelings broke out uncontrollably; I had to express them or burst and I swore without restraint at the Embassy authorities who were making our life a misery. Even in cold blood, I calculated as follows: suppose Bialoguski were the pro-Soviet progressive that he claimed to be, and these outbursts of mine found their way back to the Ambassador, they were the truth, and I was prepared to stand by them. On the other hand, if my suspicions about Bialoguski proved correct, and he reported this to the Australian authorities, I had still given away no State secrets, nothing beyond the internal squabbles of the Embassy; I had taken no irretrievable step. If the Australians took any action, I might be able to turn it to our advantage and expose some of the workings of their Security Service. My thoughts at this stage had by no means reached the point of action. I was impressed by Australia, especially by the rapid progress of the migrants I had seen, who, in a few years, were comfortably and happily established in their new land. I liked the country and the climate and the people. Now, in addition, the malice and hostility of our superiors in Canberra threatened to destroy our credit in Moscow and to wreck our future.

In May I was ordered back to Moscow to report on my M.V.D. work in Australia. I had booked my flight and was ready to go, when my eyes began to give trouble. It was a genuine complaint, not a pretence, as Bialoguski suggests. I asked Bialoguski to recommend an eye specialist, and he took me to a Dr Beckett, who had rooms adjacent to his in Macquarie Street. Beckett prescribed treatment for me and after ten days in hospital in Canberra my eyes improved. On my discharge from hospital I booked another air passage to Moscow to leave Sydney on 21st June. But on the eve of my departure I got a cable from Moscow ordering me to remain in Australia until I received further instructions.

But I was still far from any concrete decision or plan. When there is no alternative there is no choice; and I was still by no means clear about the existence of any real alternative to the career in the Soviet Service to which I had given my life. In other words, I knew in stark and real terms what I might be fleeing *from*. But I had only a vague and dubious picture of what I might be escaping *to*. There is an expressive English saying, 'Better the devil you know than the devil you don't.'

In the middle of 1953 this situation was radically altered, and a clear alternative appeared on my horizon.

Then, on the 10th July, the announcement of Beria's arrest astonished the non-Soviet world. It was heard with equal amazement, but with more reserved comment, in our Soviet ranks in Canberra.

After that, a number of minds began to work, and plans were evolved on opposing sides of the fence. As my wife has described, Lifanov and his ally Kovaliev saw in Beria's fall a golden chance to smear us with a deadly political charge; presently he sent off to Moscow the signals (which Prudnikov showed us) accusing us of forming a 'Beria group' in the Embassy.

Some weeks later Beckett sent me a message through Bialoguski to say that he would like to examine my eyes again. On the 23rd July, I went with Bialoguski to Beckett's surgery. Bialoguski intended to stay with us, as he usually did, during examinations; but on this occasion Beckett excused him, saying he would be some little time. When we were alone he began to examine my eyes, and, after a few minutes, he remarked:

'You are going back to Moscow, I hear?'

'Yes, I am going.'

'I don't know that I would want to go back, with all the changes taking place there. This man Beria——'

'It is my duty,' I interrupted. My whole training put me on guard instantly. 'Look out for traps,' it said. Friends could be more dangerous than open foes. I was alert for any attempt by the Embassy authorities to 'frame' me on the eve of my return to Moscow.

'What do you think of this country?' continued Dr Beckett easily. 'Don't you like it?'

'Oh yes, it is a fine country, plenty of food, plenty of everything——'

'You wouldn't like to stay here?'

'It is my duty to go back.'

'Well, if I were in your place, I'd stay here.'

His manner and personality were natural, genuine, direct. I took a cautious step, that committed me to nothing.

'It is very hard to get a job like that.'

I was fencing with him to see what he would say next.

'A job? Not if you know the right people. It's a tradition in our countries that we look after people who are in difficulties or in such a situation—such as the Czech Consul who was here. I have friends who know all about these things——'

I said nothing. For what seemed an interminable time Dr Beckett bent over me in silence, treating my eyes. I felt as though I was in a whirlpool of conflicting emotions—fear, hope, doubt, confusion. I must steady myself, I must have time.

To break the silence, I said: 'That Czech, yes, he has a restaurant, I know the street.'

'He's done well,' agreed Dr Beckett. 'But you must be helped by the right people.' Then he added, 'That's all.'

I thanked him and left the surgery. In the street, waiting for Bialoguski to pick me up, I strove to get this startling interview into perspective, to plan my course right.

As to Dr Beckett's *bona fides* I had no doubt whatever. His position, his frank, casual Australian approach, his grasp of the facts and presentation of the possibilities, convinced me that he was honest, authentic and would be as good as his word. I did not doubt that he was acting in some way on behalf of Australian Security.

Secondly, the interview deepened my suspicions about Bialoguski's connection with Security. Since Bialoguski had introduced me to Beckett I concluded (wrongly, as it turned out) that he had known all about the interview from the start.

When he came up, I said: 'Michael, we will have to look out for this fellow Beckett. He seems to have some connection with the Security people,' and I described the interview. At the time I disbelieved his apparent astonishment. But, in fact, Bialoguski was as startled by this new development as I was.

'Well,' I concluded, 'it's a strange situation. It will be interesting to see how it develops.'

Bialoguski in his account of the matter in his book disparages the part played by Beckett. He commented at the time, 'A most unsuitable man was selected who, due to his clumsy action, has ruined every chance of success that was there.' In fact, though I was far from any decision at that point, Beckett had given me my first plain direct assurance that I would be helped to settle in Australia if I wished to; and I was impressed by his straightforward manner.

I went back to Canberra from this visit with a cloud of whirling confusion in my mind. I told no one at the Embassy of my interview with Beckett. That in itself was a serious step. I did not even tell my wife.

Her position was the thing that preyed most on my mind. I myself had no relatives left behind as hostages in the Soviet Union, but I knew her devotion to her family in Moscow. If I proposed directly to her that we escape to refuge in Australia, the conflict in her mind would be too great to bear. Whenever I even hinted at the possibility she fiercely and furiously rejected the very suggestion. Doosia would not come. With this conviction I put the thought away and pinned my hopes on the arrival of the new Ambassador, Generalov, who, I had heard, was a good fellow. Perhaps he would usher in a new era at the Embassy, abandon the campaign to isolate us from our colleagues and discredit us with Moscow, and make it possible for us to return to our home and jobs in Moscow without fear for our lives.

And so, when I saw Dr Beckett a month after the interview I have described, and he brought the subject round to living conditions in Australia, I plunged at once into a eulogy of life in the Soviet Union, and made plain to him that I had no wish to discuss the subject of staying here any further. He got the impression that I had dismissed the matter from my mind, and that the whole proposition was a 'dead duck', which was just what I intended him to think.

With the arrival of the new Ambassador at the beginning of October, our hopes of a new deal collapsed abruptly. Instead of an improvement in the situation, the opposite happened. Generalov proved a more blatant enemy than Lifanov had been and his wife encouraged the other Embassy women to boycott and ostracize Doosia more maliciously than before. The pie-throwing incident was only one example. Within three days of his arrival Generalov reported to Moscow that 'conditions in the Embassy were far worse than he had expected'; he sent for me and censured me 'on behalf of the Central Committee' for allowing my dog Jack into the Embassy; he dismissed my wife from her position as Secretary, contrary to regulations, as she had been appointed in Moscow. Where Lifanov had been a bland autocrat, Generalov in personal interviews was tortuous, and looked at you sideways, as though he were squinting down the barrel of a rifle. When I protested about my wife's dismissal he said, 'Oh, I've nothing against you personally, Comrade Petrov, but your wife is—er—inefficient.' It was a palpable lie; but the alarming thing was that Generalov had apparently had discussions about us in Moscow before he left or he would never have dared to take these steps so swiftly.

As the evidence piled up that the ranks were closing against us without anything to suggest that we could count on help and support in Moscow, resentment gave way to fear. The strain sapped our nerves and tempers. At times I cried to Doosia, 'I would rather kill myself than live in terror of my life'; at other times, 'Their lies and slanders have won—there's no future for me in Moscow!' Sometimes our frustration and alarm turned us against one another.

From the time of my interview with Beckett, Bialoguski began to press me hard to make up my mind to stay in Australia. He had already made the suggestion that I should lend him £500 so that he could go into partnership with George Chomentowski, the Polish proprietor of the Adria Restaurant. I went so far as to put up this idea to Moscow, suggesting that we might be able to use Bialoguski to better effect if he was installed in such a position; but Moscow rejected the plan.

Now Bialoguski proposed to help me buy a chicken-farm, 'Dream Acres', owned by his wife's sister, as a quiet spot where I could settle down in Australia. Twice he drove me out to see the place, and introduced me as 'Peter Karpitch', a migrant newly arrived in Australia. He was very keen to push the deal through.

For my part, I made a show of interest in the proposition to see where it would lead. But I did not take it seriously. I knew that the major questions that confronted me would only be resolved when I was in touch with official representatives of the Commonwealth who could assure me asylum and protection. And I still hesitated on the brink of that crucial step.

Doosia remained the burning question in my mind, Doosia with her mother, sister, father and brother back in Moscow. It was too agonizing a choice for flesh and blood to make. I could not, dared not, ask her to make it deliberately. I was convinced that our fate would be sealed now, after all that had happened, if we went back. I had seen too many similar cases. But I did not believe that she could be persuaded of that herself.

I decided that I would stay; that I would then urge the Australian authorities to get her to join me; but that I should also provide for the possibility that she would refuse to come. In that case, she must be able to disclaim all knowledge and part in my act, and to denounce me as a traitor who had deceived her as well as the Soviet Government. These are the deceits that a régime of ruthlessness and terror enforces on the closest human relationships.

At my next meeting with Bialoguski I gave vent to my overwrought feelings in a violent outburst, in which all the pent-up resentments and stifled criticisms of the system I had served, and its representatives in

Australia, tumbled out uncontrollably. There was an article about Malenkov in the paper. 'Look at that man!' I shouted. 'He and his clique live in luxury, just as the Czars did, while the masses of Soviet people grovel in poverty! Three million Russians refused to go home after the war. They were better off as prisoners of the Nazis! But if you go to Russia and say these things they'll cut your head off! Look at Beria—killed after he himself had killed thousands! Why do we have to shoot each other? And those b——'s in the Embassy here, they're just the same—intrigues, jealousies, slanders! We don't fool anybody; foreign diplomats can see for themselves the real state of affairs! I'll stay here, I'll fix them all, I'll write a true story, if it's the last thing I do!'

Bialoguski poured me a drink and said nothing. It was a turning point.

One other incident is worth mentioning. On the 24th December 1953, on the Cooma road, some miles out of Canberra, my car overturned and was completely burnt. I was lucky enough to escape serious injury, but I received some painful bruises and abrasions, as well as severe shock. My Australian acquaintances, when they heard of it, showed sympathy and concern about my welfare. Not so my diplomatic colleagues at the Embassy. I am a human being, and, at the psychological moment of choice between two worlds, I was struck by this contrast.

Dr Beckett believed that his overture had been rebuffed, but in fact he had opened a door; and now I walked through it. I told Bialoguski that I would like to see Beckett again. Soon afterwards Beckett invited us to have dinner at his home. Things were moving now. After dinner and coffee, Mrs Beckett excused herself, and the three of us were alone. The conversation turned from 'doing well' in Australia to what I could do; and it was then that I told Beckett, 'I am just a countryman.' 'Well, what about a chicken-farm?' he asked brightly. I might have concluded that the minds of Australian Security Intelligence moved along a single track from one chicken farm to the next; had they no other ideas? But, in fact, it was pure coincidence. Chicken-farming happened to be a spare-time hobby of Dr Beckett's.

That evening, and again at a second meeting at his house, I told Dr Beckett: 'I have decided to stay here. It is very dangerous; they could shoot me. I will need the protection of the Australian Government, I will need help to get settled here. I would like to see a Security man, a top man, with his documents. It is very important and very secret; otherwise . . .' I put my finger to my forehead, and made the gesture of a man firing a revolver.

Dr Beckett said that everything would be arranged and promised to put me in touch with his friend Richards, 'Head of the Security Department here.'

As Bialoguski drove me away in his car he remarked, 'Beckett is a decent sort of fellow, Volodya; you can trust him.'

'Yes,' I answered, 'I don't think he is out to shoot men like me.'

That was more than I could say of my Soviet countrymen.

Anyone who has read my story so far will understand that these fears of mine were not illusion but sheer sober realism. I thought of Trotsky's file; I thought of my colleague Bokov, and of the Soviet Ambassador in the Middle East. If my plans had been discovered, I could be certain that Moscow would be directing similar action against me. That fact should not be forgotten.

On Saturday, 27th February 1954, my road reached its point of no-return. I sat in Dr Bialoguski's comfortable flat in Sydney's old respectable suburb of Point Piper. It was half-past six in the evening. Bialoguski turned down the wireless in order to telephone.

'Hullo. Yes, yes, it is. I have my friend here with me and he would like to see you. In twenty minutes? Good.'

He hung up and turned to me.

'He's coming round now. Cigarette?'

I took one and he lit it for me.

'Drink?'

'No thanks.' I needed all my wits about me now. Already the room seemed far away, like something seen in a dream or the early stages of an anaesthetic. But I needed to shake off any sense of an anaesthetic. I must watch every step. Traps, pitfalls and dangers were everywhere.

We smoked in silence and Bialoguski turned the wireless up again. It was announcing the Randwick race result when there was a knock on the door and Bialoguski let in Richards. I remember that as Bialoguski turned the wireless down, Richards made some jocular remark about having a bet.

He turned to me: 'Mr Petrov?'

'Yes.'

'I am Richards, Head of Security here. I expect you would like to see my credentials.'

'I am Third Secretary and Consul of the Soviet Embassy.' That was as far as I meant to go for the present.

I examined the two documents carefully and handed them back to him. The man opposite me was strongly built, swarthily handsome, and spoke in a quiet, business-like tone. I felt confidence in his authenticity and in him personally.

This was it, the meeting of Soviet spy-chief in Australia and a chief of Australian Security. It would take a lot of explaining in Moscow, this meeting.

I broke out into a sweat, and my voice sounded high and cracked. But I knew what I was doing.

'Dr Beckett has been in touch with me,' Richards was saying. 'He tells me that you want to see me and that you are serious in your wish to stay in Australia.'

'Yes, I am serious,' I answered, 'I wish to stay. My wife is the main trouble. I will try to persuade her to come with me, but in any case I will stay. I will need your protection—this must be between the three of us—and I will need help and assistance to start my life again.'

'Mr Petrov, I am authorized to speak on behalf of the Australian Government. I assure you that you will be granted political asylum if you request it and all arrangements are ready. Would you like to sign this now?'

He showed me a piece of paper. It said simply in English and in Russian: 'I, of my own free will, request political asylum in Australia.'

'No,' I answered. 'Not now. When I come then I will sign.'

That would be soon enough. That would be soon enough. That paper would be my death warrant in Moscow—or even in Australia if it got into certain hands. I told Richards about the campaign against us in the Embassy and the reports that had been sent to Moscow and said that I proposed to make my break about mid-March.

'And I will tell you what they will do in the Embassy. They will ask your police to find me—I hope they will not succeed—they will suggest I have killed myself; they will say I am off my head; they will charge me with some crime against Soviet law; and will ask you to hand me back.'

Richards nodded and I felt sure that all these points would be taken care of. Then he said, 'You understand, Mr Petrov, that the Australian Government will want to be satisfied of your good faith and desire to help Australia.'

'I understood and expected this,' I answered. 'I will tell all I know about the work of the Soviet Government in Australia.'

'What do you mean by "tell all"?' he asked.

'Mr Richards,' I replied, 'I know what you do. I can tell you all you want to know and I will do so; but that is later.'

At eight o'clock Richards took his leave, friendly but official. I felt impressed and reassured by this meeting, but I raised with Bialoguski the fear that haunted and dogged me still. 'What if the Government betrays Richards? Then I will be in a mess.'

I had seen a number of Government betrayals in my time as an official of Soviet State Security.

That same evening I received a telephone call which helped to re-assure me that the Australian Security were on the job and were alive to my danger. It was a brief warning that my M.V.D. colleague Plat-kais, had been seen near the hotel where I was staying. I felt encouraged by this evidence of vigilance.

Three weeks passed without any cause for alarm, while I carried on my many Embassy duties. Then, on 19th March, I again met Richards at Bialoguski's flat. Richards told me that his Director-General appreci-ated my need for material assistance and had authorized the payment of £5,000, which would be mine when I finally sought asylum in Australia.

I put up the plan I had worked out for my actual break and pressed urgently for some attempt to persuade Doosia to come with me. I even suggested that Richards should go to Canberra and try to persuade her. He naturally rejected this idea. From the Australian point of view it was diplomatically out of the question, but the problem gnawed at me ceaselessly. It gave me no rest. If only we could find a way.

While Bialoguski was out of the room preparing sandwiches, Richards said, 'I have a feeling that you would like to see me alone on this matter.'

'Yes, can you give me a number to ring? We could meet and talk together without the Doctor.'

Next day at twelve noon, I sat on a bench in King's Cross Park read-ing a paper. Richards came from behind me, walked past and gave a prearranged signal that the coast was clear. Presently I got up and fol-lowed him across Macleay Street into a block of flats called 'Cahors'. In silence we travelled up in the lift together. He got out and I followed him to his flat.

I felt more at ease than ever before as we faced each other alone. My confidence was growing.

'Can you tell me,' asked Richards, 'whether you know of any Australians who have passed on to the Soviet people in Australia infor-mation about their country which could endanger its security?'

'I don't know them all,' I answered. 'No one does. But I know some and I will tell you what they do. Some of it was before I came to Australia. During the war and after the war there was a very serious situation for Australia in official circles. There was a group bringing out official documents. I will tell you when I come.'

Later I told Richards, 'The Doctor talks a lot about money for me. I am not worried about that. I trust you to take care of me. I think the Doctor is trying to be a good friend to me. I trust him for that but not with this other; he doesn't know anything about it. My wife knows a lot,' I added. 'If she stays she could help you.'

That was the nearest I came to revealing our M.V.D. functions before my final break.

We met again with Bialoguski the next day, 20th March, and discussed the possibility of Doosia staying, but I could see that Richards was doubtful of her staying if I, her husband, could not persuade her.

Back in Canberra, I kept turning over my best method of escape with the documents which I shall describe presently. Richards also came to Canberra to stand by in case of an emergency and stayed at the Kingston Hotel, right opposite the Soviet Embassy. He told me that his Director-General was also at hand, but we did not meet then.

Richards and I had several meetings in Canberra at night in his car. To the first of these I took along my Alsatian dog, Jack, who sat in the back seat with me and breathed down Richards' neck as we talked. It was just a general precaution. I was excited and optimistic. I reported that all my arrangements in the Embassy were complete and undetected, and that I could come to Sydney to meet some new arrivals from Moscow who were due on 3rd April. I felt so confident that I proposed to return to the Embassy with them, and glean the latest news about developments in Moscow before making my break.

The next night, 31st March, I was two hours late for our rendezvous. The Party meeting in the Embassy, which I had expected to be over by eight o'clock, had lasted till ten. This was the stormy meeting at which Generalov had renewed his previous charges against Doosia, including rudeness and the pie-throwing story. When she defended herself he answered, 'Petrova, Moscow knows all about you; they know what sort of a bird you are.' By weight of his authority as Ambassador, he compelled the meeting to delete her name from a motion commending the work of all the Party women in the Embassy.

It seemed a petty business, but we understood its significance. Generalov, like Lifanov before him, was determined to convince Moscow on the eve of our return to the Soviet Union that the charges against us were backed up by the vote of the whole Party organization. It was the familiar pretence of democratic procedures cloaking dictatorship from the top.

When I arrived at the Embassy next morning, the chief cypher clerk asked me to step into his office for a moment. He closed the door with an air of importance.

'Comrade Petrov, I must mention a serious matter. Last night the Ambassador and I carried out a raid on the safes. In your safe we found documents which should not have been there.'

Documents! My heart was in my mouth. 'What documents, Comrade?' I heard myself asking, as the sweat gathered on my forehead.

'Oh, drafts of cables and other secret material left in the safe in your Consular office.'

My Consular safe!

With a wave of relief I realized that he was not talking about my envelope of documents for the Australian authorities. That had not been discovered. It was still safely hidden upstairs in the secret section. Still, the matter was serious enough.

'Where are these papers? Give me them—I'm working on them!'

'The Ambassador has them,' he answered.

I hurried to Generalov, who was obviously expecting me. Satisfaction and severity struggled for predominance in his demeanour.

'Comrade Petrov, are these your documents?' He showed them to me but retained them. I looked at them. Yes, they were mine. There was a memorandum from the Australian Communist Party on improving the work of the Australia-Soviet Friendship Society and some draft replies to cables. Tired and distressed, I had put them away the night before in the safe of my Consular office downstairs, instead of taking them upstairs to the safe in the secret section. No actual harm had been done, but I was guilty of a breach of regulations.

'I shall have to send Moscow an adverse report on this laxness,' said Generalov stiffly. My decision to defect had already been made, but these words dispelled any lingering doubts. This new charge, coming on top of the others, would be a deadly weapon in the hands of my enemies; I could get ten years in a labour camp for that offence alone.

That night, as we drove through the quiet suburbs of Canberra, I told Richards, 'I will come to Sydney on 2nd April and I will not come back.'

I told Doosia nothing of my plan. She was a target for the attacks; her anguish and alarm almost equalled my own. She will tell her own story presently. But I was clear in my mind that I could involve her no further; the decision and action must be mine alone. When I left for Sydney she had no inkling that I had decided not to return, nor had she any knowledge of the documents which I took with me in my bag.

I must explain exactly what these documents were, and how I chose and secreted them. Although I was the M.V.D. chief in Australia, it was not a simple matter under our strict security regulations, which had been rigorously tightened up in all Soviet posts abroad after Gouzenko's flight. I had to make sure that neither my wife, who handled all M.V.D. correspondence, nor Kislytsin, who was constantly in and out of the M.V.D. office, got wind of my plans.

Communications between our M.V.D. office and Moscow were of two kinds. We had no wireless link. For urgent matters we used cables, which were received and dispatched over the ordinary commercial cable lines, but of course in top secret cypher. All the cables that came to our Embassy from Moscow appeared to originate in the Soviet Ministry of Foreign Affairs. But our chief cypher clerk could tell from one indicating group of figures the cables which he had to pass on to the M.V.D. office, though he could not decypher them, as he did not have access to our cypher books. We kept a copy of each outgoing cable for three days and then destroyed it. Incoming cables were destroyed as soon as they had been deciphered and understood. If I had been deliberately planning over years to assist the Australian Government, I might have made copies of the cables before they were destroyed, but it would have been difficult and dangerous. In fact, I brought no cables at all with me.

Secret correspondence, on the other hand, travelled in the diplomatic bag on microfilm negatives, which could be destroyed by exposure to light. Parts were coded, and a key to the code was sent separately. Many were the hours that I sweated in our small dark-room at Canberra, photographing our own letters for transmission, or developing and printing the letters from Moscow.

The main documents that I brought from the Embassy were our single prints of the 'Moscow letters' for the year 1952—that is, the letters of instruction from M.V.D. Headquarters in Moscow to our office in Canberra. I did not bring copies of our own letters to Moscow, as these had to be destroyed as soon as we heard that Moscow had received the original negatives. Moscow's whole security policy towards M.V.D. stations on foreign soil is to leave the cupboard as bare as possible.

However, there was one exception to this rule. We were permitted to keep Moscow's letters for about a year, after which we were under orders to destroy them and render a certificate of destruction. Leaving the Embassy as I did early in 1954, I could not bring the 1953 letters, which were still retained for current use. But I could bring the 1952 letters, rendering a false destruction certificate. I organized this carefully. After Doosia had checked through the letters with me, I took some papers to the stove which we had for that purpose and said, 'There go the 1952 letters; they're overdue for destruction.' She had put her signature on the destruction certificate without suspicion, and that certificate was in the M.V.D. safe when my successor Kovalenok took over the office from her.

My whole plan was so designed that after I had disappeared, no one need ever know that any documents had left the Embassy. To that extent, Doosia would be protected in her fight for life in Moscow.

That is why, when the Royal Commission was first set up, Moscow declared my documents to be forgeries and may actually have believed it at the time.

I began these preparations after my first interview with Richards, but I still had to conceal my envelope of documents between that time and my actual flight. I took it from our special M.V.D. safe, and put it in a tray in another safe in the secret section where Doosia kept her cash box and other accountancy odds and ends. She never noticed the unobtrusive envelope.

The Ambassador had not dared to include the secret section in his raid. The authority of the M.V.D. had not sunk so low as that.

Now I had to get my documents out of the Embassy.

I had a rendezvous with Richards for that evening; I must leave myself clear for that. It was mid-morning; everyone was busy about their usual jobs. I went to the safe, took out the buff-coloured envelope, slipped it inside my shirt, under my waistcoat and buttoned up my shirt again. Then I walked downstairs and out of the front door at my usual leisurely pace and took the road to our house at 7 Lockyer Street. On the way I passed two Embassy women, wives of the duty staff.

'Greetings, Vladimir Mikhailovich.'

'Greetings, greetings.'

I walked on without altering my pace. At home I put the envelope under the mattress of my bed (Doosia had gone to the office). Then I called up Kislytsin, who came round. He had been slightly unnerved also by the raid; we discussed it gloomily.

'How do you feel, Volodya?' he asked.

'Terrible,' I answered. 'This campaign is driving me off my head.'

Leaving my dog Jack in charge of the house, I walked back with Kislytsin to the Embassy. We were still discussing the raid in my Consular office when Doosia came in, and heard about it. Her nerves were on edge, and she flew at me.

'You idiot!' she cried. 'Fancy leaving documents in this safe! Now you've really given them something to report to Moscow. Don't you realize you can get ten years in a labour camp for what you've done?'

She spoke truer than she knew. She little guessed that at that moment, under the mattress of my bed, were the Moscow letters destined for the Australian Government.

I was stunned, exhausted, inert.

'Can't you answer?' she stormed. 'Are you deaf? You walk about waving that air ticket as though you were out of your mind!'

In my abstracted state, I was clutching my air ticket to Sydney, perhaps in the unconscious realization that it was my one remaining passport to life and freedom.

For the moment, the worst torture of all, indecision, was over. Before going to bed, and unseen by Doosia, I wrapped my envelope of documents in a copy of *Pravda*, packed it in my usual travelling bag and put the bag by my pillow. That night I slept badly, but woke with a feeling of strange lightness, almost elation, which must have been noticeable to Doosia. By this time all normal feelings had been numbed and suppressed by the mental conflict I had been through. Any action was a relief. I moved in a sort of unreal dream, following almost mechanically the path I had mapped out for myself.

The keynote of my departure had to be a casual, nothing-unusual impression which Doosia could report under interrogation. When the car arrived, I waited till the last moment, then ran down the path, clutching my bag containing the documents without pausing to say good-bye. 'Back on Saturday or Sunday at the latest,' I called.

At Canberra airport there was an amusing incident which I was not even aware of at the time. Richards, who followed in another car, told me of it later. I was late and afraid of missing the plane. As I rushed into the passenger lounge, followed by Richards, I almost collided with a passenger who was coming out. He was the Australian Prime Minister, Mr R. G. Menzies, who had just returned from an electioneering visit to West Australia.

Richards and I travelled to Sydney on the same plane, but did not speak or exchange signals on the journey. I arranged to stay the night with Bialoguski and I spent the morning making travel bookings to Canberra for the new comrades whose ship was due into Sydney next morning. Everywhere I went I carried my bag. We were inseparable.

On that afternoon of 2nd April I met Richards at his King's Cross flat and there, at last, I signed the paper requesting the Commonwealth

Government to grant me political asylum in Australia. Soon afterwards the Director-General of Security, Colonel Spry, arrived, cool and alert. He and his organization had accomplished a stroke of major importance for the security of the Commonwealth; but what struck me then was his quiet, modest manner. We had a drink and a talk. I showed them my envelope of documents, which they looked at but did not then examine. It impressed me greatly that they seemed interested in me as a man, not merely in the usefulness of the documents I had brought. I also spoke a little about my secret work in Australia, and confirmed for the first time to anybody in all these long-drawn-out negotiations that I was the Soviet's M.V.D. chief in Australia.

I then went to Bialoguski's flat for the night taking my bag, which still contained the documents. I slept with it under my pillow. How Bialoguski's eyes would have popped if he had guessed its contents! Next morning I was down at the wharf early to meet the new comrades and escort them to the plane for Canberra. I carried my bag with me. How strange and lost-looking they were as they stepped ashore on to this perilous foreign territory! And how relieved they were to have one of their own people from the Soviet Embassy to meet them, in the person of Comrade Petrov, who knew his way about and seemed quite at home on the alien soil of Australia.

'Comrade Petrov, I am Kovalenok.' We shook hands. We could not betray the fact to the rest of the comrades, but we recognized each other; he was my M.V.D. successor at the Embassy.

A little later, when we were alone, he said, 'I bring you greetings from Topeshko; he asked me to tell you that you have no need to worry about how you will get on back in Moscow.' I thanked Kovalenok for his message, but inwardly I read its meaning as clear as day. How futile are systems of deception which do not deceive! I was the worst subject for such tricks. I had been too many years on the inside of the machine; the principles of SK security work were an open book to me, because I had myself handled such cases both in Moscow and abroad.

Topeshko, a senior M.V.D. officer, was a good friend of mine; I had nothing against him. But not for one moment did I imagine that this casual reassuring message had been sent to me as a spontaneous word of private friendly encouragement.

The most delicate aspect of SK cases, as I knew full well, was the limited power which Moscow has over its subjects while they are on foreign soil. The sovereign principle is to employ every artifice to lull the suspicions of the suspected person and get him back as expeditiously as possible to Soviet territory where Moscow can exercise its powers without embarrassments and limitations.

The die was cast for me already; but Kovalenok's message was conclusive proof of what I had long assumed—that I would be in deadly peril if I crossed the frontier of the Soviet Union.

At Mascot aerodrome I shepherded my flock to the ticket desk and luggage scales, saw that everything was in order, and then watched them straggle through the passenger gate out on to the tarmac and into the plane for Canberra. Then, without waiting for the plane to take off, I walked out of the passenger lounge, still carrying my bag, stepped into the back seat of Richards' car which was waiting opposite the Overseas Terminal, and drove away to the protection of the Australian Government as a political refugee in Australia.

But as I sat in the car, something bothered me. I had not quite finished my work for the Soviet Union. I spoke to Richards. He stopped the car, I got out, hailed a taxi and drove on towards the Kirketon Hotel.

Just before we reached it our two cars stopped alongside each other at some traffic lights. On a nearby truck a Communist orator was declaiming an election speech in the tones and language I knew so well. I looked across at Richards and my look was eloquent.

At the Kirketon, I found Comrade Elistratov, who was on his way to the Soviet Legation in New Zealand. I gave him his ticket and £10 travelling expenses, and wished him good luck in his new job. Later I posted to the Ambassador's new secretary Elistratov's receipt for £3 10s. od., the balance of the cash, and my used air ticket, which was required for accounting purposes. I did not want to leave any untidy ends or unfinished business behind me.

My journey back to the rendezvous with Richards was not quite direct and took a little time. When I settled back in the car and we were on our way to the safe house, he asked anxiously, 'You were longer than I expected, what happened?' I explained that, feeling thirsty, I had looked in at a bar for a quick one on the way.

At the house he gave me the £5,000 that had been promised, and I put it away in a safe. From my bag I took my envelope, still wrapped in its copy of Pravda, and gave it to him. Up to that point I had forced myself to concentrate and keep cool. But now the stress of my emotions began to tear and pound me, like a violent pain when the anaesthetic wears off. My hands shook, my voice trembled, my head was splitting. Nevertheless, I went through the documents I had brought, giving Richards a general idea of their contents, as well as a short account of my life and work, which he took down in his own handwriting.

I ended my statement with these words: 'I no longer believe in the Communism of the Soviet Leadership. I no longer believe in Communism since I have seen the Australian way of living. My wife would like to stay in Australia but she is afraid for her family in Moscow, and says that she must go back. There is a possibility that she might change her mind and stay here, but it is very difficult for her . . .' Then I collapsed, finished.

'Very difficult for her'—the futility of words, especially when translated into cold print in a foreign language!

In the succeeding days, such days as I hope never to live through again, I suffered agonies of fear, suspicion, doubt, remorse. It was not remorse for my defection from a ruthless, cynical and inhuman system —I did not feel it then, I do not feel it now—but remorse and fear for my wife's fate.

It was one thing to tell Richards, 'Even if she does not stay here, I will stay.' It was another thing to have stayed, to have acted on my own and to know nothing more.

Constantly I raised this question with Richards and with the Security officers around me, and urged them, 'Could you not go for my wife? Could someone see her? Could some arrangements be made? She is a clever woman, she could help you a lot, she could answer many questions.'

But behind their replies I read the question, why did she not come with her husband? Why didn't he arrange this in the first place? Does she want to come, anyway? As I read the story in the papers and learnt that she had been taken to the Embassy, pending her return to Moscow, I realized the worst.

'They will shoot her now!' I told the Security officers. 'She will never see her family again after what I have done! Why do you not kidnap her and rescue her?'

But they explained that such a thing was out of the question. She could only come at her own wish and choice; and how could that be discovered now? Over and over we discussed what possibilities there were of getting in touch with her, of finding out what her real wishes were, of offering her the chance of asylum. But what chance was there when she was a virtual prisoner in the Embassy?

I wrote to her through the Australian Department of External Affairs, telling her that I was safe and well and asking for an interview with her. I doubted whether she would ever see the letter and had little hope of my request being granted. My scepticism was justified. As I discovered later, she was compelled to refuse and to say that she was afraid of falling into a trap. And the reply was held back until the day she left Canberra. I received the message after she had gone.

On the day of her departure from Sydney my state of mind was terrible.

Preparations had been made for the possibility that she would appeal to see me at Mascot airport. During the arrival of the Embassy cars and her progress towards the plane, I was lying on an inner-spring mattress under a cover in the back of a utility truck, which was parked close by. I heard the noise in the distance. But presently my driver and guard told me that it was no use. The excited crowd had ruled out any chance of contact; my wife was now on her way to Darwin.

Darwin was our last hope. It was a bad night. Early next morning a Security officer put through a call to Darwin and presently, unmistakably, I heard Doosia's voice at the other end of the line.

'Doosia! Doosenka!' I cried, and poured out my appeal to her to stay; nothing but the worst fate now awaited her in Moscow and she would never see her family again. But I had not been speaking long when I heard her exclaim, 'No! No!' and bang down the receiver. That seemed the end.

I left the 'phone in the depths of despair, convinced that she did not believe that it was really I who was speaking to her.

We were all depressed and silent.

After an interval, the Security Officer got through to Darwin again, for a final report on the situation.

Suddenly he rushed from the 'phone. All his official reserve had disappeared as he shouted in delight, 'She's staying! She's staying!'

An elderly Australian lady who looked after the domestic arrangements of the house was there with us. The Security officers usually called her 'Mum'. I put my arms round her and hugged her as we danced round the room together, Soviet defector and Australian 'Mum' shouting, 'She's staying! She's staying!'

XXV

Alone

VOLODYA was strangely cheerful on that Friday morning of 2nd April. The last ominous Embassy meeting and the raid on his safe had reduced him to a wreck of his former self; his hands would shake and tears spring into his eyes; at times I thought he was on the brink of madness. Now suddenly he was himself again. He came hurrying from the bedroom to consult me.

'Doosia, should I wear my new suit, do you think? You know that I have to meet the new comrades from Moscow, including my successor, Kovalenok. It would be well to make a good impression.'

'Keep your good suit for a more important occasion, Volodenka, it's just another trip.'

I quickly plugged in the iron to press the trousers of his working suit, and at that moment there was a knock on the door. It was Lavrentiev, the chauffeur, who announced that the Embassy car was waiting outside. As I ironed he sat on the edge of the sofa, asking how long Vladimir Mikhailovich would be and exclaiming that they must leave immediately if they were to get to the airport in time to catch the Sydney plane. There was the usual rush as Volodya collected his things. Seizing his old bag he hurried down the path to the waiting car, in his haste not even pausing to say good-bye to me or Jack, the dog. Standing in the porch I watched the car whirl him away in the direction of the airport and as I did so a chill of fear and foreboding passed over me. How should I interpret this sudden cheerfulness, after the agony and strain that I had seen gripping him in recent months? I did not know; but I felt vaguely afraid.

The morning was sunny and inviting, but I turned uneasily back into the house. The breakfast things stood on the table, and the sitting-room needed dusting; but I had no heart for these household chores either. I decided to go to the Embassy. It was only a short walk and soon I was in sight of the terra-cotta brick building behind its high cypress hedge and the Red Flag floating from its flag-pole. Volodya and I had chosen a house close to the Embassy so as to be as independent as possible of official Embassy cars. One could never be quite sure of the chauffeurs; it was better to take no unnecessary risks. There were a few office matters to attend to, but today they somehow seemed unimportant and remote. I went out to the nearby centre of Manuka to do some shopping, but I couldn't keep my mind still.

Volodya and I were booked to return to Moscow in a few short weeks and the great question that overshadowed everything else was—what lay in store for us? All our personal plans—seeing my mother and family, settling into our flat again, meeting old friends at M.V.D. Headquarters—all these lay under the sinister cloud of slanders and accusations that had been sent back to Moscow by the Ambassadors. Many were petty, but together they were a formidable accumulation—insubordination, impertinence, splitting the 'collective', forming a 'Beria Group' in the Embassy and now Volodya's fatal slip in the matter of his safe.

I shivered and glanced over my shoulder. I had the sense that someone was following me. Several times I turned round quickly and scrutinized the streets I had just traversed. But my main fears did not centre round the possible attentions of Australian Security, but round the hostile intrigues in our Embassy, who were watching for every chance to trap me into some error.

I came back to the house, wandered round it aimlessly, lighting cigarette after cigarette. I couldn't settle to anything.

After nibbling at some food I went to the Embassy for the weekly film evening. Various other Embassy wives who were there in the main reception room greeted me with formal politeness, but they avoided me. I knew only too well what was going on in their minds. Once the cue to avoid us had gone out from the Ambassador and his wife, the subservient juniors hastened to fall into line. It was the odious ostracism that becomes obligatory in our Soviet society whenever someone falls under an official cloud. Stronger than all my bitterness at their behaviour was the sense of being utterly friendless and alone. The film afforded the relief of darkness and a measure of distraction. I don't remember very much about it, but it was quite a good Russian historical film, I think about the composer Glinka and his opera *Ivan Susanin*. As usual I did not stay to talk, but went straight home as soon as it was over.

That night I slept badly and woke several times from meaningless nightmares. Next day, Saturday, I got up late, and went to the Embassy to meet the new arrivals from Moscow. Among them was Volodya's M.V.D. successor, Kovalenok, who told me that Volodya had met them in Sydney and had said that he might not be back in Canberra before Monday. There was nothing surprising about that in our work, but I remembered Volodya's recent state of mind, and my anxiety was not dispelled.

Later, when we were alone, I asked Kovalenok if he knew anything about the Ambassadors' campaign against us.

'Yes,' he answered, 'I heard about it at Headquarters before I left Moscow. I can tell you that you have nothing to fear and that your husband has no need to worry.'

Unlike Volodya, I did not detect the sinister implication behind the message and I felt a little encouraged.

Back at the house our cat and her three kittens were mewing and running about at the kitchen door. As I fed them and talked to them, I felt a measure of relief, even of relaxation, in their company, after the cold hostility at the Embassy. An old proverb came to my mind; I could not tell when I had first heard it, but it seemed exactly suited to my situation at that moment—'The more I see of people the more I like to be with animals.' As I stroked her fur, I said, 'Pussilka, you and your family always give me a warm welcome, don't you?'

Jack, the dog, was jealous of this attention to Pussilka; he looked straight into my eyes and whined, as though to say, 'As long as I am with you, isn't that enough?'

As always when Volodya was away, Jack missed him and was restless. He lay on the floor and from time to time would sigh heavily. Whenever a car came by in the street he pricked his ears, lifted his head, and raised himself to see if his master were at the gate. Then as the car disappeared he would sigh and lie down again. Sometimes we would both walk out into the street looking up and down in both directions; then we would go back into the house and I would say, 'No, Jack, it doesn't look as if he's coming yet. We must wait a little longer.'

Jack was an important member of our household at 7 Lockyer Street. Volodya had bought him as a pup on one of his early visits to Sydney, soon after our arrival in Australia. I was in bed when he got home, and I remembered how he came into the bedroom, said, 'Here's a present for you,' and threw the wriggling, snapping puppy to me. He grew quickly and left the usual train of chewed slippers and torn chair covers that betoken a puppy in the house.

But, as Volodya has described, even Jack was used in the campaign against us.

Sunday dragged by and Monday came without any sign of Volodya. Early in the afternoon I had a call from the Duty Officer at the Embassy to say that the Ambassador wished to see me. Generalov was sitting in his office when I entered and held a folded paper which he twisted in his hand. He spoke abruptly, without inviting me to sit down. His sly face was pale and worried.

'Has Petrov rung you?'

'Petrov has not rung me. He is not in the habit of ringing me up when he is on duty.'

I said this acidly. The Ambassador had to know of our M.V.D. functions, of course, but just how we managed our affairs was none of his business.

'Did he tell you when he was coming back?'

'Yes, he said he would be back on Saturday or Sunday. But Kovalenok told me that Petrov had an assignment and would not be back till today.'

'Very well. That's all.'

As I left I felt sick and alarmed. What did Generalov know? What was he contriving? I went upstairs to Masha Galovanov's room and found her alone. She and her husband Ivan had remained our friends through all our troubles. Now, as I faltered out to Masha my fears about Volodya's state of mind, and the schemes of our enemies, the tears that I had kept in check for so long broke their barriers and poured down my cheeks. Masha put her arm round me and tried hard to comfort me, saying that there was no need to be alarmed, since Vladimir Mikhailovich was often away for long periods. I was not convinced, but I was grateful for her sympathy all the same. I stayed with her, crying and talking, till the small hours of the morning. Masha persuaded me to eat a little and invited me to stay the night with her, but I did not like to leave our house all night and went home to sleep.

The goodness of Masha and Ivan is among the few happy things that I remember from the Canberra Embassy. I still see her plain, kindly face, round and full, with its turned-up nose and almond eyes, a typically Russian cast of face, as she comforted me through my tears in the only ways she knew. Masha could not write, and could only read with difficulty, but she had a warm, generous heart. Masha came regularly to help me with the housework at 7 Lockyer Street. Ivan in his spare time worked a plot which we had given them in our vegetable garden. Volodya, who liked simple people, used to spend hours talking to him about his own early life in Siberia. We were glad to help the Golovanovs to supplement the limited salary which Ivan received in his modest position of Night Duty Officer. Their honesty, kindliness and homespun worth, are qualities that persist under Communism as they did under the Czars, among the humble, simple people of Russia.

On Tuesday morning events took an alarming turn. The Duty Officer rang me from the Embassy to say that the Ambassador wanted to see me. As at our previous interview, Generalov looked nervous and pale but he spoke politely. 'Evdokia Alexeevna, I am now seriously worried about your husband. You remember that motor accident of his last Christmas? Well, I have the same premonition as I had then that something is wrong. I feel it my duty to report to the Australian Government that he has failed to return and to ask them to investigate his whereabouts. I must also inform Moscow. You, too, must agree that the situation is serious. This is Tuesday and he said he would be back on Saturday or Sunday at the latest.'

I answered, 'Nikolai Ivanovich, I know my husband had several assignments in Sydney, and he may have been delayed. I suggest you need to make sure of your facts before you report to Moscow.'

'We shall see about that. I tell you this purely for your own information. Whether I report it or not is my own business. I don't need your advice. Moreover, on account of your husband's disappearance, I now require you to take up residence in the Embassy building. We must forestall any possible attempts to kidnap you.'

Generalov ordered Kovalenok, who had been a silent witness at this interview, to escort me to my home in the Ambassador's car in order to collect my belongings and bring them to the Embassy, where I was to be kept in the room occupied by the Golovanovs.

At 7 Lockyer Street, Kovalenok stayed in the car with the chauffeur and I went in alone. I saw Ivan Golovanov working in the vegetable garden and beckoned him into the kitchen. Kovalenok and the chauffeur saw this and followed as far as the garden, but did not come into the house. 'Ivan, I have been ordered to stay at the Embassy; I am to be kept in your room.' He paled and his face clouded. 'Our room? This is the first I've heard of it.' Then, 'What do they think?' he exclaimed. 'Are they accusing Vladimir Mikhailovich of something wrong?' After a moment's thought, he added, 'Whatever has happened is their fault, not his. Even a machine can't go on for ever; it breaks down some time. All the more with human beings. Flesh and blood can't stand persecution for ever. It cracks in the end.' Disturbed and troubled he went back to the garden. I did not immediately begin packing, because I was still turning over ways and means of making my own inquiries about Volodya. First I rang the two airlines, T.A.A. and A.N.A., to see whether he had booked a return seat from Sydney to Canberra. Both reported that he had not. I then tried to ring Dr Bialoguski in Sydney, but he was out. Kovalenok had now come in

from the garden and began to walk up and down in the corridor
urging me to hurry up.

I collected bed linen and night attire and locked the house behind me.
Back at the Embassy, the first thing I did was to book another call to
Dr Bialoguski. While I was waiting for it to come through, I was sum-
moned again to the Ambassador.

Brusqueness had replaced his usual sly hesitancy. 'Evdokia Alexeevna, I am aware that you are making independent inquiries about your
husband. I order you to stop, because the matter has been reported to
the Australian Department of External Affairs, and in future all inquiries will be made by them.'

I said nothing and left the room.

A little later I got through on the telephone to Dr Bialoguski. With
tears in my eyes and struggling to control the tremor in my voice, I
asked whether he had seen Volodya in the last few days. 'Strangely
enough,' he answered, 'I have already had an inquiry for him from
Platkais and Antonov. Unfortunately I can't be of much help to you.
He hasn't called here and I haven't seen him lately. But what are you
worrying about? I'm sure he's all right. You know how busy he is
when he visits Sydney. I'm sure that's the explanation. I wouldn't
worry. A man isn't a needle, he'll be found all right.'

'Well, I hope so, but do make any inquiries you can and let me
know, please.'

'Of course; I'll do my best and ring you if I find anything.'

'Thank you, ring me at the Embassy, will you?'

'Not at home?'

'No, at the Embassy.'

I went up to the Golovanovs' room, sat down on a sofa and began to
cry. From then until I left Canberra tears were never far away, as waves
of terror and weariness passed over me. Sometimes I would feel as
though gripped in a vice, and would sob and sob for half an hour at a
time; then the fit would pass and for a while I would be dry-eyed and
outwardly calm. That was generally when I had some call upon my
concentration, or when some particularly stupid piece of officiousness
or deception by the Embassy authorities stirred me to fresh resentment
and resistance.

The room which was to be my prison for the next thirteen days was
of medium size, on the first floor, with a window looking on to the
Embassy grounds. In one corner was the Golovanovs' bed, in another
Masha's dressing-table, in a third a wardrobe. A bookcase along the
inner wall and a small dining table completed the furniture, except for

the sofa, which had been brought in specially for me to sleep on. It was far too short even for me. When I protested to Sanko, the Ambassador's chauffeur and Embassy caretaker, and asked for a bed, he said he had no orders about that. I spent the first night uncomfortably trying to slee· on the sofa. Next morning I went to Generalov.

'Nikolai Ivanovich, I demand a bed. That sofa is far too short for any human being; I can't sleep on it.'

With bad grace he told Sanko to bring a bed from our own house, which was installed in place of the sofa. Several times I asked Ivan to bring some more of my things from the house, and gave him the door key; but he came back saying that Sanko had confiscated the key.

I was not supposed to leave this room, nor be left alone there; if Ivan was not there himself, Masha had to be. No arrangements had been made about my food. I had to insist on my right to go down to the kitchen to get something to eat for myself; I had brought some rolled oats from our house, and I made myself some thin porridge. When Masha discovered how I was being treated, she insisted on sharing their meals with me, and only reluctantly accepted the payment which I pressed upon her before I left.

Now I tasted, as never before, the bitter experience of anyone in our Soviet system who falls under official disfavour. Apart from the Golovanovs, who did their best and kindest as warders, I had not a friend in the place whom I could trust. No one spoke to me or came to see me except Kovalenok, and he came only to summon me to the Ambassador, or on official M.V.D. business. He had no ill-will towards me, but he was under orders and he had to look after his own skin now. Once when I went out for some fresh air and sat on the bench by the volley-ball court, he came up to me, obviously uncomfortable and apologetic, and explained that it was not quite safe for me to be outside the building, as there was danger of an attempt to kidnap me. I fumed, but did as ordered; it was plain that in all but name I was under arrest.

Every action by Generalov and his staff seemed designed to enrage and frighten me. Perhaps most galling of all were the petty irritations and stupid deceptions, which did not deceive me for a minute.

I asked for newspapers and got them for the first couple of days by going to the office of Kharkovetz, the Press Attaché. Then, without a word, they were all removed. I asked the Ambassador's permission to read the papers. He assented, but later I was told that I was only to get *The Canberra Times*, as 'the same news was in all the other papers'.

For the first week I was allowed a radio in my room, but as soon as the news about Volodya's disappearance broke, the set was removed, and I heard that the Ambassador required it 'for his own use'. I then went downstairs to the big radio in the lounge, but I was not allowed to stay there, and was told that the set was 'out of order'. I tried the office of the Counsellor, Klimov, where there was a set and listened there before lunch. When I went back after lunch, the set had gone. Kharkovetz later told me that it was out of order. I asked another of the wives who lived in the Embassy, if she would mind me listening to her radio set. 'I'm sorry, Evdokia Alexeevna, it's out of order.' Even in the Ambassador's car, on my fateful journey to Sydney, I was told that the car radio was out of order when I asked to have it switched on.

It would have been ludicrous in less serious circumstances, but I was simply angered by these insults to my intelligence.

In my isolated state I desperately needed someone with whom I could talk things over and unburden myself. But I had my lesson about this. In a weak moment I poured out my troubles to Kharkovetz, who was a decent sort of fellow; he had been recruited as an M.V.D. agent in Moscow and had worked for us in Australia. I mentioned that General-ov had told me not to hope for Volodya's return. Kharkovetz immediately reported the conversation to the Ambassador, who rebuked me severely for talking to Kharkovetz.

I had become an untouchable. Everyone avoided me, or merely acknowledged my greeting if I spoke first. Conversations would stop when I passed; I would see little groups of women gossiping and sneering with malicious pleasure at my misfortune. Mrs Generalov, who hated me, was the ringleader. On the first Sunday, clearly at her instigation, a group of women gathered under my window, chattering and laughing in obvious mockery at my predicament.

Though I despised their spitefulness, I could understand what made them do it. Apart from venting their hostility and jealousy, they could now feel smug in the assurance that according to Soviet teaching, persecution was not only justified but even commendable against anyone who was linked with an 'enemy of the people' and Generalov's actions already suggested that he regarded Volodya in that light.

On top of the isolation, I had to submit to a series of interrogations, some of them lasting for hours. Soon after I was taken to the Embassy, the Ambassador summoned me.

'Evdokia Alexeevna, a telegram from Moscow asks that you elucidate certain questions which might assist in the search for Petrov.'

'What are they, Nikolai Ivanovich?'

'As follows: One: On what terms were you with your husband? Two: Did he take any articles of clothing with him? Three: Did he have any money with him? Four: Did he say anything to you before he left? Five: Has he ever hinted that he meant to take his life? Six: Was he preparing to leave for the Soviet? What preparations did he make?'

I replied that he had taken no extra clothing, and was wearing his old suit; that he had about £30 to buy suitcases; that we were almost ready to leave for the Soviet Union; had bought some wooden crates to pack our belongings in and had begun our packing; he had booked passages for us for the 8th May; that I thought he was in such a nervous state that he could easily commit suicide. 'You know how agitated he was,' I said to Generalov. 'He knew of all the hostile reports that had gone back; he feared that, false as they were, he might not be able to disprove them in Moscow. But he always said that no matter what happened to him, he still had his hands, and he could always work with them.'

Generalov then asked me whether I could help locate Petrov. I said, 'If I could help, I would not be making inquiries myself.'

Back in my room, the defiant front which I had put up to Generalov's interrogation suddenly crumbled. I was utterly helpless and alone, without a friend in the world, beset by a pack of ravening wolves united in their determination to destroy me. All my defences collapsed; the conviction swept over me that I was lost and doomed; there was nothing I could do about it. Yet there *was* something I could do! I could beat them yet; I could snap my fingers at them all, I could escape —in the one way left open to me.

There was no one in the room; Masha had gone out on some errand. Working with the energy of desperation I took the flex from the electric iron, doubled it and went to the high, built-in wardrobe. Inside against the wall there was a row of hooks some inches above the level of my head. Quickly I put the doubled flex over one of the hooks, knotted it in a rough slip-knot, and put the loop round my neck. In a few moments Masha might return, or my courage might fail. With wild resolution I lifted both feet off the floor, so that the full weight of my body hung on the flex. It tightened round my neck; for a second, everything went black; then I crashed to the floor with the flex slack. Looking up I saw that the hook had broken under my weight.

I picked myself up, shaken and trembling, and sat down on the bed. The shock of my attempt and failure left me frightened and weak; all the fight had gone out of me, for the time being. I put the broken piece of the hook into the wastepaper basket, wrapped the flex round the iron again, and covered all traces of the incident. I told no one, not even the Golovanovs, and I made no further attempt of that sort during the

rest of my stay in the Embassy. However, I did not finally put the idea
of suicide out of my mind, as I shall tell presently.

For a week I waited in anguish and uncertainty. What was the truth
of the matter? What had really happened to Volodya? I knew well
enough his state of mind, which at times was near madness. I knew the
hints he had dropped about suicide and about the possibility of staying
in Australia, which I had always fiercely rejected; it was clear that Dr
Bialoguski had been encouraging him in this direction too. But how
could I know? The treatment I was receiving suggested that Generalov,
and Moscow, believed Volodya to have decamped of his own free will,
but surely he would never have taken such a step without telling me?
Could it be that the Australian Counter-Intelligence had found out
about his M.V.D. role and had actually kidnapped him? How could I
know, how could I discover? The silence and uncertainty were the
worst torment in the world. Meanwhile, I handed over the M.V.D.
office to Kovalenok. Together we checked the codes and cyphers, the
equipment and the documents, including the Destruction Certificate
for the 1952 Moscow letters (which we little dreamed were at that
moment being studied by the Australian Security Service). I also turned
over to Kovalenok the secret M.V.D. funds, which we used for paying
agents and other clandestine purposes. There was about £A2,000 in
ready cash. Kovalenok checked it, agreed with my accounts, and signed
for it as correct.

After that I was no longer allowed into the secret Cypher Section of
the Embassy where for three years I had worked hard as Captain of
State Security and M.V.D. cypher clerk.

Suddenly, on Tuesday, 13th April, the blanket of silence was shattered. Over the nine o'clock news of the Australian Broadcasting Commission, I heard a summary of Prime Minister Menzies' statement,
made an hour before to the Australian Parliament, that 'one Vladimir
Mikhailovich Petrov', Third Secretary of the Soviet Embassy in Canberra, had requested and had been granted political asylum in Australia.

I rushed downstairs to the Ambassador.

'Nikolai Ivanovich, you have heard the radio announcement?'

'What announcement, Evdokia Alexeevna?'

'About my husband, Petrov?'

'No, I didn't hear it, what did it say?'

I told him briefly.

'Well, thank you. You may go.'

Even at this stage, in my agitation and distress, I did not feel sure that
Volodya had not been kidnapped. Why should I believe the word of

any Government? All my training was against it. In the Embassy no
one told me anything; there was no one I trusted except the Golovanovs and they knew nothing. Whom could I trust? What could I
believe?

Two days after this, Generalov called me again to his study and
handed me a letter from Volodya, which had been forwarded to the
Department of External Affairs. I took it with studied calm and
examined it carefully; there was no doubt that it was from Volodya
and in his own handwriting. He said he was well, had sought refuge in
Australia of his own free will and asked me to meet him.

'Obviously he wrote it under pressure,' said Generalov. 'It was dictated to him.'

Could I be sure that he was not right?

He told me to sit down and write a reply in accordance with a draft
which he gave me. I incorporated some of his phrases, but rejected
others. It was not a situation to encourage me to pour my heart out; but
I let Volodya know where and how I was, and asked him to think of
me; at least he would know that I was alive and still in Australia; he
would be able to guess the rest.

I saw the Ambassador pin my letter to an official note addressed to
the Australian Department of External Affairs; and I thought that
Volodya would have it in a day or so.

But three days later Generalov sent for me once more and said that he
had received a telegram from Moscow with instructions as to how I
should reply. Clearly my first letter had never been sent. Generalov had
been frantically cabling Moscow for instructions before allowing any
communication to go from me to Volodya. The key sentence of the
reply drafted in Moscow was, 'Under the conditions laid down by the
Department of External Affairs for meeting you, I cannot meet you,
because I am afraid of falling into a trap.'

For four hours I fought Generalov and Kovalenok on this issue of
saying that I feared a trap. I was afraid that the phrase would finally end
all possibility of my seeing Volodya, and finding out the truth. In the
end, worn out and exhausted, I gave way and wrote what they wanted.

'You say my husband wrote under dictation,' I remarked bitterly.
'I am certainly writing this under dictation, and my husband will
realize that these are not my own words.'

They were quite impervious to any such arguments in their panic
subservience to every detail of Moscow's instructions. Generalov went
even further. I had begun my letter with the affectionate diminutive
that I always used when I wrote to Volodya, 'Dearest Volodenka'.

'No, no!' objected Generalov. 'That won't do at all, this is no time
to be sentimental. Don't address him at all.'
'Not at all? Then he will know it is not from me. Shall I write "Dear
Volodya"?'
'Yes, all right.'
I was furious at his interference, but, as ordered, I wrote the more
formal 'Dear Volodya'. By this insistence Generalov made quite certain
that Volodya would know that the letter was not my own composition,
but had been written under official dictation.

After this I was allowed a brief visit to our house to collect the rest of
my belongings. Kovalenok and Sanko accompanied me in the car and
Vislykh, the First Secretary, and Masha Golovanov came too. As we
hurried into the house we passed two men, who, we thought, might be
press correspondents. In the bedroom I was horrified and enraged to
see a great mound of our belongings piled in the middle of the floor
where they had obviously been thrown when our cupboards and
drawers were searched. Shirts, shoes, hats, coats, underclothing—everything was heaped together indiscriminately. I turned on Vislykh, who
was in charge of the party. 'Aren't you ashamed of yourself? Just look
at that pile! How could I ever sort my things out of that mess?'

He was apologetic but abstracted; the sight of the press correspondents had frightened him badly; he was responsible for my custody.
'We must go back at once. Leave all these things here, they can be
collected later. Hurry, there may be a dangerous incident.'

In their panic they hustled me to the car and drove me back to the
official confines of the Embassy. Then, between nine and ten, when it
was dark, they brought to the Embassy the jumbled pile of our clothes,
with the trunks and crates we had got ready. I stayed up all night sorting and packing. I was careful to put aside everything of Volodya's. I
knew what construction could be put upon it if I took any of his things.
No one would believe that they were for my father or brother. In the
nervous tension which gripped the Embassy authorities in these days, I
knew that I could be shot if I gave anyone the slightest impression that
I was planning to follow my husband.

Even with my own packing I took elaborate precautions. For example, I wrapped my shoes in brown paper only. Australian newspapers found in my suitcase could be used as incriminating evidence
against me once I crossed the guarded frontiers of the u.s.s.r. Printed
matter and gramophone records were regarded with particular suspicion.

No one told me what was to happen to me, but from various signs I gleaned that I would be leaving soon for Moscow. Golovanov mentioned that he had seen a request to External Affairs for a taxation clearance for me; and I was given a series of rushed injections (the doctors were brought to the Embassy for this purpose). Then, on 17th April, the Ambassador told me, 'You are leaving for Moscow by air on the nineteenth.'

So that was it. The Soviet authorities were convinced that Volodya would not return, either because he had in fact left of his own free will, or because he had been kidnapped and was being held under duress by the Australian authorities. In either case I must go on to Moscow alone, to face—what? The question had assumed an urgent importance. If only I could discover some more facts! During these months of strain and suspense, and particularly since Volodya's disappearance, my family in Moscow had been constantly in my mind—my mother and sister, my father and brother. I had, of course, said nothing in my letters to them about what we were going through, but in some way I believe that my mother had sensed and shared my sufferings since I came to Australia. I knew how much she longed to see me again, how she would be counting the days till my return. But what awaited me in Moscow now? Whom could I trust? How did I stand myself? I was to travel with an escort officially provided for my protection against attempts to kidnap me. But their first task, I had no doubt, would be to deliver me safely at m.v.d. headquarters in Moscow. And what then, after all that had happened? What could I expect but the worst?

Two conversations greatly intensified my alarm. I asked Kovalenok, as an m.v.d. colleague recently arrived from Moscow, what he thought would happen to me when I got back. He shrugged his shoulders.

'There are special provisions of our Soviet penal code in such cases—you must know all about them, Evdokia Alexeevna.'

'I can guess,' I answered as bravely as I could. 'But I still want to know what you think will happen.'

He answered slowly: 'Oh, various things could happen—perhaps a labour camp—possibly even the death sentence, since by the look of things your husband deserted of his own free will.'

'There's no proof of that!' I flared. 'No one has seen him—you wouldn't let me talk to him!'

Kovalenok did not reply, but his words focussed in sharp relief a fear that I had never yet faced in its stark and terrible reality.

The other incident was quite as alarming. As soon as I got wind that preparations were afoot to send me back to Moscow, I went to Generalov.

'Nikolai Ivanovich, I don't mind telling you that I'm very worried about what will happen to me in Moscow after all this. I've handed over the office in perfect order; I myself am entirely innocent, yet I fear punishment on account of my husband.'

Generalov's manner towards me had changed completely. He was now all solicitude and reassurance.

'Certainly you are completely innocent, Evdokia Alexeevna. You have nothing whatever to worry about. However, if you feel anxious I'll give you my personal guarantee that you'll be all right in Moscow.'

'I'm not asking for your guarantee,' I answered, 'I'm asking for a guarantee of immunity from the Soviet Government.'

'By all means, I'll send off a telegram at once for such a guarantee.'

On my last morning in the Embassy I asked Kovalenok if he had heard anything about the guarantee which I had requested from Moscow.

He answered ironically, 'Ask the Boss.'

I went to Generalov and repeated my inquiry.

'Your guarantee from Moscow? No, I have not yet received it.'

After these two conversations I was really frightened. My mind began to work frantically and furiously. But I thought of my family, and I still meant to go back.

XXVI

Flight

I WOKE on the fateful morning of my departure with one burning question in my mind—what had really happened to Volodya? Everything else hinged on that; the thought of going back to Moscow with that overwhelming question unanswered was agonizing, unbearable.

From the way I was being treated, I was clearly regarded by Generalov, acting on Moscow's authority, as the wife of an enemy of the people, who had deserted to the capitalist camp.

But could that be the true story? Or had Volodya in fact been kidnapped and compelled to write to me under duress? Was Generalov really afraid that I too might be abducted? All these possibilities seemed quite feasible to me then. I knew very little about the realities of democratic life, but I knew a lot about our own M.V.D. methods. It seemed quite possible that the Australians had found out about Volodya's intelligence work and had kidnapped him by force.

On the other hand, there was the terrible strain, fear and near-madness which the Embassy campaign had imposed on him. There were the hints that he had dropped from time to time, and the plainer hints of his friend Bialoguski, about staying in Australia. All these pointed to a voluntary decision.

But I couldn't believe that he would have left without telling me. I remembered a conversation we had had a few months before his disappearance. That evening I was alone at home, in the depths of misery. Volodya had been in a state of tension for days and I began to imagine all sorts of things. When he came in about ten o'clock I burst out, 'Volodya, where have you been? I've been worried to death about you. I even wondered whether you could have left us, or been kidnapped!'

'Didn't you know I was on duty?' he answered. 'Surely you didn't think I would leave you?'

His words kept ringing in my head as I questioned and argued with myself, this way and that. I would never rest until I had seen him. Whatever happened, I must see him. Somehow, somewhere, I must satisfy myself as to what had happened. I must discover the truth. Even my own fate seemed less important than that.

The morning was fine, but overcast. I ate a little breakfast, took some headache and sleeping powders and put the finishing touches to my packing. My four suitcases were ready; Kislytsin would take them ahead and book them through to Moscow. As personal luggage for the journey I had a small valise and a shopping bag. I had received Volodya's salary for his last days of work up to the time he left the Embassy. I got the remainder of my own M.V.D. salary up to the time I handed over my cypher duties and I had some money which I had saved. These sums made up about £300 in all, in Australian money. Later, I discussed with the couriers what I could do with this remaining Australian currency and they advised me to spend it on my way through Switzerland, which I decided to do.

An hour before I was due to leave, I was summoned to my last interview with the Ambassador. Generalov's manner was heavily official. 'Your plane leaves Sydney at ten o'clock tonight. You will be accompanied to Moscow by Second Secretary Kislytsin and Diplomatic Couriers Jarkov and Karpinsky. Your first stop after Darwin will be Singapore. You will not leave the airport there, and you will not go to any hotel. You will spend the night in the public lounge of the airport; there you will play cards with the couriers, in order to give the appearance of a casual party of tourists, and you will laugh.'

I said nothing, though I boiled inwardly at this callous disregard of my real feelings.

'Your escorts have orders,' he went on, 'to guard and protect you constantly and not to leave you for a moment.'

'Not even when I go to the toilet room?'

'Not even then.'

Again I felt nothing but disgust and contempt at his ponderous severity. But his next words chilled me with real fear. 'Bear in mind that the couriers are armed. If there are any attempts on the part of the Australian authorities to force you to stay here, they may use their weapons.'

A new terror laid hold on me at those ominous words. What did the threat really imply? My M.V.D. experience had taught me to look behind the façade of things for the hidden deception. Instances of people I had known personally, or had heard about indirectly, came crowding into my mind. Was it not possible that plans were already far advanced for my own 'disappearance'? Why, the couriers might even now have secret orders to shoot me somewhere along the route, under the pretext that I was trying to escape, or that the Australians were trying to kidnap me. That fear never left me all the way to Darwin. I had seen too much myself. The greater the reassurances, the greater my misgivings.

A considerable crowd had gathered outside the Embassy gates to see my departure. Isolated from my colleagues, cut off from almost all channels of news, I had gathered only a vague confused impression of the reactions of the outside world. I did not realize the tremendous public interest and sympathy which my situation, headlined across the non-communist world, had aroused. I was not at all certain that the Australian crowd were not waiting to vent their rage upon me as one who had helped my husband in his M.V.D. work against Australia. As the Golovanovs' room was on the side of the Embassy away from the street, I could not see this crowd, but I heard descriptions of it from the alarmed discussions of the Embassy employees.

Apparently Generalov got in a panic lest some riotous incident should occur. He sent out Ivan Golovanov and a clerk, Chizhov, to photograph the crowd in order to disperse them; later Vislykh also pretended to be photographing the throng of reporters and others who clustered round the gates, but he was too scared to open the car windows.

Now, looking back, I see a tremendous significance in the incident, in the ridiculous belief that an Australian crowd might be dispersed by photographing them. It showed clearly the great gulf between our countries, and revealed how great was our ignorance, even after years of life in Australia, of how Australians thought and behaved. In Moscow, the crowd would have melted away as if by magic. Why? Because a photograph is a record which can be used against you with deadly effect. In a country where the only safety from political arrest lies in being anonymous, it is a perilous business to be photographed, especially by foreigners and in unknown company. During the purges, Volodya had been investigated because a photograph, which included him, had been found on the person of an arrested man.

But the Australian crowd ignored the clicking cameras; some people even waved. Disappointed, our nervous strategists had to think out another plan. It was decided to send out one of the cars half an hour ahead of the one in which I would travel; the chauffeur would drive Mrs Antonov and Mrs Vislykh in order to mislead the crowd and draw off anyone who planned to follow us. I got a view of this stratagem being prepared. From the Golovanovs' window I looked down on the back courtyard of the Embassy, and saw the two ladies getting into the car. Klimov, the Counsellor, was instructing them and I heard him say to Mrs Vislykh, who was a blonde like myself, 'Take off your glasses and cover your face, so that they will think you are Petrova.'

I poked my head out of the window and called down to him, 'Comrade Klimov, do not be so naïve; they know perfectly well who's who.'

So it proved. The decoy car dashed out of the gate with a great flurry, but entirely failed to draw off the crowd, who were still there when I left half an hour later.

At one-thirty it was time to leave. I said good-bye to Masha and Ivan, thanked them for all their kindness and went down to the car which was waiting in the back courtyard.

Apart from Antonov, the Tass agent, not one of the Embassy staff came to say good-bye to me.

I was placed in the back of the car with the two diplomatic couriers, Jarkov and Karpinsky, who were to escort me back to Moscow, while Kislytsin, my other travelling companion, went in another car. I sank back in my seat, and at high speed we roared out of the gates of the Embassy and headed in the direction of Sydney.

The four-hour drive from the Embassy to Mascot aerodrome remains a blurred, painful memory; I remember that I felt exhausted, miserable and utterly alone, and cried a good deal of the way. Sitting in the car there was nothing to do, no one to see, nothing to take my mind off my situation. A few miles out of Canberra we formed a convoy with the other two Embassy cars and travelled on in company.

Somewhere near the little township of Collector, I asked them to pull up for a few minutes. I crossed the road to the side where there were some sheltering trees. Two of the women came with me. Dully I wondered whether we were being followed and whether the Australian authorities were planning any measures of the kind the Ambassador had hinted at. I looked back, but there was not a sign of anyone following us.

To return I had to cross the road again. It was the last day of the Easter holidays, and a steady stream of cars flashed by going back towards Canberra; I had to wait some time before there was a break in the speeding procession. Standing by the side of the road, I was seized again with the impulse to end my life. My attempt in the Embassy had failed when the hook broke, and I had never again had the opportunity or the resolution to try again in cold blood.

But now it would be so quick. I could throw myself in front of one of the oncoming cars before my companions had a hint of what was in my mind, and the endless cycle of fear, pain, and loneliness would be over for me.

For a moment I hesitated. But an even stronger force held me back— some supernatural influence, it may be, or the dread of being crippled, which I have always feared more than death. I waited till there was a break in the traffic, crossed the road carefully and got back into the car.

For perhaps fifty miles we travelled on in silence, through the undulating Australian countryside, past huge paddocks dotted with occasional clumps of sheep, on through patches of bush, the grey trunks of the gum trees merging into the grey-green monotony of their leaves. I stared in front of me, listless and unregarding.

A fresh spasm of misery gripped me and I began to sob again. Someone judged this a suitable time for diversion. The cars stopped by the roadside, picnic baskets were produced, food was spread out and the rest of the party got out and stood around, eating. I stayed in the car. After a few minutes Vislykh approached and offered me a glass of brandy; at first I refused, but afterwards drank a little. He then began to soothe me, adopting a confidential and sympathetic tone.

'Evdokia Alexeevna, I understand very well how distressed you feel about this whole unfortunate business and especially now that you are on your way to Moscow. But you really have no need to worry. None of us believes that Vladimir Mikhailovich left of his own free will. Why, I've had many conversations with him and never once did he suggest that he felt any dissatisfaction with our Soviet régime. I'm quite sure the whole thing will be cleared up once you get back to Moscow; that's all you have to bother about now. *You'll* be all right. You'll soon be at home again, settling down to work in your old job.'

I said, 'Alexandre Georgevich, don't try to cheer me up or pretend it isn't serious, after all I've heard and seen at the Embassy.' In my misery I thought, 'I am utterly alone; there is no one I can trust. I will never see Volodya again. And as for my family in Moscow—will I be able to help them? Or will I simply involve them in penalties and suffering along with me?' It was a terrible question which I had neither strength nor facts enough to answer at that point.

The food was packed up, and we drove on without stopping till we reached the approaches to Mascot aerodrome. It was dark before we got there. Sanko and Vislykh went ahead to reconnoitre, and returned to warn us that there was a large excited crowd at the airport. We drove on cautiously. There were cars everywhere. As we got near to the airport buildings, the crowd spotted us and surged round the car, a pushing, shouting tide of angry and excited people. It was a terrifying experience. Faces peered in the car windows; photographers and reporters seemed to be everywhere. One man put his head right inside the car and asked in English, 'Mrs Petrov, will you make a statement? Do you wish to return to Russia, or do you want to stay here?' I shrank back in the car and said nothing. I felt sick and paralysed with fright. This was a very different crowd from the collection of curious spectators who had gathered at the Embassy gate in Canberra; this crowd was turbulent, violent, out of control; the noise was deafening. Coming on top of all that I had been through, the sight and sound of them terrified me; perhaps they really did mean to tear me in pieces because of the work that Volodya and I had done for the Soviet in Australia.

Sanko and Karpinsky took my arms and dragged me through the crowd on to the tarmac. It seemed a very long way; I heard afterwards that they had made a mistake and stopped the car at the T.A.A. buildings instead of the Overseas Terminal. We went first to an aircraft which turned out to be the wrong one; then we had to pass round in front of the T.A.A. buildings to reach the right plane, all the time surrounded by shouting, running, pushing people. Under the floodlights of the airport I saw the milling crowd like a roaring sea around us. I lost my right shoe, and asked my escorts to get it back for me, but they would not stop. 'Don't hold me so tight—I can walk all right—you are humiliating me and yourselves in front of the crowd,' I cried to them, but they took no notice, and continued to drag me across the tarmac. They had one object only—to get me on to the plane. Half dragged, half hobbling and stumbling, I at last reached the great looming shape of the plane. On the way I made out some of the shouts of the crowd, mostly in Russian—'Don't go!'—'Stay here with your husband!'—'If you go, it's a labour camp or death for you!'—'You'll never see your family!' But in that hectic, confused uproar I felt stunned; all I wanted was to get away from it; I did not dream of answering. I could not even think.

As we got near the mobile gangway up to the plane, the crowd became more and more violent. When I had climbed two or three steps, they tried to pull me off; as I reached the top and was about to step into the plane, the gangway was suddenly pulled away, and I almost fell between. Police helped to push the gangway back into place, one of the plane's crew reached out and steadied me, and I stepped aboard and sat down in the nearest seat. At that moment it seemed a haven of refuge.

A member of the crew, perhaps the captain, came up and put a hand on my shoulder and another on my hand as though to comfort me. I squeezed his hand and said, 'Can I see my husband?'

He said nothing, but patted my shoulder, and gave me a glance of sympathy. I asked him if my shoe could be recovered; he answered that time was short, but they would do their best. He went off, but presently came back and said that there was too great a crowd; the shoe could not be found.

Sitting there, in the relative quiet of the plane's interior, with the shouts of the crowd in the distance, my mind cleared a little, but my overwhelming feeling was exhaustion. I felt like a straw tossed about by wild forces outside my control; I was grateful even for this brief respite.

It was said in press reports that while I was sitting there a white-haired Russian was allowed on board the plane, and appealed to me to stay in Australia, but that is not true. Apart from the crew member and the air hostess, nobody spoke to me. Of our Embassy people, only Mrs Antonov came to say good-bye to me; the others no doubt were too frightened of the hostile crowd and too relieved to see me delivered on board the plane.

As I recovered a little from my fear of the uproar, I began to think more clearly and my despair deepened. If the Australians had planned to kidnap me there was no sign of it in what had happened. I had seen the police helping to control the crowd, so that my escorts could get me successfully on to the plane. It seemed that my last chance of seeing Volodya was gone now; I would go back to Moscow with the aching question in my heart unanswered. I would never know the truth.

Now there was activity aboard the plane. It must be nearly time to start. My three travelling companions had also got safely aboard by this time, and the air hostess came along and showed us to our proper seats. I was by a window, with Kislytsin beside me, while the two couriers, Jarkov and Karpinsky, sat behind us.

The plane door was shut and locked with a sense of finality; one after the other, the engines roared to life and we taxied away from the lighted buildings to the lonely darkness of the aerodrome. 'This really is the end,' I thought; 'I will never see Volodya again now,' and the tears sprang to my eyes; that chapter was finished for ever.

The plane turned, paused, raced forward and lifted itself into the air. As we circled in a wide sweep over Sydney, I looked down on the myriad of jumbled lights scattered below us—streets and ferries and bridges and houses in a confused maze of glimmering pin-points of light and in my heart I said, 'Good-bye Volodenka, my husband; somewhere among the million lights of Australia you are hiding now, but where, I cannot tell.'

How ironical that (as I later found) Volodya at that very moment was waiting at Mascot airport, where he had been brought by his friends in the Australian Security Organization, in case I should appeal to see him. But I had no inkling of this. Even if I had, the clamour and confusion of the crowd would have made any such move on my part out of the question.

Soon the clustered lights were left far behind and we flew on in complete darkness. Karpinsky leaned forward from his seat behind and praised me for my courage at the airport. He and Jarkov were obviously immensely relieved at the way things had turned out and presently they were both leaning back sound asleep.

Then a curious thing happened. A little man who was sitting in the seat in front of me screwed round and whispered to me in Russian, 'Do you want to stay in Australia?' I took no notice, and indicated by studying some papers that I did not wish to discuss the matter with him. I thought that he must be an agent of the Australian Security Organization who had been placed there to approach me and observe me. The impression was confirmed when I noticed him consulting with two other men passengers further down the plane, and also when he took photographs of me as I lay back, apparently asleep.

He was not, in fact, a representative of Security at all, as I discovered later. I suppose that he was a press man from one of the Australian papers. At the time I decided to be on my guard and to watch him carefully.

After a while I got up to go to the ladies' rest-room at the rear of the plane, then realized that I was limping, and remembered my lost shoe. I went back to my seat, took off the other shoe and walked along to the rest-room in my stockinged feet. Both the couriers and Kislytsin had settled down and made no attempt to follow me. In the rest-room there was a bed and wash-basin; a lavatory opened off it. I had begun to tidy myself up when the air hostess came in. She spoke to me in a friendly tone and when she saw me in my stockings, offered to lend me a pair of her own shoes. They were black suede sandals, with high heels, and although they were rather too big, perhaps fours, while my size is three —I accepted them gratefully.

'How do you feel?' she asked with real kindness in her voice. I tried to reply but broke down and sobbed. When I had recovered a little she asked, 'Would you like to lie down for a while? You could have my bed here,' indicating the bed in the rest-room, but I answered 'No, thank you.' I explained that I was too wrought-up to sleep and had not slept properly for a fortnight.

'I understand what you've been through and how you feel,' she said, 'I'll do anything I can to help you. Do ask me if there's anything at all you want.'

'I want to see my husband,' I said. 'Do we stop at Melbourne?' From newspaper references I knew that the headquarters of the Australian Security Organization were in Melbourne. I concluded that Volodya was in their hands, and I snatched at this last hope of seeing him. She shook her head, 'Oh no, Darwin is our first stop.'

My heart sank and I sighed aloud. 'Then it is impossible. I shall never see him.'

My grief overcame me again. The hostess gave me a glass of water to cool and calm me, and I saw tears in her eyes. I was grateful for her sympathy. I felt sure it was genuine.

When I got back to my seat I saw that the little man in front was drinking a glass of beer, and I asked him whether he had got it from the steward. (I felt thirsty and I also thought I would test him out to see what his intentions were.) He said, 'Yes', and I asked him to order beers for the four of us, Kislytsin and me and the two couriers behind, whom I woke up. He did so, but did not try to engage me in conversation again.

While we sipped our beer, Kislytsin became his usual confidential and affable self. 'Doosia, may I come and visit you in Moscow next May Day? You know I've always been a good friend of yours, and always will be. Whatever happens when you get back, I promise that it won't make any difference to our friendship.' 'You say that now,' I answered, 'to reassure me and calm me down. But back in Moscow, it may be a different matter. Suppose I'm dismissed and disgraced, as the wife of a traitor to the Soviet Union, suppose I'm condemned and punished—that will be the end of your friendship with me.'

'Doosia, I can see you don't know me. I'm ready to risk even my career to prove my friendship. After all,' he went on confidentially, 'you and I don't need to keep up pretences, we can be frank with each other. Actually, I feel my own position is very similar to yours.'

'How do you mean?' I asked.

'You know as well as I do that Lifanov, Generalov and Kovaliev have sent Moscow unfavourable reports on me too.'

It was true enough; he had been mentioned unfavourably in the cabled reports about Volodya and me. Kislytsin had always been very decent to us. During my detention in the Embassy he had obeyed Generalov's instructions and had not spoken to me, but I knew it was not out of any personal hostility to either of us, and that in itself was something to be grateful for.

'Well, thank you anyway for your encouragement; I appreciate it.

Do come and call on me at home on May Day—that is, if I'm ever allowed to see my home again.'

'I'm sure you will be. This whole business may turn out quite differently. You may find yourself a heroine instead of a victim. After all, who is in a position to say that Volodya willingly left the service of the Soviet?'

Who could say, who could say? Presently Kislytsin dozed off. The plane roared on through the night, crossing the vast breadth of the continent to Darwin, its last port of call in Australia. My mind was wide awake now, recovered from the frightening experience at Mascot, working furiously. The flight from Sydney to Darwin was a chance, the first real chance I had had, to consider things in relative calm, to get the whole nightmare of the last few weeks into some sort of perspective. Not only the last few weeks, though; it covered the last two years, since the first launching of the campaign to isolate us in the Embassy and discredit us with Moscow.

It was a menacing total—Lifanov's accusations about us, culminating in the charge of forming a 'Beria group'; Generalov's continuation of the campaign of denunciation, the last ominous Embassy meeting, the incriminating raid on Volodya's safe. And now, on top of all that, my imprisonment in the Embassy, Kovalenok's warning about the penalties, the non-arrival of Moscow's guarantee and my recall to Moscow under armed escort.

The signs were clear enough for a blind man to read. As the plane thundered on and my mind wrestled with these problems, the various incidents gathered and focused in one burning query—'If they do this to me here in Australia, what will they do to me back in Moscow?'

I glanced round at the couriers. Their eyes were closed, they seemed relaxed. The diplomatic couriers, Jarkov and Karpinsky, have been pictured as brutal ogres; 'diplomatic gorillas' was one vivid phrase used to describe them. Actually, they were a type I knew well enough, men who had reached their trusted position through long service rather than ability. They were clumsy and slow thinkers, rough rather than cruel. They were not brutes by nature. But that was beside the point. They were armed and they were men under orders, orders which they alone knew, which they would carry out to the letter, for fear of the consequences to themselves if they failed.

I remembered Generalov's ominous words and shivered.

So far everything pointed one way—to the madness of going back to Moscow. But the thought of remaining was equally frightening. What could I really expect here? What had happened to Volodya?

Would we not be shot as spies against Australia? Then with a wave of anguish I thought of my family in Russia. If there was a chance of helping them, and they needed my help, I was ready to risk anything that might happen to me. But was there such a chance? How could I know, how could I discover the truth, how could I decide? The agony of my thoughts tore me in two.

I got up and went again to the rest-room. The hostess was there; she smiled at me, asked how I felt now and gave me an ice compress for my aching head.

Then she said, 'I do realize how awful it must be for you not being able to get in touch with your husband. Do you want to stay in Australia too?'

I answered, 'I want to see my husband.'

'You look very frightened; what are you afraid of? Is it the people who are escorting you?'

'Yes, the couriers; they have guns.'

'Don't be afraid. Stay here a moment while I see the captain.'

Soon she came back with the steward. He, too, asked if I wanted to stay in Australia, and again I said that I wanted to see my husband, and that the couriers were armed.

I went back to my seat, sat still for a time, decided to go to the rest-room again. But first I woke up one of the couriers. 'Comrade, I wish to go to the ladies' room; don't you think it's your duty to escort me?' He got up, still half asleep and lumbered after me to the rest-room; he drank a glass of water outside the door, saw that I was tidying myself up and went back to his seat.

While I was there the steward came back and asked me how I felt. Again I repeated that I would like to see my husband, but was afraid of the couriers and their guns.

'Don't worry,' he said, 'you'll be all right. But do you want to stay in Australia yourself?'

I understood quite clearly the issue before me; but I was not pre-pared to tell them that I wished to stay in Australia. It was a huge and terrible step for me, I expected traps and dangers everywhere, and I had not decided.

Instead, I asked him directly, 'Can you help me find my husband? Can you help me to see him?'

He murmured something like 'Everything will be all right', and left me.

Unknown to me at the time, another drama was being played out which was to answer my question and determine my fate. The captain of the aircraft was in radio communication with the Director-General of the Australian Security Organization, Colonel Spry, who was in Canberra, in touch with the Australian Government throughout the night. He had asked the captain of the aircraft to find out how I was, physically and mentally, whether I was afraid of my escort and whether I wished to remain in Australia. My conversations with the air hostess and steward were the basis for the reply which the captain radioed back to Canberra and for the final instructions which Colonel Spry then telephoned to the Acting-Administrator in Darwin as we sped towards our landing there.

But all this I only discovered later. After this conversation with the steward I went back to my seat and did not leave it again until we reached Darwin. Presently, at about five a.m., the lights inside the plane were switched on and it was evident that we would soon be landing. I began to repair my ravaged make-up and, as I did so, succumbed to fresh fears as to what might happen when we did reach Darwin. I had no picture of it, but I dreaded a repetition of what had occurred at Mascot, but perhaps worse, with mob violence and indiscriminate shooting. What would the couriers do if the situation became really desperate?

The contrast of what actually happened took me by surprise. As the plane bumped and rolled across the runway in the darkness before dawn, Kislytsin reminded us that we were to remain on board throughout the short stop. The plane came to a halt, the door was unlocked and opened, a gangway was run up. All the other passengers began to shuffle off to wash and have breakfast. Soon the four of us were left alone in the plane. A steward came along and explained politely that we would have to disembark, as passengers were not allowed to remain on board during refuelling. There was nothing else for it. The couriers went first, then Kislytsin. I was the last passenger to leave the plane. As I emerged I noticed a small group of grey figures close to the gangway, but there was no commotion or disturbance. As I reached the bottom of the gangway and stepped on to the tarmac under the aerodrome lights, a man approached me and introduced himself with the words— 'I am Mr Leydin, the representative of the Australian Government.' He spoke quietly but firmly. 'I have been authorized by the Australian Government to ask you whether you wish to remain here, and to seek political asylum in Australia.'

Quickly I looked round to see where the others were. Kislytsin was a little distance away, talking to someone whom I could not see clearly. Each of the couriers was standing about twenty yards away, separated from me and from each other by a number of armed and uniformed police. None of them was within earshot. It had all happened very quickly, without any disturbance that I had noticed.

I began to speak to Mr Leydin, but my stress of feelings was too much for me, and I cried aloud, 'My mother and sister and father and brother —I want only to die—can you give me poison?' He said, 'I am not here to give you poison, but to ask you whether you wish to stay here, or whether you wish to go home. I am your friend, not your enemy. I understand your situation very well, I sympathize with you very much, but you must decide yourself what is best for you.'

'I don't know, I don't know,' I groaned, with my eyes shut. 'What has happened to my husband?'

'Your husband is alive and well,' he answered, 'and you too——'

'I don't believe you!' I burst in. 'I know my husband and I know he would not have left me! Where is he? Can I speak to him?'

He answered, 'I assure you that your husband is alive and well and that if you decide to stay in Australia, you will be taken to join him as soon as possible.'

His manner impressed me. He was tall, neatly dressed, and his face, which reminded me strangely of a pleasant Russian type of face, seemed kindly in its expression. I had a sudden feeling of confidence in him.

But I checked it quickly. After all, it was the business of a person in his position to seem genuine and to inspire confidence; I was determined not to be deceived by anyone. I had suffered too often before. Without positive proof, without seeing Volodya and speaking to him, I would not move a step. And then there was my family.

'I don't know, I can't choose,' I groaned again. 'My father and mother and sister and brother are in the Soviet Union. What you ask is too hard for me. I can't choose, I can't decide.'

I glanced round again and saw one of the couriers looking over in my direction; my heart leapt with fear. (I did not know till later that their guns and ammunition had been taken away by the Australian police.)

Mr Leydin listened to what I had to say and made no effort to convince or persuade me to stay; he only asked that I should think the matter over carefully. There was no need for me to hurry about it; he would leave me alone to think it over, but he would like to see me again later.

I was again impressed by the calm and authority of his manner, without hustle or pressure; it contrasted strongly with the panic, rudeness and inhumanity of the treatment I had endured in our Embassy at Canberra.

I asked Mr Leydin if I might rejoin Kislytsin and the couriers. He said, 'Of course', and walked away. As I approached the couriers and Kislytsin, the police made way for me. One of the plane's crew asked if we wanted breakfast, but we refused and all four of us went to the airport buildings and sat down in the lounge. Kislytsin was very worried and depressed. 'Who was that person talking to you?' he asked me. 'What did he want?' 'Oh, he said he was an Australian official,' I answered. 'He asked me what sort of a trip I'd had, how I felt, and inquired whether I had any intention of remaining in Australia. I didn't reply.'

The couriers were glum and shaken; they described how they had been disarmed by the Australian police, who told them that it was illegal to carry firearms and ammunition in the aircraft. Muttering about infringement of diplomatic immunity, they said they would demand their weapons back before they left Darwin.

Neither Kislytsin nor the couriers asked me any more questions. They seemed satisfied that the crisis was over; perhaps they were simply dazed and bewildered by the turn things had taken; they were obviously convinced that I still intended to go on with them to Moscow, as indeed I did.

There we sat. No one seemed to be taking any notice of us; the other passengers had all gone off to breakfast. We sat in silence for perhaps half an hour. At last I exclaimed, 'Well, why do you sit here doing nothing? Aren't you going to ring the Embassy and report what's happened?'

The couriers in an apathetic sort of way agreed that it would be a good idea and Kislytsin went off to put a call through to the Ambassador. He came back after a short while. 'Yes, I got through to the Embassy all right. I could only raise the cleaner, Mrs Karasev; I had to give her the account of what happened here and tell her to pass the message to the Ambassador.'

I laughed ironically at that. How well I could picture what had happened! No doubt there had been a celebration last night, as they congratulated themselves on getting me safely on to the plane and off their hands; discipline had probably gone to the winds, and this morning they were sleeping it off.

We sat on in the lounge for another half-hour, while it got fully light. Presently the plane's crew walked through the lounge and out on to the tarmac to board the plane; in another half-hour we would be taking off. I watched them, numb and paralysed. Physically and emotionally I had come to the end of my tether; I was exhausted, I had no reserves left, I had not the energy for any positive decision. In a last wild irrational craving to escape further conflict, to make an end of crises, to have things settled at last, I turned to my escorts, 'Look, the plane crew are going on board; let's go on board too.' But Jarkov disagreed, 'No, I think we should wait till the rest of the passengers start going on board; then we can mingle with them and be less conspicuous.'

That piece of prudent commonsense possibly settled my fate. As we sat waiting, a man whom I took to be an aerodrome official came up to us and said, 'Mrs Petrov, your husband is calling you on the phone.' Trembling all over, I got up to follow him and casually asked the couriers and Kislytsin to come with me. The man led me to the foot of some stairs. On the landing above I saw Mr Leydin pacing up and down. He had received the call which Volodya, with Security's help, had put through to me.

'Ah, Mrs Petrov! Your husband wishes to speak to you on the telephone. Will you take the call up here?'

'Can I take it downstairs, please?'

He agreed and had the call switched downstairs. I was led to an office phone; my escorts followed and stood behind me. I lifted the receiver and said, 'Hullo.'

'Doosenka, it is I, Volodya.' It was his voice, plainly and unmistakably Volodya's. I said nothing.

'Doosenka, it was the lies—all the lies that they told about me, all the slanders that were thrown at us at our Party meetings, which Moscow seemed to believe—those were what forced me to stay here. I stayed here of my own choice, I wasn't kidnapped.'

I forced back the torrent of questions that raced through my mind. I couldn't afford one false move, with the couriers at my elbow. As Volodya talked I kept saying, 'No, no!' and 'That is not him, that is not my husband.' I let him do the talking. 'It is I, I, Volodya!' he went on, 'don't you recognize me? Doosenka, I know it is you. Again I tell you, I stayed here of my own accord. I am alive and well. I beg you, face facts before it is too late. I ask you to stay, not just because you are my wife, but as one human being to another. You still have life ahead of you if you do. If you go back now you will never see your family anyway, because of what I've done. Doosenka, believe me, you will never cross the threshold of your home.' All I answered was, 'No, you are not my husband, good-bye,' banged down the receiver and walked out of the office.

It was Volodya all right. From the fog of confusion and doubt two facts had emerged like mountain peaks above cloud. Volodya had stayed in Australia of his own free will; he was alive and wanted me to stay with him. And he had confirmed my worst fear of all—the fear that even if I did go back to Moscow, after what he had done I would never see my family again. My mind was made up; I had decided.

Kislytsin and the couriers went out of the office first. I followed. Opposite the door I saw Mr Leydin standing and I gave him an emphatic wink as I passed to indicate that I wanted to speak to him.

He understood my signal, came up to us and asked me, 'Would you like to speak to me alone?'

I began to reply when Kislytsin interrupted angrily, 'She does not want to talk! She can come with me and the others!'

I said firmly to Mr Leydin, 'Yes, I would like to speak with you.'

I followed him into the office where I had taken the telephone call. We were alone this time, but I was terrified lest the couriers in desperation should resort to violence. I noticed that the room had frosted glass windows, and I was afraid that they might break the windows and force their way in. I asked Mr Leydin to shut the door quickly and to have the room surrounded by police. I said to him, 'Mr Leydin, I have decided to stay because there is no other way out.'

He asked me to sign a statement that I was seeking political asylum in Australia of my own free will, but I said, 'I will sign it when I see my husband.'

Then I followed him out of another door to a car, and drove with him to Government House, Darwin.

★   ★   ★

The kindness and consideration of Mr and Mrs Leydin in those first few hours is a story in itself; for the first time for weeks I managed to sleep and found I had some appetite. That same afternoon, after a pleasant lunch, I sat with them on the veranda of the house in the warm sun, while a cool breeze from the sea fanned us and rattled the palm leaves in the garden. Next day Mr Richards, of the Australian Security Service, arrived with a Russian interpreter and a woman companion to be with me at this crisis. It was a thoughtful step which I greatly appreciated. I was still stunned and dazed, like a patient after a serious accident. Despite everyone's kindness, I was taut, tense and watchful. I would trust no one until I had seen Volodya and had heard the whole story from his own lips. There were so many tremendous questions of the past and the future to be resolved. I had to see him first.

Not until Volodya and I met at the house provided for us in Sydney, did I begin to relax my attitude of wary suspicion towards my Australian protectors. The Soviet couriers had been there to 'protect' me with loaded revolvers that they would have turned against me in a crisis. How could I be sure about my new escorts? Might they not be arranging some trap or stratagem? I would say nothing, sign nothing. The lessons of a lifetime were in my attitude.

One small example illustrates my frame of mind in those first days, and the mistrust of everything and everyone that my M.V.D. training, and my life in the Soviet Union had instilled into me. One of the Security Officers with us was always referred to by the others as 'Jack'. I assumed automatically that this must be a code-name and that we would never be permitted to hear the real names of Australian Security people. It was months later that I met him and found that his name really was Jack.

Laughing over the incident with one of his colleagues, I said, 'You see, it is still in me.'

Bit by bit I discovered how groundless and unjustified my suspicions were. Volodya was well, far better than he had been in those last dreadful days in the Embassy, and he reassured me completely about our reception. He was receiving the best of treatment, had full trust in the good faith of the Australian authorities and said that we should help them in any way we could. As I bombarded him with questions, so many things that had baffled and tormented me in the weeks since his disappearance became clear. Especially, I understood why, believing that I could never bring myself in advance to the decision to accompany him, he had acted alone, hoping that I would follow him, but covering my retreat as best he could by hiding from me his decision, his departure-date and his removal of the documents.

Above all, I saw with absolute clarity what madness it would have been for me to choose differently at Darwin, and to go back to Moscow in the vain, tragic hope of seeing my family again.

XXVII

Aftermath and Prospect

VLADIMIR PETROV: As we come to the last chapter of our book, it is more than a year since first I and then my wife fled from the Soviet Service to political asylum in Australia and crossed the frontier from one world to another. It is time for us to say something of our experiences in the strange interlude of these months, something of what we have found as guests of the Australian people and Commonwealth, something of what has been going on in our own minds since, with such violent abruptness, one life ended for us and another life began.

EVDOKIA PETROV: Gradually we have relaxed our fears and suspicions. Our story is the best explanation of these suspicions, instilled into us by our training as M.V.D. officers and by the whole background of our lives in the Soviet Union.

I tried to convey to one of the Security officers just what it means in practice to live under a régime of universal fear, where at least every tenth person is an M.V.D. informant, and where the sheer hunger for enough to eat drives people to spy and report on their neighbours. I said to him, 'Suppose you are my friend in the Soviet Union. We talk, visit each other's homes, go to the theatre, meet in the office or at Party meetings, but I do not tell you what is in my heart. Never, not to anyone, not to my best friend. Perhaps only to the closest in my family circle—perhaps only to one.' The training of a lifetime does not disappear overnight. But we have found the Australian Commonwealth as good as its word. We have been protected, looked after, and provided with what we need and we believe the assurance of the Commonwealth Government that we will be helped to establish ourselves in comfort and security as citizens of our new country. That is our earnest desire.

With the Security officers whose task it is to guard us, we have formed friendships going beyond mere official relationships. On Christmas Day several of them brought their families to visit us. The house and the Christmas tree were decorated with tinsel and coloured lights and I enjoyed myself in the part of Father Christmas. Wearing a jovial mask and Volodya's old dressing-gown, I distributed the pile of presents to grown-ups and children, while Volodya watched and en-joyed the occasion. There was one thing we soon noticed about the Security officers, who were our first direct contact with Western life on terms as close as must occur in living continually with people under one roof; they seemed to trust each other, and worked together without apparent friction or cross-currents of jealousy, suspicion or intrigue. The contrast with the conditions we had left behind us among our own people in the Embassy was striking. And yet it was not because human beings in one country are absolutely different in their nature from those in another country.

Our story shows that Soviet people have the same basic desires, instincts and aspirations as people in other countries. The difference is better explained in words which I used under cross-examination before the Royal Commission—'Two systems which contradict each other'.

VLADIMIR PETROV: One passionate desire which I voiced to Bialo-guski when I decided to leave the Soviet Service, was to write a book which would tell the truth.

Soon after my wife joined me in Australia, we were powerfully reminded of what happens to truth in the Communist world we had left.

A weekly newspaper in Poland (one of the so-called 'Peoples' Democracies') reprinted a picture taken at Mascot aerodrome on the night of her departure from Sydney, which showed her being hustled to the plane between Sanko, the Embassy driver, and the courier, Jarkov.

Under the heading 'Gangster Methods used by Australian Fascists', the paper described how 'a group of Australian Fascists, assisted actively by the police, abducted Mrs Petrov from the airfield (*see picture*) and beat up the First Secretary of the U.S.S.R. Embassy, A. Vislykh, his wife, and the U.S.S.R. diplomatic couriers'.

Ludicrous though such perversions seem to people outside the Iron Curtain, the effect of a continual diet of them should not be under-estimated. I myself, while in the U.S.S.R., without any outside standard of comparison, accepted the 'revelations' of the great Moscow trials of 1937 and 1938 and believed the 'confessions' of leaders like Kamenev, Rykov, Bukharin, and Yagoda, confessions which were incredible and palpably false to the outside world at the time as they are to me now.

Soviet leadership does not seem to realize the effect of its gross false-hoods on public opinion in free countries—perhaps because on the home front it has so effectively muzzled all honest discussion and criticism of fundamental issues. Thus a recent article in *Pravda* signed 'Observer', and quoted by Moscow Radio claimed that the 'so-called Petrov case' was fabricated by the Australian authorities under the direct guidance of the Australian Prime Minister, Robert Menzies, and added:

'Neither the petty criminal Petrov nor the Australian Premier managed to blacken Australian citizens, and to discredit the Soviet Foreign Service, whose members, unlike those of some other Powers, discharge no functions except diplomatic ones.'

Our evidence has made plain enough the degree to which the obtaining of secret intelligence—in plain words, espionage—is a primary objective in all Soviet establishments abroad. I have seen Rear-Admiral Rodionov, a high-ranking Naval Intelligence officer, who was appointed Ambassador to Sweden in 1949. Alexander Panyushkin, my Moscow chief during my service in Australia, a professional M.V.D. officer, was appointed Soviet Ambassador to China and then to the United States. Georgi Zarubin, the present Soviet Ambassador in Washington, was Ambassador in Canada at the time of the Gouzenko revelations (though there was no evidence of his involvement in espionage) and later in London. My colleague Kislytsin served under him there and told me that in the Committee of Information period, Zarubin, though not a professional Intelligence officer, acted as supreme Intelligence chief in the Embassy and used to sign letters and signals concerned with secret Intelligence operations.

As M.V.D. officers appointed to carry out espionage in Australia under diplomatic cover, we cannot help having some reservations about the truth of *Pravda's* pronouncement. We, like thousands, and even millions, of other Soviet citizens had become aware of the deceits and contradictions of the régime we served long before we ever thought of leaving it. There lies a perpetual source of weakness and insecurity to the Soviet Government—the need for such constant falsification and concealment.

In this respect, our impressions of Australia had continued and reinforced a process which had begun long before, in Sweden, and even earlier.

From our earliest days in Australia we had been impressed with the prosperity, cheerfulness and contentment of the people; many of them talked about Australia as 'a country to dream of'. They did not correspond with the Soviet picture of oppressed masses in foreign countries. We often recalled May Day processions in Moscow and the unconscious irony of the hard-worked, hungry, ill-clad, badly housed Soviet workers, as they marched through the Red Square under the banner, 'Workers of the capitalist countries, fight on for better conditions of life'.

Even Party members in Canberra could not ignore the fact that Australian workers were better dressed than many of our Embassy staff. Pakhomov prevailed upon all the non-diplomatic members of the staff to write requests for an extra allowance on this account; and Lifanov forwarded these requests to Moscow with a letter from himself supporting their claim. It was 'not approved', and Lifanov was reprimanded for lending his support to a 'strike'.

Then there was the contrast between Fascist Australia and Soviet Democracy. At Party meetings and in Soviet papers, the Australian Prime Minister, Mr Menzies, was always described as having 'Fascist tendencies' because of his vigorous anti-communist programme and especially because of his proposed Bill to dissolve the Communist Party of Australia. This Bill had been rejected in the Courts and later in a referendum.

Here again we saw an astonishing paradox, if Communist theory was to be believed. For in this 'Fascist' régime, the leader, the Prime Minister, having failed to get his proposal made law, accepted this veto and continued to govern within the limits imposed on him by a vote of the people.

Throughout the whole Soviet system democratic forms are preserved. There are abundant meetings, committees and elections.

Do not imagine that elections in the u.s.s.r. are taken lightly. The Government and the Communist Party take them very seriously. Voting is universal and compulsory; everyone has his part to play. But the part allotted to the ordinary voters is that of a flock of sheep. Things are arranged at the highest level and handed down from the top. The Government need have very little fear of interference from below. There is, of course, only one party, the Communist Party. The Central Committee of the Communist Party selects the candidate Deputies and through the Party machine arranges for these candidates to be proposed and recommended to the people of their electoral districts. The Party secretary makes speeches on behalf of the proposed Deputy, detailing his biography, record and general qualifications. Once before the election the Deputy himself appears, and makes a resounding speech, in which he promises (if elected) to serve the people and be their worthy representative. The people are then invited to come forward and express any divergent views about their candidate.

Nobody does.

They are also permitted to propose rival candidates.

Who would bother?

The ordinary voter in the Soviet Union needs all his time and strength to glean for himself and his dependants the bare material necessities of existence. He would not dream of courting trouble by questioning the Deputy whom the all-powerful authorities have chosen to 'represent' him.

Ministers and Chiefs of the State all have to go through this 'democratic' system of standing for election for some district. Thus, for instance, Stalin was proposed as candidate for a district of Moscow.

He was elected. He was repeatedly re-elected. In Western democratic terms, he was returned unopposed.

There is a story which ought to circulate as widely as possible in the Soviet Union, 'Peoples' Democracies' and all Communist countries. Dulles and Vyshinsky were discussing which of their respective countries accorded their citizens the greater liberties. Dulles claimed the prize for the United States. 'Why, in my country,' he said, 'any citizen can take a plane to Washington and march up and down in front of the White House shouting, "Eisenhower is crazy!" and nobody will arrest him.'

Vyshinsky was unimpressed.

'There's nothing remarkable in that,' he retorted. 'In the u.s.s.r. also any citizen can take a trip to Moscow, can go to the Red Square and can march up and down outside the Kremlin shouting, "Eisenhower is crazy!" and nobody will interfere with him!'

The Royal Commission itself was the most surprising revelation to us of the pains which a democratic country takes to be scrupulously fair to its political enemies. Communist after avowed Communist appeared in the witness-box assisted by able and energetic lawyers, defended himself, and in many cases attempted to use the box as a platform for Communist propaganda.

Coming from a country where anyone who is even suspected of political opposition disappears quietly overnight, and where people suffer severe penalties for an unguarded grumble about shortages, we found the tolerant Western attitude astonishing and at times mystifying. We accepted it as part of a system which we are still learning to understand.

To us, the most extraordinary example was that of Mr E. F. Hill, a member of the Central Committee of the Communist Party of Australia, and the Party's secretary in the State of Victoria. As a qualified barrister he appeared for many of the Communist witnesses and took the lead in cross-questioning us. We heard him constantly referred to by the lawyers assisting the Commission as 'my learned friend'; he was treated with courtesy by the judges; and was accorded all the privileges granted to the other barristers at the Commission.

Mr Hill asserted that he was a Communist and said in his evidence that he did not want to make any secret of the fact that he spent more time proportionately in his Party work than in his profession. Yet if the Communist Party ever came to power in Australia, the whole system of justice which guaranteed Mr Hill these rights would be swept away instantly. Every vestige of a law which could ensure the political rights of individuals against the State would disappear, as it has disappeared in every country where a Communist government has gained control.

In Communist countries the idea of tolerance for political enemies is unthinkable. In the Soviet Union the death penalty has been abolished for murderers and criminals; but it is retained for political offenders. In the prisons and labour camps ordinary criminals are allowed the right of correspondence with their families. Such right is denied to political offenders, because the Government views all forms of political opposition as equal to treason.

We were indeed confronted with two contradictory systems.

By going into the witness-box of the Australian Royal Commission on Espionage, which heard practically all evidence in open court, my wife and I made history for Soviet refugees in our position. At the Canadian Royal Commission Gouzenko gave all his evidence in secret session. Up to this present moment he has declined to show his face to the public, and appears on film and television programmes with a sack over his head. More recent refugees from the Soviet, like Captain Khokhlov and Yuri Rastvorov, whom my wife knew in the M.V.D. in Moscow, though they have been photographed, have told their stories in secret session, in closed court, or to discreet representatives of Western Intelligence agencies.

Not one of them has been submitted to the gruelling experience which we have been through, in our repeated appearances in a public court-room over a period of eleven months, under cross-examination in a foreign language (however brilliantly interpreted) and in utterly unfamiliar circumstances, by able barristers who used all their skill to test our credit as witnesses and were alert to detect us in contradictions, confusions and damaging statements.

We have already quoted in our Foreword, the Royal Commissioners' opinion of us as witnesses. What we alone can know fully is the strain of that experience and the mental and physical effort involved.

It is an ordeal that we have willingly endured, as part of our duty to our new country, and as something which we have been prepared to do to help the Commonwealth of Australia. But we would like others to understand what it has demanded of us.

EVDOKIA PETROV: Volodya, in the witness-box, appeared impassive and detached, but the experience took a great toll of him in nervous strain.

After a lifetime's training in security, conspiracy and secrecy, we suddenly found ourselves standing in the full glare of world publicity. As we entered and left the court in Melbourne, pressmen and photographers clustered round us. Newspapers in Australia, Great Britain and other countries carried pictures, news and special articles. We were photographed together on the first day of our public appearance.

I found myself publicized like a film star. Men and women reporters noted every detail of my clothes, my make-up, appearance, voice, behaviour, manner; I was like some strange creature never seen before.

One reporter described my first appearance on 6th July 1954 as 'a spy-film heroine's entrance'. Another commented on my 'magnificent performance' and added, 'There was artistry in every touch—downcast blue-grey eyes, an appealing smile, momentary sadness, furrowed concentration giving way to dimpling laughter. . . . It was difficult to realize that this was an espionage inquiry, and the story she told so lightheartedly was terrifyingly real.'

I would have been a strange woman if I had not been flattered by this unfamiliar blaze of public interest. But I felt far from lighthearted as I told my story.

The night before my first appearance in the witness-box I suffered nightmares through apprehension and as I faced the door to the court (the first court I had ever been in) I trembled with nervousness. But as I climbed the steps, I said firmly, 'Take yourself in hand'. Perhaps some gesture then gave observers the impression that I was assuming a part. Once in the box I was reassured by the encouraging smile of Major Birse, the distinguished interpreter (who had interpreted for Stalin and Churchill at Yalta) and by the calm kindliness of the three judges. As for the people in the body of the court, they were at first an indistinct blur, but later I made out faces, mostly friendly, but some hostile. The hostile ones I took to be Australian Communists. But even then I looked at them more as Australians than as Communists, and I thought, 'If you knew the truth about life inside the u.s.s.r. you would not hate me for appearing in this box.'

My evidence which seemed to some observers an accomplished performance did not feel so to me. As I told the story of my life, culminating with the treatment we had received in Canberra, my husband's
disappearance, my recall under escort to Moscow, and my decision to
join him in Australia, forsaking my country and leaving my family in
the Soviet Union, I relived those frightening and agonizing experiences
so vividly that at times I broke down and wept. My tears were anything but an act.

On the third day of my evidence I faced cross-examination by Mr
Hill. When I was told that he was an important official in the Australian
Communist Party and that under Australian law he was entitled to
cross-question me, I felt very afraid. A lifetime's habits of thought
are not shaken off overnight. All my life I had struggled to make
good in Communist organizations in my own country—first as a
Pioneer, then as a Komsomol, then in the Party itself. I had only
achieved admission to this privileged *élite* body in 1950, not long before
we left for Australia. The Communist Party is the new aristocracy in
the Soviet Union and I wanted to be part of it. Always I had striven to
prove myself a correct and conscientious Communist, especially
under the attacks which followed my first husband's arrest and in face
of those which were later launched against us in the Embassy at
Canberra.

I broke with Communism when, in pain and fear, I chose to leave
the Soviet service and start life afresh in Australia. But I had not completely cast off the surviving fears; Mr Hill, as a Communist official,
perhaps understood the situation very well.

Before I entered the witness-box I had taken an oath on the Bible,
using the name of God, to tell the truth.

Mr Hill got me to agree that in my years as a Komsomol and Party
member I had been a keen student of dialectical materialism (as indeed
we all had to be).

He then asked, 'By taking the oath, Mrs Petrov, do you know
exactly what you have done?'

'I know what I have done,' I answered.

'What have you done?'

'I am not to blame.'

'But what do you mean, Mrs Petrov, when you say you understand
what you have done in taking the oath?'

'That I have abandoned my country.'

'You would agree with me that dialectical materialism involves the
rejection of a belief in God?'

I answered, 'I am not now a Communist, and that which is denied by dialectical materialism does not apply to me.'

As I stood in the witness-box, apparently calm and collected, strange fears and hallucinations raced through my mind. At one moment I had the illusion that this was all a dream and that I was, in reality, back in Moscow, undergoing interrogation in an M.V.D. cellar.

For a few seconds I was terror-stricken. Then, with a flood of relief, I realized that this was a witness-box in an Australian court and that my fears were ridiculous.

Then a fresh spasm of terror took hold of me. Even though this was Australia, could I rely on that fact to protect me? Could not the long arm of the M.V.D., of the Administration of Special Tasks, the assassination department, reach me even here? Had we not Soviet agents everywhere? Why not in this very court?

Then again I realized that I was giving way to extravagant fears. Such operations on foreign territory are not so easy, even with Moscow's resources. For such a job they would need time to plan with the utmost care and detail, to select and train their special agents and to move them into position to strike. There was no need to panic; not here, not now, not immediately.

I have described the thoughts that pursued each other through my mind just as they occurred, because they will help Western readers to understand the background and mental climate of life in the empire of fear that I had so recently left.

VLADIMIR PETROV: Mr Hill is a clever man and I do not question the sincerity of his Communist beliefs. Thus he got my wife to agree with the statement that there is no exploitation of man by man in the Soviet Union. This is perfectly true according to Communist definitions; for the U.S.S.R. is at present considered to be a socialist state, in which, since private ownership of the means of production, distribution and exchange has been abolished, there is no longer a class of capitalists and therefore no private individual is in a position to exploit another.

Our book is not written to justify exploitation by capitalists or anyone else. It is written to make clear the truth that the vast, oppressed, silent, needy masses of the Soviet people are exploited by the Soviet Government to a degree hardly conceivable in capitalist countries. Their distress and discontent is huge but ineffective. It does not count. Thirty-eight years after the Revolution the cry is still, 'Priority for heavy industry. Goods for the people must wait. Build for the future, and future generations!' Deeply disillusioned, the Soviet masses toil in vain for the coming Utopia that never comes.

But poverty is not the worst thing.

The most terrible thing about life in the Soviet Union, and through the whole length and breadth of the Communist empire, is not the material hardship but the insecurity of life under a system which destroys faith and trust between man and man, or between the citizen and his Government. That is what Soviet Communism does, methodically, ruthlessly and effectively, as our story shows. Where faith, trust and honesty survive, as they still do in the Soviet Union, it is in spite of, not because of, the régime in power.

That is why, when I telephoned my wife at Darwin in the early morning of 20th April 1954, I spoke with life-and-death urgency, begging her to face the fact that if she returned to Moscow she would never see her family again, no matter what assurances she might have received.

Stalin declared, and it is a clause written into the Soviet constitution, that 'The son is not responsible for the father's actions, nor the father for those of the son.'

No piece of legislation in history has ever been more cynically disregarded.

The story of Borzov has probably never been told before, but it is a story which should be known everywhere, especially among former Soviet citizens abroad who may be moved by a yearning to see their native land and their loved ones again.

I remember reading in 1949 a small paragraph in *Pravda* to the effect that three Soviet airmen had been forced by petrol shortage to land in the American Zone of Austria; two of them had gone over to the Americans, the third had insisted on returning to his Soviet homeland.

The man who returned was the radio operator, the two who went over to the Americans were the pilots, Pirogov and Borzov. I have just read with great interest Pirogov's book in which he describes the careful planning of the escape, the flight, the arrival in the American Zone, the International Commission which examined their case, the arguments of the Soviet representative who strove to induce them to return to the Soviet Union. They disbelieved his promises and went to America, where they gave interviews and made speeches. Pirogov is presumably in America still.

But Borzov after a time began to pine for his wife and his four-year-old son, whom he had left behind. In the end he could bear it no longer, and approached the Soviet authorities in the United States, who encouraged his hopes and arranged for him to be repatriated to the Soviet Union. That is where I take up the story.

One day in 1950 at M.V.D. headquarters in Moscow, my colleague Igolkin, who worked in the American section of the S.K. department, told me of Borzov's return and said that he was interrogating him in his cell in the Taganskaya Prison. Igolkin had a series of interviews with Borzov, who supplied a mass of valuable information. He was talking freely and was describing every detail of his experiences in American hands, in the hope of working his passage back to pardon, and of being permitted at least to see his wife and son again. As Igolkin described it to me, 'Each time I go to see him he looks at me like a dog that wags its tail and gazes at you in the hope of a bone.'

They kept Borzov about eight months in prison because he had so much interesting information to supply and because so many senior M.V.D. officers wanted to check up on various points in his story.

Of course, no one told him that he had been sentenced to death while he was still in America. When they had finished with him they shot him without letting him see his wife and son again.

If this story helps some waverers who are hesitating on the brink of returning to their Soviet homeland, it will have been worth the telling.

What will happen in the next ten years in the U.S.S.R.? What chance is there of fundamental changes taking place from within? Without question there is widespread disillusionment with the hypocrisy and cynicism of the system and with its failure to produce the long-promised improvement in living conditions for the people. But the Soviet Government, having seized power by revolution, has set up a machine unique in its elaboration to ensure that no second revolution shall be possible. We, who have been part of that machine, see little hope of a spontaneous popular revolt among the divided and intimidated masses of the Soviet people.

And yet we believe that some day, somehow, the miracle will occur and even the Soviet masses will enjoy the freedom, scope and well-being of their brothers and sisters in happier countries. Even now the Soviet Government cannot entirely ignore the feelings of its own people and, in spite of contrary appearances, it is far from indifferent to opinion in Western countries. Major changes in Soviet policy are possible in the years ahead. But it is important for the free countries to understand one point very clearly in all dealings with the Soviet Union.

The rulers of the Soviet Union respect one thing only—strength.

The rulers of the Soviet Union have no respect at all for those whom they can intimidate or deceive.

If our book helps people in the free world to understand the truth about the Soviet system and the Soviet people, it will have done something to advance the possibility of relations based neither on panic, nor on illusion, but on reality.

As for us, who have escaped from the empire of fear and have told our story, who can say what the future will hold for us? Perhaps we shall never escape from its shadow entirely; will never be able to enjoy as we would wish the quiet, freedom and security that ordinary citizens of this fortunate country of Australia take for granted. There is enough in our story to give grim reality to the question.

Perhaps, on the other hand, that privilege will in time be ours, together with the greatest freedom of all, the freedom from fear.

EVDOKIA PETROV: Perhaps the experience of my very first hours on Australian soil will turn out to be a portent. We arrived at Canberra airport in darkness and were taken to the house occupied by one of the Embassy drivers as a temporary lodging, as our own house was not ready.

That first night on strange alien territory, so far from home and family in distant Moscow, I was a prey to fears. I had heard a lot about the bitter anti-Soviet migrants whom we must expect to find in Australia and in the middle of the night I woke screaming from a nightmare in which I thought that some enemy was trying to get in the window to attack us.

It was pure illusion; Volodya sleepily told me not to imagine things, and I went off to sleep again.

Next morning, before I was properly awake, I was aware of the most wonderful torrent of musical sound I had ever heard. I lay there bathed in it for a moment, wondering if the old religious fables of my mother's girlhood were true after all, and I had been transported to heaven in my sleep.

Then I woke up properly. Outside the window it was a glorious tingling sunny morning; the sound, which I still could not identify, seemed to echo the vibrant stimulating sunlight.

Each morning in the days that followed I heard this sound and it was some little time before I discovered that it was the song of the Australian magpie.

That strong, buoyant song was one of the things I loved best in those early days in Australia. Perhaps that first night and morning are a symbol. Perhaps also in our life a night of fears is ending and a new morning is beginning.

Appendix by Vladimir Petrov

SINCE we wrote our book, Dr Bialoguski has published his book which he calls *The Petrov Story*, though, as the *Sunday Times* of London pointed out, it should have been called 'The Bialoguski Story'. As his account is inaccurate and misleading at a number of points we wish to offer the following comments dealing with a number of statements made by him:

1) Bialoguski greatly exaggerates his own part in the matter and the extent of his own knowledge. So far as life inside the Embassy was concerned, his knowledge was superficial. Even after the facts had been clearly revealed at the Royal Commission, he described our Communist Party meetings as 'staff meetings . . . designed to increase staff efficiency and boost personal enthusiasm'. (See page 151 of his book.) The meetings were in fact meetings of the Communist Party members of the Embassy staff.

2) On page 125 of his book he writes: 'Strictly from an espionage point of view, it did not matter much whether he, Petrov, defected or not, so deeply had I penetrated into his activities.' He further describes a list of names which he found in my notebook when I was asleep, as 'the key to the whole Soviet espionage system in Australia'. (See page 107 of his book.) These claims are absurd. The names in my notebook were of little value in themselves and the real key to Soviet espionage in Australia was provided by the documents which I brought from the Embassy and handed to Mr G. R. Richards on April 3, 1954. To this day Bialoguski has never seen these documents and he did not know of their existence until the news was made public by the Australian Prime Minister when he made his announcement of my request to be granted asylum in Australia.

3) Concerning Antonov, Bialoguski writes: 'One of his main tasks appeared to be to maintain contact with the Russian Club and seek out any likely candidates for return to the Soviet Union.' Antonov never had this task. This line of inquiry was in the first place in my hands and later in the hands of Platkais, as I explained in my evidence at the Royal Commission.

4) Bialoguski describes (on page 91) how I coached him in photography and suggests that I did this in order to prepare him for

an important espionage task. In fact I had no such plan for him, for, as I have explained in our book, I had suspicions about his true role. I certainly had never dreamed of appointing Bialoguski to be the head of Soviet espionage in Australia, as he suggests on page 125 of his book.

5) Bialoguski in his book represents himself as having single-handed persuaded me to defect from the Soviet Service and he minimises the vital part played by Dr Beckett. My own account puts these events in their right perspective.

6) On page 148 Bialoguski describes how my wife discussed business openings in Sydney with him. She is most emphatic that no such discussions ever occurred, especially as she then fully intended to return to the Soviet Union.

7) Bialoguski has also stated in an article published by him that I warned him of the dangers he was facing and advised him to wear a gun for his own protection. I never gave him any such advice.

8) As I have made quite clear, Bialoguski's part in my decision to defect was simply that of an intermediary.

Index

345